LAW WITHOUT A LAWYER

LAW WITHOUT A LAWYER

SECOND EDITION

FENTON BRESLER

Century · London

Published by Century in 2000

1 3 5 7 9 10 8 6 4 2

Copyright © Fenton Bresler 2000

Fenton Bresler has asserted his right under the Copyright, Designs and
Patents Act, 1988 to be identified as the author of this work

First published in the United Kingdom in 2000 by Century
The Random House Group Ltd
20 Vauxhall Bridge Road, London SW1V 2SA

Random House Australia (Pty) Limited
20 Alfred Street, Milsons Point, Sydney,
New South Wales 2061, Australia

Random House New Zealand Limited
18 Poland Road, Glenfield
Auckland 10, New Zealand

Random House (Pty) Limited
Endulini, 5a Jubilee Road, Parktown 2193, South Africa

The Random House Group Ltd Reg. No. 954009

A CIP catalogue record for this book is available from the British Library

Papers used by Random House are natural, recyclable products made
from wood grown in sustainable forests. The manufacturing processes
conform to the environmental regulations of the country of origin

ISBN 0 7126 8091 8

Typeset by SX Composing DTP, Rayleigh, Essex
Printed and bound in Great Britain by Biddles Ltd, www.Biddles.co.uk

FOR MY BROTHER,
HAROLD BRESLER

CONTENTS

INTRODUCTION

WHAT THIS SECOND EDITION IS ALL ABOUT

In the five years that have passed since 1995 when the first edition of this book was published, there has been an enormous outburst of new law. The late Lord Taylor, when Lord Chief Justice, accused John Major's Tory Government of 'legislative diarrhoea' and I hate to think how he would describe the deluge of new statutes and ministerial regulations that have poured out since Tony Blair's New Labour Administration took over in May 1997. Nor is that all: big business has become even bigger, the corporate outlook is for many the only outlook. Life has become even more complex and, for many, more stressful. The only protection we all have is the law.

That is why this edition is so much larger than the first edition and the number of chapters has swelled from 20 to 33. If you want to stand up for yourself against our political and economic masters, you have first to know what your rights are.

This book is for the articulate, the determined and those who believe that knowledge is power. The nanny state has become also the bossy state, with the consequence that never before have lawyers been so necessary. But sadly never before have they been so expensive or inaccessible to so many people. State legal aid has become meaningless to most people in this country who want to fight or defend their case in the civil courts or before the various tribunals that now abound (criminal cases are in a different category) – and this edition, even more than its precursor, is aimed at them.

The cost of going to law these days or even seeking skilled legal advice can be prohibitive. Hence, the need for this book.

Primarily its purpose is to help you to be your own lawyer, while recognising the necessary limitations, the occasions when you inevitably have to seek expert help. It is directed at an audience of reasonable intelligence and reasonable education who have the desire – and the ability – to stand up for themselves. If you have never firmly but politely queried a bill in a restaurant, or think that you would not like to because it would be too embarrassing or demeaning – or because you do not have the courage – please do not bother to read on. This book is not for you.

But in countless situations in everyday life today people need to know what the law is in order to be able to protect their own legitimate interests.

This is not a manual: that would be boring and unreadable. This is, I hope, a readable book, which will give you the knowledge to enable you whenever possible to battle for yourself.

I have practised at the Bar and also been a legal journalist for a long time. An elderly barrister once dismissed me with a perceptible sniff as 'a populist'. I happily accept the title.

But this book is not comprehensive. That is a will-o'-the-wisp in a single book of this length. I have chosen instead those sections of law which I think will be of most value to my readers. You will find no reference to the legal problems of the homeless or the complex laws dealing with social security. But you will read about birth and death, divorce and marriage, eating out in restaurants and wine bars; about landlord and tenant, buying and selling your home, holiday problems, motoring law, wills, schools, the vast range of modern employment law, maternity rights, coping with the police, jury service, etc., etc., and all put in their historical and social context, with true-life cases, so that you can understand them better.

The aim is to give readers the particular kind of information that they require – which, at the moment, they cannot easily find elsewhere. There are other books on everyday law available but most read like legal textbooks; most are the product of several people's efforts. What I claim for my 'one-man-band' effort is that it presents one person's view of the law. I have written only on subjects that I know about myself, often from practical experience at the Bar or in legal journalism, and which I believe to be of special interest to the sort of person likely to pick up this book and turn over its pages.

I also believe immodestly that it is more readable, more reliable and more up to date than the others.

In general terms, the law is stated as of 1 January 2000. It will vary in some respects for Scotland and Northern Ireland but I have done my best to make it as accurate as possible for England and Wales, although I can accept no liability to anyone if unwittingly I have erred in any specific instance. Halsbury's *Laws of England,* the semi-official statement of the law found in every lawyer's office and on the shelves of most public reference libraries, runs to approximately 70 volumes and reissue volumes.

PART 1

YOU AND YOUR FAMILY

1

PRE-BIRTH

The law – and medical science – used to be simple. You were born and your life was said to start, both legally and factually, when you left your mother's body and, kicking and perhaps screaming, you started an independent existence taking in your own air and your own food. As Mr Justice Brett told a jury back in 1874: 'A child is born alive when it exists as a live child, breathing and living by reason of its breathing through its own lungs alone, without deriving any of its living or power of living by or through any connection with its mother.'

His Victorian lordship never had to consider the legal ramifications of a newborn babe going straight on to a ventilator or of an 'unborn' child aborted late in pregnancy by the prostaglandin injection method who, small but perfectly formed, manages to survive, struggling for breath for minutes or even hours. It is impossible to speculate what the learned Mr Justice Brett, now long lying dead in his coffin, would have thought of the first-ever coroner's inquest in April 1979 on an aborted baby: a 23-week-old girl foetus who survived for 36 hours at a hospital in Barnsley, South Yorkshire, and was actually given a name – Emma.

Medical science has not stood still. In recent years judges, lawyers – and Parliament – have had to rethink many of the concepts involved in the whole complex gamut of rights and legal situations brought about by the modern hi-tech phenomenon of birth: from conception through to delivery.

In fact, we have to start even before conception. It is a truism that not every couple who have sex want to have a child: rarely do those who have had a 'one-night stand' or a brief affair want to complicate their lives by the birth of a child and nowadays all married couples and long-term partners, except those whose religious principles forbid it, use modern scientific methods to try to select when they have children.

What is the law on contraception?

It takes two forms: birth control and sterilisation – and the law on both has changed very much in recent years.

BIRTH CONTROL

Birth control is almost as ancient as mankind. No one knows when the first coupling pair used any of the 'natural' methods of contraception. But tattered fragments of Ancient Egyptian papyri tell us that, about 1,850 years before the birth of Christ, upper-class Egyptian women were trying to stop themselves becoming pregnant by using – of all things – crocodile dung as a primitive vaginal pessary, while Egyptian men some 500 years later were putting on ill-fitting, uncomfortable, handmade sheaths.

Nowadays, of course, it is all very different. Condoms are readily available, slickly packaged and, so we are assured, a pleasure to wear. As with many other modern forms of contraception for both sexes, including the 'morning-after Pill' for women, they are available free on the National Health Service at family planning clinics, most hospitals' genitourinary (GUM) clinics and from some GPs. In fact, when a woman in Dorset claimed that 40 condoms a month were not enough for her needs, her local family planning clinic duly gave her more, free of charge. People can, of course, buy their own with no legal difficulty (regardless of age) in most chemists' shops – and if they find that too embarrassing, as many still do, there is the comforting anonymity of vending machines in the lavatories of countless public houses, motorway cafés and discos.

But how 'safe' does a condom, wherever bought, have to be in law? According to a report in *The Times,* an average purchaser uses 102 condoms a year. Yet for years there was no specified legal standard. The British Standards Institute issued its Kitemark quality standard for condoms (No. 3704) in 1989 but, like most Kitemarks, it has no legal effect. In August 1993 the Consumers' Association warned that they had tested condoms produced by 34 different manufacturers – and nine makes had leaked or split in use. Disturbingly, three of those nine carried the British Standards Kitemark.

Nowadays, this is all history. In August 1996, after long deliberation, the European Commission in Brussels finally settled on a legal standard,

EN600, enforceable throughout the European Union for natural rubber latex male condoms. The English-language version of this legal standard runs to 50 pages, including tables, diagrams, appendices and testing procedures. It also specifies the dimensions of a legal Euro-condom: average length 170mm with a width of 44mm to 56mm. Ever since 14 June 1998, all medical devices – and that term includes 'condoms intended for contraception or as protection against sexually transmitted infections' – marketed throughout the EU, including Britain, must carry a CE marking on the pack to tell purchasers that it complies with EN600. CE applies to all goods supplied in accordance with EU legal require-ments and means, in French, *Certification Europienne* or, in translation, 'Certificate for Europe'.

But despite all this there is still no legal guarantee of complete security and, if you read the rest of the small print on the pack you will see that no manufacturer is so foolhardy as to give any such assurance. The result is that no one can sue if a condom fails and a baby is born – or a sexually transmitted disease is contracted.

The only legal protection for users is that extravagant claims should not be made. The 1968 Trade Descriptions Act says that *all* retail goods must not bear a 'false trade description' – and this applies equally to condoms:

The case of the 'supersafe' condoms

In 1987, trading standards officers in the London suburb of Greenwich, alerted by complaints about foreign-manufactured 'Supersafe (Ribbed) Condoms' on sale locally, found that nineteen out of a hundred had holes in them. In the first prosecution of its kind, Greenwich Magistrates' Court fined the importers £1,000 and £500 costs for selling goods with a false trade description. Whatever the quality of the condoms may have been, they were most certainly not 'supersafe'.

Most men probably prefer women to take the precautions against pregnancy and, with the first contraceptive pill going on the market in the United States as far back as May 1960, it is estimated that today at least three out of four women in England, both married and single, choose it as their preferred form of contraception. At present there are about 35 brands, but, again, no legal guarantee is given.

What about the young? Some may find totally unacceptable the current state of the law where a doctor or family planning clinic may prescribe the pill or other contraceptive device to a child under 16 without insisting that she first obtain her parents' consent – or even tells them.

That was decided in the famous case of *Gillick* v. *West Norfolk Area*

Health Committee and the DHSS in October 1985 when a devout Roman Catholic mother, anxious about the future welfare of her four young daughters under 16, went to court for a declaration that her local area health committee had acted unlawfully in refusing to promise her not to give them the pill without her prior knowledge or consent. The case went up to the House of Lords, the ultimate court of appeal, and Lord Templeman would have granted the declaration:

> I doubt whether a girl under the age of 16 is capable of a balanced judgement to embark on frequent, regular or casual sexual intercourse fortified by the illusion that medical science can protect her mind and body and ignoring the danger of leaping from childhood to adulthood without the difficult formative transitional experiences of adolescence. There are many things a girl under 16 needs to practise but sex is not one of them.

But the four other law lords disagreed. Lord Scarman's judgment was typical of their philosophy: 'Parental right yields to the child's right to make her own decisions when she reaches a sufficient understanding and intelligence to be capable of making up her own mind.' All four law lords said that doctors should normally seek parental consent but unanimously ruled that it was not legally necessary so long as their young patient was, in the words of Lord Fraser of Tullybelton, 'capable of understanding what is proposed and of expressing her wishes'.

To comply with this majority decision, the British Medical Association (BMA) laid down guidelines that a doctor must first decide if an underage patient understands the risks of taking contraception and having sex. He should then 'encourage' her to tell her parents but must take into account whether she is likely to have sex without protection if help is refused. Finally he must determine whether contraception is likely to have any harmful effect on her physical or mental health and must 'consider' whether making it available without parental consent is in her own best interests.

But in no circumstances must he himself tell the parents that their young daughter has asked for or been given help with contraception.

That seems clear enough; but doubts about confidentiality persisted among young people and in November 1993 the BMA announced it was sending leaflets to every surgery in the land stressing its importance. 'All the evidence shows that concern about confidentiality is the main reason that prevents underage girls from seeking advice,' said the BMA's Dr Fleur Fisher. 'There is general confusion among the public but we are quite clear in the medical profession that confidentiality must be regarded, whatever the age of the patient.'

Not every parent would agree. Or be happy with the fact that the same largesse seems to apply to schoolteachers. In October 1994, it was announced that three teaching unions and the National Children's Bureau had obtained an opinion by a leading QC that, although the matter had not been tested in the courts, teachers could, in his view, safely ignore Education Department guidelines on sex education limiting teachers' discretion to give contraceptive advice to children under 16 without telling their parents. The opinion said that the guidelines had 'no special legal status' and teachers need not comply with them if, in their professional judgement, a child's best interests were better served by confidentiality. That is still the situation today.

Yet whatever the rights and wrongs of the moral debate, in practical terms the law is quite clear: parents do not have to be told and birth control for girls under 16 is obtainable virtually on demand.

There are many examples. In early 1992, for instance, there was a great furore in the press because a school doctor at Marlborough, one of the country's most prestigious co-ed establishments, had prescribed the pill to a 15-year-old girl unbeknown to her parents and she had been found in her 17-year-old boyfriend's bedroom. The headmaster expelled them both but maintained vehemently that his school had been 'unfairly picked on'. He protested: 'There is nothing that happens here that doesn't happen in many other schools.'

Seven years on, in March 1999, it was much the same. In that month, a community health adviser to the Royal College of Nursing proposed at the Royal College's annual conference that school nurses should be able to prescribe emergency contraception to girls as young as 11 – without having to wait for a doctor. Family campaigners immediately said it was grossly irresponsible but the Brook Advisory Service, which specialises in family planning services for youngsters, welcomed it. 'We have been at the forefront of calls for a nurse-led contraceptive service,' proudly said a spokesman. 'This would free up the service because there wouldn't have to be a doctor there all the time. It would streamline the service.'

Yet there is a disturbing paradox: despite this easy legal availability of contraception for children, Britain still has the highest teenage pregnancy rate in Western Europe. In March 1999 it was disclosed that teenage pregnancies had risen in England and Wales to a record rate of 9.4 conceptions for every 1,000 girls between 13 and 15. In this age group there were 8,829 conceptions in 1996 compared with 8,034 in 1995 – and these were all girls still at school.

STERILISATION

Unlike birth control, this is primarily a modern phenomenon. It really only began to be medically possible on any large scale in the 1970s; but already the law is well established, evolved by the judges themselves in several precedent-making cases. Parliament has had little to do with it.

Sterilisation is legally just like any other operation: the surgeon must not only use reasonable skill and care in carrying out the operation itself but must also ensure that beforehand the patient understood and agreed to what was going to happen. Any surgery without consent is 'trespass to the person' and the patient could recover substantial damages from the surgeon or the NHS authorities. With sterilising a man, there is usually no problem: he will have chosen quite deliberately to have his vasectomy and signed the normal consent form without demur. With women, the situation can be much more delicate – and doctors overlook the need for consent at their peril.

Two doctors who went too far

In 1980, a 33-year-old married woman who already had four children and whose religion forbade sterilisation entered hospital for a minor gynaecological operation. During the operation the surgeon saw that her womb was ruptured and sterilised her there and then. She won £4,000 damages for the loss of her ability to conceive again and £2,750 damages for her distress at what had happened to her.

In 1978, a 35-year-old Roman Catholic woman was about to be wheeled into the operating theatre to give birth to her second child by Caesarean section, for which she had already signed a consent form, when she was asked to sign a second form for a sterilisation to take place at the same time. She understood what that physically meant but, in her trauma, no one sufficiently explained the psychological implications to her. She won £3,000 damages.

Does a surgeon have to satisfy himself that the spouse or live-in partner of his patient also consents to the sterilisation? After all, they are intimately involved. The British Medical Association recommends this as a courtesy – but there is no legal obligation.

What happens if the operation fails? The risk of natural reversal of a male vasectomy is lower than that of a female sterilisation; but there is still no absolute guarantee that any sterilisation will work for all time. Yet, if the operation fails and a child is born, you can, in this increasingly materialistic world, generally still sue for damages if (a) the surgeon did not warn you there was a risk, however slight, of failure or (b) you can prove he was negligent in carrying out the operation. This second possibility will require expert evidence from other medical practitioners which, because of the professional freemasonry of doctors, is not always easy to obtain.

In the early 1980s some judges objected on moral grounds to this sort of litigation but now it is clear that parents are entitled to recover reasonable damages for what Mr Justice Brooke called in January 1992, in *Allen* v. *Bloomsbury Health Authority,* a mother's 'discomfort and pain' in carrying and bearing an unwanted child, and much more substantial damages for the cost of bringing up the child through to adulthood. This can, in appropriate circumstances, include the mother's loss of earnings in not going back to work for a while – and the cost of private education. As Mr Justice Brooke said: 'If an unplanned child is born after a failure by a hospital doctor to exercise the standard of care reasonably to be expected of him and the child's parents have sent all their other children to expensive private boarding schools for the whole of their education, then it appears to me that a very substantial claim for the cost of private education of a healthy child of a reasonably wealthy family might have to be met from the funds of the health authority responsible for the doctor's negligence.'

In July 1997, the legal right to sue for an unsuccessful sterilisation was extended to the case of a mother who had been unaware that she was already pregnant with her fourth child when she had a sterilisation operation at a Newcastle upon Tyne hospital. Mr Justice Langley, using sporting language that only an English judge would use, said that the consultant gynaecologist who had carried out the operation had 'taken his eye off the ball' in not advising her that the operation should be delayed until she had taken a pregnancy test. The judge awarded the mother £113,982 damages, of which £102,521 was to cover the cost of bringing up her son to the age of 21.

As we have seen, attempts to prevent conception with birth control or sterilisation in this imperfect world do not always succeed. So let us now look at what the law says about that other main form of preventing childbirth.

ABORTION

For more than half this century, most abortions in England and Wales were sordid, illegal, backstreet affairs with large quantities of gin and a hot bath or knitting needles as the principal tools to hand. The only abortions legally allowed were medical terminations of pregnancy

performed by a doctor when the child was not capable of being born alive
or when necessary to save the life of a pregnant woman who would
otherwise have died or, as Mr Justice MacNaughten said in a classic 1939
case, 'have become a physical or mental wreck'. By 1967, about 50,000
abortions were estimated to be taking place every year – of which more
than 30,000 were illegal.

Then the 1967 Abortion Act, introduced as a Private Member's Bill by
David (now Lord) Steel, then a young MP, revolutionised the law. A
woman could thenceforth obtain a medical abortion within the first 28
weeks of pregnancy if two doctors signed a certificate to the effect that:
(1) continuing the pregnancy would involve risk to her life or to her
    physical or mental health or to that of her other children; or
(2) there was substantial risk that the child would be born with a serious
    physical or mental handicap.

Subsequent decisions in the courts have made clear that, once a woman
obtains those two vital signed certificates, it is only *her* decision that
counts. A man cannot stop his wife or girlfriend having an abortion, even
though he admits the child is his. And (except with a girl who is mentally
backward or ill, where the courts decide the issue) parents cannot obtain
an injunction to stop their teenage daughter from having an abortion. She
has the legal right to do what she likes with her own body.

How many abortions do you think took place in England and Wales in
the twenty-three and a half years between April 1968, when the Abortion
Act came into effect, and December 1991? According to figures released
by the Office of Population, Censuses and Surveys, the staggering total
was 3.5 million, of which 2.9 million (nearly 83 per cent) were performed
on women living in this country: the other 600,000 came from abroad to
profit from more liberal laws than in their homeland. Although Lord Steel
has always denied that was his intention, his Act effectively created legal
abortion on demand – at least, within the first 28 weeks of a pregnancy.

That time limit has since changed. In 1990, Parliament amended the
1967 Act and reduced the period to 24 weeks – but only when the
woman's physical or mental health or that of any of her existing children
is at risk. In fact, today a legal abortion can take place well beyond 24, or
even 28, weeks if, even at that late stage, it becomes apparent that there
is a substantial risk of a seriously handicapped child being brought into
this world. In such cases, unknown to many people, there is now no time
limit whatsoever.

THE OTHER SIDE OF THE COIN – MODERN METHODS OF ASSISTED CONCEPTION

What about those people who, far from not wanting a child, passionately want one even though God seems to have decreed otherwise? It is estimated that as many as one in ten couples, perhaps more, have difficulty in conceiving naturally and seek medical help. What are their legal rights to use modern science to conceive and deliver a child against all the natural odds?

Within the past 25 years 'reproductive medicine', as it is called, has grown out of all recognition to form a whole new section of science – for which a whole new set of legal rules has had to be created. The subject is highly complicated and the law is still evolving and extremely complex. Only those cursed with a natural blight on their ability to have children can truly understand the yearning and the anguish.

The situation takes a variety of forms:

Artificial insemination

Back in the 1960s this was the only kind of assisted conception available. An estimated 1,700 children are still born this way every year. It can be done if the problem is with the man, not the woman: i.e. if for some reason he cannot have normal sexual intercourse and penetrate the woman naturally with his penis so that his sperm can travel within her body, mingle with her eggs and bring about fertilisation.

It is, however, a comparatively simple procedure to start the fertilisation process by artificially inserting his sperm into her. If necessary, this can even be done without medical assistance. In fact, animals have been artificially inseminated for more than two centuries: the first recorded instance of a puppy being born to a bitch from a dog's sperm inserted artificially into her vagina was back in 1780. The process has for many years been extensively used in rearing farm animals, especially cattle; and there are several statutory regulations on the subject with such marvellous titles as the 1964 Artificial Insemination of Pigs (England and Wales) Regulations and the 1984 Importation of Bovine Semen Regulations.

By the 1960s artificial insemination was also becoming available for humans.

There are two kinds: DI ('Donor Insemination') where the sperm does not come from the woman's husband, and AIH ('Artificial Insemination by Husband') where it does. AIH has seldom caused any legal complications: a child conceived in this way is as much the couple's legitimate child as any other and generally no outsider even knows it has occurred.

With DI it is different, and for one obvious reason: a third party is necessarily involved. Originally the Church condemned the process as adultery, although in January 1958 the Court of Session held that was not so – at least, in Scottish law. But up to 1987 a child born as a result of DI was still born into a legal limbo. Even if husband and wife had agreed to the wife being impregnated by another man's sperm (as nearly always happens), the child was treated as *their* illegitimate child and not the child of the married couple. That has now changed. The 1990 Human Fertilisation and Embryology Act says that, if the woman is married and has the treatment with her husband's consent, the baby is the legitimate child of their marriage, and the husband, not the donor, is the legal father. If the couple are unmarried but seek treatment together, the child is illegitimate just as if it had been born naturally, but the male partner is recognised as the father and can obtain full parental rights by seeking a 'parental responsibility' order in the courts under the 1989 Children Act, just like any other unmarried father.

Unmarried couples can now use DI without having to worry about undesirable legal consequences.

Test-tube babies

This is the generic term for all babies produced with the help of modern science – other than by artificial insemination.

In its simplest form it is designed to aid a woman who can produce eggs normally from her ovaries but whose Fallopian tubes are, for some reason, blocked so that she cannot conceive naturally because her eggs cannot travel through the tubes to meet male sperm entering her body and so be fertilised. Mrs Lesley Brown was just such a woman. In November 1977 Dr Patrick Steptoe implanted direct into her womb one of her own eggs after it had been fertilised – in a test-tube – by her husband's semen. Eight months later, in July 1978, she gave birth at a hospital in Greater Manchester to the world's first test-tube baby: a perfectly normal, healthy baby called Louise. The Latin for 'glass vessel' is *vitrum* so the new process was formally named *in vitro* fertilisation (IVF for short).

Immediately hope was given to thousands of couples around the world. 'Yet,' as Professor Margaret Brazier has commented, 'for every man and woman who rejoiced at what the doctors could now do, there were as many who condemned the technical advances as unnatural and contrary to the will of God.'

Improvements and refinements of the technique soon followed and, in answer to continuing public disquiet, the Thatcher Government established an official committee under Dame Mary (now Baroness) Warnock to draw up legal guidelines for the future. Its report was published in the summer of 1984 and six years later, in the summer of 1990, after vitriolic debate in Parliament and two further Government reports, its somewhat modified recommendations became law as the 1990 Human Fertilisation and Embryology Act – which even today many people know little about.

The Act came into effect in August 1991 when its creation, the Human Fertilisation and Embryology Authority, began functioning. Based in London's East End, the 21-member Authority has over the years included doctors, geneticists, psychiatrists, lawyers, bishops, a rabbi, a well-known actress (Penelope Keith) and other lay members. It is responsible for inspecting and licensing all clinics, whether private or NHS, which provide any form of fertility treatment where any part of the fertilisation process takes place outside a woman's body (with the one exception of artificial insemination by her husband) and all clinics which store human embryos or carry out research on them. No such clinic can operate lawfully without the Authority's licence and its staff and procedures are strictly monitored and controlled. In has, for instance, intervened to ban clinics from providing treatment which would allow parents to choose the sex of their offspring unless there was a risk the child could be born with an inherited disease.

The Authority has licensed over 100 establishments, and anyone wishing to know the address of the nearest clinic can telephone the Authority on London 020 7377 5077.

Yet fertility treatment carries no guarantee: legal or otherwise. Every year in Britain, 10,000 women attempt to have a test-tube baby but only 1,500 births result. It is believed that IVF pregnancies are perhaps more likely to end in a miscarriage than normal pregnancies because women undergoing IVF tend to be older or are more likely to have other fertility problems.

Free treatment is available on the National Health Service but, as ever, funding is limited. As Professor Robert Winston has written in his 1999 book *The IVF Revolution*, 'Only a fraction of the couples who might benefit from IVF receive it. IVF is primarily a treatment for those who can afford to pay for it. Probably less than 10 per cent of IVF in Britain is carried out through the NHS. Nor do private medical insurance companies, to their eternal shame, fund any part of IVF treatment. Indeed, in Britain it is increasingly difficult to get any free advanced fertility treatments.'

Nevertheless, test-tube babies are no longer supplied only by 'traditional' IVF methods. Even more advanced technical refinements are available and discussed below.

Surrogacy

This is a further stage on from normal DI. It applies when a woman gives birth to a child through ordinary artificial insemination – but she is not intended to be the 'real' mother once the child is born. She is merely 'lending' her womb to another couple to help them bring into the world their child, even though genetically half the child may be 'hers' with her own egg fertilised by the would-be father's semen.

Kept within the family and with no money changing hands, surrogacy usually causes no major legal problems. It often takes place between sisters, one of whom may have had her womb removed by hysterectomy. Or even, as happened in Darlington in December 1996, when 51-year-old Mrs Edith Jones gave birth to her own granddaughter, having carried the child for her 21-year-old daughter who had been born without a womb.

But in January 1985 the first known English case of *commercial* surrogacy occurred – and the courts at once became involved. Mrs Kim Cotton, a 28-year-old housewife from north London, with a husband and two other children of her own, gave birth to a baby girl after she had 'leased' her womb for £6,500 through a professional agency to another married couple to carry the husband's child. They had no form of sexual relations. She never even met him. As Mr Justice Latey later clinically explained in the High Court: 'He had come to England for the sole purpose of providing seminal fluid for insemination of the surrogate mother. The semen was introduced into the mother by a qualified nurse. The father and surrogate mother never met. Conception resulted from the insemination. It was agreed that at birth the baby would be handed to the father and his wife.'

Using the traditional legal yardstick in all cases dealing with children, of what is best for the child, Mr Justice Latey ruled that the couple should bring up the baby and look after her – although Mrs Cotton was undoubtedly her genetic and legal mother.

Parliament has twice intervened since then. The 1985 Surrogacy Arrangements Act outlawed all commercial arrangements negotiated through an agency or other intermediary, although not many people realise that the Act still allows a married couple to negotiate direct with a surrogate mother and even to pay her a fee, so long as no 'middle man' is involved.

What about a fee dressed up as 'expenses'? Although the 1985 Act says nothing one way or the other about expenses, case law says that 'reasonable expenses' are allowed. Allegations have been made over the years that these can be unrealistically high, in fact amounting to a concealed fee. In October 1998, a Government-appointed committee reported that the sums paid were often double what they should be. The Government promptly promised to bring in tighter new laws – but we have not yet seen any, and are unlikely to do so for quite some time.

The second relevant piece of current legislation is the 1990 Human Fertilisation and Embryology Act. This lays down that no surrogacy arrangement can be enforced in the courts. A mother cannot be made to hand over the child; nor can a commissioning couple be made to accept it. Even today the surrogate remains the child's lawful mother and a married couple can only become the child's legal parents by adopting it or by obtaining a 'parental order' under the 1990 Act. But this latter course is only available if they are married and the child is genetically related to at least one of them. If unmarried, their best hope is to persuade a court to make a 'parental responsibility order' or a 'residence order' under the 1989 Children Act – which will give them somewhat lesser rights.

The girl who lost a child to her own mother

A teenager in Lancashire agreed to bear a baby for her own mother because the older woman was eager for a baby after remarrying but had suffered two miscarriages and been told another pregnancy was dangerous. The daughter handed over the child at birth but some six years later changed her mind after quarrels about how the little girl was being raised. She applied to Fleetwood magistrates' court for the child to be returned to her. The result was a Solomon-like decision whereby she withdrew her application and the child's grandmother – for that was her legal status! – obtained a 'residence order' saying the child should live with her but the daughter won a 'contact order' giving her contact at certain weekends.

As Andrew Bainham says in his book *Children – The Modern Law*, 'English law is ambivalent about surrogacy. On the one hand it is seeking to discourage the making of agreements, whilst on the other it is providing mechanisms for giving effect to a proportion of them.'

Hormone treatment, egg donation and embryo transplants

Sometimes intensive hormone treatment can help a woman who does not ovulate naturally to start ovulating and so release her eggs into her reproductive system with the result that a child may be conceived. Since this treatment is all internal and within the woman's own body, it does not have to be supplied in an establishment licensed under the 1990 Act and there are no national rules or guidelines.

It all depends on where you live. For instance, at one time, couples wanting treatment in south Cumbria had to be in a stable relationship for two years, while in west Essex the period was four years. Some decisions seem highly questionable, as in a famous example when sextuplets in Grimsby were born to a single woman to whom a local NHS hospital had chosen to give drug fertility treatment, although she already had one child and did not even live with the father who already had three children of his own by someone else.

But, if hormone treatment does not work, infertile women may be helped by egg donation, which is a later variant on 'normal' artificial insemination and is within the Human Fertility and Embryology Authority's remit. Eggs are taken from a fertile woman, fertilised in the laboratory with male sperm – usually but not always (as we shall see) from her husband – and the resulting entire embryo is implanted in her womb. One cycle of treatment costs between £2,000 and £2,500 and couples have been known to remortgage their homes and sell their cars just to try it.

But there is a limit to the lengths to which the Authority will permit a couple to go in their search for a child. There are no legal restrictions on the age of a woman who can be offered fertility treatment under the 1990 Act, but, in July 1993, when commenting on a case reported widely in the press where a 58-year-old Englishwoman had gone to Italy for fertility treatment denied to her in Britain, Professor Colin Campbell, then the Authority's chairman, said it did not 'encourage' treatment of women over the age of menopause but did not actually forbid it. In November 1997, a widow named Liz Buttle became the oldest woman to have a child in Britain with the aid of fertility treatment when she gave birth to a healthy baby boy at the age of 60 – but she had lied about her age, saying she was only 49. When the Authority's Code of Practice was revised eight months later, in July 1998, its attitude had hardened and the Code said specifically: 'Gametes (eggs and sperm) should not be taken from female donors over 35 and from male donors over 55 unless there are exceptional reasons for doing so.'

Both the Act and the Code are silent on the question of fertility treatment between the races and the Authority has allowed a licensed clinic in Cambridge to make a black woman pregnant using eggs from a white donor; but it said the reason was that the black woman's husband was of mixed race – and so the child would have been born of mixed race anyway. Mrs Flora Goldhill, the Authority's then chief executive, commented that they would not have followed an earlier Italian example where a black woman was helped to have a white baby solely because she felt it would have a better life. 'That smacks of social engineering and the creation of a designer baby which would not be acceptable to the Authority,' she said. Within a fortnight it was announced that a licensed clinic in Nottingham, operating under the Authority's control, had refused an Indian couple's request for a donor egg implant from a white male.

The Authority published a detailed written questionnaire to which the general public was asked to send in its replies on the subject of whether women should be allowed to become pregnant using eggs from aborted foetuses. That will sound appalling to many people but the Authority explained that the shortage of donor eggs was so great that clinics had waiting lists of three to four years for women whose only chance of becoming pregnant was to receive a viable donor egg – from some source or other.

'The use of donated adult, cadaveric or foetal ovarian tissue could provide many more eggs than are currently available,' said its somewhat chilling press release in January 1994. Six months later, after having considered 10,000 responses from the public to its questionnaire, the Authority announced that it was banning the use of eggs from aborted foetuses but that they could be used for research purposes. In November 1994 the Criminal Justice and Public Order Act made it a criminal offence to use eggs from aborted foetuses for fertility treatment in Britain.

One final question: should fertility treatment be available to women who are not married to their sexual partner?

Section 13 (5) of the 1990 Act says not too helpfully:

A woman shall not be provided with treatment services unless account has been taken of the welfare of any child who may be born as a result of the treatment (including the need of that child for a father), and of any other child who may be affected by the birth.

What does that legal mumbo-jumbo, hurriedly cobbled together while the Act was going through Parliament (it was not in the original version of the Bill), actually mean? In practice, not very much: it was a sop to the traditionalist lobbies in Parliament. You do not have to be married to qualify for fertility treatment. It is available to both unmarried women in stable relationships and to single women living on their own. In 1991, there was even a much-publicised 'virgin birth', in which a single woman who said she had never had sex with anyone, lawfully gave birth to a child assisted by DI.

Doctors in modern Britain rarely make moral judgements about candidates for fertility treatment. And who is to say they are wrong? A quarter of the children born this year will see their parents separate before they are 16 and, when families break up, almost half of all fathers lose contact with their children. So is lack of a father necessarily a good reason for denying a woman the right to have a child?

In reality, if the staff at a clinic or hospital licensed by the Authority believe that a single woman without a partner, let alone a stable one, has the right to a child and will probably do a good job of bringing it up, they will treat her. As Dr Jack Glatt, then medical director of the Infertility Advisory Centre in London, has told a *Daily Express* journalist:

> The Human Fertilisation and Embryology Act encourages clinics not to discriminate against single women. . . We see single women in stable unions, single women who live with a man and single women without a partner. We treat each case individually. If we are satisfied by her special circumstances we go ahead.

A baby has somehow managed to overcome the hurdles of birth control, sterilisation and abortion. Now one last question has to be asked:

WHAT ARE THE LEGAL RIGHTS OF THE UNBORN CHILD?

Lying in its mother's womb, it has no legal rights at all. In 1989, a young Liverpool woman had just nine days of her pregnancy to go when a drunken motorist drove into her on a pedestrian crossing. The impact threw her across his car bonnet and into the road. Her baby girl was stillborn after an emergency Caesarean section. Despite a string of previous motoring convictions, the driver was jailed for only three months for reckless and drink driving. He could not be charged with the more serious offence of causing death through reckless driving because, as defence counsel explained in words that he may afterwards have regretted, 'in law, of course, the unborn child does not count'.

Indeed, it has no separate legal existence – and therefore no legal rights – until at least it is born. In January 1993 an 18-weeks pregnant woman in Leeds lost her unborn baby when she was stabbed in the stomach while struggling with a street mugger and the police had to admit that the attacker, if caught, could be charged with attempted murder of the woman or grievous bodily harm upon her – but not with any offence concerning the 'death' of the unborn baby. Five months later, in June

1993, a woman driver three and a half times over the alcohol limit was jailed at Winchester Crown Court for three and a half years on charges of causing the deaths of a heavily pregnant mother *and* her child – but the baby, delivered by Caesarean section, had survived for 36 hours.

This governing principle that an unborn baby has no legal rights until actually born was first set out by Sir George Baker, then Family Division President, in the High Court in May 1978. A Merseyside steelworker, whose pregnant wife had just left him, had applied for an injunction stopping her from going ahead with an abortion without his consent. But he lost his case – on two grounds. Sir George ruled that he had no legal right, merely because he was the woman's husband, to prevent her from having an abortion and that he had no such right as a spokesman for the unborn child itself. Indeed, Sir George rejected the idea out of hand, saying somewhat tersely: 'The foetus cannot in English law, in my view, have any right of its own – at least until it is born and has a separate existence from the mother.'

This doctrine has been developed in subsequent decisions. In January 1988 the Appeal Court specifically ruled that a child, while still unborn, has no legal rights as against its own mother. There is a limit to legal intervention in the miracle of childbirth. No woman can be ordered to behave in such a way that no harm comes to the foetus within her. This was in the case of *Re F (in utero)*:

> London social workers had applied to the High Court for an unborn child to be made a ward of court (and therefore protected by the full authority of the Law) because its mother, a mentally disturbed 36-year-old drug addict, had gone missing, not for the first time, and they considered she was a danger to the foetus, now only a few weeks off its expected date of birth.
>
> Said Lord Justice Staughton: 'This court is in no position to inquire into the problem of mothers who may neglect or harm their children before birth or to decide in what circumstances and with what safeguards there should be power to restrict the liberty of the mother in order to prevent that happening. The court cannot care for a child or order that others should do so until the child is born; only the mother can.'
>
> Mr Justice Hollings refused the application and the Appeal Court ruled he was quite right.

But, once a child is born, the House of Lords has said that a court can rightly take into account events that happened while it was still in its mother's womb. This was in December 1986 when five law lords ruled that Berkshire County Council had been right to take into care a baby girl born prematurely to a heroin addict and suffering from heroin withdrawal symptoms caused by the mother's addiction – even though that inevitably meant taking into account what had occurred before the child had been born.

Similarly, once born, a child can sue for damage sustained through someone else's negligence while it was still in its mother's womb, as when a negligent driver smashes into a car in which the pregnant woman is a passenger, or when a doctor or nurse is negligent while the child is actually being born. In May 1992, a six-year-old boy made legal history by winning £700,000 damages against his own mother (but paid by her insurance company) after he had been born disabled because, while pregnant, she had negligently crashed the car she was driving.

This is a rapidly developing part of the law. In October 1992 a 30-year-old 'born-again' Christian was in labour with her third child. The baby was lying transverse with its elbow through the cervix. There was a high risk of rupture of the uterus and, unless a Caesarean section was performed, it would be impossible for the baby to be born alive.

But the woman, supported by her husband, refused the operation.

After the woman had been three days in labour, her gynaecologist applied to the High Court for a declaration that the operation could be performed lawfully without the mother's consent. Within 18 minutes – and with no one in court to argue the mother's case – Sir Stephen Brown, then Family Division President, granted the declaration. 'The surgeon's evidence is that we are concerned with minutes rather than hours and that it is a life-and-death situation,' he explained.

The operation was performed – but the baby still died. Two days later Alexander McCall Smith, a reader in law at Edinburgh University, wrote forcefully in *The Times:*

Pregnant women should be afforded the normal courtesies when they make decisions about their health. They must be entitled to refuse treatment, even if their refusal is dangerous to them and to the foetus they carry. If their conduct causes the death of the foetus, then that is a matter for their consciences, and it should weigh very heavily indeed.

The consequences of allowing compulsory treatment, though, are just too unattractive to accept.

What will be a judge's ruling when the situation arises – which assuredly it will – that an operation is required which would certainty save the life of the unborn baby but might kill the pregnant mother? I would not wish to hazard a guess. It would all depend on the individual judge and how the law has developed by then.

But sometimes one can try and be too legally watertight, cross too many 't's and dot too many 'i's in the attempt to lay down too many wide-embracing principles in advance.

There is often a simple way round most legal problems. When over thirty years ago my wife's gynaecologist, whom I knew to be Roman Catholic, arrived to deliver our first child, with my wife already in labour, I said to her: '*If* there is any problem, any question of risk in the birth, you are to save my wife's life – even if it means the baby dies. I want you to agree that now, before you go into the delivery room' – and she did.

That vital exchange formed a legal contract between us. If she had then gone back on her word and saved the baby at the cost of my wife's life, I could have sued her. Whether I would have chosen to do so is a different matter.

2

BIRTH

Even being born can have legal complications nowadays. It has been reported in *The Times* that the number of babies born by Caesarean section had more than doubled in recent years. And why? One reason advanced was that doctors and midwives were frightened of being sued if something went wrong during childbirth.

Such cases used to be extremely rare but no longer. Legal aid is now available to young children and teenagers under 18, irrespective of their parents' financial status. The result is that more young people can now sue if something goes wrong when they are being born. Ironically, today many middle-class children have better access to the courts than their allegedly too wealthy parents.

Caesareans are less risky than natural childbirth. Therefore there is less risk of being sued. So many doctors and midwives, forced to practise what they call in the United States 'defensive medicine', nowadays prefer, if at all possible and there is any likelihood of complications, to advise their patients to have a Caesarean. In the US, it is even worse: one in four babies is now born by Caesarean and exorbitant premiums for medical malpractice insurance have driven many doctors out of maternity care altogether. One can only hope that this is one instance where we do not too slavishly follow the American pattern.

But what happens if a pregnant woman, for reasons of her own, refuses her doctor's advice to have a Caesarean? In the mid-1990s there was a flurry of High Court cases in which hospitals sought emergency orders, often outside normal court hours, in order to enable them to conduct what they claimed were life-saving Caesarean sections. The Official Solicitor was usually involved but only to advise the court or to represent the interests of the baby. Seldom, if ever, was any lawyer in court to argue on behalf of the woman. In all these cases, different judges ordered the woman to submit by force, if necessary, to a Caesarean, having accepted the medical evidence that it was the only way to save the baby's life and the woman's objections could be discounted.[1]

Yet in 1993 Lord Donaldson of Lymington, then Master of the Rolls, had ruled that a mentally competent person had an absolute right to refuse medical treatment, and such a refusal could be 'rational, irrational or for no reason at all'. So how could it possibly be lawful for a woman to be compelled to accept so highly intrusive a piece of surgery against her own passionate objections, however misguided? The answer, of course, was that another human life was involved: that of her unborn child. But not one of the Family Division judges based their decision on that – more honest – ground. They all said that, as is true, it was accepted law that a patient was to be deemed incompetent of giving a valid consent to treatment, if unable to understand or retain the relevant information or unable to make a decision based on the information given – but they virtually invented the doctrine of 'temporary incompetence' on the basis that, as one judge put it, the woman 'was called upon to make the decision at a time of acute emotional stress and physical pain'. Quite a few people, both within and outside the law, found that view offensive to women and I am glad to say that it was finally and uncompromisingly rejected by the Appeal Court in *St. George's NHS Trust* v. *S*, reported in (1998) 3 All England Reports 673.

Lord Justice Judge's words make good reading: 'While pregnancy increases the personal responsibilities of a woman, it does not diminish her entitlement to decide whether or not to undergo medical treatment . . . Her unborn child's need for medical assistance does not prevail over her rights. She is entitled not to be forced to submit to an invasion of her body against her will, whether her own life or that of her child depends on it.'

Thankfully most parents do not have to think in these terms. Their child is born healthy and with no problems. Their only legal need is to choose a name and register the birth.

NAMING AND THE BIRTH CERTIFICATE

Some young couples panic because they still have not agreed on a name even after the child has been born. They need not worry. The 1953 Births and Deaths Registration Act gives parents up to six weeks in which to supply all the details – including the name – and register the birth at the local register Office. Only then is it crunch time and you actually have to commit yourself.

You can call your child anything you like. There is no law about it. 'Coloured parents often call their babies "Prince" or "Princess",' a helpful official at a London register office has told me, 'and we raise no objections. Why should we? It would only become a problem if in later life they became con artists and tried to pass themselves off as royalty. In the same way, we would not object to registering "Lord" or "Lady" as a first name. But we do object to profanity. I would refuse to register a newborn babe as "Little Bleeder" or "Bloody Awful" – but I cannot actually point to any legislation which gives me the right to do so.'

She actually knew of a baby named Little Joy – but 'Little' was legally the first of the baby's two first names, as stated on the birth certificate. A Christian name is, of course, only a child's baptismal name. Only someone who has been christened bears a true Christian name.

In any event, whatever name you register, you can always afterwards change your mind and get the birth certificate altered. If you do so within a year, the registrar cannot question your decision. After that he will need to be satisfied that you have in fact been calling the child by a different name from that stated on the certificate. In later life, the child, when grown to adulthood, can change his or her own name – but we will come to that later.

Who can register the child? Here immediately we run into one of the few remaining – but important – differences between children whose parents are married when they are born and those who are not. The 1987 Family Law Reform Act is supposed to have removed the unfair stigma associated with illegitimacy and to have put the two kinds of children on virtually the same legal basis.

But it has not fully happened.

'Illegitimate' is no longer a politically correct word and the fashionable term nowadays for children born to single mothers is 'non-marital'. Yet, as we shall soon see in the section on illegitimacy, this bland phraseology masks a still-imperfect reality.

It is popularly believed that having the short version of a birth certificate shows that a child is illegitimate. Unlike the full certificate, this does not give full details of the parents. But many people, both legitimate and illegitimate, only have a short certificate: it is provided free at the time of registration whereas the full one costs £3.50.

The truth is that, irrespective of short or full certificate and despite everyone's good intentions, an unmarried mother can all too soon discover that the law puts her and her child into a different category from others. This is how it works:

(1) If the couple are married, either she or the father can register the child and sign the birth certificate. In practice, the birth certificates of legitimate children usually have only one signature: that of the father or mother who happened to register the birth. It does not matter which.

And please note that a baby is born legitimate if its parents are married to each other *when the baby is born*. It does not matter that they were not married to each other when the baby was conceived – or even if at that time one or both were married to someone else. It is their marital state at birth which counts – except (and there is all too often in the law a sentence beginning with 'except') if a couple are married to each other when their child is conceived but, by the time the child is born, they are divorced or the father has died. Then the child is still born legitimate and can be registered as such. In that specific instance, the law takes account of the couple's marital state when the child is actually conceived.

(2) If the couple are not married to each other (and never have been) at the time of the birth, only the mother can register the birth by herself and her signature alone will appear on the birth certificate. The father cannot register the child by himself and the only way in which his signature can appear on the birth certificate is alongside the mother's if they both go to the register office and register the child jointly.

It is unusual for both parents to register a child's birth, if they are married, so both parents' signature on the certificate is often a sign of illegitimacy: it tells the world even today what your child in later life may not wish everyone to know.

(3) Even without his signature, an unmarried father's name can still appear on a birth certificate – but only if both father and mother consent *or* the mother asks for it and produces a written statutory declaration signed by him (i.e. a statement sworn in front of a solicitor) declaring that he is the father *or* she produces a court order to that effect, which is rare.

Sometimes a problem arises when a pregnant woman lives with her boyfriend and has adopted his surname but, for some reason, he is still married to another woman when their child is born. Can the child be registered in his name, even though he is still married to someone else and the child is not his wife's? The answer is 'Yes'. The child is undoubtedly illegitimate but his mother has chosen to use her lover's surname, so there is no legal reason why she cannot register her child in that name. If the father thereafter becomes free to marry and marries the mother, that will automatically – ever since the 1926 Legitimation Act – legitimise the child with retrospective effect as from birth and either parent can then, as a married parent, go to the local register office, re-register the child and obtain a new birth certificate with that tell-tale solitary signature.

One last matter: a baby can legally be given *any* surname, not necessarily that of either parent. You could call your child John Windsor, if you liked, giving him a spurious air of bearing the royal family name and perhaps being a distant cousin of the Queen.

ILLEGITIMACY

Back in October 1989, Marina Ogilvy, daughter of the Queen's cousin, Princess Alexandra, announced that she was expecting a baby. She was single and said she had no intention of marrying her boyfriend, Paul Mowatt. Overnight a bitter feud erupted between her and her parents, duly reported in loving detail in certain sections of the press. At first, Marina claimed that her parents had tried to trick her into an abortion and that her father had cut off her trust fund allowance. Then, within a month, she and Paul changed their minds and announced they would marry after all.

'They said if I had the baby without getting married, it would change history and bring disgrace on the monarchy,' said Marina. She was exaggerating. In Britain at the turn of the century just one in 23 babies was born illegitimate. But by 1978 the proportion had increased to one in ten and in June 1994 the Office of Population Censuses and Surveys (now the Office for National Statistics) reported that almost one in three of all children was being born outside marriage. Furthermore, the number of illegitimate births registered by both parents, a sure sign of a stable non-marital relationship, had doubled since 1961.

Since World War II there has been a constant process of legal change to keep pace with this sustained development in moral and ethical values. It culminated in the 1987 Family Law Reform Act, which is virtually the Bible of illegitimate children's rights. Before the Act there were still considerable, if somewhat bizarre, injustices. For example, if someone died without making a will their illegitimate child shared in the estate in exactly the same way as a legitimate child, but that did not apply if grandparents, brothers or sisters died: in that case, the illegitimate grand-child, brother or sister was ignored.

But the 1987 Act proclaimed roundly the general principle that in future all references in statutes or private legal documents to 'any relationship between two persons shall be construed without regard to whether or not the father and mother of either of them, or the father and mother of any person through whom the relationship is deduced, have or had been married to each other at any time'. What could be simpler? The Act means what it says: legitimate and illegitimate children are now, as a general rule, treated by the law in exactly the same way – except (and I warned you earlier of 'except'!) that an illegitimate child is not entitled as of right to British citizenship and still cannot succeed to a hereditary title.

But many people do not realise that it is possible to contract out of the Act: it only applies 'unless the contrary intention appears'. This means that if, for example, you want to ensure that only the legitimate children of your children living at your death benefit from your estate, you state in your will that the bequest is 'to my legitimate grandchildren living at my death' instead of simply 'to my grandchildren living at my death'. The result would be different if you did not make a will and your estate was shared out between your family on the basis of the 1952 Intestates' Estates Act. Then *all* your grandchildren living at your death, illegitimate as well as legitimate, would inherit.

So old-fashioned grandparents should take note: to ensure that your wishes prevail, you should seek expert advice in making a will – which, as we shall see later, is true of everyone anyway.

But the 1987 Act not only gave a new sense of legal equality to illegitimate children. It also bestowed new rights on their parents. For the first time, unmarried mothers were put in the same position as wives to make claims for the financial support of their children. Until then, unmarried mothers could claim only in their local magistrates' court, whose austere and often depressing atmosphere is generally more appropriate for minor criminals and shamefaced motorists on drink-driving charges than for women with an unpleasant problem in their personal life. Now such women have the option of going to their local county court or High Court, which provide a far more agreeable atmosphere.

It is not only the setting that has improved: under the old law, a mother claiming maintenance had to take the baby's father to court within three years of the child's birth. Now there is no time limit. Previously, mothers had still to be single to claim. Now they can already be married to someone else. In the old days, they could not obtain a lump sum order from the father of more than £1,000. Now there is no limit on the amounts that a man can be ordered to pay on top of his monthly or weekly payments.

This is all very well and fine. But not every father of an illegitimate child happily admits that he is the father. How does a mother prove it in court? Until recently blood tests were never conclusive: they were able to establish that a man could not be the father rather than prove positively that he was. But now the blood is submitted to modern DNA testing methods and the results are claimed to be 100 per cent accurate.

The ex-policeman who was proved to be a liar

In the late-1980s, a former policeman swore in court that he had never had sexual intercourse with a baby girl's mother. The magistrates believed him and she lost her case. But later DNA testing became available – and proved he was the father. At Gloucester Crown Court in May 1989, he was jailed for six months for perjury.

The court always has discretion to grant or refuse a test in what it considers to be the child's best interests. What happens if a man refuses to take a test ordered by a court? The worst is presumed against him and he can be made to pay for the child as if he was, indeed, the father. This course of action was approved by the Appeal Court in July 1993 when a wealthy Midlands businessman, who had always denied that a young girl was his daughter but refused DNA testing, was ordered to pay maintenance plus a £1,000 lump sum. The mother claimed that she had given birth to the child after a brief office fling nine years earlier.

Normally, of course, it is the woman who asks for the alleged father to be tested but he has the right to ask to be tested to prove that he *is* the father – when she is denying it! However, in such cases, the court is generally wary.

The end of the affair

A woman had been having an affair with another man while still sleeping with her husband. She became pregnant but insisted that it was her husband's child. The affair ended and several months later a baby girl was born. She and her husband (whom she had told about the affair) believed it was their child and intended bringing her up as such, but the ex-lover still insisted it was his and asked the High Court to order DNA testing to prove he was right. The baby was then eight months old. Judge Callman refused. He said that, in the circumstances, it would disrupt the family unit and not be in the child's best interests. In February 1993, the Appeal Court upheld his decision.

Formerly, only the unmarried mother had legal rights over her child. She had sole legal control: she alone had the legal right to decide its name, its school, its religion, where it lived – in fact, its whole general upbringing. The father's only effective 'right' was to ask a court to be allowed to see the child – at risk of being ordered to pay towards its maintenance.

Nowadays an unmarried mother still starts off with sole legal control – now called 'parental responsibility' – but a father who wants to act like a father (even though not marrying the mother) also has substantial rights. As Lord Justice Balcombe recognised in the Appeal Court in November 1990 in *Re H (No. 2)*: 'The position of the natural father can be infinitely variable. At one end of the spectrum his connection with the child may be only the single act of intercourse (possibly even rape) which led to conception. At the other end of the spectrum he may have played a full part in the child's life from birth onwards, only the formality of marriage to the mother being absent.'

Parliament has acknowledged that reality and the 1989 Children Act gives every unmarried father the right to acquire joint parental responsibility along with the mother. They can either agree this amicably between themselves or he can go to the High Court or nearest family hearing centre (via the local county court) and ask for it. A judge will order joint responsibility, if he considers it in the child's best interests – which will, of course, depend on all the circumstances. As Lord Justice Balcombe also said in *Re H* , 'The court will have to take into account a number of factors of which the following will undoubtedly be material, although there may well be others: (1) the degree of commitment which the father has shown towards the child, (2) the degree of attachment between them and (3) his reasons for applying for the order.' He does not have to be living with the mother: in *Re H,* for instance, the Appeal Court made the order although the parents were living apart.

In fact, the Children Act so encourages unmarried parents to function, at least in this respect, as if they were married that couples can easily give themselves joint parental responsibility without even going before a judge. All they need do is ask a clerk at their nearest county court office for a Parental Responsibility Agreement form. Its wording is extremely simple. They merely fill it in, sign it and post two copies to the Principal Registry of the Family Division, First Avenue House, 42-49 High Holborn, London WC1V 6HA. No fee is required.

My only word of warning is that they should do this only if they are sure – at least, as sure as anyone can be of anything in this world – that they will stay together during the child's early years. A parental responsibility agreement lasts until the child comes of age on his 18th birthday. It should not lightly be entered into.

But not everyone can have children or is prepared to undergo artificial methods of reproduction. Ever since the original 1926 Adoption Act, the law has provided a widely used alternative.

ADOPTION

Until they actually get involved in trying to adopt, most people do not realise that the factual basis of adoption has changed fundamentally in recent years. This is inadequately reflected in the current legislation, which is still based on the old 'total transplant' idea, as enshrined in the most recent Adoption Act dating from 1976: this assumes that adoption irrevocably transfers a child from one family to another. It does this by vesting joint parental responsibility in the adopters and by extinguishing the parental responsibility of the natural parents. Mr Justice Thorpe has actually gone so far as to rule that the natural mother of an adopted five-year-old boy was no longer legally his 'parent' and so required the leave of the court before applying to see him again after having handed him over for adoption four years earlier – which leave he refused.

An adopted child is treated in law in almost every way as the adopters' child with exactly the same rights of inheritance and nationality as their blood child. One so-called exception trotted out by most law books is that it does not apply to the 'prohibited degrees of relationship' within which two people cannot marry, so that, for instance, an adopted woman can marry her adoptive brother but not her genetic brother.

But this, of course, is hardly a practical problem, since most adopted people will not know who are their genetic brothers or sisters. In fact, a case in August 1993 highlighted a tragic loophole in the law:

The young mother killed by the pill

When a 22-year-old Birmingham divorcee, who already had one child, decided to go on the pill to help beat period pains, her doctor asked her the usual family medical history questions. But the doctor did not know that she had been adopted and she herself did not know that her natural mother had suffered from thrombosis. If the doctor had known about the thrombosis, she would never have prescribed the pill – which killed the young woman with a massive blood clot. 'Accidental death' was the jury's verdict and afterwards her adoptive mother told a reporter: 'There should be a way of checking if a patient is adopted and find out if the natural mother had suffered from thrombosis.'

But, as the law now stands, that is impossible. An adoption order virtually amounts to a legal rebirth. The Registrar-General enters the adoption in the Adopted Children's Register. This is kept at the Office for National Statistics' headquarters at Smedley Hydro, Southport PR8 2HH and certified copies may be obtained, for a small fee, either in person at the Office's London address at the Family Record Centre, 1 Myddleton

Street, London EC1R 1UW or by post from Smedley Hydro. An entry states the child's sex, date of birth and new name and gives the adopters' names and occupations plus date and place of the adoption order. Although each entry has a number linked secretly to the original registration of birth, it does *not* give the natural mother's or father's name or address.

This is effectively the child's new birth certificate. The new parents can even request a short-form certificate which makes no mention of the adoption.

This legal framework seems very enlightened. The problem is, as shown by the sad story of the young divorcee who did not know of her natural mother's thrombosis, that it is largely out of date. It relates back to a time when, as Professor Stephen Cretney says in his book *Elements of Family Law,* 'Adoption was primarily seen as a method whereby a healthy, white (and usually illegitimate) baby would be placed with a childless couple who would bring him or her up as their own child with preferably no contact at all with the child's birth mother or natural family.' In practice, adoptions of this kind are no longer typical. Nowadays, candidates for adoption are much more likely to be older children who often already know at least one of their parents or family background or they are stepchildren or close relatives of at least one adoptive parent.

Also many adopted children are now of mixed race, handicapped or with emotional or behavioural problems where it can sometimes be useful for some kind of monitored link to be maintained with their previous existence.

The result is that silence about antecedents is no longer the sacred cow it used to be. As far back as 1975 an earlier Children Act tried to remove some of the secrecy by providing that all adopted persons over 18 who want to trace their natural parents can apply to the Registrar-General for the information needed to find their original birth entry – which would, of course, give their mother's name and her then address and possibly also that of their father. If adopted before 12 November 1975, an applicant had first to see a counsellor because until that date parents were assured their offspring would never know their names. For those adopted later, counselling was optional.

But, because the details given were only those on the original birth registration, in practice it proved difficult for people to trace their genetic parents. So the 1989 Children Act instituted an alternative streamlined process. It set up an Adoption Contact Register, also kept by the Registrar-General, on which parents and other relatives (including anyone related by blood or marriage to the child) can inscribe their names and current addresses. These updated details can then be passed on to adopted children who apply to be registered; but, as the Registrar-General has emphasised in an official leaflet, this will happen only if both parties want it: 'Birth parents and other relatives who have decided that they would prefer not to have contact with an adopted person need have no fear that the introduction of the Register will put them at greater risk.'

We are, alas, still a long way from a thoroughly thought-out modern law of adoption. As Andrew Bainham says in his *Children – The Modern Law*, 'There has been a growing realisation that the "exclusivity" of adoption, perhaps the cardinal feature of English adoption law, would have to give way to a more flexible concept which admitted greater "openness".'

So, after all this, what is the actual process of adoption? Only 7,000 children are adopted each year in Britain – with 100,000 couples wanting to adopt. They face a virtual obstacle course.

The first hurdle is to get accepted by one of the 200 authorised adoption agencies: all are forbidden by law to exact a fee for their services. Most are run by social services departments of local authorities but some are independent voluntary agencies. Since the law was changed in 1982 (by an amendment to the 1976 Act), 'private' adoptions are no longer legally possible: even adoptions within a family must first be vetted by the local social services department and require, like all others, an adoption order by a court.

Adoption law is somewhat two-faced. The Act itself lays down only the most minimal qualifications for adopters: they must usually be at least 21 but there is no upper age limit. Most adoptions are joint, in which case the Act specifies that the couple must be married; but single people, whether unmarried, widowed, separated or divorced, may apply. Contrary to popular belief, there is no law that says the adoptive single parent and child cannot be of the same sex. Heterosexual unmarried couples and homosexual couples cannot jointly apply – but a sole application by one (with the other in a sort of legal limbo) is technically possible, although in practice unlikely to succeed. Lesbian couples (with one as the actual adopter) are sometimes successful but male gay couples almost never – whatever the sex of the child.

In fact, the law of supply and demand is more rigorous than the law of the land. Just because, in this age of extensive birth control and unmarried mothers, there are many more would-be adopters than children available for adoption, the agencies have wide scope within the law to pick and choose those they accept.

There are no hard-and-fast rules: acceptability, like beauty, is in the eye of the beholder. All agencies require would-be adopters to submit to medical examination and regular 'assessment' home visits by social workers. Most set an upper age limit of 35 for the wife and 40 for the husband. Couples do not have to be particularly well off but they must all be able to show they can afford to take on a child.

Some agencies will not accept people who have been divorced and most insist that the marriage is at least three years old. All agencies accept people from all kinds of ethnic origin or religious background but some only allow them to adopt children of similar origin or background. Believe it or not, smoking can be a reason for refusal: several social services refuse to accept couples one or both of whom smoke as candidates to adopt children under 10, while the co-ordinating body, British Agencies for Adoption and Fostering, has told all social services and voluntary agencies that children *under two* should not generally be adopted by people who smoke. When the British Agencies announced in March 1993 these new national guidelines, Tim Yeo, then Junior Health Minister, commented: 'It would be wrong for a child to be denied the chance of a loving home solely because there is a smoker in the household. There is no room for dogma or ideology in any aspect of adoption. Each case has to be judged on its merits, using common sense and compassion.'

Few people would argue with that but, in the same month, the British Agencies gave two reporters from the *Daily Telegraph* this revealing profile of ideal candidates:

> Non-smoking, heterosexual couples under the age of thirty-five, with a comfortable home, plenty of friends and no criminal convictions. There is only one factor which absolutely rules anyone out for adoption: a conviction for child abuse or molestation.

A particularly disturbing case was subsequently picked up by the media where a white Englishman and his Asian-born wife were told by Norfolk social services after three years of 'assessment' by social workers that, because they lived happily in the country far from any deprived inner city, they were 'too racially naïve' to be accepted as adoptive parents for a youngster of mixed race. The furore prompted Peter Thurnham, a backbench Tory MP, to tell the *Sunday Times* of his own experience of the adoption process:

The MP's story

In 1983, Mr Thurnham and his wife, who had four children of their own, want to adopt a child with special needs. 'The social workers thought our house was too neat and tidy. They didn't like the fact that we sent our children to boarding school and, because I am in a Tory marginal, they thought my job was insecure,' he said. But they persevered and six years later they succeeded in adopting a boy who was severely mentally handicapped.

One day – hopefully – the position will change for the better; but we should not hold our breath. Back in November 1993 John Major's Government published a White Paper, *Adoption – the Future*, which proposed that children aged 12 or more would have to agree to their own adoption, couples over 40 would no longer be barred as adopters and it would be made easier for step-parents. Above all, 'common sense' was promised as the watchword of the selection process. In 1996 a draft Bill was proposed along those lines but, in May 1997, Tony Blair's Government took office, the draft Bill was dropped and a change in the law seems as far off as ever.

For now, acceptance by an agency remains only the first stage in the long, drawn-out process of adoption. After acceptance comes the agonising wait to be tried out for a specific, available child – and that too has its problems, as witness this letter published in the *Sunday Times* in July 1993 which still applies today:

The adoptive parent is the lowest of the low

We are a white, middle-class married couple. We have a large, tidy house in the country with a good-sized garden. I am a university lecturer, aged 49, and my wife (48) is a teacher. We have lived and worked in Africa; we have fostered a Mauritian boy for eight years and we have three children of our own (two grown up, and a 10-year-old son at home). We want to offer a home to a disadvantaged child or children.

We are approved as adoptive parents and have been receiving visits from various social workers over the past three years without success. Many reasons have been given as to why we were not suitable: we are too old; we live in the country, which is not suitable for town children; we will have too high an expectation of children academically; etc., etc.

Recently we were short-listed for a group of three children and then we were dropped because 'the other two couples dropped out and so it was not possible to offer the selection panel a choice'.

We fully appreciate the principle that the child's welfare is paramount and we have no argument with it. However, we feel that the system has gone overboard in its search for ideal parents. Time and money seem no object as social workers search for months for the end of their rainbow. In this regard the best is so often the enemy of the good.

The position of the adoptive parent is the lowest of the low. Judgements are made about your suitability by social workers who visit you for two hours, and there is no right of reply. There is no way they will allow you to present your case at their panel discussions. Someone described to us the rejection you feel as having a psychological miscarriage. We can vouch for that feeling, as I am sure many others can.

So much for would-be adoptive parents. What about the rights of the adoptive child's natural parents?

The fear of many adopters is that at some time in the future the child may be taken away from them, reclaimed by its natural parents. They read cases in the newspapers such as that of two-year-old Jessica DeBoer in the United States and wonder: 'Can that happen to us?'

The adoption girl taken from the only parents she knew

Cara Clausen in Iowa was twenty-eight and single when she waived her parental rights on the birth of her unnamed daughter and put her up for adoption. She had broken up with her boyfriend Dan Schmidt, and felt unable to cope as an unmarried mother. Mrs Roberta DeBoer, who had a hysterectomy after a honeymoon illness, heard of Cara's plight through a friend, drove through a snowstorm to see the baby and a private adoption was agreed. Cara wrote to Roberta and Jan DeBoer: 'I know you will treasure her and surround her with love. God bless and keep you all.'

Then she had second thoughts and filed a court motion to reclaim her baby, exactly a month after the birth. The news devastated the DeBoers. They argued they should retain custody as they were the only parents Jessica (as they called her) had ever known. By the time the case eventually came to court, Cara had married Dan Schmidt and had another child. So the judge ordered their first baby must be returned to complete their family.

In August 1993, the Iowa Supreme Court upheld that ruling and Jessica, by then two years old, was carried in tears from the only home she had known and handed over to the Schmidts. They at once said they would rename her Anna and refuse all visits to the DeBoers.

In fact, despite all the continuing imperfections in our adoption law, that could never happen here. It is a fundamental rule, enshrined in the 1976 Adoption Act, that natural parents must 'freely, and with full understanding of what is involved, agree unconditionally to the making of the order'. If the parents are married, both must give their consent. If unmarried, only the mother must – unless a court has granted the father an order sharing parental responsibility or (most unlikely) a residence order saying the child must live with him. In all cases, the baby must be at least six weeks old for the mother's consent to have any legal validity and the actual adoption can only take place when the child is at least 19 weeks old: two vital differences between the law in this country and that in the US.

Generally, the agreement takes the form of a properly executed and witnessed document but it can also be by word of mouth. But, whether written or oral, it can be withdrawn at any time before the adoption order is made. The only major exception is that, if consent is withdrawn too late in the process, a judge may rule that the parent has unreasonably withheld consent to the adoption – and overrule it.

Unreasonable refusal of consent to adoption by a natural parent is one of the few instances envisaged by the 1976 Act when consent can be dispensed with. But the courts do not lightly come to that conclusion. In one case, a young mother changed her mind after she and the child's father decided to marry and bring up the child with the help of her family. A judge ruled this was reasonable – and the adoption did not go through.

As Judge Stephen Willis has said, 'Many adopted people start looking for their roots, particularly in adolescence . . . adoption should only be the last resort where no one in the wider family is available and suitable to look after a child. Parentage is not always perfect but parentage in the family is preferable to the unknown risks of adoption.'

The 1976 Act says that a child must be placed with its prospective new parents for at least 13 weeks – in practice, usually much longer – before they can apply (usually to a circuit judge at the nearest family hearing centre) for an adoption order. But even this formal 'placement' does not guarantee success: if the agency believes that things are not working out satisfactorily it can, on giving the would-be adopters 14 days' notice, remove the child and 'place' it elsewhere.

The last stage in this long process is, of course, when the prospective parents ask a judge to make an adoption order in their favour. The 1976 Act states:

> In reaching any decision relating to the adoption of a child a court or adoption agency shall have regard to all the circumstances, first consideration being given to the need to safeguard and promote the welfare of the child throughout his childhood; and shall so far as practicable ascertain the wishes and feelings of the child regarding the decision and give due consideration to them, having regard to his age and understanding.

In practice, the would-be new parents have been so thoroughly vetted and the child will already have lived happily with them for so long that the decision is almost a formality. The adoption will nearly always be approved. A new life will begin for both child and parents.

Note

1 One woman had a phobia of needles; one had painful memories of the after-effects of a previous Caesarean and would rather die than have another; a third was, in the words of the judge, 'unable to weigh up information in order to make an informed decision'.

3

CHILDHOOD AND
GROWING UP

To many a parent you remain a child, however old you are: 'Small children small worries, big children big worries,' is an old Jewish saying. That is almost the view of the law, for the legal line between childhood and adulthood is extremely blurred. Indeed, the word 'adult' has no precise legal significance. When the law treats you as 'grown up', which again is a concept with no precise legal meaning, will depend on what aspect of life one is looking at.

If it is the criminal law and your responsibility to be held to account for your criminal acts, the 1933 Children & Young Persons Act says you are a 'child''until you are 14, when you become a 'young person', which you remain until you are 18. In divorce and family law, the 1989 Children Act keeps you a 'child' right up until you are 18. With contract and general business law, the 1969 Family Law Reform Act says you are not a 'child' but a 'minor' until 18, when you legally come of age: it used, of course, to be 21.

But even these divisions are far from watertight. The age at which you can and cannot do things legally is a jigsaw with some very odd little pieces tucked away. Here is a guide to the puzzle:

As soon as you are born: You can sue or be sued in the civil courts but, until you are 18, an adult will need to act as your 'next friend', if you are suing or being sued. A bank or building society account can be opened in your name and you can claim the single person's tax-free allowance so that, if the interest is less than £4,195 a year (as from April 1999), you will not have to pay income tax. You can also open a National Savings bank account but normally the money cannot be withdrawn until you are seven. You cannot hold shares or unit trusts in your own name but an adult, usually a parent or grandparent, can buy them and hold them as your trustee until you are 18, when they can be re-registered in your name and an income tax refund claim made to recover the tax credits. Until October 1998, you had to be named on an adult parent's passport but since then you can *only* have your own passport.

When you are five: This is the first major legal stage in growing up. You are no longer entitled to travel free on buses, trains and the London Underground (although only two youngsters under five are allowed free per adult) and a reduced 'child fare' becomes payable until you are 16. You still cannot go into the bar of a public house except when en route to some part of the premises which is not a bar (garden, restaurant, etc.) and 'there is no other convenient means of access or egress'; but you can now drink alcohol in private, although up to this age any adult giving you an alcoholic drink, however small, could have been fined up to £200 except if doing so on doctor's orders, in sickness or 'for other urgent cause'. You can go to the cinema – but, if the film is PG rated, you must be accompanied by an adult. Most important of all, you must start going full-time to school.[1] No law says that you must first go to a nursery school, although they usually are available from about three; but the 1996 Education Act states that a local education authority must serve on any parent whose child of five years old or more is not receiving suitable education 'either by regular attendance at school *or* otherwise' a school attendance order. If the parent does not then satisfy the authority that the child is receiving such an education, he or she can be summonsed in the local magistrates' court and fined up to £1,000.[2] By 'or otherwise' the Act means that a suitably qualified adult can teach you at home – but I warn you that it is not easy.

When you are 10: Until now you have enjoyed complete immunity from criminal prosecution: in *Walters* v. *Lunt*, in 1951, the parents of a seven-year-old boy were charged with receiving a stolen tricycle from their young son but, since he was legally incapable of theft, the tricycle was not 'stolen' and they were acquitted. But at 10, although still legally a child, criminal responsibility starts: you can be convicted of any crime, even of a sexual nature, although until the 1998 Crime and Disorder Act the prosecution had specifically to prove that you knew it was 'seriously wrong', as for instance, Mr Justice Morland told the jury in the tragic case of the two 11-year-olds convicted in November 1993 of Liverpool toddler James Bulger's murder.[3] A similarly discarded Common Law principle was that a boy under 14 could not be convicted of rape or any other sexual offence involving penetration because he was conclusively presumed to be physically incapable of sexual intercourse, although as far back as 1839 there is a case in the Law Reports where a 12-year-old had shown that was nonsense but the 1993 Sexual Offences Act abolished that doctrine and there have since been several cases of under-14-year-olds being charged with rape. I suppose that some people might call that progress. Except for murder or manslaughter, as in the case of James Bulger's two child murderers tried at Preston Crown Court, you will be tried in a youth court (the old-style juvenile court) and your parents must be present unless this is 'unreasonable'. It is a sad comment on today's world that the 1994 Criminal Justice and Public Order Act allows 10-year-old children, convicted of serious non-homicidal crimes such as rape or indecent assault, to be locked up in young offender institutions.

When you are 12:   You can buy a pet and, for the more adventurous, you can be trained to participate in dangerous public entertainments so long as you get a licence from the local authority.

When you are 13:   You can be employed and paid for your work but there are many restrictions, sometimes shamefully unobserved in practice. You can take on light work such as a paper round but not during school hours nor before 7 a.m. or after 7 p.m. and for not more than two hours on school days and Sundays and, in any event, for not more than a total of 20 hours a week. Many local authorities also have by-laws allowing those under 13 to do limited work for their parents, on a farm, or at weekends or during the holidays – and modelling or professional acting, subject to special arrangements to avoid missing school.

When you are 14:   You are now a 'young person' and can be convicted of most crimes without restriction and without the prosecution needing to show that you knew it was wrong. If convicted, you can be fined up to £1,000 (between the ages of 10 and 14, the limit is £250) but the youth court must order your parents to pay the fine unless 'it would be unreasonable, having regard to the circumstances of the case'. In practice, a court will try to avoid imposing a fine: a wide range of other sentences, all non-custodial, is available. You become responsible for fastening your own seat belt in a car but no longer have to wear a safety helmet when horse riding, although it remains advisable at whatever age. You can own an airgun and its ammunition. You can go into a bar with an adult but cannot buy or consume alcohol. You can be a spectator in a courtroom: until now you could only have been present in court if you were an 'infant in arms' or giving evidence as a witness, although all alleged victims under 18 of sexual or violent crime now usually give evidence from outside the courtroom via closed-circuit television.

When you are 15: If convicted of a crime, you are now termed 'a young offender' and can, if the youth court thinks there is no other appropriate way of dealing with you, be sent to a young offender institution for not less than 21 days or, as from early 1995, more than 24 months. You can now work up to 30 hours a week.

When you are 16: This is another major step forward. You can leave school[4] and work full-time but not at night, except in certain industries such as iron and steelworks, glassworks and paperworks, and, if you work in a factory, you cannot be made to work more than 48 hours a week and not on Sundays. Unless you are continuing in full-time education, whether at school or college, Child Benefit will cease to be payable to your mother. Even if named on your parents' passport under the old rules, you must now reapply for your own passport in your own name. You can drink beer or cider in a pub but only with a meal in a part of the pub that serves meals. You can buy fireworks. You can buy cigarettes and not be at risk of a police officer confiscating your pack if he finds you smoking in the street or other public place (you can smoke legally at any age provided you do not, if under 16, buy cigarettes yourself or smoke in public) and *thinks* you look under 16. You can be ordered to pay your own fine for a criminal offence without your parents necessarily being ordered to pay it for you. You can drive a moped or motorcycle of up to 50 cc. You can join the armed forces with parental consent. You can marry with parental consent but, if it is refused, you will have to get the consent of a magistrates' court (this holds true until you are 18). A girl must be 16 or over to agree to sexual intercourse – unlike boys, who can do it at any age although they still cannot consent to homosexual acts until they are 18, a Bill to lower the age to 16 having twice been thrown out by the House of Lords.

When you are 17: You can drive a car or any motorcycle. You can go into a betting shop but cannot place a bet. You can have an airgun in a public place. You can be arrested and questioned at a police station, as if you were an adult: until this age the official Code of Practice under the 1984 Police and Criminal Evidence Act would have required the police to inform your parent or other 'appropriate adult' that you had been detained. If that person wanted to be present during the questioning, the police would have had to wait until he or she arrived, except in urgent cases involving immediate risk of personal harm or serious damage to property. (Police failure to obey the Code could lead to a court throwing out any confession as improperly obtained.)

When you are 18:   This is the legal age of majority. You can vote, sue or be sued in your name, marry without parental consent, change your name, own land or other property, enter into binding contracts, obtain credit (including hire purchase) and have a cheque card or credit card, serve on a jury, buy any drink in a bar, off-licence or supermarket, donate your blood or any body organ, bet, make a will and join the armed forces without parental consent. If a witness or defendant in any court proceedings (many people wrongly think the embargo applies only to cases involving sex), your name and identity can be disclosed in the media, the minimum age having been raised from 17 by the 1991 Criminal Justice Act.[5]

When you are 21:   For centuries, until 1969, this was the legal age of majority – because 21 was the age at which knights in the eleventh century were deemed to reach majority – but vestigial restrictions still exist until this birthday. Only after that momentous day can you stand as candidate in a parliamentary or local election, apply for a liquor licence, drive a lorry or bus – or be sentenced to gaol (except that, for all first offenders of whatever age, the court must first rule that no other penalty would be appropriate).

When do you legally reach any particular age? At the first minute after midnight on the start of your birthday.

In later life, one's time is divided between work and non-work, but at this stage the division is between school and non-school. Let us look at non-school first.

BABY-SITTERS, CHILDMINDERS, NANNIES AND AU PAIRS

There is no such thing in English law as 'a right not to be left alone', at whatever age. Britain has a growing number of one-parent families and adults under pressure to go out to work. That, coupled with a lowering of moral standards and an appalling lack of childcare facilities – Britain has fewer provisions than any other country in Western Europe – means, sadly, that thousands of children, even including babies, are left on their own. And at risk.

The law is totally inadequate to protect the young and vulnerable. There is no such crime as 'leaving a child on its own'. The 1933 Children and Young Persons Act makes it an offence for a parent – or anyone else over 16 – who has responsibility for a child under 16 'wilfully to neglect, abandon or cause unnecessary suffering or injury' to that child. There is no specific reference to leaving a child on its own or unattended but such an event is undoubtedly covered by this wide wording.

Yet there are no time limits within which a child can be left – nor any specific age at which it can or cannot lawfully be done. *The Times* has reported that nearly a million children under 10 are regularly left at home alone after school or in the holidays; but prosecutions remain rare. The National Society for the Prevention of Cruelty to Children says that social services are reluctant to prosecute because of the difficulties of proof and because it can cause further distress to the child.

There is not even a legal minimum age for **baby-sitters**. Many decent, concerned parents believe they cannot legally ask anyone under 16 to baby-sit. That is not so. It all depends on the intelligence and maturity of the particular child. In Scotland, all baby-sitters, without exception, legally have to be at least 14; but not south of the border.

Some parents believe that 14 is old enough or, at least, give themselves the benefit of the doubt. But Judge Thomas MacKean disagrees. In March 1993 he was presiding, as Southampton Coroner, over an inquest on a 23-month-old baby boy who, when left alone, had accidentally strangled himself when trying to climb out of his cot. His unmarried mother had gone out 'for a few drinks' on a Friday night leaving him with a 14-year-old schoolgirl who had then pocketed her £5 baby-sitting money and gone to a disco, leaving the baby asleep in an empty flat. Said Judge MacKean: 'It is not my function to blame people but the public must feel that mothers who leave their children at night have a duty to ensure the baby-sitter is a responsible person. There is nothing in law which specifies a minimum and maximum age of carers, but clearly a 14-year-old girl may not be thought responsible enough . . . it really was unacceptable to have left this baby alone.'

But no law was broken.

Childminders are in a different legal category.[6] They must be approved by the local council, which has to maintain a register on which parents are supposed to be able safely to rely. The 1989 Children Act says this applies to anyone who is not a parent or foster parent who looks after a child *under eight* for payment for more than two hours a day. 'If either a childminder or Council is negligent, the parent can sue for damages,' Mr Justice Scott Baker laid down in the High Court in January 1994 in the case of:

The childminder who damaged a baby's brain

When 33-year-old single parent Cora Dowling phoned the Surrey County Council childminding officer to inquire about placing her six-month-old son

Thomas with a local registered childminder so that she could go out to work, he did not tell her that three months earlier that same childminder had been under investigation when a small baby in her care had suffered severe brain injury. But, as Mr Justice Scott Baker laid down: 'He should have told her whatever he knew that a prudent parent would wish to know before placing a tiny baby with a minder.'

As it was, the newly engaged childminder shook little Thomas so hard that he ended up partly blind and brain damaged. His injuries were so horrific that a priest had to give the last rites.

After a four-year-long legal battle, Mr Justice Scott Baker awarded Ms Dowling damages (the actual amount to be assessed later when Thomas's medical prospects were clearer) against both Surrey County Council and the childminder who had by then been de-registered.

Sadly the legal procedures are not always so watertight as they should be:

The childminder who killed a baby

In July 1998 at Norwich Crown Court 41-year-old registered childminder Helen Stacey bowed her head and sobbed as the jury found her guilty of having shaken to death a six-month-old baby in her charge because he 'had been in my earhole for the best part of 10 minutes and it was beginning to go through me.' Although a convicted prostitute and shoplifter, she had got herself on the register through lying on her application form and failing to give social services her former married name. Sentencing her to life imprisonment for murder, Mr Justice Blofeld demanded a 'searching inquiry' into the checks made by Norfolk county council and the police. The National Childminding Association promptly said that it would be calling for childminders to have nationally standardised registration and constant police vigilance – but it has not happened.

Does a childminder have the legal right to smack a child?

In December 1994, Virginia Bottomley, then Tory Health Secretary, announced new Government guidelines allowing childminders to smack children in their care, but only rarely and always with parental consent. This replaced earlier guidelines that banned all form of corporal punishment for children. 'We've got political correctness on the run,' claimed Mrs Bottomley. 'The guidelines are a victory for responsible parents who know that children need control as well as care.' But John Bowis, her junior Health Minister, emphasised that childminders should smack only as a last resort and then only if they had secured the parents' consent. That is still the legal position.

Nannies are employed by parents to look after children in the family home. They can cost anything up to £350 a week. Full-time professionals, they were for years almost exclusively an upper-middle-class phenomenon. But in the mid-1990s, as more and more middle-class mothers were going out to work, nannies became increasingly popular over a wider social spectrum. Finally, in April 1999, Tony Blair's New Labour Government published a free, easily available 20-page booklet *Need a Nanny? A Guide for Parents* aimed at all working mothers, regardless of class. In sometimes over-simplistic language, including a section on 'What is a Nanny?', it tried to popularise the concept and at the same time allay widespread fears caused by an Old Bailey case two months earlier when Louise Sullivan, a 27-year-old Australian nanny, had been convicted of killing a six-month-old baby girl in her care by shaking her. The booklet said that parents should employ people to look after their children only if they agreed not to smack them and said it was important for parents to discuss 'positive discipline strategies with prospective nannies'.

But it resisted calls for a legally enforceable national register for nannies and insisted that it was for parents to establish a nanny's credentials, with little, if any, help from the state. Our inadequate law on child protection continues.

For most of the decades since World War II, many middle-class households with young children would not have known how to survive without **au pairs** from abroad. Until January 1994, they always had to be young women but Home Office rules then changed to allow young men[7] as well as young women to be au pairs and a clearer distinction was drawn between au pairs from inside and outside the European Union.

Nowadays all EU nationals have, in theory, the untrammelled right to live and work in all the member countries, so EU au pairs do not need a work permit. And they can legally take on other domestic jobs besides pure au pair work. The specialist employment agencies that traditionally supplied the domestic market with au pairs from Western Europe nowadays do as much, if not more, business with these other categories.

Yet the term 'au pair' still has a precise legal meaning for non-EU nationals who enter the United Kingdom on what is now officially called 'the au pair scheme'. They must be single men or women without dependants and aged between 17 and 27 who come here to study English and live as a member of an English-speaking family. They can be asked to help in the home for not more than five hours a day (including baby-sitting!) in return for 'a reasonable allowance' (recommended as not less than £35–£40 a week) and a room of their own. They do not qualify for a minimum wage, are not to be treated as servants or underpaid domestic labour and cannot be expected to do more than 'light housework and taking care of children'. They must have at least two full days off each week and be allowed to attend language classes and religious services, if they wish.

Furthermore, non-EU nationals only qualify for the scheme if they are nationals of Andorra, Bosnia-Herzegovina, Croatia, Cyprus, Czech Republic, Faeroe Islands, Greenland, Hungary, Liechtenstein, Macedonia, Malta, Monaco, San Marino, Slovak Republic, Slovenia, Switzerland or Turkey. They can be here for a maximum of two years and can change host families within that time: they are not tied to their first employer.

But they must have come into the country as an au pair. They cannot try to switch once they first come in as a visitor.

DISCIPLINE

It was back in the seventeenth century that the satirist Samuel Butler first paraphrased the Bible and coined the phrase 'Spare the rod and spoil the child' and until very recently that was the robust view of Her Majesty's judges. But no longer. Technically parents still enjoy the right of 'moderate and reasonable chastisement', as laid down in several Victorian judgments, but today's judges are likely to interpret those words in a modern and non-authoritarian sense.

Stern, even though loving, parents seem to be going out of fashion. In June 1990 Princess Diana made front-page headlines, complete with photographs, when she gave the wilful Prince William, then seven years old, a public smacking at his school sports day. She called him to go home at the end of the events but he ignored her and ran off to play with his friends. Clearly angry, she dashed after him, caught him by the arm and gave him a firm smack on the bottom. The future King of England burst into tears but was pushed into the back of the royal car, given a good telling-off and driven back to Kensington Palace.

But, unless you relish battling with over-zealous officialdom, do not be too quick to follow the royal example. Princess Diana was lucky that no bystander reported her to the local council's social services department. If so, she might have found her young son put on their children's 'at risk' register. Do not laugh. If a non-royal mother had been seen to act in that way, it might have happened – and the decision could have been upheld in the High Court. I refer you to the 1991 case of *R.* v. *East Sussex County Council:*

A young mother in East Sussex smacked her six-year-old son with a wooden spoon because he spat in her face. His teachers noticed bruises and called in local social workers. When questioned, the boy said his mother had hit him for being 'too lippy' and she claimed: 'Every mother corrects her child.' Her son – *and his untouched five-year-old sister* – were put on the 'at risk' register.

She appealed to the High Court to delete her children's names from the register. But Sir Stephen Brown, President of the High Court's Family Division, ruled that the social workers had not acted unreasonably.

'It may seem to some that this was simply an exasperated parent spanking a child,' he said. 'However, what came to the attention of the authority were the marks of injury. Fortunately they were not very serious but what they did suggest was that there was a basis for concern as to the treatment this boy might receive in the future.' So this cheeky little boy was protected *in advance* from any stern future disciplinary action – which many people might think was one thing he needed.

In the words of the latest (1999) edition of *Street on Torts*, a leading legal textbook: 'Changes in social *mores* and in the status of children have diminished parental rights of discipline. A growing body of opinion supports outlawing any right of physical punishment.' Indeed, in June 1999, a 48-year-old school teacher became the first parent in Britain to be convicted of smacking his child. At Hamilton sheriff court in Scotland, he was found guilty of assaulting his eight-year-old daughter by smacking her bottom in a dentist's waiting room after she refused to have a tooth extracted. Mind you, his conduct was a bit extreme: he pulled down her trousers and pants and put her across his knee. Sheriff Dan Russell could have fined him or gaoled him for up to three months but he chose merely to 'admonish' him, as is allowed by Scottish law. Even so, it gave the man a criminal record.

ACCIDENTS AND CHILDREN

These are of two kinds: (a) those that children cause and (b) those that happen to them.

Accidents caused by children

The law does not expect a parent to keep their child under lock and key all day. But if you do not properly control your child, you can be held liable to compensate anyone who has been injured or whose property has been damaged by her. This is not so much because the child has misbehaved as because you have been negligent in preventing her from doing so.

Not every risk of injury or damage can be avoided, even by the most careful parent. Their only legal duty therefore is to take 'reasonable care' in all the circumstances, which will include the child's age, intelligence and past behaviour.

So if, for example, a 10-year-old girl is playing football in a quiet residential street and accidentally kicks the ball into a nearby window, her parents would probably not be liable. But if they were to allow that same 10-year-old access to a sharp kitchen knife and she accidentally stabbed a young friend while playing Cowboys and Indians, they probably would be liable.

The question always is, as Lord Goddard said, when Lord Chief Justice: 'Is it the child's negligence alone or that of his parents?'

Accidents that happen to children

We will come to accidents at school in a moment but, even out of school, children present a particular problem to the law. They are, after all, particularly vulnerable.

Even giving your small child a birthday party can cause legal problems. In the High Court in May 1989 a north London mother, who had given a toddlers' birthday party for her young child, was ordered to pay £20,000 agreed damages to a girl who, as a one-year-old baby, had been a guest at the party. She had been badly scalded when a pot of hot tea fell from a table while the children were playing.

How did the pot of tea fall? The mother denied that she had been negligent. She said that she had done her best when coping as a harassed hostess with a clutch of small children in party mood and denied that she had left the pot too near the edge of the table. But she still had to go along with the agreed settlement, albeit without any formal admission of liability. She was covered by her household insurance and the company paid out. As an insurance specialist commented afterwards, 'It appears likely that, if she had not got cover, she would have had to pay out of her own pocket.'

The moral is clear: 'Accidents will occur in the best-regulated families,' as Mr Micawber said, and a prudent householder will make sure that his household contents policy contains a personal liability section (at very little extra cost) for injury to visitors. Especially child visitors.

In more general terms, the 1957 Occupiers' Liability Act says that occupiers of all types of premises, from private houses to cinemas and from schools to supermarkets, owe their visitors a duty to take reasonable care 'to see that the visitor will be reasonably safe in using the premises for the purpose for which he is invited or permitted by the occupier to be there'.

Children are allowed to have less sense than adults. The Act expressly says: 'An occupier must be prepared for children to be less careful than adults.' While adults should take care to avoid obvious dangers (and have any damages reduced because of their own 'contributory negligence' in not taking proper care for their own safety), children are not expected to have the same degree of reasonable caution.

So, when a four-year-old child fell through a gap in railings adjoining a public staircase on a south London council estate and the gap was not wide enough for an adult to fall through but was wide enough for this child, the Council was held liable. They should have realised that unaccompanied children were likely to use that staircase running between two floors of flats.

That case was decided in the mid-1960s; but the principle is of general application and dates back to long before the 1957 Act. On this point, Scottish law is the same as English law and as far back as 1921 Glasgow Corporation was held liable to the father of a seven-year-old child who had died from eating poisonous 'deadly nightshade' berries from a shrub in a public park controlled by the Corporation. The berries were attractive and accessible to children and, although the Corporation knew that children were frequent visitors, they still had done nothing to fence off the shrub or provide some other effective protection.

But what about parents' own responsibility? Should householders or other occupiers of land foot the bill for an accident if the true culprits are the child's own parents in allowing him to be out on his own?

The late Lord Devlin gave the authoritative answer in December 1954 when he was a High Court judge. A five-year-old boy, out picking blackberries with his seven-year-old sister on a piece of open land soon to become part of a Kent council estate where he lived, broke his leg when he fell into an open sewer trench which his sister had safely negotiated. In clearing the Council of blame, Mr Justice Devlin laid down that landowners and others are entitled to expect that 'prudent parents' would not allow their small children to go out unaccompanied in areas where there was likely to be 'an obvious danger', such as an open trench. 'The responsibility for the safety of little children must rest primarily on the parents,' he said.

That remains the law. In 1983, for instance, the Appeal Court had to consider a case where a seven-year-old girl slid down a Welsh mountainside on a picnic blanket. The mountain had a steep slope which became very steep at the bottom from which she fell 30 to 40 feet on to the road below and fractured her skull. Was the Rhondda Borough Council legally responsible? The answer was no. The appeal judges ruled that the Council neither had to fence off the slope nor to warn of the sharp drop – even though they knew unaccompanied children were prone to play in the area. A 'prudent parent' would have warned his children of such an obvious danger. As Lord Justice Dunn remarked, an occupier is not bound to fence every tree simply because a child might climb it and fall out of it.

But children have not changed over the years. As Lord Justice Hamilton said back in 1913, 'In the case of an infant, there are moral as well as physical traps. There may accordingly be a duty towards infants not merely not to dig pitfalls for them but not to lead them into temptation.'

So where the danger is not obvious but latent or concealed, like broken glass at the bottom of a children's paddling pool, or is made particularly tempting for a child by what the law calls an 'allurement', like a defective escalator in a department store, the occupier will be liable – despite the fact that it is irresponsible of parents in the area to allow small children to wander around unaccompanied.

What if the children are trespassers? There can nowadays be liability, although the law is still unclear as to the actual extent. Trespassers used to trespass at their own risk: except when malicious or deliberate injury was involved, they could not complain if they were hurt. But in 1972, in a case where a six-year-old boy got on to an electrified railway track through an unrepaired gap in a fence, senior appeal judges in the House of Lords literally invented what they called 'a common duty of humanity', which remained remarkably vague in its application.

Then, in 1984, a new Occupiers' Liability Act tried to improve on this situation, with not much success. For it says that, if an occupier has reasonable grounds to believe that a danger exists on his premises, and the consequent risk is one against which he may reasonably be expected to offer 'some protection', then he will owe a duty to trespassers and other uninvited entrants, of whatever age, who he might reasonably believe would try to enter.

Please do not ask me precisely what is the meaning of this turgid double-talk (which, believe it or not, I have tried to simplify). The only reliable word to latch on to in all this verbiage is 'reasonable'. So, for instance, burglars can expect little or no protection. But, if children are known to be likely to trespass, occupiers must give them some protection – however mischievous the children may be.

What is that protection? The Act is not specific but does say that occupiers can escape liability by putting up warning notices. However, the test of reasonableness still applies. DANGER. KEEP OUT CONCEALED TRENCHES would probably be a defence to a claim by an injured 11-year-old, who can reasonably be expected to read and write – but to a claim by a six-year-old? I simply do not know. The answer will partly depend on the intelligence of that particular six-year-old.

Notes
1 The actual date of your compulsory first school day is the first day of the first term after your fifth birthday, although some schools may be prepared to take you before.
2 This is more theory than reality. The law lacks rigorous enforcement. Department of Education figures consistently show that school truancy is a disgrace nationwide – and not only in socially deprived inner-city areas.
3 The two young defendants were ordered to be detained at Her Majesty's pleasure, which is still the only custodial sentence available for children between 10 and 14 convicted of murder or manslaughter. No other child criminal under 15 can be 'locked up' but they can be placed under probation service supervision or, as a last resort, put in secure accommodation for a limited period of time.
4 The actual date is not your 16th birthday. There are two school-leaving dates in the year. If your birthday falls on or between 1 September and 31 January, you can leave at the end of the spring term; and, if it falls on or between I February and 31 August, you can leave at the summer half-term.
5 The ban not only applies to the child's own name or identity – but to that of any adult from whom its name or identity could indirectly be revealed. On 31 December 1993, Mr Justice Ewbank rejected a plea by three newspapers to lift a ban on identifying a 59-year-old woman who had given birth to twins on Christmas Day after being artificially inseminated at a Rome clinic. He said it was not an issue of public interest, merely curiosity.
6 Technically childminders, who look after children on domestic premises, are different from day-carers, who do so on non-domestic premises; but the Children Act applies equally to both.
7 At the end of 1992 a young Swede named Johan Engelstedt tried to come into the country as a male au pair and, when he was turned back, there was such amusement in the press that the then Home Secretary, Kenneth Clarke, decided the rules must be revised.

4

SCHOOL AND UNIVERSITY

SCHOOL

The world is divided into those who say that their time at school constituted the happiest days of their life and those who do not. For some, as they look back, school is a delight to be recalled misty-eyed and with a smile. For others, it is one long nightmare. Personally I think that something must be wrong with your life if you can only pinpoint as the happiest part of it the period you spent before you fully began to live.

But the law does not concern itself with such philosophical niceties. It answers practical questions. So let us examine those aspects of our schooldays where the law has most impact, and we will start at the beginning:

Choosing the school

There is an obvious difference between fee-paying independent schools – which I shall call by their old-fashioned, and still generally known, name, 'public schools' – and state schools.

The restriction on parents' choice of a public school is primarily a financial one: what can they afford? According to the latest (1998) edition of the *Good Schools Guide*, one should expect to pay, per term, between £1,000 and £4,000 for day pupils and between £1,400 and £4,500-plus for boarders. There are over 2,200 public schools in Britain, educating about 550,000 children, or 7 per cent of the school population. The Independent Schools Information Service (ISIS), with its national headquarters in London, keeps a list of most of these schools but, unlike those in the state system, public schools do not by law have to provide information about themselves.

Education at a public school entails a legal contract between school and parent. And, to make sure your choice is properly exercised and that you are assured of your legal rights (and those of your child), you should examine the prospectus carefully, just as you would the basis of any other written contract, and satisfy yourself that you know exactly what you are letting yourself – and your child – in for.

You should check particularly whether important information has been omitted or updated, such as what happened to last year's school leavers; and watch out for euphemisms: 'catering for all abilities' may, in truth, mean 'desperate to recruit'. One should also read carefully what is written about extras: before setting the seal on your choice you should check whether fees include such items as lunches, instrumental tuition, elocution lessons, specialist sports coaching or even books and stationery.

With state schools, education is of course free (a specific legal requirement imposed by the 1996 Education Act) but parents' choice of school is very much restricted by other provisions of the Act and by the many other recent Education Acts (since 1979 there have been more Acts of Parliament dealing with education than with any other single subject, so great has been official twisting and turning on policy, often depending on which political party is in power).

There used to be a 'Parents' Charter' which contained a section boldly headed 'The Right to Choose': it stated that parents could choose the school they would like their child to attend. This was misleading and, indeed, the Charter went on to make clear that parents have merely the right to express a preference for a particular school – which is, of course, not at all the same thing.

Admittedly the 1996 Education Act requires local education authorities (LEAs), which control and organise state schools, to 'have regard to the general principle that, so far as is compatible with the provision of efficient instruction and training and the avoidance of unreasonable public expenditure, pupils are to be educated in accordance with the wishes of their parents'. But this requirement (first introduced by the 1980 Education Act) has always been more a pious expression of hope than a legal guarantee.

Today the 1996 Education Act spells out categorically that an LEA need not accept any parent's stated preference. Section 9 says it is only to prevail 'so far as compatible with the provision of efficient instruction and training and the avoidance of unreasonable public expenditure'. In the years before the 'parent power' revolution of the 1980s, families were expected to send children to the nearest comprehensive, regardless of whether it was a good school. The result was selection by mortgage or postal codes, with better-off middle-class families buying homes in the catchment area of good schools while those unable to move were left with places at inadequate comprehensives. But in 1989, in the classic case of *R. v. Greenwich London Borough Council*, the Appeal Court ruled that an LEA's policy of favouring applicants in its own area at the expense of applicants living outside was unlawful. The popular belief still exists that local children have priority but where a child lives is nowadays only one of the factors to be taken into account, such as whether space is available, the child's ability and aptitude or whether a sibling already attends the school.

To be honest, this is a grey area in both law and practice, as proved by Mr and Mrs Tony Blair's decision to send their sons to the highly achieving London Oratory rather than the less successful comprehensives in their own pre-Downing Street home area of Islington.

Unhappy parents have a right of appeal against refusal, usually within 14 days, to an LEA appeals committee. A simple letter will usually be enough to start off the process but you should always state your reasons for preferring that particular school: for example, that your child lives in its catchment area (that is still a plus!) or that his brothers or sisters go to the same school. You will be able to amplify those reasons in person at a private hearing and, if that fails, you can appeal direct to the Education Secretary that the decision was 'unreasonable' – but few, if any, of these further appeals ever succeed.

School transport

With public schools, this is solely parents' responsibility. It is entirely up to you how you get your children to and from school in time. With day schools, the 'mothers' rota' is an accepted part of urban life, although traffic wardens or parking attendants sometimes harass women who get to school too early in the afternoon and sit in their cars causing a minor traffic jam while they wait patiently to collect their charges. Waiting in a

'No Waiting' street is unlawful, even in a worthy cause, and the authorities are technically within their rights in threatening you with a ticket unless you move on.

With state schools, local education authorities are under a statutory obligation to provide free transport for children to and from school, if they live more than 'walking distance' away. This is defined by Section 444 of the 1996 Act as two miles (or 3.218688 kilometres!) for a child under eight and three miles (or 4.828032 kilometres) for a child over that age 'measured by the nearest available route'.

What does that mean? How available is 'available'? The phrase first appeared in the 1944 Education Act and the courts have restricted its meaning to 'the nearest route along which a child can walk to school with reasonable safety when accompanied by an adult'. Such a route does not fail to qualify because of dangers which may arise if the child is unaccompanied.

So, when the shortest public route between a 12-year-old Essex girl's home and her school was 2.94 miles but it lay partly along an isolated, unmade and unlit track where, particularly in winter, it would be both difficult and dangerous for a young girl to walk on her own, the House of Lords ruled in October 1986 that Essex County Council was *not* in breach of its statutory duty in failing to supply free transport. The route would have been perfectly safe if she had been accompanied by an adult and it was up to a responsible parent to see that she was accompanied rather than expect her bus fare to be paid out of public funds.

A local education authority may provide free transport in such cases, but it is a matter for its own discretion. It is under no legal compulsion to do so. Except with children who live more than 'walking distance' away, parents even today have the ultimate responsibility for ensuring that their children attend school – not the school authorities.

School holidays

Schools, both public and state, are perfectly at liberty to fix their own holiday dates – but have parents the right to take their child away on a family holiday during term time? This often causes problems, especially when one or other parent is constrained through work or some such pressing reason to take the children away on holiday at some time other than late July, August or early September, the traditional holiday season.

Schools can sometimes be 'difficult' about this, and the law is firmly on their side. Section 444 of the 1996 Education Act says that schools, whether private or state, only have to give leave of absence by reason of the child's sickness, religion (e.g. the Day of Atonement for a Jewish child or Ramadan for a Muslim), absence of free transport when the local education authority is under a legal duty to supply it – and 'unavoidable cause'. This last category is the heading under which you should try to persuade the head teacher to let your child miss school for a family holiday: 'We are really sorry about this but my husband has just been promoted at work and this is the only possible time he can take us all away with him.'

Technically, this should not suffice because Lord Goddard ruled in the High Court back in 1949 in *Jenkins* v. *Howells* that 'unavoidable cause' must mean unavoidable for the child, and not the parent. But since then the 1995 Education (Public Registration) Regulations say that a school may grant leave of absence of up to 10 days during the year. In fact, most head teachers, properly approached, will usually do their best to be helpful except, understandably enough, in a senior exam term.

Size of classes

There is no legal guarantee, with either a public school or state school, as to how many other pupils will be in your child's class. The only exception is where a public school gives a specific assurance in its prospectus, or otherwise, as to the size of its classes.

Sex education

Public schools can provide this as they please, and normally the prospectus will say whether or not this is the case.

Most state schools have no legal obligation to provide sex education. Section 403 of the 1996 Education Act merely says that, where sex education is provided, the head teacher must 'take such steps as are reasonably practicable to secure that it is given in such a manner as to encourage pupils to have due regard to moral considerations and the value of family life'.

But can you legally refuse to allow your child to take the classes? The 1993 Education Act first gave parents this right 'insofar as the subject is not comprised in the National Curriculum'. Section 405 of the 1996 Act repeats this provision. Since there is precious little sex involved in the National Curriculum's mandatory subjects, this gives parents plenty of scope to exercise their right of refusal.

National Curriculum

Until 1988 state schools were free to teach any subject they liked but the Education Act of that year, brought in by the Thatcher Government, created a National Curriculum which the Education Secretary was to 'revise whenever he considers it necessary or expedient to do so'. Twelve years later, as from September 2000, of the original 10 prescribed subjects, only English and watered-down versions of mathematics and physical education will remain compulsory for all pupils aged 5–16. In a forthcoming revision of the National Curriculum announced by the Blair Administration in May 1999, the original Tory idea of compulsion was replaced by 'flexibility' to 'enable teachers to use their professional judgment'. A new era was said to be ushered in with a 'basic framework within which schools can develop their own approaches'.

In fact, legally that had always been the situation. In a little-known case in 1995, the Appeal Court accepted, to many educationists' surprise, that teachers were not under a statutory duty to implement the National Curriculum. It is not the rigid strait-jacket that many people still believe.

Religious education and collective worship

Although most public schools provide both RE and a daily act of collective worship, they are under no legal obligation to do so. And whether you wish to exclude your child from both or either is a matter for you to sort out with the head teacher.

With state schools, it is different. The 1988 Education Reform Act – and now the 1996 Education Act – says they must provide both and must 'reflect the fact that religious traditions in Britain are in the main Christian whilst taking account of the other principal religions'. There is still no unanimity among school authorities over what exactly this means or what is the correct balance to be adopted between Christianity and the other main British religions: Judaism, Buddhism, Hinduism, Islam and Sikhism. Official guidelines have suggested that pupils should study three major non-Christian religions by the age of 11 and all five by 16. Many parents will probably agree with the *Daily Telegraph*'s comment: 'A grotesque formula for religious indigestion.'

When in February 1993 two Christian mothers complained to the High Court that 'multi-faith' morning assemblies at a primary school in Manchester were unlawful, Mr Justice McCullough ruled against them. But one thing is clear: parents of all religious beliefs, and those of none, can withdraw their child from either RE or daily worship or both. This is about the only untrammelled legal right that parents enjoy in modern state education law and, if you want the exact reference, it is Section 389 of the 1996 Education Act.

Truancy

The child commits it but the parent – either one! – commits the offence. The 1996 Education Act says that an LEA can summons any parent of a registered pupil who 'fails regularly to attend at school' before the local magistrates' court where they can be fined up to £1,000. On the other hand, schools must also bear some responsibility. When children fail to appear in class, schools must register them as missing and act accordingly. Most schools used to follow Government guidelines first laid down in 1994 and wait until the second day of a child's absence before alerting parents unless the pupil had a record of playing truant. But in January 1999, after a distressing case in Sussex where parents did not know that two little girls had not arrived at school in the morning until they did not return in the afternoon and they were then found several days later in a stranger's flat, new guidelines were issued which recommended that, as soon as a child is missing from class, a teacher should contact the parents.

School uniforms

Who should decide whether children have to wear a school uniform or not – the child, the parents or the school? Although some parents may feel the decision should lie with them, it is, for both public and state schools, the head teacher who the law says has the final word.

As long ago as 1954, Lord Goddard laid down the law in these uncompromising terms:

> A headmistress has the right and power to prescribe the discipline for the school and in saying that a girl must come to school wearing a particular costume, she is only acting in a matter which must be within the competence of the headmistress of any school, whether it is one of the great public schools or a modern state school.

This ruling that the head teacher's views must prevail applies to boys as well as girls, and there are only two exceptions. The first is medical: if, for example, a child is allergic to one of the fabrics used in a school uniform, she can get a doctor's certificate exempting her from wearing it. And the second is non-discriminational: as in the case of two Muslim sisters in Altrincham, Lancashire, who, after a somewhat acrimonious dispute, were eventually permitted to wear to school the headscarves required by their religion.

In the 1954 case a west Derbyshire mother claimed that she was 'the best judge of what her daughter should wear' and insisted on sending her to school in long trousers, although she knew the headmistress would send her back home. The head-on conflict ended with the mother being fined in the local magistrates' court for failing to send her daughter to school, although every morning she had diligently sent her on her way – wearing the forbidden trousers. The mother appealed to the High Court only for Lord Goddard to uphold the fine and make his historic decision.

Since then, the ruling has been extended to other breaches of school rules. So when parents have sent boys to school with long hair or girls with hair streaked with bright colours, knowing that they would be sent home, this has amounted to failing to send the child to school and the parents have been fined up to £1,000.

But the Sex Discrimination Act gets into everything these days. In June 1999, the *Sunday Times* carried the story of a woman professor at Leeds University who had started legal proceedings against her 13-year-old daughter's comprehensive school because the girl had been told she could not wear trousers instead of the regulation skirt. Under the 1975 Act, different dress codes for males and females are allowed but it is illegal if the dress code of one sex disadvantages the other and the professor claimed that her daughter was disadvantaged by having to wear skirts because swapping to trousers would be warmer and cheaper. She also said: 'Times move on. You won't go to many places now where you don't see women in trousers, including Cherie Booth and government ministers.' It will be interesting to see how her case works out.

Discipline

We have already seen that this is an area where Lord Goddard has ruled that the law concedes to head teachers an undoubted 'right and power' in both public and state schools.

Corporal punishment used to be perhaps the most popular way – among some teachers – of enforcing discipline. I am happy to say that it is now totally illegal.

The 1986 Education (No. 2) Act began the process by outlawing it in state schools and later regulations banned it for the 27,000 academically bright children from low-income families who attended some 295 public schools under the Assisted Places Scheme with their boarding fees paid out of public funds. Pupils in those same schools whose fees were paid for privately could still technically be caned but no school would operate one disciplinary code for children whose fees were paid privately and another code for those whose fees were paid by the state, so in practice no one in these schools was caned – even after the Blair Government abolished the scheme in 1998.

Yet, as a matter of law, all pupils in public schools whose fees were paid privately could, even after 1986, still be caned or otherwise physically chastised in accordance with long-standing judge-made law that, for instance, once said a blow which broke a boy's jaw in two places was 'reasonable' because of the need to protect society from 'an excess of sentimentality or sloppy thinking'.

But then the 1998 School Standards and Framework Act came into effect in September 1999 and totally banned corporal punishment for all pupils in all schools.

Detention used to be legally a grey area. Before September 1998, when yet another Education Act – that of 1997! – came into effect, detention after school might in some circumstances have been unlawful but in others lawful. The yardstick was laid down by Lord Lane, then Lord Chief Justice, in *R.* v. *Rahman* in 1985 when he ruled that detention by a parent of his own 14-year-old child could be unlawful when 'for such a period or in such circumstances as to take it out of the realms of reasonable parental discipline'. The same vague principle applied by analogy to schools

But the 1997 Act now makes the legal situation crystal clear. It not only says that all detention 'must be reasonable in all the circumstances', part of a known disciplinary policy and imposed only by a head teacher or another authorised by him or her. It further lays down that the pupil's parent must have been given at least 24 hours' written notice in advance.

Expulsion

Nowadays called legally 'exclusion', this is the ultimate sanction against serious or persistent offenders. Public schools are traditionally loath to expel, not only for economic reasons but because it is regarded as so draconian a measure as to be employed in only the clearest cases. But the schoolchildren of today are different from those of yesterday.

Many, but not all, public schools are increasingly vigilant about drugs, and possession, at least of hard drugs, almost always leads to expulsion. But, like many parents, schools are more liberal nowadays towards modest drinking and some boarding schools even have their own sixth-form bars. Bullying (if sufficiently serious and capable of being proved) is, however, now an expellable offence in many public schools.

But the law makes a fundamental difference between expulsion from a public school and a state school. With a public school, neither parents nor child have any form of legal redress. There is no appeal procedure and no recourse can be had to the courts.

The alleged bully who could not clear her name

A 16-year-old girl and her parents appealed to the High Court after she had been expelled from school for allegedly being a bully and the ringleader of a gang which terrorised other girls. The headmaster admitted they had not been told of the allegations until after she was expelled but explained that he feared the pupils she was said to have bullied might have suffered reprisals.

Mr Justice Brooke appealed for private school heads and governors to ensure pupils received 'fair play' when accused of offences which could lead to expulsion but ruled that he had no jurisdiction. The only legal option open to aggrieved parents was to sue the school for breach of contract. Only state-school pupils could seek judicial review in the High Court to protect their rights to natural justice. He expressed concern at this 'anomaly'.

Expelled state-school pupils are in a much more favourable legal position. They enjoy a statutory right of appeal within the state education system which, according to at least one teachers' leader, Mr David Hart of the National Association of Head Teachers, is so prejudiced in pupils' favour that classroom discipline has become eroded as schools have been forced to readmit an increasing number of pupils expelled for serious offences.

Recent examples of schools ordered to take back seemingly undesirable pupils include four 15-year-old boys excluded for pushing drugs on the premises, a teenager who had assaulted a teacher, two 14-year-old boys who had sexually assaulted a girl pupil, and two 15-year-old boys allegedly caught smoking marijuana.

The moral is that, if your child is expelled from a state school, you stand a pretty good chance of getting him readmitted. The 1996 Education Act says that a head teacher must tell you and your child of your right of appeal to the governors and/or the LEA. If the LEA upholds the expulsion, it will have to find your child an alternative place within the embattled state system so there is considerable pressure to order the child's reinstatement in the same school hoping that he has learned his lesson. But if you are still not satisfied, you have a final right of appeal to a local appeal committee staffed by local worthies who will have nothing to do with the school and – allegedly – little sympathy for, or understanding of, its problems.

Accidents at school

The occasional grazed knee, scraped elbow and bruises are all part of growing up; but a school cannot use youthful high spirits as an excuse to avoid its legal responsibilities. As long ago as 1893 Lord Esher, a distinguished Victorian judge, laid down a school's duty: 'A schoolmaster is bound to take such care of his boys as a careful father would take of his own son.'

But the world has moved on since then. Lord Esher was talking of a small private school where a young boy won damages after his chemistry master had left a bottle of phosphorus lying about. Today, even public schools have larger classes than they used to, while state schools struggle against budget restraints and are often chronically overcrowded or understaffed.

Yet the law, in theory, remains the same for both. As Lord Justice O'Connor said in the Appeal Court in June 1989, 'The law imposes duties on all schools simply because they are schools. These duties are of general application whether the school be provided by the State or privately, and regardless of whether it be fee-paying or free.'

With a public school, the pupil sues the proprietor or governing body; with a state school, he or she sues the local education authority. That is supposed to be the only difference. In practice, it does not work out quite like that. In all cases of alleged negligence, whether in relation to children or adults, the judges must look at all the facts. They must, therefore, always have regard to reality. A teacher looking after, say, only 18 pupils in a class will be expected to supervise them more effectively than someone with double that number to cope with.

In fact, nowadays when judges apply the 'careful parent test', as it is called, to an accident in a state school, they usually add the qualifying words 'parent of a *large family*'. This term was first coined by Mr Justice Hinchcliffe in March 1969. He was giving judgment against the Hertfordshire County Council regarding an eight-year-old boy who hurt himself badly when crashing into the sharp-flinted wall of a crowded playground while running a race with other young children. They were all habitually left to their own devices, without supervision, for ten minutes on arriving at their primary school in the morning.

Ruled the judge, a robust Yorkshireman: 'If one lets loose young children in a playground of this sort with inherently dangerous walls around it, one is simply asking for trouble.'

In all types of school, the judges try to impose a reasonably high standard of teachers' care. Cases have been won by a 14-year-old west London schoolboy blinded in one eye when a classroom prank misfired during a chemistry lesson and by a seven-year-old primary-school pupil injured when his teacher gave him sharp scissors to work with instead of the blunt-edged variety; but lost by a 12-year-old boy whose leg was broken in a playground accident when the only teacher on duty had been called away to deal with another incident.

The judges try to draw the line between what Lord Goddard once said, 'If every master is to take precautions to see that there is never ragging or horseplay among his pupils, his school would be too awful a place to contemplate', and the view expressed by Mr Justice Veale in a case when a state school tried to argue that a 12-year-old girl's damages should be cut because of her own 'contributory negligence' in putting her hand out to stop a door with too thin glass swinging back on her instead of trying to catch the handle: 'If the defendants allege this as negligence on the part of a child of twelve,' he said, 'how very much more negligent it was on their part!'

Of course, accidents are particularly prone to happen on a school sports field and here the judges, perhaps with memories of their own schooldays, have tended to be reluctant to find liability proved against a school. But in recent years a new element has crept into their judgments: the possibility of insurance. In the 1989 Appeal Court case of *Van Oppen* v. *Clerk to the Bedford Charity Trustees,* a 16-year-old boy had been seriously injured playing an inter-house rugby match at Bedford School nine years earlier. He made a flying tackle to try to bring down an opponent but ended up crashing into him. His spine was fractured and he had to spend six months in hospital, paralysed in all four limbs. The school, which at that time (back in 1980) considered it had no legal responsibility to insure pupils against sporting accidents, denied liability.

But the boy, supported by his parents, took the school governors to court claiming they were to blame for failing to coach him properly – and for not insuring him against sporting injury. The Appeal Court supported the trial judge's rejection of his claim on both counts: the coaching had been impeccable and, as these matters were understood in 1980, the school could not be faulted for failing to insure him. But all three appeal judges made clear that opinions had changed within the teaching profession since 1980, at least in the private sector, and it had become good practice for a public school to take out personal accident insurance so that its pupils were covered for accidental injury sustained in *any* properly authorised school activity, including outings, adventure camps and organised foreign trips, not only sporting events or authorised games.

If a similar accident were to happen now to a public-school boy on the rugby field or while playing any other authorised game, and the school had not taken out personal accident insurance to protect him, the school would be liable.

But remember that this decision does not apply to state schools, where pupils are still usually only insured against injury at sports meetings, school outings and expeditions – not while playing normal games, however dangerous.

Bullying

This has always gone on, as I remember from my own schooldays of quite some time ago; but nowadays it has, if anything, become even more prevalent. The same basic principle applies as with school accidents. Parents can sue if their child is injured as a result of bullying which has taken place only through lack of proper supervision.

It is as much a school's legal duty to take reasonable care to prevent bullying as to prevent potentially dangerous horseplay and, in recent years, several successful actions have been brought. This applies to both state and public schools.

The public school boy who was bullied

A bright 10-year-old arrived home covered in bruises just three weeks after enrolling at a leading public school in West Sussex. He told his parents he had been the victim of systematic 'dormitory punishments' by older boys.

His parents complained to his teachers but claimed that, despite being assured that the bullying would be stamped out, the boy was attacked twice more when he returned. They withdrew him from the school and threatened through solicitors to sue for negligence and breach of duty of care towards their pupil.

The school denied liability but agreed to pay £2,500 in an out-of-court settlement which was approved, as settlements for under 18-year-olds must always be, at Horsham County Court in May 1999.

UNIVERSITY

The law on this subject for most people boils down to money. Supporting a son or daughter through university was always an expensive business. But since the scrapping of student grants in the autumn of 1999, it will be a heavier burden.

Despite loud student protests, the Blair Administration refused to back down over the imposition of tuition fees for university students. And with maintenance grants being phased out in the 1999–2000 academic year to be replaced by means-tested loans, many parents will feel that financially they have to help out their undergraduate children even more than before.

In fact, students whose parents earn a combined salary of over £23,000 a year only have to pay tuition charges on a sliding scale but those whose parents earn more than £35,000 must pay the whole sum.

In the autumn of 1999, tuition fees went up from £1,000 to £1,025 per year. This means that students on a standard three-year degree course are now faced with having to pay as much as a total of £10,000 for their higher education to include living expenses. To make ends meet, most are forced to take out special student loans. They will not have to start paying them back until they have left university and earn more than £10,000 per annum. Employers will then be legally empowered to deduct repayments from salary instead of leaving it to former students to make their own arrangements, and the interest rate will be 9 per cent of income above the £10,000 threshold.

In the years to come, many undergraduates will have to 'work their way through college', both while they are still at university and for several years after.

5

GETTING MARRIED

All right, you are one of the couples who still form the majority and want to get married: what does that entail?

For a start, there is no legal obligation to get engaged, although many people still do. Yet it no longer creates a binding contract to get married, which it used to do. Until 1970 a girl could sue for breach of promise of marriage if her fiancé jilted her – although it never worked the other way round.

But engagement ring and engagement presents still remain in a special legal category. If either party breaks off the engagement (it does not matter which one), the girl is entitled to keep the engagement ring – except when the boy specified when he handed it over that he would want it back if things did not work out. This seldom happens, one would have thought.

It is different with engagement presents. In law, they are not outright but only conditional gifts. They are given on condition that the marriage will take place and, if not, they should be returned whence they came – if their original donors want them back. They should, at least, be given the option of refusing.

Thomas Hardy, the Victorian novelist, cynically defined marriage as 'a licence to be loved on the premises' but the classic legal definition was coined by Lord Penzance in *Hyde* v. *Hyde* in 1861: 'The voluntary union for life of one man and one woman to the exclusion of all others.' That still remains true but nowadays the essence of a valid marriage has to be looked at more closely. It must be voluntary, between two single people who are both over 16, of the opposite sex and not too closely related and the wedding ceremony must have taken place with due legal formality.

If any one of these essential elements is lacking, there is no true marriage. The courts will not grant a decree of divorce which pre-supposes that there *was* a marriage until the court's judgment ended it. Instead there will be a decree of nullity which, in effect, declares that there never was a valid marriage anyway.

Let us examine each of these basic requirements in turn:

VOLUNTARY

All is fair in love and war. There is a limit as to how far the courts will examine just how 'voluntary' the agreement was. I know of no case where a marriage has been annulled because a man told a woman that he was much richer than he really was or a woman tricked a man into marrying her by deliberately making herself pregnant through not taking the pill. 'Shotgun weddings', with the couple getting married because the girl is pregnant and her father is metaphorically holding a shotgun to the boy's head, have always been fully binding in law, although it would be different if the father was *literally* holding a shotgun to the young man's head, as actually happened in an American case back in 1928 when a judge later annulled the marriage because, as he said, 'if there had not been a wedding, there would have been a funeral'.[1]

Technically, duress is a factor that *can* invalidate a marriage but the only cases I know of, in recent years, concern arranged marriages within the Asian community. Even so, the judges draw a fine line – as shown by these contrasting cases:

The Sikh marriage that was legal

A young Sikh girl had never seen her husband before the marriage, and only went through the ceremony out of 'proper respect' for her parents and Sikh traditions. But she was bitterly unhappy and asked for her marriage to be annulled on the grounds of duress. In 1971, the High Court refused her petition because there was no evidence of fear. 'Respect' for her cultural and ethnic background was not enough.

The Hindu marriage that was void

A 19-year-old Hindu girl was forced into an arranged marriage because her parents said that otherwise they would throw her out of the house, leaving her homeless and destitute. In 1982, the Appeal Court annulled the marriage on the basis that 'the crucial question in these cases ... is whether the threats, pressure or whatever it is, is such as to destroy the reality of the consent and overbear the will of the individual'.

It is still uncertain to what extent the bride or groom must actually be put into a state of fear. In an Irish case in 1989 (which is not binding in Britain but merely of 'persuasive authority'), a pregnant woman was pressurised by her parents into getting married and her employer told her she would lose her job if she did not. There was no question of her being put in fear but the marriage was still annulled: there had been no true consent.

BETWEEN TWO SINGLE PEOPLE

Fairly obviously, neither party can be already married and, if either is divorced, the former marriage must have been fully ended by what is called a decree absolute.[2] The 'decree nisi' which is pronounced at the actual divorce hearing does not end the marriage. It merely entitles the person obtaining the divorce (the 'petitioner') to apply to the court office for the decree to be made absolute after six weeks and one day. This is only a paper formality that does not involve the judge; but until it takes place neither husband nor wife is free to remarry.

Sometimes problems arise because the 'respondent' (i.e. the other spouse) has already met someone else and wants to remarry as soon as possible and the petitioner is vicious or embittered and is in no hurry to facilitate their plans. So what happens if the petitioner does not obligingly ask for the decree to be made absolute after six weeks and one day?

In dire emergency, where for example a speedy remarriage is necessary for a child to be born legitimate, the respondent can apply – personally or through a lawyer – to the judge at the actual divorce hearing to cut the normal six-week period. Otherwise a respondent can make a paper application to the court office but only after a further three calendar months have elapsed: in those circumstances, the total time between decree nisi and absolute can be as long as six weeks and one day *plus* three further months.

It is generally believed that bigamy, where someone goes through a ceremony of marriage while still married to another person, does not happen nowadays. That is simply not true. Bigamy cases still occur but the Crown Prosecution Service tends only to prosecute where the bigamous person has acted maliciously or fraudulently:

The bigamous oil rigger

A 29-year-old Newcastle oil rigger was jailed for four months in February 1993 at Durham Crown Court after pleading guilty to leading a double life for almost a year, dividing his time between his legal wife and a young office clerk whom he had married illegally. Each woman was in complete ignorance of the other, although they lived just 15 miles apart in houses shared with the same man. They believed his regular absences were due to his working abroad.

The truth only came out when the bigamous marriage soured after the office clerk became pregnant. He told her to get rid of the child – and he soon stopped coming 'home'. Desperate to trace him, she drove to Wallsend where she had last dropped him off. A car pulled up – containing her 'husband' and his real wife.

Sometimes genuine misunderstandings can occur when a married couple have been separated for many years and have lost all contact with each other. You do not even know whether your partner is alive or dead. What then? After seven years you can go to court and obtain a declaration of presumption of death and, after only five years, you can obtain a divorce on the grounds of at least five years' separation. But not everyone leads such a tidy life. The 1861 Offences Against the Person Act (and that date is not a misprint) says that it is a defence to a charge of bigamy if the missing spouse 'shall have been continually absent for the space of seven years and shall not have been known to be living within that time'.

There has been no modern interpretation of this mid-Victorian wording but it *could* mean that you do not actually have to take positive steps to trace your missing partner during those crucial seven years. It might suffice if you merely did not know they were alive, although you could have done more to try and find out.

OVER SIXTEEN

It may surprise some people to know that before the law was changed, back in 1929, the minimum age for marriage for boys was 14 and for girls a staggeringly low 12.

But although children of 16 can now get married legally, until they are both 18 years of age, they will need their parents' consent and, whether the parents are still married to each other or divorced, *both* parents must give their consent. If the parents are not married to each other and never have been, only the mother need consent – except where the father has 'parental responsibility' under the 1989 Children Act, when again they must both give consent.

And if they refuse? The 16-year-old or 17-year-old denied consent can go along to the local magistrates' court and ask the Bench to allow the wedding to take place without it. There will be a private hearing in front of all the parties and, especially where one set of parents are supportive or (more problematically) the girl is pregnant, the odds are that the Bench will agree.

Incidentally, there is no legal upper age limit for marriage as long as the officiating priest or registrar is satisfied that both parties are still 'compos mentis', i.e. appreciate fully what they are doing. In January 1993, an 81-year-old couple, both in their wheelchairs, were married at St Mary's Church, Old Basing, Hampshire having met at a local old people's home.

OF THE OPPOSITE SEX

Gay 'marriages' between two people of the same sex are not legally recognised in this country, although they are accorded some legal effect in Denmark and Holland.

In Britain there is no way that two men can go through a legal ceremony of marriage, even though one is dressed as a woman, looks like a woman and considers herself to be a woman. But two people *can* legally get married, who both look like women, talk like women and behave like women even though one of them was in fact born a man.

This follows from the fact that the yardstick of sex, in English law, is the sex with which you were born. A man may have had his sexual orientation changed by surgery. He may now consider himself to be in every way a woman but legally he remains a man. As Mr Justice Ormrod, a doctor as well as divorce court judge, ruled in February 1970 when annulling the marriage seven years earlier of April Ashley, the first British recipient of a sex-change operation, having been born George Jamieson:

Having regard to the essentially heterosexual character of the relationship which is called marriage, the criteria (for deciding the sex of the parties) must, in my judgement, be biological, for even the most extreme degree of transsexualism in a male or the most severe hormonal imbalance which can exist in a person with male chromosomes, male gonads and male genitalia cannot reproduce a person who is naturally capable of performing the essential role of a woman in marriage.

Well put. But the bizarre consequence of this sensible ruling is that in August 1993 two people, each with a woman's name, were given permission to marry at Fareham register office, Hampshire because one of them had been born a man and, although having had a sex-change operation 15 years earlier, still was legally a man and, therefore, of the opposite sex to her partner – who presumably is now legally her 'wife'.

NOT TOO CLOSELY RELATED

In the eyes of the law, one can be too closely related to someone to marry them. The subject is similar to, but not the same, as incest, which (only since an Act of 1908) is the crime of having sexual intercourse with a member of your immediate family (parent, grandparent, child, brother or sister, half-brother or half-sister). The range of close relations whom you cannot marry is much wider and more specific. The general belief still persists that first cousins in Britain cannot legally marry each other but in fact ever since the reign of Henry VIII, that has not been the case.

The present law is extremely complex and is mainly governed by the 1949 Marriage Act which refers to the 'prohibited degrees of affinity'. Some are obvious: parent, child, brother or sister, grandparent, grandchild, parent-in-law, daughter-in-law, son-in-law, step-parent, stepchild, uncle-in-law and aunt-in-law. The rest are perhaps not so obvious: the wife or husband of a grandparent who has married more than once, the wife or husband of a grandparent-in-law, a stepchild's wife or husband, the wife or husband of a grandchild.

The general rule was that these restrictions applied even after the relationship technically no longer existed. For example, a woman whose husband had died could not marry her son-in-law, even if he had divorced her daughter especially to do so. He was stuck for ever with being within the 'prohibited degrees'. In the rather lovely old language of the law books, 'A husband is of affinity to his wife's kindred and a wife is of affinity to her husband's kindred.' My wife's stepmother, however young and attractive she may be, is legally considered my stepmother too and therefore I can never marry her.

Over the years, Parliament has made a few specific exceptions to this otherwise rigid rule. A man can now marry his dead (or divorced) wife's sister, aunt or niece; and he can also marry the ex-wife of his brother, uncle or nephew. The most recent change in the law was the 1986 Marriage (Prohibited Degrees of Relationship) Act which enables a man to marry his stepdaughter or a woman her stepson, as long as the couples are over 21 and did not live together as a family when the younger person was a child. A man can also now marry his ex-wife's grandmother or his grandson's ex-wife. He can even marry his ex-mother-in-law or ex-daughter-in-law, if both former partners are dead. This also, of course, applies the other way round, with a woman able to marry her dead – or divorced – husband's brother, etc.

WEDDING TOOK PLACE WITH DUE LEGAL FORMALITY

Although others can legally perform a marriage ceremony, only two categories of people can give legal approval for that ceremony to take place: a Church of England clergyman for church weddings of Anglicans, and a state superintendent registrar for everyone else, including Roman Catholics, Quakers, Jews, other non-Christians and those, irrespective of their religion, who simply want to have a civil wedding in a state register office.

There are thus two stages: the preliminaries and the actual ceremony.

Preliminaries

Anglican marriages in church   The traditional procedure is **'calling the banns'**: On at least three consecutive Sundays the couple's names are read out in the parish church of the district where they live, so that anyone who knows of a legal obstacle to their marriage can come forward. If no one materialises, they can marry at any time in the next three months. Then there is **common licence**: if a couple do not wish banns to be published, they can apply, at a cost of £55, for a common licence from the bishop in whose diocese either of them has lived for at least the past 15 days. That too will allow them to be married at any time in the next three months. Finally, there is the **special licence** issued only by the Archbishop of Canterbury which requires no residential qualification and authorises a marriage at any time and in any place. It costs £120, more than double the cost of a common licence, and is restricted to special cases (e.g. where someone wants to marry in the church of the parish where they were brought up but from which they have long moved away) or cases of exceptional urgency. It will require character references, letters of approval from parents and from the vicar of the church where the couple want to marry.

All other marriages (including Roman Catholic marriages)

A **registrar's certificate** costing £23 is issued after notice of the couple's intention to marry has been displayed for three weeks at any register office of the couple's choice. It authorises a marriage at any time in the next three months. A **registrar's licence** – sometimes wrongly called a special licence – costs an extra £46.50 but authorises a marriage after one clear working day. There are special preliminaries to facilitate the marriage of the terminally ill, the housebound, prisoners and people in mental hospitals.

The ceremony

There are five permitted types of ceremony. (1) **Marriage according to the rites of the Church of England**. This must be celebrated by an Anglican clergyman in the presence of two or more witnesses. By church law, it is usually unavailable to anyone whose previous marriage has ended in divorce and the ex-spouse is still alive, although a remarriage in a register office may be, and often is, then 'blessed' in church.[3] The clergyman will use the rite laid down in the Book of Common Prayer or authorised alternative form of service. (2) **Register office wedding.** The bride and groom each has to make two fundamental declarations. First: 'I do solemnly declare that I know of no lawful impediment why I (full name)may not be joined in matrimony to (full name).' And then: 'I call upon these persons here present to witness [there must be at least two witnesses and 'with open doors'] that I, (full name), do take thee, (full name), to be my lawful wedded wife (or husband).' As soon as both have made that second declaration, they are legally man and wife. The presiding registrar does not proclaim them man and wife, and placing a wedding ring on the bride's finger forms no part of the legal ceremony of marriage. (3) **Marriages in a registered place of religious worship.** Roman Catholics, Nonconformists and, in modern multi-racial Britain, Muslims, Sikhs, Hindus and Buddhists can marry in their own church, chapel, mosque, temple or other place of religious worship so long as it is registered by the Registrar-General. The form of the ceremony, and the words used, are entirely a matter for the parties and their own religious principles, except that at some stage the bride and groom must make the same two fundamental declarations as in a register office wedding. They must do so in either English or Welsh but ironically there is no specific legal requirement that the couple understand what they are saying.

(4) **Jewish and Quaker weddings.** These are in a special legal category. So long as religious laws are complied with, they do not have to take place in a registered building and the only requirements of English law are that a registrar's certificate or licence has been obtained beforehand and that afterwards the marriage is registered at the local register office. (5) **Civil marriages not in a register office.** Until the 1994 Marriage Act, which started out as a Private Member's Bill introduced by Gyles Brandreth, civil marriages could take place only in register offices. But now they can take place in any other building specifically licensed for that purpose by the local council. It was originally thought that only stately homes, hotels, castles and suchlike would qualify – but in May 1999 a thousand shoppers became 'honorary guests' at Britain's first marriage in a shopping mall. It took place at the Belfry Shopping Centre in Redhill, Surrey. It was a great success; the bride came up the escalator radiant in white and later said that her mother had always expected her to have an unusual wedding.

WHAT HAPPENS IF SOMETHING GOES WRONG?

It has never been the law that the parents of the bride pay for the wedding and that the parents of the groom are merely responsible for the flowers. That was, at best, a social convention that now is less often observed. But *someone* has to pay for the ceremony and the reception: what rights do they have if the food is sub-standard, the band does not turn up or the DJ operating the mobile disco is drunk?

Formal weddings nowadays can be very expensive: according to a recent survey, the average white wedding in London costs about £13,000 while outside London it will leave little change from £10,000. The result is that many people take out wedding insurance to cover cancellation or mishap.

If not, normal legal liability remains, as for any other breach of contract, if something goes wrong – except that the damages may be greater because a wedding is involved. And this does not only apply to large-scale 'Society' weddings or lavish middle-class functions with a marquee in the garden, as shown by a case at Blackwood county court in October 1993:

The wedding reception that was a disaster

A mother in Gwent, North Wales booked a room at a local club for her daughter's wedding reception. It was not to be a very grand affair. She paid a fee of £205 which was to cover £35 for the hire of a room and a disco and buffet food at £2 a head for 85 people. Guests were to buy their own drinks at the club's bar.

The county court judge ruled that it was implied in the contract that there would be a reasonable sufficiency of food provided for the guests and that proper facilities, in particular toilet facilities, would be available.

In fact, the food was enough for only 30 people so that some guests had nothing to eat at all while others left the reception to go and buy food at a local fish and chip shop. The bride and groom were so embarrassed that they left their own wedding reception in their wedding clothes to go and buy more food for their guests. And the toilets were 'messy' with wet floors.

The judge awarded the bride's mother £485 damages, £85 being to reflect the lack of food and £400 for her inconvenience and distress. She had been unwell for a week afterwards because of what had happened.

Money is no guarantee of satisfaction. In May 1997, a caterer in Maidstone, Kent who had served warm seafood mayonnaise at a wedding reception costing £4,785 in a mock Tudor house in nearby Sissinghurst was jailed for four months at Tunbridge Wells magistrates' court. He had used raw eggs in the mayonnaise, mixed it with prawns and left it in covered dishes for up to four hours in a marquee. Temperatures on the day had reached 85 Fahrenheit and more than 200 people, including the groom, went down with salmonella poisoning. 'You, as a professional, had a duty of care under the food regulations to provide food which was fit for human consumption. Quite evidently, it was not,' said the chairman of the Bench.

ONE FINAL QUESTION: DOES A WOMAN HAVE TO CHANGE HER SURNAME?

No. It is only a social convention that a woman takes her husband's surname on marriage. There is absolutely no legal obligation. So the authorities have no choice but to respect your wishes. In particular, your passport will not need to be changed and, if you are still of the same mind when it comes up for renewal, the new passport will be issued in the same name.

As for the Inland Revenue and the DSS, all you need do is write to the relevant office saying you are getting married but wish still to keep your existing surname. There should be no problem.

Notes

1 A more tolerant attitude prevails today. The *Daily Telegraph* has reprinted this item for sale in a local newspaper: 'Wedding Dress. Ivory in colour. Designed to hide pregnancy at approximately seven and a half months.'

2 A polygamous marriage where a man can have more than one wife at the same time cannot take place legally in Britain but a valid polygamous marriage abroad can be recognised here.

3 In recent years the General Synod of the Church has allowed local clergy to remarry in church someone who has been divorced, as distinct from allowing a mere blessing, if the diocesan bishop allows it.

6

LIVING TOGETHER –
AND BREAKING UP

For many people contemplating marriage in modern Britain today, one of the first questions must be: why bother? The old days have long since gone of marriage being the norm for any heterosexual couple in love and wanting to live together and have children. As the late Sir George Baker once said, when England's senior divorce judge, 'There is an increasing tendency, I have found in cases in Chambers, to regard, and indeed to speak of, the celebration of marriage as "the paperwork". The phrase used is, "We were living together but we never got round to the paperwork".'

But that was way back in the mid-1970s. Nowadays, marriage is even more an institution under attack. Official figures show that more couples are cohabiting than ever before and that more than a quarter of all homes are now one-person households. Even Buckingham Palace, with three broken marriages among the Queen's four children, has bowed to the pressure: those invited to the traditional summer garden party are nowadays allowed to bring 'companions', and so established a bastion of the legal profession as the South Eastern Circuit Bar Mess provides for organised trips abroad for barrister members of the Circuit 'and their partners'.

As part of this (largely piecemeal and unplanned) development, the legal differences between being married and living together have shrunk considerably, even to the extent that Gordon Brown's 1999 Budget completely did away with the married couple's allowance for anyone under 65 as from 5 April, 2000. The fundamental difference remains that a husband and wife are under a legal duty to maintain each other during and sometimes even after the marriage but that is never true of cohabitees (the ugly word increasingly being used for those who live together without being married). Palimony does not exist in English law.

But otherwise a wedding ring now brings few extra legal benefits – except with property rights, as we shall see in a minute. Both a married and an unmarried mother can go to the Child Support Agency for help in making the father of the child pay maintenance for the child. Both husband and wife automatically have an equal say in their child's upbringing but an unmarried father will only get it, if the mother agrees or a court grants him shared parental responsibility under the 1989 Children Act. A married woman can obtain a state pension in her own right or, in certain circumstances, on the strength of her husband's contributions whereas a cohabitee must rely on her own contributions.

If a person makes inadequate provision for their spouse or unmarried partner in their will or makes no will at all, the 1975 Inheritance (Provisions for Family and Dependants) Act says that either can go to court for 'reasonable provision' out of the estate but a cohabitee only has this right if 'wholly or partially maintained' by the lover at the time of death. In practice, this qualification makes very little difference when a man dies, as cohabitees tend to have been at least 'partially maintained' by their partner. Yet an ex-spouse, who has not remarried, can ask for 'reasonable provision' from the estate, which an ex-cohabitee, with no new live-in relationship, can never do.

Even so, the 1995 Law Reform (Succession) Act further narrowed the gap between marriage and cohabitation by saying that anyone living with the deceased 'as man and wife' for the last two years can also claim 'reasonable provision'. In December 1998, in the first case under this new Act, Mr Justice Neuberger awarded £24,000 or £2,500 a year for life to be paid out of a £200,000 estate to a 67-year-old woman who had lived with a retired teacher for ten years, cooking and looking after him but not sharing his bed. He ruled that, in all the circumstances, they were living together 'as man and wife'.

If a person is killed through someone else's negligence, for example in a road accident, their husband or wife can claim damages for their own and their children's financial loss plus £7,500 'bereavement damages' for their own emotional loss. In 1976, the Fatal Accidents Act extended the definition of 'husband' or 'wife' to include 'any person living with the deceased as husband or wife for at least the past two years'. But only a husband or wife can claim 'bereavement damages'. However long or loving the relationship, a live-in partner of either sex does not qualify.

Yet the acid test for the legal difference between marriage and living together comes with the division of property rights when a marriage or relationship ends; and particularly for the woman.

I do not want to be pessimistic but the grim reality is that, as revealed in February 1999 in a study carried out by the Office for National Statistics, couples who cohabit are three or four times more likely to split up than those who marry. For many people, getting married still entails a greater commitment than merely choosing to live together; and the law respects that fact. It is all very well for Jack Straw, then the Home Secretary, to declare in a speech in June 1999 that the institution of marriage is less important than the quality of relationships and that nobody should 'get into a paddy' about the decline of formal marriage since 'the most important thing is the quality of the relationship and not the institution in itself', the fact remains that, if a relationship does break up, however great its 'quality', the law is not so generous to the woman as it would have been if the couple had been married.

That is a fact of legal life.

When a relationship breaks up, the woman (or man but it is nearly always the woman who finds herself in this position) can only claim what is legally hers: she has no automatic right to any share of her ex-lover's assets. This shows itself in two main areas:

Pensions An unmarried non-contributing cohabitee will not automatically get pension payouts if their partner dies, or they split up. Many pension companies say they are not entitled to anything at all unless the pensioner has nominated their partner, and the pension company trustees are happy to accept that.

Family home If a woman has been so foolish as to allow the house to remain in her lover's sole name, and it is surprising how many women still do, she can usually claim only something less than a full half-share in the legal ownership, and then only if she helped pay for the property in the first place (e.g. by contributing to the original down-payment or sharing in the mortgage repayments) or if she has since increased its value (e.g. by physically helping to modernise it, as one cement-mixing Amazon did in a classic case in 1972).

Her non-financial or non-physical contribution does not count.

The case of the unmarried housewife

A woman kept home for her businessman lover in Southgate, North London for twenty years and bore him two sons. He would not marry her because he was married to a Roman Catholic who would not divorce him; but she had changed her name by deed poll and they openly lived together as a married couple. She was an old-fashioned housewife in everything but name, looking after the house, cooking and bringing up the family.

Sadly the relationship deteriorated and eventually she left but, when she claimed a share in the house (which was in his sole name), the Appeal Court ruled she was entitled to nothing. Said Lord Justice May: 'When one compares this result with what it would have been if she had been married to the defendant, I think that she can justifiably say that fate has not been kind to her. In my opinion, however, the remedy for any iniquity she may have sustained is a matter for Parliament and not for this court.'

That was back in July 1983 but Parliament still has not taken up the invitation to intervene, although the position has slightly improved by virtue of later cases that have made some minor improvements to the law.

Even in these days of increasing economic parity between the sexes, whether you are a man or a woman, you should seek skilled legal advice before going to live in your lover's home on any long-term basis. Indeed, this is even more advisable if you decide to buy a place together: whether in both names or only one. This does not mean going to the first High Street solicitor you can find but asking around friends or relations until you find a solicitor with particular experience in this field. Otherwise, I suggest you send a stamped addressed envelope asking for a list of local members to the Solicitors Family Law Association (SFLA) at PO Box 302, Orpington, Kent BR6 8QX (Tel: 01689–850227).

In the meantime, I can give these pointers for starters:

(1) If you reach the stage when you and your lover really think your relationship is going to last, that is wonderful but, in sheer prudence, you should not allow your home to remain indefinitely in your lover's sole name. It is just too dangerous legally. You are a hostage to fortune in your lover's house and he or she can, after giving you reasonable notice, have you evicted as a trespasser – which is what you will have become.

(2) If you are buying a new place jointly or, subject to financial adjustment between the two of you, transferring your lover's home from sole ownership into joint ownership, you should consider very carefully which form of joint ownership you want. There are two kinds. **Joint tenancy** is where you both own the whole property and do not each own merely a share. This is usually to be preferred for married couples and for those contemplating a permanent unmarried relationship: the advantage is that, when one dies, the other automatically becomes the sole owner of the property without need of a will. The disadvantage is that, in their joint

lifetime, both parties have to agree on a sale and, if they have not sorted out in advance what is going to happen (e.g. that the person remaining in the property shall have a reasonable time, say six months, to raise the money to buy out the other before selling to an outsider), one will have to take the other to court and ask a judge to order what he thinks is fair in all the circumstances – which causes delay and expense.

Tenancy in common is where you each own a separate share in the property, although not necessarily equally. This is preferred when two people share ownership on what is probably going to be a temporary basis, as when two working women club together to buy a flat. If one were tragically to die early (for instance in a road accident), the other does not automatically become sole owner and the dead person's share forms part of their estate to be disposed of according to the terms of their will or, if there is none, it will go to the next-of-kin.

(3) There is a way round these difficulties. It may not be very romantic or dewy-eyed but, as the law now stands, a couple contemplating a long-term relationship should, at a very early stage, discuss between themselves and agree on what is going to happen if they eventually break up and part.

The case of the couple who said nothing

A woman went to live with her lover in his rented Council flat. After a while they jointly bought his flat from the Council as tenants in common, although, in their happy state, nothing was said as to the shares in which they owned the place. Did they own it 50/50 or what? The subject was ignored. In fact, the man provided 75 per cent of the down payment and the woman 25 per cent and they agreed to pay off the mortgage equally.

After some years the relationship broke down and the woman left. The flat was to be sold but they could not agree on how to share the net proceeds of sale, after deduction of mortgage.

The man went to court for a decision. The judge ruled it should be 50/50 on the basis that, although neither had said anything about it to the other, each had in their own mind an 'uncommunicated belief or intention' that they were to share ownership equally.

The man appealed and, in March 1992, the Appeal Court said the division should be 75/25, as with their original down-payments. Lord Justice Dillon said that, when a couple buy jointly, they hold the property, in the absence of evidence of 'a common intention' to the contrary, in the same proportion as they made the original down payment. He ruled – perhaps surprisingly – that agreeing to pay the mortgage equally was *not* evidence of 'a common intention' to own the property equally; and he poured scorn on the idea that there might be 'a common intention' to share equally that neither had communicated to the other.

He said the court would refuse to 'do palm tree justice' to try and provide a fair decision, and gave a swingeing rebuke to solicitors for not thinking about the future when unmarried cohabitees buy property and, in particular, for not advising couples about the need to make provision for what should happen if the relationship broke down and they separated.

(4) So, in plain self-interest, two lovers starting to live together on a long-term basis should enter into a formal signed **Cohabitation Contract** with each other. The words 'contract' and 'lover' may not seem to have much in common; but that is the cynical reality of life today.

I would be doing more harm than good by drafting specimen cohabitation contracts (or 'living together agreements' or 'declarations of trust', as they are also called) and printing them in this book. Each such document should be tailor-made to the requirements of the couple who have to think through every single one of its detailed terms.

This really is one instance where you need a skilled lawyer's individual help. But it should not cost a fortune. In the last ten years or so, such contracts have become much more common. If you are buying a home together, you almost certainly will be using a solicitor anyway – so why not ask her or him to draft this extra document at the same time? *If you write out beforehand a rough plan of what you both want*, even if then the solicitor spends time asking you to consider certain eventualities you might not yourselves have contemplated, it should not cost much more than about £125 plus VAT for the solicitor to put your draft into legal language. And it will be money well spent.

TO SUM UP

Depending on how strong is an unmarried couple's love for each other or how 'practical' they are ready to be, there are four golden rules for improving the legal position on break-up:

1. Make sensible wills.
2. Insist, if at all possible, on your partner being made a beneficiary in your private or company pension.
3. Put all property, savings and investments into joint names.
4. Sign a 'cohabitation contract' setting out exactly what is to happen in a wide range of future eventualities.

ONE FINAL QUESTION: WHAT IS COMMON LAW MARRIAGE?

Some people like to refer to each other as 'my Common Law husband' or 'Common Law wife'. But how does this concept fit into the scheme of things, and what exactly does it mean anyway?

In truth, very little. It is a myth based on a total misconception of the true significance of this ancient legal term. Sir Robert Megarry, when Vice-Chancellor of the High Court's Chancery Division, described the phrase as 'a polite cloak for fornication or adultery of the less ephemeral type' and Judge Michael Corley described its use in a case at Southend County Court as 'slovenly, silly and suitable only for Americans and criminals'.

Most couples who live together in what they call a Common Law marriage do so because they have decided not to get married, or at least not for the time being. But the whole essence of a real Common Law marriage is that the couple are free to marry each other and would dearly love to do so – but cannot! The concept dates from centuries past when, under the old Common Law of England, a couple became legally married merely by saying to each other in front of witnesses: 'I take you as my husband' and 'I take you as my wife'. They were then married in the eyes of the law.

But the 1753 Marriage Act ended all that when it introduced the calling of banns and the modern church wedding. Since then Common Law marriages have had no legal validity whatsoever *except when a couple wish to marry but cannot because of prevailing local or temporary conditions*. Examples have been cases in the early British colonies where no law had yet been established or in prisoner-of-war camps and foreign internment camps. Couples declared they were married in front of witnesses, and so they were. Only divorce can end such a marriage, as actually happened to some real Common Law marriages that took place in World War II internment camps.

If a woman lives with a man these days and shares his life on a permanent or semi-permanent basis, we have seen that the law gives her rights that are in many ways not much less than those enjoyed by a full wife. Nigel Dempster, the *Daily Mail* gossip columnist, has coined the more honest phrase 'live-in girlfriend' or 'boyfriend'. But whichever label is used, the one thing that such a person is not is a Common Law wife or husband.

7

GETTING DIVORCED

The statistics are appalling. Britain has the highest divorce rate in Europe. More than 160,000 British couples divorce each year, compared with under 30,000 thirty years ago. More than 2 million children are being brought up in one-parent families. Almost one in ten new marriages do not even get as far as the seven-year itch: they break up within two years, compared with one in a hundred thirty years ago.

Marital unhappiness has been with us for centuries. In the sixteenth century poet John Donne could lament his elopement with a bitter poignancy: 'John Donne, Anne Donne, Undone.' Matters had not improved by the late eighteenth century when Samuel Taylor Coleridge described unhappiness as: 'Those habitual ills/ That wear out life, when two unequal minds/ Meet in one house and two discordant wills.'

But now couples are no longer content to accept their misery. They are battering down the doors of their self-built prisons on a scale never known before. They go out into the world seeking new happiness, although whether they always find it is perhaps open to question. According to figures published in June 1999 by Euromonitor's *World Marketing Data & Statistics*, Britain's annual rate of 3.25 divorces for every 1,000 inhabitants is the sixth biggest in the world.

Divorce has become an essential part of our way of life. Nowadays nearly all divorces are uncontested or, after protracted negotiation, end up that way: dealt with in private far from prying eyes or ears, usually quite literally through the post with no one going to court. For most, it is mailbox justice. A man or woman who has committed adultery with a married person is still sometimes concerned about having to be named in their divorce. They no longer need be worried: ever since October 1991 the courts accept a spouse's written admission that they have committed adultery 'with a woman (or man) whose name I am not prepared to disclose'.

A divorce is not what it was in the old days before the 1969 Divorce Reform Act modernised the law and swept away the grim charade of couples revealing to the world the most intimate details of their private life in front of elderly judges and crowded public galleries, with the details of the more 'juicy' cases trotted out for general delight later in the newspapers.

The basic framework is remarkably simple.

No divorce is possible within the first year of a marriage but thereafter there is only one ground of divorce: that the marriage has irretrievably broken down. The 1973 Matrimonial Causes Act (which soon re-enacted and replaced the 1969 Divorce Reform Act) says that this single ground of divorce can be established by proving one of five possible 'facts': i.e. adultery, unreasonable behaviour (which can mean almost anything you want it to mean, from 'he was always coming home late' or 'her love-making was passionless and made me feel used' to more traditional allegations of physical violence or abuse),[1] two years' desertion, two years' separation and consent and five years' separation without consent.

Despite the stern words of the Act itself, the more liberal tone of the New Divorce Age was early set by Lord Denning as Master of the Rolls and senior Appeal Court judge, back in February 1973, when hearing an acrimonious dispute between a dentist and his wife from Streatham in suburban south London. 'Divorce today,' he said, 'carries no stigma but only sympathy. It is a misfortune which befalls both parties. No longer is one guilty and the other innocent.'

That message has been highlighted and strengthened by Part 2 of the 1996 Family Law Act which went on to the Statute Book in July 1996. It created new divorce laws for this country that were fundamentally different from the old yet still within the same generous spirit enunciated by Lord Denning 23 years before. For Section 1 of the Act states the general principles of the new regime in these clear-cut words:

(a) The institution of marriage is to be supported;

(b) the parties to a marriage which may have broken down are to be encouraged to take all practical steps, whether by marriage counselling or otherwise, to save the marriage;

(c) a marriage which has irretrievably broken down and is being brought to an end should be brought to an end –

(i) with the minimum of distress to the parties and the children;

(ii) with questions dealt with in a manner designed to promote as good a continuing relationship between the parties and any children as is possible in the circumstances; and

(iii) without costs being unreasonably incurred in connection with the procedures to be followed in bringing it to an end;

(d) that any risk to one of the parties, and to any children, of violence from the other party should, so far as reasonably practicable, be removed or diminished.

That is all very fine and commendable. The only trouble is that the wonderful new laws to which these splendid principles were to be applied were in themselves hopelessly flawed by legislators who could not bring themselves to acknowledge or accept the fundamental contradiction implicit in an Act designed to protect the institution of marriage and at the same time to make divorce easier. It was from the very start doomed to failure as a practical blueprint for endeavour, and had to be driven through by John Major's Conservative Government against bitter opposition from both religious figures and more than a hundred Tory MPs, including William Hague.

As early as in January 1996, Lord Mackay of Clashfern, then Tory Lord Chancellor, had to admit that it would be two years before the scheme could be brought into effect because of the need for pilot studies on its two most controversial innovations: compulsory 'information meetings' for all would-be divorcing couples and official encouragement for mediators to persuade them *not* to divorce at all or at least to agree on property and child disputes without involving the courts. When Lord Irvine of Lairg, the new Labour Lord Chancellor, took over in 1997 he announced that even more pilot studies would be required and further training schemes which would inevitably entail that implementation would be pushed back another two years, to 2000.

But even that was not enough. In June 1999 the Government virtually threw in the towel and announced that the project was shelved indefinitely. Lord Irvine gave the reason as the failure of the various pilot studies. The results had been 'disappointing', he said. In fact, the pilots had shown that only 10 per cent of couples had opted to attend the information meetings which under the Act would be compulsory and, of those, only 7 per cent had been diverted into mediation and 39 per cent said they were more likely than before to go to a solicitor. As Chris Barton, Director of the Family Studies Centre at Staffordshire University, commented: 'These flawed proposals would have been like Snakes and Ladders without the ladders.'

Yet Part 2 has not been formally abolished. It remains on the Statute Book and, at least in theory, could still one day be brought into operation. The reality, however, is that anyone contemplating divorce within the foreseeable future will still need to know about the old law.

So, to go back to the basic framework of the five 'facts' needed to establish irretrievable breakdown of the marriage under the 1973 Act, there are, of course, nuances. The Act allows the parties to continue living together (and having sex together) to try and work out their differences for a trial period of up to six months before parting irrevocably. And, even if the real reason for continuing to have sex is simply that they enjoy it, irrespective of the possibilities of reconciliation, these six months do not have to form one long continual period:

An example of how the six months trial period works

A wife discovers in January 2000 that her husband has been committing adultery. She tries to forgive him but she cannot. One month later, in February, she asks him to move out on a 'trial separation', and he goes. But in July 2000 he returns to see if they can save the marriage. She then has five more months until December 2000 to decide whether to divorce him on the basis of his 'old' adultery, although of course this would not affect a divorce on the basis of any 'new' adultery.

Furthermore, two or even five years' separation does not necessarily mean that you must have lived under separate roofs during all that time. The courts accept that there can be financial or economic reasons why people have to go on living in the same house, or even the same flat, without actually living *together*. It suffices if there have been 'two separate households under one roof': i.e. you may have shared the same kitchen and bathroom but not the same bedroom or living-room. And you should most definitely not have cooked for one another or have spent evenings together happily watching television; but, in all conscience, who really is to know if occasionally you have done?

With the 'fact' of five years' separation without consent, the 1969 Act tried to throw a lifebelt to people who were, for the first time in our history, being divorced against their will and with nothing alleged against them. So the Act said that a judge could refuse a decree if he thought it would cause 'grave financial or other hardship and that, in all the circumstances, it would be wrong to dissolve the marriage'. Like so many parliamentary compromises, this proved of limited effect. The judges ruled that the 'hardship' must be only financial and not emotional so that divorce, even in these circumstances, became almost inevitable –

except that a husband would be ordered to give his wife a larger annuity or extra finance for a little more security in an insecure world.

ALTERNATIVES TO DIVORCE

For the sake of completeness, we must look at the three alternatives to divorce, whether under the old or new law. They are far from frequent but still of considerable importance:

Legal separation

This is often not so much an alternative as a temporary stage on the way to divorce, as it was with both the Queen's two older sons, the Duke of York and the Prince of Wales. In fact, it does not entail going to court. Couples who no longer want to live together agree between themselves on most, if not all, of the practical issues that normally arise when a marriage sours: what is to happen to the children, the family home and the furniture, where they are both going to live, whether one will pay maintenance to the other and, if so, for how long and how much, etc. etc.

Couples can simply exchange letters setting this all out but it is safer to ask a solicitor to draw up a formal deed which you then both sign. If there are future difficulties, a judge is much more likely not to tamper with the terms of a separation agreement in a deed than one merely contained in letters written without legal advice.

Judicial separation

This is half a stage on: it is a sort of reluctant semi-divorce. You have to go to court but you need not wait for a year. A judge will grant a decree of judicial separation in much the same way as a decree of divorce – *but it does not end the marriage.* That is why it remains quite popular with people, mainly women, who have a religious objection to divorce. Also it is easier because you do not have to prove that your marriage has irretrievably broken down. It is enough to prove one of the five basic 'facts': adultery, unreasonable behaviour, etc.

There are only about 1,600 decrees a year, of which this is a good example:

The vet who lost his case

A 49-year-old veterinary surgeon who complained that his 50-year-old wife criticised him in front of others for being over-sexed was refused a divorce for 'unreasonable behaviour'. But Judge Watts granted the wife a decree of judicial separation on the grounds of the vet's adultery. He said the couple remained 'in a state of holy deadlock.'

In fact, the deadlock does not have to be for all time. Judicial separation does not prevent either party later getting a divorce, if grounds exist. This veterinary surgeon, for instance, should be able eventually to divorce his wife, even against her wishes, after they have been separated for five years.

Nullity

A decree of nullity ends a marriage not because the marriage has broken down irretrievably, as with divorce. It is because of a fundamental flaw in the marriage itself. Once a marriage has been annulled, it is as if it had never existed not, as with divorce, that it existed but has now been brought to an end.

The law distinguishes between two types of annulled marriage: void and voidable. There is little practical distinction between the two. But a void marriage never was a valid marriage and technically did not need a decree to bring it to an end whereas a voidable marriage was a perfectly valid marriage until it was annulled. The children, if any, of both kinds of marriage are legitimate except that, with a void marriage, at least one parent must reasonably have believed that the marriage was valid when the child was conceived – which, of course, will usually be the case.

We looked at void marriages in Chapter 5 when considering the essentials of a valid marriage but let us now briefly look at the five kinds of situation that make a marriage voidable:

Incapacity to consummate   A marriage is consummated when what an early Victorian ecclesiastical judge once called 'ordinary and complete' sexual intercourse has taken place. There must be both erection and penetration for a reasonable length of time. There does not have to be ejaculation. As Professor Steven Cretney has wryly commented, 'It is not necessary for either party to have an orgasm', and the House of Lords has ruled (in *Baxter* v. *Baxter* in 1948) that a marriage is consummated whether or not a condom is used.

When one of the parties is incapable of consummating a marriage because of his or her incapacity to do so, *either* can ask for a nullity decree. Impotence can, of course, be either physical or psychological and, if physical, the court has power to order a medical examination and may draw adverse inferences from a refusal to be examined. Whether physical or psychological, the law does not expect the other partner to go about sex like a bull in a field. There must be tenderness and understanding – and time. In a case of my own, I once managed to persuade Mr Justice Barnard that a wife was entitled to leave after only one week of her husband's inadequate love-making. The case, under its strange anonymous title of *B. (otherwise S.)* v. *B.*, established something of a legal precedent and is reported in (1958) 2 All England Law Reports at page 76; but other less robust judges might disagree.

It is sex between the parties after marriage that counts and not pre-marital sex. In another case of mine, a man and woman had lived happily together for several years without being married, enjoying full and frequent sex. Then they got married – and at once she refused him sex, and continued steadfastly to do so. The truth was that she could not help herself. As a young teenager, she had been raped by her father and, once her lover was in a close formal family relationship with her, she could not bear him to touch her sexually. It was all very sad. She did not contest his nullity petition.

Wilful refusal to consummate   With a more liberal generation of judges on the Bench, this is now the basis of most nullity decrees, although of course it is usually word against word since there is no question of physical abnormality. Even so, decrees are granted when, on an analysis of the whole history of the marriage, there is a 'settled and definite decision' by one spouse to refuse sexual intercourse to the other that has been 'come to without just excuse'.

Not surprisingly, it is only the aggrieved spouse who can ask for the decree. But I emphasise that you can only go for nullity on this ground and for incapacity (which, unlike divorce, you can always do within the first year of marriage), if you have never had sex with your spouse after marriage *at all*.[2] If you have had sex, even though only once, but then you are refused further sex and that destroys the marriage, you will have to go for divorce (on the grounds of unreasonable behaviour) – and wait a full year from your wedding day.

Lack of consent at the time of the marriage   We have already looked at this when talking about 'shotgun weddings', duress and arranged marriages in the previous chapter. It is irrelevant whether or not the marriage has been consummated.

Venereal disease, pregnancy by another man and mental illness   In practice, all of these cases are very rare but if, at the time of the marriage, your spouse was suffering from venereal disease in a communicable form (it is unclear whether AIDS is a venereal disease for this purpose) or, unknown to you, was pregnant by someone else or was suffering from mental disorder within the meaning of the 1983 Mental Health Act, you can ask for a nullity decree – provided you do so within three years. Again, it is irrelevant whether or not the marriage has been consummated.

To all these different kinds of voidable marriage petitions, there is one possible overall defence. It used to be called 'approbation': you could not seek nullity if by your conduct you had 'approbated' the marriage. Now Section 13 of the 1973 Matrimonial Causes Act more specifically says that a court shall not grant a decree when 'the petitioner . . . with knowledge that it was open to him to have the marriage avoided, so conducted himself in relation to the respondent as to lead the respondent reasonably to believe that he would not seek to do so . . . and it would be unjust to the respondent to grant the decree'.

An obvious case in which such a defence would succeed would be where an elderly widower weds a woman, of whatever age, on the understanding that they are not to have sex together and that their marriage is 'for companionship only', and then he later changes his mind and asks for sex – which she refuses. If he then petitions for nullity on the grounds of her 'wilful refusal to consummate', she can almost certainly get his petition dismissed (if she wants to!) on the basis that it would be 'unjust' to grant him a decree.

We have sufficiently examined the practical alternatives, now let us return to the main subject of divorce.

HOW TO GET A DIVORCE?

Anyone can go to court and get their own decree. You will not have to engage in courtroom advocacy which, for the non-professional (except when arguing a civil case in the small claims court), can be dangerous territory. So any reasonably intelligent person can do it themselves. It is almost too easy and, although most people do not risk doing it themselves but use a lawyer, the process is often called a 'quickie' divorce. All you need do is go along to your local county court office (or telephone them) on any weekday between 10 a.m. and 4 p.m. and ask the name and address of your nearest *divorce* county court. It will be either the same court or not very far away.

You then collect from that court's office a Petition form and, if you have children under 16 or between 16 and 18 but still at school or training for a career, a Proposed Arrangements for Children form (Form D8A) and fill them out. None of this is more complicated than filling in a passport application, but if you have any problems, the court office staff are always very helpful and they can supply a free 30-page explanatory booklet. This should be sufficient to get you through. If not, your local citizens' advice bureau will generally assist and several useful DIY divorce books are on the market, of which perhaps the best is the *Which? Guide to Divorce* (1998) at £10.99.

When you have completed the forms, send or take them to the court office (together with your marriage certificate or a copy) and £150 court fee, hugely increased from only £40, along with all other court fees, in January 1998. The office will then post these forms to (the legal phrase is 'serve them upon') your spouse and anyone you have named as their partner in adultery (i.e. the co-respondent).[3] They should then post to the court their reply in Form D10, the 'acknowledgement of service', saying whether they are defending the divorce, and your spouse must say whether he or she agrees to the proposed arrangements for the children. If the divorce is to be defended, the case will then be transferred to the Family Division of the High Court: this does not necessarily mean you will have to go to the Law Courts in London since some High Court judges are always out on circuit sitting at large provincial cities. But whether in London or the provinces, you really will now have to get yourself a solicitor, even if you had not engaged one before.

You will need a good one, experienced in family cases and with the right attitude to you and your personal problems. I will come back to this in the next chapter.

You will also need this right kind of solicitor if your spouse replies in Form D10 saying that the arrangements for the children will be contested. The case will stay in the divorce county court and your divorce will continue to go through as undefended but it will not be finalised (and you will not be free to remarry) until the judge has made a ruling on the future of the children. Incidentally, property disputes do not hold up the granting of an undefended divorce. Couples are often divorced and even remarried before their differences over the family assets have been resolved. We shall look at this whole question of 'ancillary relief', dealing with disputes over property, money and children, in the next chapter.

But in most cases Form D10 confirms that the divorce is undefended and the proposed arrangements for the children are agreed. Your petition will then go smoothly on.

There will be some more paperwork, including a sworn affidavit in which you state your version of the particular 'fact' on which you rely: adultery, unreasonable behaviour or whatever. The No.2 judge at the divorce county court, 'the District Judge', will read the papers in the case and decide whether all is in order and you are entitled to your divorce. She almost certainly will say 'Yes', and you will receive another form (D84A) stating the date and time at which the full judge will grant your decree in open court. You need not attend nor be represented. The names and court numbers of cases will be read out in batches and the judge will simply say: 'Decree nisi granted.' Not very romantic or impressive.

Even so, your marriage is not yet ended and you are still not free to remarry. Decree nisi comes from the Latin word *nisi*, 'unless'. It means that you will get your divorce soon *unless* someone comes forward to prove there has been a fraud on the court. In the old days, this served some valid purpose: divorces were sometimes obtained fraudulently, usually by the parties themselves trying to lie their way around the strictness of the pre-1969 law. Nowadays 'collusion', as it used to be called, is hardly necessary and, even when it exists, it seldom gets brought to the attention of the court. Ideas have changed. Yet a decree nisi is still the general rule.

What will happen next is that you will have to apply to the court office for the decree nisi to be converted into a decree absolute. You do this on yet another form (D36) and with your cheque for a £20 court fee. This is only a paper formality that does not involve the judge; and you will have to wait six weeks and one day.

Sometimes problems arise because your spouse has already met someone else and wants to remarry as soon as possible. You may be in no hurry to help. So what happens if you do not obligingly ask for the decree to be made absolute after six weeks and one day?

In dire emergency, your spouse can apply, in person or through a lawyer, to the judge at decree nisi to cut the normal period. But usually the application will only succeed if he or she wants to remarry urgently before a child is born. Otherwise they will have to wait a full three months before asking for a decree absolute: posting their own Form D36 and £20 cheque. In that case, the total time between decree nisi and absolute can be as long as six weeks and one day *plus* three further months. So, if you are the petitioner and you want to be bitchy, whatever your sex, there is plenty of scope – even at this late stage.

How long will a 'quickie' divorce take? On average, about three months. It could hardly be quicker.

A WORD ABOUT SOLICITORS

If you are among the majority who prefer to use a solicitor, even when you and your spouse have agreed all outstanding issues in a civilised fashion, that is of course your privilege. It would also be understandable. Many people might find it disagreeable, to use no stronger word, to do their own dirty work in ending a marriage that doubtless began with so much joy and hope. Depending on the part of the country where you live, the cost would be around £350 to £500 plus VAT, including court fees. Provided you choose what I have already called 'the right kind of solicitor' (and we shall discuss later how to find one), many people might think that was well worth the price.

As for legal aid, it simply is not available for undefended or 'quickie' divorces except for the Green Form Scheme. This is very limited in effect. Taking its name from the colour of the application form, it is available only to those with a net income of not more than £83 a week and with less than £1,000 disposable capital (with allowances for dependants). It entitles them, in matrimonial cases, to up to three hours of a solicitor's time, which can sometimes be extended. In that time the solicitor can help with drafting a divorce petition, giving general advice and perhaps writing a few letters – but not much else.

Full legal aid, including representation in court, is available, subject to the usual property and income limits of £6,750 disposable capital and £130 a week disposable income, in the few defended divorces that still occur and – much more important – in disputes about 'ancillary relief': i.e. children, property and maintenance. But unlike legal aid generally, this can benefit some middle-class wives (at least, those who are not working) because their disposable income is likely to be less than £130 a week and the capital value of the family home, which is usually the subject matter of the dispute, is ignored. They are often legally, as well as factually, poor enough to qualify.

That is the set-up as it is due to continue indefinitely. However, for the sake of completeness, we must now turn to look briefly at the new divorce laws that remain on the Statute Book and, if ever implemented, would change the whole process.

Notes

1 The district judge in your local divorce county court who must approve most divorce petitions before they go to the full judge for a decree knows that the case is undefended and that your spouse wants a divorce at least as much as you do. Unless the allegations are too blatantly frivolous, he (or she) is often likely to let things go through 'on the nod', although no one will officially admit this.

2 Some solicitors, particularly of the older generation, can be remarkably shy about getting the correct details from their client. Some years ago, I had a case where a solicitor brought a woman down to chambers for me to obtain the background needed to draft a divorce petition on the grounds of her husband's unreasonable behaviour. By the time she left I had ascertained that they had

never had sexual intercourse together. Eventually she obtained a nullity decree on the grounds of his wilful refusal to consummate.

3 You may have lost all contact with your spouse and have no current address. What happens then? The answer is time-consuming but effective: you first write to the last known address asking for your letter to be sent on. If that fails and you also draw a blank with the DSS national computer or your spouse's trade union, trade association or last known employer, the court office will help you swear an affidavit detailing your efforts and you will almost certainly be allowed to 'dispense with service of the petition'. Your divorce will go through without your spouse even knowing about it.

8

THE NEW DIVORCE LAWS

If ever they come into effect, these laws will make fundamental changes which, however far off in time they may be, the reader may be interested to know about.

Irretrievable breakdown of marriage will remain the sole ground of divorce but it will no longer be necessary to prove any of the five 'facts' needed by present law to support that allegation. Adultery, desertion, unreasonable behaviour, etc. will sadly continue as a reality of marital life but they will no longer be any concern of the law. There will not even be divorce decrees any more but only 'divorce orders'.

There will be no allegations of fault made by one spouse against the other and no need for them to live apart for any period of time, as for instance with present-day desertion. Instead one party will give notice that they want a divorce and, after jumping a number of legal hurdles, the divorce will be made. The courts will be unable to refuse it. For the first time in legal history, the judges will not be able to refuse a divorce.[1]

But, as we have seen, the 1996 Act was a bitterly fought-over compromise seeking to make divorce easier and at the same time encouraging couples to reconsider whether they want to carry on with it.

Throughout the parliamentary debates on the Act, a constant theme was the attempt to identify and encourage opportunities to save saveable marriages. Amazingly, about 40,000 divorce petitions filed each year are not proceeded with, mainly because there is a reconciliation. So, as David Hodson and Gillian Bishop wrote in the *Solicitors Journal* in January 1997, 'Parliament was anxious that the new divorce process should not lead the couple on to a roller coaster from which they felt unable to get off if a reconciliation seemed possible.'

That is, of course, a laudable idea but what many people still do not realise is that the result is that the new divorce process, if ever brought in, will take much longer than the usual three months for present-day 'quickie' divorces. Here is a brief outline of how it will work.

As with the present law, the process cannot start until the parties have been married for at least a year.

Anyone wanting a divorce must first attend a compulsory **information meeting**. The Act is vague about what exactly is supposed to happen at this meeting but Lord Mackay of Clashfern, when Lord Chancellor, explained in a speech in the House of Lords: 'This will not only mark the seriousness of the step being taken but also ensure that essential information is conveyed. [That] will include information about the various services available to help people, including marriage guidance, mediation and legal services . . . It will also deal with alternative options to divorce and the consequences of divorce for the parties and their children.' If both parties have agreed on the divorce, it is anticipated that they will generally attend together. If not, at least the one person wanting a divorce will have to attend – whether or not the other party does. Couples will be encouraged to talk to a marriage counsellor, whose services will be free to those on the lowest scale of legal aid.

If the couple – or the one wanting a divorce – decide not to proceed, that will be an end of it. But if a divorce is still desired, they cannot simply go ahead. They must wait for a **cooling-off period** of three months before the legal process can begin. This will no longer be by lodging with the court a divorce petition but by lodging a much more prosaic written document called simply **statement of marital break-down**. This will state that one or both parties believes the marriage has broken down (with no details as to why!) and will confirm that they understand the nature of the legal process which is now to begin.

Then they will have to wait for, at least, a further nine months for what the Act calls 'reflection and consideration'. In this time, in the finest tradition of the modern nanny state, couples are expected to reflect on whether the marriage can be saved and if not, to consider and make the arrangements appropriate for their future lives apart, as a pamphlet by the

Lord Chancellor's Department somewhat pompously relates. Mediation will be available and encouraged, funded by legal aid for the lower-income couples who qualify financially.

Even though for many this process may so far have amounted to a complete waste of time, they will now have gone a whole year since lodging the statement of marital breakdown. But where there are children of the marriage under 16 or one of the parties requests it, this nine-month period for 'reflection and consideration' will be extended for another six months to a total of fifteen months.

In other words, whereas now a couple with young children who are intelligent, civilised human beings and can work out their destiny for themselves can obtain a 'quickie' divorce in three months, the quickest they will be able to do so under the new regime is exactly five times that length of time.

That is what some people call progress.

Notes
1 Technically, a judge's existing power to refuse a divorce on the ground of 'hardship' will be preserved but, as now, it is likely only to hold up the inevitable divorce, not ban it outright.

9

PROPERTY AFTER DIVORCE

When a marriage breaks down, people feel lost, despondent, angry. The trauma is deep and can be frightening. Falling out of love with someone, shattering the mould of your everyday existence, is heart-breaking enough in itself but when you add the uncertainty of the future, the worry about how you are going to make ends meet, the potential loneliness and the almost inevitable drop in living standards that will follow (at least, for a while), the broken heart can easily harden to steel.

FINDING THE RIGHT SOLICITOR

Despite the expense, this is when a lawyer is needed, and what I have already called 'the right kind'. An able divorce solicitor or barrister (who will generally also be needed in the more difficult cases) must have at least as much understanding of the human spirit as of law books and statutes. But all too often lawyers, instead of making life easier, seem to make it worse. Some become too involved in their cases and too partisan so that their judgement is warped, and instead of pouring oil on troubled waters they set a match to it. I know of one case where a woman solicitor acting for a wife found a perfectly normal but tough letter written by a rather aggressive male solicitor on the other side so 'repugnant' that she had to let several days pass before she could bring herself to pass it on to her client and, in the end, wrote back a letter that was so angry and insulting that it torpedoed what would have been an eminently reasonable settlement of the dispute.

Other lawyers are inexperienced in the specialist world of family law or bumbling incompetents or quite honestly money-grabbing and lacking in basic humanity. I genuinely believe that many solicitors and barristers, although decent, honourable folk, charge far too much for what they do: that is the going rate – and they go along with it. This not only increases the cost, it also prolongs the agony. When every hour with your solicitor can cost you anything from £100 to £150 plus VAT, or even more with a top London firm, it is easy to become obsessed with getting your money's worth. Couples see the pound coins clocking up and become trapped in endless – and expensive – rounds of bidding over who gets the mortgage, the Mercedes, the second home in Cornwall or Spain.

In *Evans* v. *Evans*, in January 1990, the legal proceedings were so drawn out and acrimonious that the costs incurred by the husband and wife amounted to £35,000 and £25,000 respectively. The wife had wanted to remain in the matrimonial home but the house had to be sold to pay the legal bills. Mrs Justice Booth commented forcefully: 'If they are united in nothing else, this husband and wife must be united in bitterly regretting the dissipation of their assets which has so unfortunately occurred.' With the concurrence of the senior divorce judge, the president of the High Court's Family Division, she laid down guidelines for all divorce lawyers. Eight are matters of detail but three deserve to be reprinted here for you to remind your own solicitor:

(1) All professional witnesses should be careful to avoid a partisan approach and should maintain proper professional standards.
(2) Solicitors and counsel should keep their clients informed of the costs at all stages of the proceedings.
(3) The desirability of reaching a settlement should be borne in mind throughout the proceedings.

To refresh your solicitor's memory, you can photocopy for yourself the whole of these guidelines and hand them over to him. You will find them at pages 148 and 149 of Mrs Justice Booth's judgment in Volume 2 of the (1990) All England Law Reports. These law reports are available at most major public reference libraries.

The question still remains: how are you to find the right kind of solicitor with the right kind of experience? That is more important than choosing the right kind of barrister for you have first to choose your solicitor who then selects the barrister, and he is likely to be on the same wavelength. Unless you have a personal recommendation to a suitable solicitor, there are two possibilities. One is that you consult a list of solicitors accredited by the Law Society as experts in this field with the right non-confrontational attitude and called the Family Law Panel. This scheme only began in January 1999 and the aim is eventually to publish the list in telephone directories and Yellow Pages, as well as agencies such as citizens' advice bureaux. The much longer established alternative is to send a stamped addressed envelope for a list of local members to the Solicitors Family Law Association (SFLA) at PO Box 302, Orpington, Kent BR6 8QX (Tel: 0689–850227). This association, formed in December 1982, has a formidable track record and is a group of some 4,000 divorce solicitors 'who promote a constructive and conciliatory approach rather than an aggressive or angry one' (their own words). They are dedicated to conciliation and restraint. Many other solicitors share this view but, if you want to be certain of getting someone committed to this attitude, you should consult either the Law Society's Family Law Panel or the SFLA.

Ever since an Appeal Court decision in 1975 in *Calderbank* v. *Calderbank* a solicitor with the right kind of approach can pressure the other side into accepting a reasonable offer of settlement by writing in the latter stages of protracted negotiation what is called 'a Calderbank letter'. Taking its name from a letter written by a solicitor in that case, it restates the client's final offer and gives this warning: if the other spouse rejects the offer and the judge ultimately makes an award *around the amount offered*, the judge will be shown the letter and asked to order the rejecting spouse to pay the costs of both parties as from the date of the letter. If this ploy works, it can very much blunt the financial edge of any apparent victory. Judges are usually happy to co-operate and, since the costs incurred after the rejection of the letter are usually the greatest (since they include the actual court hearing, probably lasting for several days), a shrewdly timed Calderbank letter can concentrate an opposing solicitor's mind marvellously.

A Calderbank letter that worked

In 1990, a wealthy businessman was in dispute with his wife over money. Negotiations were dragging on between the solicitors on both sides. Finally a week before the hearing the husband's solicitor wrote the wife's solicitor a Calderbank letter offering her £400,000. The solicitor, having (presumably) checked with his client, wrote back rejecting the letter – but did not make any counter-offer. The case went on.

After several days in court, the judge awarded the wife £435,000, only 8.75 per cent more than the figure she had earlier refused. He was then shown the Calderbank letter – and ordered her to pay the costs of both sides from the date of her refusal, which probably cost her the better part of another £35,000!

WHAT ABOUT LEGAL AID?

As we saw in the last chapter, many middle-class wives who do not go out to work are eligible for legal aid to fight their claims for 'ancillary relief' (concerning the home, money or children) because their husbands' income and the value of the family assets in dispute are ignored.

This is obviously good so far as it goes but there are two main drawbacks:

(1) It is difficult to find a competent solicitor, experienced in this field, who is prepared to take on the case at the measly rates paid by the Legal Aid Board, which will be replaced in April 2000 by the Legal Services Commission. As a London suburban solicitor has said, 'For private work I charge £110 an hour but for legal aid work I get £60. My partners want me to stop but I am committed to it, not least because my mother sorted out her divorce only because of legal aid. Maybe outside the South-East there are firms that find the legal aid rate profitable' – it has since gone up marginally – 'but fewer and fewer in this area will touch it. Many of my clients travel for more than an hour to see me because so few firms will do this work. In almost every family dispute, especially during the recession, at least one party qualifies for legal aid.'

A by-product is that, even when a competent solicitor with the right attitude takes on legal aid work, he is under constant temptation to cut corners and employ inexperienced or even unqualified staff to handle sensitive matters. Solicitors should not have to be philanthropists. They are professional people doing a professional job.

(2) There is a financial trap which many women often discover only late in the day. It is this: if a wife is legally aided, anything over the first £2,500 of the 'property preserved or recovered' (i. e. anything over the first £2,500 in value of her share in the family home or the first £2,500 of any lump sum settlement) is subject to a statutory charge – a sort of mortgage – in favour of the Legal Aid Board. When she wins her case, the judge may make no order as to costs, in which case the parties are thrown back on their own resources, or, as more often happens, the judge will order the defeated husband to pay his successful wife's costs.

But this does not necessarily mean the Board will get back all the money it has spent on her representation. This can be either because the husband is himself legally aided which means that the Board will be reimbursing itself, which is a nonsense, or because he simply does not have the means to pay his own legal aid contribution *plus* his wife's costs. In these circumstances, the Board can enforce its charge on 'the property preserved or recovered' by the wife to claw back the Board's fees to her lawyers: i.e. her home. The Board (or the taxpayer) does not suffer: she does.

And remember that this is when the wife wins her case! If she loses, there will not be any statutory charge because there is nothing to which the charge can attach. She will often have to pay something towards her husband's costs but that will only be what the judge considers 'reasonable'. This usually amounts to the same again as her legal aid contribution to her own costs: a comparatively small sum.

The bizarre (and unfair) result is that, if the Board enforces its statutory charge on her winnings, it can cost her more to win than to lose. Nothing is for nothing with divorce legal aid.

But to revert to the statutory charge: if, as often happens, the judge orders that the home has to be sold and the wife is to receive the net proceeds of sale, the Board will often demand immediate repayment of its costs from these proceeds of sale – before she gets anything herself. If the house is not to be sold, usually because it is being transferred into her name as a home for herself and her children, the Board may magnanimously allow the charge to remain unenforced until the property is eventually sold: with interest ticking happily away in the meantime. Sometimes the Board will even agree to the charge being transferred to a new property if needed as a home for the wife and children. It is all a matter for the Board's discretion.

These principles were laid down by the House of Lords in May 1980 in *Hanlon* v. *Hanlon* where a nurse from Waltham Cross, Hertfordshire divorced her policeman husband after seventeen years of marriage. She had won a protracted courtroom battle to have her home, valued at £10,000, transferred into her name – only to find that the house had to be sold under the statutory charge to pay her unrecovered legal aid costs of £8,000. All five senior appeal judges were reluctant to come to this decision and called for Parliament to change the law. Lord Edmund-Davies, who had earlier achieved nationwide fame with the 30-year prison sentences he imposed in the Great Train Robbery trial, specifically said: 'We live in a busy world and the demands made on the legislature are endless but the present state of affairs could, if permitted to continue indefinitely, substantially erode our present pride in the legal aid system of this country.'

That pride continues to be eroded. Parliament has done nothing to reform the law, despite a new Legal Aid Act in 1988.

So much for solicitors. The delicate and difficult legal problems involving children on divorce require a chapter on their own. But let us now look, in some detail, at the law on property and money disputes.

ANCILLARY RELIEF: PROPERTY AND MONEY ON DIVORCE

Pre-nuptial agreements

It is often written, and sometimes by legal commentators who should know better, that these are not legally binding. That is a crude over-simplification. 'Pre-nuptials', as they are familiarly called, carry considerable weight in the courts. They do not have the force of law. The judges are not bound to accept every single provision and every single sentence – but increasingly judges are taking them into account.

As we shall see, Section 25 of the 1973 Matrimonial Causes Act, as amended by the 1984 Matrimonial and Family Proceedings Act, says that judges, when deciding on the proper disposal of a couple's assets after divorce, must consider many different factors. And as far back as July 1980, Lord Justice Ormrod ruled that the couple's own views, as expressed in a 'pre-nuptial', can be one of those factors. He said: 'Formal agreements properly and fairly arrived at with competent advice should not be displaced unless there are good and substantial grounds for concluding that an injustice will be done.'

Traditionally, the courts do not like decisions being taken out of their hands by the parties themselves. Some judges also consider it contrary to public policy to give legal recognition to an agreement before marriage which presupposes that the marriage will not endure.

So judicial attitudes to 'pre-nuptials' have varied since Ormrod's pioneering words. In 1985, Mr Justice Balcombe favoured them. In 1995, Lord Justice Thorpe said they should be 'of very limited significance'. But in 1997, both Mr Justice Cazalet and Mr Justice Wilson said they could not be ignored.

So what is the result of all this? Namely that a 'pre-nuptial' will generally be taken into account – but not slavishly followed – by the courts. And that will only occur if both parties have been separately advised by their own lawyer: i.e. the 'competent advice' referred to by

Lord Justice Ormrod back in 1980. This has much logic behind it; but is it not sad that parties contemplating marriage should also need to be contemplating divorce – and getting their own skilled professional advice in advance?

The overall picture

Basically, unless the parties can sensibly sort out matters between themselves (hopefully helped by their lawyers) or they have well-drafted pre-nuptial agreements, everything is up for grabs. The slate of the family assets, property as well as income, is wiped clean and, since you have not reallocated your resources yourselves, a judge does it for you. He will do so 'in chambers': unrobed and unwigged, sitting in court in private session with only the parties and their lawyers present. He will conscientiously bear in mind various factors set out for his guidance in Section 25 of the 1973 Matrimonial Causes Act, but the result will still be the same. The old set-up will have gone for ever, and in its place will be a new reality. The eggs will have been cracked and made into two different omelettes.

These are the factors that Section 25 says a judge must consider:

- the income, earning capacity, property and financial resources of the parties both now and 'in the foreseeable future';
- their present and future needs, obligations and responsibilities;
- their standard of living prior to the breakdown of the marriage;
- their ages and for how long they have been married;
- any physical or mental disability;
- any contributions they may have made to the family;
- their conduct during the marriage 'if such that it would be inequitable to disregard it';
- the value of any benefit (for example a pension) which either party may lose because of the divorce.

These are all unexceptionable and, one would have thought, reasonably fair. They are also self-explanatory – except perhaps for two items:

Conduct that cannot equitably be disregarded   What exactly does this mean? Precious little, in fact. The old idea that a 'bad' wife should be entitled to a smaller division of the family assets or a 'good' husband to a larger share went out of the window with the old pre-1969 law. As Lord Denning said in his classic Appeal Court judgment in *Wachtel* v. *Wachtel* in February 1973:

It has been suggested that there should be a 'discount' or 'reduction' in what a wife is to receive because of her supposed misconduct, guilt or blame (whatever word is used). We cannot accept this argument. In the vast majority of cases, it is repugnant to the principles underlying the new legislation. There will be many cases in which a wife (although once considered guilty or blameworthy) will have cared for the home and looked after the family for many years. Is she to be deprived of benefit because she may share responsibility for the breakdown with her husband?

There will no doubt be a residue of cases where the conduct of one of the parties is both obvious and gross, so much so that to order one party to support another is repugnant to anyone's sense of justice. In such a case the court remains free to decline or to reduce financial support.

But, short of cases falling into this category, the court should not reduce its order merely because of what was formerly regarded as guilt or blame. To do so would be to impose a fine for supposed misbehaviour in the course of an unhappy married life.

Nicely put. But many divorcing couples still do not realise this. They think that because one party has committed adultery or failed to fulfil their marital obligations in some other important or hurtful way, that can be used against them to cut their share in the family home or reduce their maintenance. In the overwhelming majority of cases today, 'conduct' is not a factor in sorting out the finances.

Pensions   Until the law was changed by the 1995 Pensions Act, the courts' ability to manage the division on divorce of pension rights – usually, those of the husband – was generally considered woefully inadequate. All that the judges could do was take pensions into account when dividing the family's assets: the husband would tend to keep his pension while the wife got perhaps a larger share of the ownership of the house but with no legal stake in any part of the pension itself. The reason was that, once a wife was divorced, she lost entitlement to a share of her husband's pension on retirement or death. If she had no private pension of her own, as often happened, she only had the basic state pension to fall back on. And if she had made reduced National Insurance contributions, she would get only a reduced pension, at that.

In most marriages, even when both parties are in full-time employ-ment, the husband usually earns more than the wife (and, if not, these rules worked the other way around. The law on this was, and is, unisex). The husband therefore was usually the only one able to look forward to a substantial private pension with the wife's rights to some extent built into that – but only so long as she continued to be his wife. A judge was supposed to take into account the value of that lost entitlement when sorting out the finances on divorce.

But there was a fundamental flaw in the law.

A judge could not get into the pension fund itself. He could only order the future recipient of the pension – who, as I say, was usually the husband – to borrow a large sum of money or otherwise juggle his finances so that the wife did not lose out too much by ceasing to be his 'wife'.

In practice, if the husband could not do this and no money could be made available to compensate for the wife's lost share in the pension, she receieved no benefit from it whatsoever, although during the marriage both parties would have looked to it as a joint fund helping to provide for their eventual retirement. That was clearly unfair to many women.

So, as from July 1996, when the 1995 Pensions Act came into effect, judges were allowed for the first time to 'earmark' pension rights: in other words, to make an attachment order against a pension fund which would bite at the date a pension became payable. This would require the trustees or managers to pay all or part of the capital or periodic sum to the party who was not the pensioner.

There were, however, two major drawbacks: the ex-spouse could not receive her or his share of the pension until the pensioner-to-be retired and all payments ceased when the pensioner died. Injustice was still being done. So in June 1998 the Government unveiled ground-breaking proposals: that the courts would not merely have the power to 'earmark' pension sharing upon eventual retirement but would be able to order actual 'pension splitting' to take effect at the time of the divorce itself – not at some remote retirement date in the future.

The Government promised that these proposals would be in place by April 2000. But in February 1999 it announced that – allegedly because of fierce lobbying from the pensions industry and problems with the Government's own computer systems – the new laws would be delayed until April 2001.

Nowadays, when writing about the law, it is no longer sufficient to write about what the law is today. All too often, one must have regard to what it will be tomorrow – or the day after tomorrow. It is always changing.

Property

Many couples still believe that, if their family home is in joint names, at least that will be safe from the potential carnage on divorce. It may have to be sold but the proceeds of sale will at least be shared equally between them, after the mortgage and other expenses have been paid off.

But, in the words of the song, 'It ain't necessarily so.' It is an old principle of the law that 'equality is equity' and many property disputes end up in a 50–50 division but there is absolutely no hard and fast rule.

The family home may be in a man's sole name but he may be ordered to transfer it into both names. The home may be in joint names, with each party thinking they share it equally, but the court may make an order giving an ex-wife only a one-third share. An ex-wife may be given a half-share plus maintenance – and then sometimes the value of that maintenance may be offset against the half-share so that in practice she ends up receiving nearer one-third than one-half. It all depends on the facts of each case and how a judge applies the Section 25 guidelines to those specific facts.

As Lord Denning has said: 'The court takes the rights and obligations of the parties all together and puts the pieces into a mixed bag. Such pieces are the right to occupy the matrimonial home or have a share in it, the obligation to maintain the wife and children, and so forth. The court then takes out the pieces and hands them to the two parties – some to one party and some to the other – so that each can provide for the future with the pieces allotted to him or her. The court hands them out without paying any too nice regard to their legal or equitable rights but simply according to what is the fairest provision for the future, for mother and father and the children.'

There are three specific problems that can arise with regard to the family home:

(1) Before you get to the actual divorce stage one party can change the locks and try to force the other out of the house. This is a dangerous ploy and can easily backfire. Regardless of which spouse owns or rents the property, the 1983 Matrimonial Homes Act, now replaced by Part IV of the 1996 Family Law Act, says that both parties have rights of occupation so long as the marriage lasts right up to decree absolute. And if one party evicts the other, they can go to court, if necessary, on a legal aid emergency certificate – and the judge will order them to be allowed back into their home.

Furthermore, if the reason why one party, usually the wife, has left is because her husband has beaten her or the children or threatened physical violence to them, not only will he be ordered to let her back into the house but he will be ordered out of it. This is known as an ouster or exclusion order. A wife's income or property is disregarded and she will qualify for legal aid – if she is lucky enough to find a competent solicitor prepared to take her on at legal aid rates.

(2) If the home is in one party's sole name, he or she may sometimes

try and sell it behind the other's back. This used to happen quite often but now there is a foolproof way to prevent it. At the slightest sign of marital discord, or in this cynical world as a sensible precaution long before it, if the property is registered at the Land Registry, as most are, the non-owner needs only to ask the Registry to enter a 'notice' on the file stating he or she is claiming their rights. With unregistered land, a Class F Land Charge must be registered against the property at the Land Charges Department.

Both procedures are simple and inexpensive. But one can ask a solicitor's help, consult a citizens' advice bureau or telephone the Land Registry on 020 7917 8888 for an explanatory do-it-yourself leaflet.

Protection is immediate. No one can then buy the property nor building society or other lender foreclose on it without respecting the occupier's rights. He or she cannot be turfed out. The property is virtually unsaleable unless they can be persuaded to leave – usually with financial encouragement.

(3) What will happen if, as in many lower- and middle-income divorces, there simply is not enough money available to provide a new home for the husband and a suitable home for the wife *and children*? Something has to give. If limited resources are available, the judges accept that one party cannot insist on their full rights: at least not until after the children have completed their education and begun to build their own lives.

In February 1973, in the early days of the new divorce law, Lord Justice Davies conceived the idea of a 'Mesher Order', taking its name from *Mesher* v. *Mesher*, the name of the case. This says that the matrimonial home must be transferred into the couple's joint names (irrespective of who owned it before) *but* when the youngest child reaches 17 or ceases full-time education, whichever occurs first, the property must be sold and the net proceeds divided (usually equally) between ex-husband and wife.

Then there was something of a judicial rethink and it was realised that this can sometimes give children too decisive a role in the life of their parents. Are they to be forced to give up their home merely because their children have grown to a certain age?

Nowadays the Mesher Order is often replaced by the Martin Order. Taking its name from the case (*Martin* v. *Martin*) in which the Appeal Court first approved it, an ex-wife is allowed to remain in the former matrimonial home, not until the children have reached a certain age, but until her death or remarriage or until she cohabits with another man for at least six months. Then the house is finally sold and the net proceeds of sale divided: not necessarily on a 50–50 basis. Quite often, depending on all the circumstances, an ex-husband may get only a 25 per cent share.

In this way, an ex-spouse, usually the ex-wife, remains for all practical purposes the owner of the place (often having to take over the mortgage), while her ex-husband keeps a financial interest in the proceeds of the eventual sale, so that he is not entirely out of pocket on the deal.

With the best will in the world, property arrangements on divorce often boil down to horse trading – with varying degrees of politeness.

Maintenance on divorce

So far as a wife is concerned, we have really already covered this when talking about the Section 25 guidelines. But four other major questions remain:

The 'one-third rule'   For some unknown reason, the judges always say this is not a 'rule' – but it is, in the sense that they all use it as what Lord Denning called in *Wachtel* v. *Wachtel*, the case of the Streatham dentist, 'a starting point'. As he said:

> There may be cases where more than one-third is right. There are likely to be many others where it is the only practicable solution. But it is only a starting point. It will serve in cases where the marriage has lasted for many years and the wife has been in the home bringing up the children. It may not be applicable when the marriage has lasted only a short time or where there are no children and she can go out to work.

Yet, in practice, despite all this talk of 'starting point' in Lord Denning's judgment and in those of several other senior judges, at grass-roots level in most cases, a wife is usually entitled to a one-third share in the house or other family assets and a third of the joint earnings by way of weekly or monthly maintenance – *before* maintenance for the children is even considered. Nowadays, as we shall see in a moment, the Child Support Agency, functioning – or, as some would prefer to say, malfunctioning – since April 1993, has revolutionised child maintenance so that there is less to go round for the couple themselves but its effect on the 'one-third rule' is still not clear.

But without the Child Support Agency complicating the issue, *Wachtel* v. *Wachtel* back in 1973 still supplies the best practical example of how the 'one-third rule' works:

Both the dentist and his wife were 47 and their marriage had lasted 18 years. He earned £6,000 a year and she earned £750 a year, and their house was worth net about £20,000. So she got £6,000 as her share of the house, £1,500 a year as maintenance – and £300 a year as a 'reasonable' sum for their daughter. How was her £1,500 a year arrived at? Joint earnings of £6,000 +£750 = £6,750; one-third of that was £2,250; deduct her own £750 – and you were left with £1,500 to make up her income to the 'one-third of joint earnings' figure. Simple!

The concept of 'clean break'   The expression was first coined by Lord Scarman back in 1979. He said that divorcing couples should be encouraged 'to put the past behind them and to begin a new life which is not overshadowed by the relationship which has broken down'. Five years later the 1984 Matrimonial and Family Proceedings Act gave a statutory basis to this noble idea. Indeed, it said that in every case a judge must consider whether it is possible: 'It shall be the duty of the court to consider whether so to exercise its powers that the financial obligations of each party towards the other will be terminated as soon as the court considers just and reasonable.'

A marvellous idea but how is it to be done? The theory is that, if there is sufficient capital available, the more wealthy of the two – usually the husband – is ordered to make over the family home to his wife and pay her a substantial lump sum immediately and/or maintenance for a limited period but sufficient to enable her to adjust 'without undue hardship' to life without any more regular payments coming in from her ex-husband. It would then be up to her to make her own financial arrangements in the future for herself and her young children.

This is superb – if the husband can afford it or equally, as many women might say, if the husband will co-operate or go along with it. But the courts have to be reasonable. You cannot get blood from a stone. As Mr Justice Waite said in 1988, there is no point in hounding 'a genuine struggler'. Men readers may be interested in the name of that case: *Ashley* v. *Blackman*, reported in (1988) 3 Weekly Law Reports at page 222.

The same principle works the other way round: if a marriage has lasted a long time and a wife is no longer young and has not worked for years or has limited future earning capacity, few judges are going to force her into a financial strait-jacket as a sacrifice on the altar of 'clean break'. And here a good case for women readers to know is *Boylan* v. *Boylan*, reported at (1988) 18 *Family Law* at page 62:

The wife who got more than the husband offered

The marriage of a successful partner in a decorating business who had made his wife a director of the company finally ended in divorce. A consent order was made giving her the home and its contents together with maintenance of £1,800 a year. He later sold his share of the business for £1.2 million. All

court orders for ancillary relief, whether orders made by consent or after a
courtroom battle, can always be varied if circumstances change, so she
applied for an increase in her maintenance. He replied offering a 'clean break'
on the basis that, in the changed circumstances, he should no longer pay her
maintenance at all but give her a once-and-for-all lump sum payment of
£40,000. She refused to accept this.

So what happened? Mrs Justice Booth said that, on the basis of this ex-
husband's new finances, his ex-wife would be entitled to vastly increased
maintenance of £16,000 a year. The court would only allow her to lose that
entitlement if the ex-husband paid her a lump sum sufficient to guarantee her
an income at that new level. £40,000 was inadequate for that purpose. So
there would be no 'clean break' and the ex-husband would henceforth have to
pay her £16,000 a year.

Two final points: (a) clean breaks are limited to maintenance for a
marriage partner only. As Lord Justice Ormrod said in *Pearce* v. *Pearce*
in the Appeal Court in 1980, 'People who have children cannot succeed
in making a clean break when their marriages are dissolved. Whether
they like it or whether they do not, they continue to be fathers and
mothers to the children. The relationship, such as it is, continues and so
clean breaks are not possible in all cases, or indeed in many cases.' This
has great relevance to present-day maintenance awards by the Child
Support Agency, as we shall see in the next chapter.

(b) It used to be the law that the poorer party (usually the wife) could
only be paid out one lump sum, as part of a 'clean break' or in any other
circumstances. There was, in effect, only one bite of the cherry; but on
1 November 1998 three paragraphs of Schedule 8 of the 1996 Family
Law Act came into effect with the result that an ex-wife (or ex-husband)
in receipt of maintenance can now come back to the court for a second
lump sum payment out of her former spouse's capital. She will be
entitled to do this if there has been a substantial improvement in his
fortunes and a judge considers it appropriate. Examples would be an
inheritance or major National Lottery win; but as yet it is too early to see
exactly how these new provisions will work out in practice.

When does a maintenance order end?   Unless it is a 'clean break'
situation when the judge will say that the order is to last for a
comparatively short time (usually no more than three years) to enable an
ex-wife or ex-husband to adjust to the new financial reality, it continues
for joint lives or until remarriage: i.e. until one of them dies or remarries.
Cohabitation does not revoke the order. If an ex-husband can prove that
he should pay less because his ex-wife's new man is wholly or partly

supporting her, a judge can reduce the amount of the order, but that is all. Cohabitation, unlike remarriage, has no automatic effect. A woman may be living with a man and still be receiving maintenance from her ex-husband. All of this also applies where an ex-husband is being supported by another woman.

STOP PRESS

On 5 June 2000 a new way of hearing maintenance cases with less input from the lawyers is due to come into effect. The process will start in a totally different new way: with a 20-page document called Form E in which the contending couples make full disclosure under oath of all their assets and state in detail how much they think they will need to live on in their new lives. It is hoped that this will be a vast improvement on the current affidavit of means in which each party, aided or influenced by their lawyers, swears on oath whatever they want on the subject, sometimes with no great regard for the truth.

Lawyers will be able to help with filling in this vital new form and will still be able to represent their clients before the judge but a much more active role is planned for the judiciary. They will be given much greater powers to determine the speed of the case and the route it will take.

When this epoch-making change in procedure was announced in June 1999, the Lord Chancellor, Lord Irvine of Lairg, presented it as a totally new Government project. In fact, it was based on pilot schemes initiated two years earlier by Lord Mackay of Clashfern, his Tory predecessor.

'It is often said,' Lord Irvine told the UK Family Conference in June 1999, 'that the costs involved in reaching a settlement are disproportionate to the value of the assets at stake. We have all heard of cases where many hundreds of pounds have been spent by couples arguing over the ownership of a relatively low-value piece of property and where settlement has only been reached after several court appearances.

'The current process is also criticised for being slow, with too much delay caused by demands for excessive disclosure of information, or for unreasonable action by the parties to the divorce. Under the current procedures, the parties and their lawyers are in the driving seat. This means that court processes can become a weapon for use in disputes, rather than a means of resolving them.'

He forecast that the new system of greater judicial control 'will make it easier to identify the issues that are important to the couple and encourage them to reach agreement. It will reduce unnecessary cost, delay and personal distress. It will also ensure that people understand at

every stage how much money they are spending on taking forward their
case . . .

'In many ways, the judge will be speaking over the heads of the
lawyers directly to the participants.'

It will be interesting to see how this new system works out, with judges
doing more and lawyers doing less.

10

CHILDREN AFTER DIVORCE OR RELATIONSHIP BREAKDOWN

Children suffer whenever a marriage or relationship breaks down: it is inevitable. All that the law can realistically hope to do is provide machinery whereby, if the parents cannot agree on the best solution, the wisdom and experience of a bench of magistrates or (more often) that of a judge is available to minimise the damage.

That is why the 1989 Children Act, which came into effect on 14 October 1991, is so important. For the first time it created the concept of 'parental responsibility', defined as: 'All the rights, duties, powers and responsibilities and authority which by law a parent has in relation to the child and his property.' As we have seen in Chapter 2, unmarried mothers and married parents enjoy parental responsibility automatically from their child's birth while unmarried fathers may obtain it with the mother's consent or by an order of the court.

In the old days, the court itself could take over responsibility for a child's upbringing when it was made 'a ward of court'. That procedure is still available but 'wardship proceedings', as they are called, are now much less common. The whole ethos of the Children Act is to encourage other close family members to take over responsibility for children rather than the courts themselves.[1] A court can, for instance, award parental responsibility to grandparents where a child is suffering through its own parents' neglect of their duties.

This power even extends to an unmarried father at loggerheads with the new husband of his ex-girlfriend. As in the case of :

The unmarried father v. his child's stepfather

The parents of a two-year-old child parted without ever having married each other. The mother eventually married someone else – and then refused to allow regular contact to continue between the father and his son because of her new husband's attitude. Although a consent order was made saying that the father was to see the boy every fortnight, the child's stepfather wrote to the father that the marriage was at risk because he was not happy with this continuing contact. The father then applied for parental responsibility and for contact, but a judge refused both applications.

The Appeal Court then made a judgment of Solomon. It ruled that the judge's refusal of contact was justifiable because the stepfather's continuing attitude would place the marriage – and the welfare of the child – at risk. But it awarded the father parental responsibility because he was 'entirely qualified' and the wife's marriage might break down anyway and it wanted the father's legal position to be preserved so that, if that happened, he could step in to safeguard his son's best interests.

Stepfathers and stepmothers are in a special legal category. They do not automatically assume shared parental responsibility when marrying the mother or father of a child. But they can specifically apply to the court for parental responsibility if they want to, although it will probably be refused if it is thought likely to create difficulties with the other parent which could rebound on the child.

Parental responsibility is a vague but essentially flexible notion. It endures until the child is 18 and continues despite divorce or remarriage. But there is nothing to sign, no piece of paper stating what exactly your rights and duties are. Parents with shared responsibility do not have to consult each other, although it would obviously be sensible to do so. Schools sometimes express nostalgia for the certainties of the old custody order when, for example, a mother breezes in without notice to take a child out of school for the afternoon, airily citing her joint parental responsibility. But the flexibility also has its advantages, as when a father does not have to obtain the mother's consent before allowing their child to have an emergency operation.

But the value of the Children Act goes much further than the new notion of parental responsibility, however important that may be.

Section 1 of the Act not only restated the widely approved basis of the old law: 'When a court determines any question with respect to a child, the child's welfare shall be the court's paramount consideration.' It went on to display a totally new attitude to the intervention of the courts. For it proclaimed this fundamental new principle: 'A court shall not make an order unless it considers that doing so would be better for the child than making no order at all.'

It is not that the courts are now hearing fewer applications with regard to children: far from it. In February 1994, Mr Justice Wall adjourned the normal private hearing of a case in chambers into open court so that he could give a public rebuke to lawyers in general for giving unrealistic estimates of the time required to hear their cases with the result that many ran over time and inordinate delay was caused to others.

The courts are used at least as much nowadays as in earlier years but, unknown to the general public and not commented upon in the press because all hearings are in private, their role has subtly changed: from *always* ending in a court order setting out parameters for the future to increasingly providing a catalyst for parents so that they can better sort out their problems for themselves. 'What on earth is the judge doing? He has deliberately put off a decision until late-July,' a retired solicitor who was also an irate (and extremely involved) grandfather complained to me recently, when a Family Division district judge in the High Court had deferred making a ruling for another four months on the solicitor's ex-daughter-in-law's application for contact with her five-year-old daughter, then living with her father who had gone back home to his parents after the divorce. I had gently to explain that nowadays, except in cases when they believe that a child is really at risk, judges tend to give parents as much chance as possible to find their own solution. I have to admit that he was not very impressed.

But he failed to appreciate the whole present-day thrust to the law of children brought about by the Act and the considerable change in judicial thinking that slowly built up in the last few years before it came into effect. As Cambridge lecturer Andrew Bainham has written in his book *Children – the Modern Law:* 'Children law is still in its infancy but is fast coming of age.' I remember, in the 1950s, a judge (the late Mr Justice Wallington) who actually once said that he would not give custody to a mother who had committed adultery because a woman who had shown that she was a bad wife could not be trusted to be a good mother. He was a prejudiced old commercial lawyer marooned by the nature of judicial appointments back in those days in the divorce court.

But it could not happen nowadays. From top to bottom, all courts that today hear child disputes are staffed by experts with specialist knowledge or experience. Family Division judges in the High Court, who were all family law practitioners when at the Bar, hear the most difficult or most sensitive cases; nominated family judges hear the everyday run of case at county court level sitting in local 'family hearing centres' and specially trained magistrates hear the lowest rung of cases at specialist magistrates' courts dubbed 'family proceedings courts'. Do not worry about which court to go to: apply at your 'ordinary' local county court or magistrates' court, and they will point you in the right direction.

People, even experienced journalists who should know better, still talk about 'custody', 'care and control' and 'access', as in a headline in *The Times* in November 1998: 'Mother's day has gone, says custody judge' and in the *Daily Telegraph* a month earlier: 'No winners or applause in child custody battles'. In fact, the use of the word 'custody' was then already seven years out of date; it had ceased to exist, along with the other traditional terms, on 14 October 1991. They had been discarded as somehow conveying the idea that a child was some sort of possession or, at best, a kind of second-class citizen. Section 8 of the Children Act now provides this range of orders (when a court can be persuaded to make one!):

A residence order   This is perhaps the nearest to the old custody or care and control order. It spells out where the child is to live. In most cases, it will be with one parent, usually the mother; and is only made after a court welfare officer has visited both prospective homes and talked to both parents and the child as well as, if necessary, grandparents and schoolteachers. This officer is terribly important for the judge will usually – but not always – follow his or her recommendation and, if not, must give reasons.

Even so, do not misunderstand me: it is the judge's decision which she will only come to after a long and anxious hearing in chambers with both parents (and sometimes other interested parties as well) giving evidence – including the child. The Children Act specifies that 'the ascertainable wishes and feelings of the child (in the light of the child's age and understanding)' must be taken into account. Normally only a child of at least nine will be asked to attend chambers and he or she will not be questioned in front of everyone else: the judge will interview them in private.[2] A residence order, like all Section 8 orders, continues until the child is 16 unless the court is satisfied that the circumstances of the case are 'exceptional'; but in practice no court will make an order against a child's wishes, once they are over about 14.

Several of the old restrictive ideas have gone. It used to be presumed that it would always be best for a small child to stay with its mother but in June 1990 (when the Children Act was already on the Statute Book but not yet in force) Lord Justice Butler-Sloss, since promoted to President of the High Court's Family Division, said in the Appeal Court: 'It may have been thought previously that young children and girls approaching puberty should be with their mothers and that older boys should be with their fathers. But that is not applicable any longer.

'Where there is a dispute, it is for the magistrates or the judge to decide which parent is better for the child: it cannot be "best" because the parents are not together. While it is natural for young children to be with their mothers, where there is a dispute, it is but one consideration, not a presumption.' (For those interested, the name of the case is *In re H (a Minor)*, reported in (1991) Family Court Reporter at page 155.)

Similarly, it used to be said that only in the most exceptional case would a 'joint care and control order', as it was called, be made allowing children to live part of the time with their divorced mother and the other part of the time with their father. As late as 1986 the Appeal Court ruled that such an order should not be made. But in *A v. A (Children: Shared Residence Order)* in February 1994, the Appeal Court ruled that, where there was 'positive benefit to the child' and the family atmosphere was harmonious with, as Lord Justice Butler-Sloss put it, 'no possibility of confusion in the child's mind as to where he would be at particular time', the present-day equivalent of a joint residence order should be made. So two children in Newcastle upon Tyne were allowed to live with their mother most of the time but to stay with their father on alternate weekends from 10 a.m. on Saturday until 6 p.m. on Sunday and half of all school holidays including school half-terms. This established an important precedent.

Where parents are failing in their responsibilities to their children, grandparents may obtain a residence order even though a judge is not prepared to go so far as to give them a parental responsibilities order. This is really a distinction without a difference, as someone with a residence order has in practice many of the rights (and duties) of someone with a parental responsibilities order. The same is true for step-parents, who not infrequently are awarded shared residence with the child's parent, even though not qualifying for full-scale parental responsibility.

The current law is all about reality and helping the child to the most, not about labels.

A contact order This really replaces the old 'access order' but is much more child-centred. It provides for the child to visit or stay with a named adult, unlike the old orders which were the other way around, allowing the named adult to 'have access to' the child. 'Access' only allowed visits or staying with someone. 'Contact' embraces all forms of contact: chats over the telephone, e-mail, letters, school outings – whatever.

A specific issue order   This is entirely new, and is exactly what it says it is: a way for someone who has parental responsibility to come to court and get an answer relating to a specific issue: for example, which school the child should go to.

A prohibited steps order   This also is new and has the effect of restraining someone with parental responsibility from doing what he would otherwise be able to do. This is most often used to stop a child's surname being changed or to prevent a child from being taken abroad for any long period of time.

Pre-Children Act, the position was clear: a child's surname could not be changed without both parents' consent or the consent of the court, which was rarely given. Nowadays, if a residence order has been made, it will automatically state that the child's surname cannot be changed without the consent of the other parent or the court. However, someone with parental responsibility (usually, a mother on remarriage) can change the child's surname without asking anyone's permission: even so, if objection is made *promptly* by the other parent, a prohibited steps order would probably be made. If there was a long delay and the child had adjusted to the new surname, it would probably be refused. As ever, the interests of the child are paramount.

As for taking a child abroad, if there is a residence order, it will automatically allow the child to be taken abroad (for example, on holiday) for up to a month but, for longer than that, all parties with parental responsibility must technically give their consent: if refused, the opposing party may well apply for a prohibited steps order. Whether it would be granted would, of course, depend on all the circumstances. However, if there is no residence order, anyone with parental responsibility can usually take the child abroad for as long as they like without anyone else's permission.

If someone with parental responsibility wants to start a new life abroad and emigrate with the child (perhaps a father who has remarried and wants to go and live with his new wife in her native country), anyone else with parental responsibility can oppose it by asking for a prohibited steps order. There have been no new cases reported in the Appeal Court but, on the basis of pre-Children Act decisions, the law is reasonably clear: courts will usually allow children to start a new life afresh with one parent, even though it will cause much heartache to the other parent and grandparents, if there is a real possibility that refusal would spark friction and bitterness within the new marriage which would, in itself, be detrimental to the happiness and welfare of the children.

On this basis, in 1986 the Appeal Court allowed two girls, aged 11 and 10, to be taken by a mother to live in New Zealand with their stepfather and two young half-brothers, despite their close continuing relationship with their father and his parents. Yet all these cases turn on their own facts: in 1989, the Appeal Court refused to allow a mother, living with her two young sons in a council house in Leeds, to start a new life with them in her parents' home in Australia because it would mean tearing them away from their father and their roots on the farm in Lincolnshire where they had grown up.

There is one factor we have missed out in all this: money. Who is going to support the child and how much is maintenance likely to be? This requires consideration of that other major new piece of legislation brought in during the 1990s to affect children:

THE 1991 CHILDREN SUPPORT ACT

This created the **Child Support Agency** which starting functioning on 5 April 1993 and has acquired the unenviable reputation of being the most unpopular Government measure since the poll tax. As an Agency press office spokesman recently admitted to me: 'There is widespread agreement that the current system is failing in its objective and that reform is needed.'

Like the poll tax, it was the brainchild of Margaret Thatcher who, when Prime Minister, was appalled by the increasing number of single-parent families and the financial burden they imposed on the state. (Of the 1.3 million single parents in Britain in 1991, nearly a million were on means-tested benefits, costing the taxpayer some £5 billion a year.) So, in a speech in January 1990, she bemoaned the fact that: 'Nearly four out of five lone mothers claiming Income Support receive no maintenance from the fathers.'[3] A Government White Paper called *Children Come First* (it should really have been entitled 'The Treasury Comes First') followed nine months later and then the Act itself setting up the Child Support Agency.

Its proclaimed task was to take over from the courts their flexible and pragmatic method of assessing children's maintenance on the basis of what was 'reasonable' and substituting a rigid system of assessing maintenance on the basis of a fixed formula which was then to be collected from what was called 'the absent parent'. Nine times out of ten, this was expected to be the father; and that is how it has worked out.

The Agency was not to take over existing maintenance orders until April 1997; but all existing Income Support cases (whether or not the parents were married) and all new cases, Income Support or otherwise, were to be dealt with by the system – except where the parties were civilised enough or sensible enough to agree maintenance between themselves. Argue over maintenance and you will find yourself enmeshed in the system: that was the message. Recourse to the courts was no longer available, with or without legal aid. In future, maintenance assessment was to be largely a paperwork job, devoid of humanity or compassion.

It was primarily, at least in the first instance, designed as a cost-cutting exercise with an announced target of saving the taxpayer £530 million in the first year alone through clawing back money for the Treasury from 'absent parents' who were paying nothing at all or a mere pittance for their children's maintenance. What was *not* announced at the time and only leaked out in January 1994, nine months after the Agency first opened its doors, was that Ros Hepplewhite, the Agency's chief executive, and her 4,939 staff at six regional centres around the country were enjoying performance-related bonuses.

This was justice with a profit motive and it was not even doing those on Income Support a great deal of practical good. In December 1993, Alistair Birt, then Social Security Minister, had to admit in Parliament that, of the £530 million expected to be clawed back from the absent parents of children whose mothers were on Income Support, only £50 million would actually go to the mothers: £480 million would go to the Treasury. And, as several stories in the press confirmed, if the amount clawed back 'floated' a mother off Income Support, all too often she was likely to lose out on other fringe benefits from the state, including housing benefit, council tax benefit and free school meals, prescriptions and dental care.

It did not make a great deal of sense.

But what soon emerged was that, although the Agency had originally been targeted at 'absent parents' whose children were on Income Support, many proved difficult to find (often the mother had no idea where the father was) and, even if they were found, no money could be clawed back from them, except perhaps for a token £2-a-week, because they were unemployed or earning low wages or themselves on Income Support. The plain truth was that the state was trying to extract money from some of the poorest in society and, to say the least, it was not an overwhelming success.

So the Agency changed direction. Instead of going for the increasingly elusive target of the feckless or missing poor, it went for the easy 'soft touch' of middle-income husbands who were not feckless or missing, *and were easily traceable*. In mid-September 1993, an internal memorandum leaked to the press revealed that Agency workers had been told to give top priority to 'good quality cases . . . where the absent parent is already paying . . . and is able to pay'.

Another memorandum quoted in a *Times* leader was even more explicit: 'The name of the game is maximising the maintenance yield. Don't waste a lot of time on non-profitable stuff.' Charming!

As part of the extensive publicity surrounding the opening of the Agency, it was claimed that average maintenance would only go up from £25 a week under the old court system to just over £48 a week per child. With the new easy target of middle-income husbands in their sights, that estimate soon proved laughably – or tragically – inaccurate. Middle-class husbands who were already paying towards the upkeep of their children were reassessed by the Agency and ordered to pay hugely increased amounts, often twice as much and sometimes three or four times higher than sums previously fixed by the courts. Second marriages were put under stress and some actually broke under the strain, at least one husband killed himself, others left the country and increased bankruptcies were forecast.

For her part, Ros Hepplewhite remained unrepentant. 'Many people were paying at quite unrealistic levels which in no way reflected what it costs to keep a family,' she said. 'Some absent parents are able to afford their current lifestyle because to some extent their first family is being supported by other taxpayers.'

But how was this New Look possible? How could court orders be overruled in this seemingly cavalier way? What about the specific provision in the Child Support Act, and Regulations made under it, that existing cases were not to be touched until April 1997? And what about the 'clean break' concept we looked at in the last chapter and under which many existing court orders were made?

Let us get the 'clean break' query out of the way at once. Despite all the hot air in the press at the time, it is invalid. Newspapers and magazines carried many distressing stories about husbands complaining that the court had imposed 'clean break' orders on them or that they had agreed 'clean break' consent orders that were now being broken. But that cannot be right. They had either been badly advised or they had mis-understood the advice. As we have already seen, most 'clean break' orders or settlements were never meant to extend to the children. As Lord Justice Ormrod said back in 1980: 'Whether they like it or whether they do not, people continue to be fathers and mothers to their children', and their needs change as they get older.

What is perhaps more difficult to understand is how the Agency came to be dealing with these cases at all, and there the answer is simple. Human greed. Mothers realising that they stood to get more money from their ex-husbands by getting themselves into the new system went to court to get their existing orders revoked and then they were 'new cases' so far as the Agency was concerned. How did so many mothers come to this realisation? They either had astute solicitors or it seems that helpful Agency staff (perhaps with their performance-related bonuses in mind) suggested it to them.

In October 1993, Judge David Bryant in a case at Teeside County Court dubbed the practice 'inappropriate' and overruled the revocation of a divorced woman's court order. She had written to the Agency and received a reply from 'Customer Services' advising her that, if she revoked the order, she could apply for assessment. So she got it revoked at Darlington County Court and the Agency promptly increased her ex-husband's maintenance for two of their three children from £123 a month to £473 a month. He was by then a health service executive earning £26,000 a year living with a girlfriend and their own two children. He claimed the increase threatened the financial stability of his new home, and Judge Bryant agreed. 'It seems to me that an assessment from the Agency is not necessarily in the best interests of the children,' he said. 'It might produce a higher figure but it may be that other matters outweigh the purely financial.'

Sadly, few judges followed this robust example and a ruling by a county court judge is not binding on other judges at that level.

The rights of 'clean break' husbands were then further undermined by a High Court decision of Mrs Justice Booth in December 1993 when she refused to unscramble the four-year-old 'clean break' consent order of a divorced £9,390-a-year wood machinist. He had handed over to his ex-wife his share in their house in Carlisle, Cumbria on the agreed basis that there would only be nominal maintenance of 5p a year for their son, then aged five, and that she would have full responsibility for maintaining him. Nevertheless the Agency had said he must pay maintenance of £29 a week, although he now lived with a new partner with whom he had two children. Mrs Justice Booth accepted that her ruling could be seen as 'harsh' and that the couple would never have made their agreement if they had thought the husband would be required to pay maintenance – certainly not of the magnitude calculated by the new assessment.

But she repeated what all family lawyers should know anyway (but do not always seem to tell their clients): that a couple are free to achieve a clean break between themselves but they cannot do so in respect of any child.

So what is the current position?
Popular anger at the Agency's consistent breaking of its own rules and dealing with cases where the courts had earlier made maintenance orders

became so great that in a second Child Support Agency Act in 1995 the official deadline for taking on such cases was shelved indefinitely. An estimated 300,000 middle-class couples were thus taken out of the Agency's grasp.

What is wrong with the Agency's maintenance formula?

Originally devised by the Treasury when John Major was Chancellor of the Exchequer, it was slightly revised in 1995 but remained widely conceived as much too rigid, based on a complex and unwieldy assessment of both parental incomes. Gone for ever were the old, more flexible rules evolved by the judges.

Criticism mounted. A Green Paper published by the Labour Government in July 1998 proposed various solutions but never found its way, in any form, on to the Statute Book. Then at last, in July 1999, came a White Paper grandly entitled *A New Contract: Children's Rights and Parents' Responsibilities* promising wholesale reform and proposing a flat-rate levy for each child with absent parents having to pay 15 per cent of their salary for their first child, 20 per cent if there were two children and 25 per cent for three. Second families would also be taken more into account, with allowances on the same percentages deducted from net income before calculations were made for the first family.

In a House of Commons statement, introducing the White Paper, Alistair Darling, the Social Security Secretary, admitted that the Agency had proved to be 'a bureaucratic nightmare'. It was too complicated, with a third of the cases taking six months to reach a decision. He claimed that his White Paper heralded 'a new system far fairer to fathers who want to support their children and far tougher on those who won't'. Those who repeatedly refused to make payments, or paid late, would face fines of up to £1,000 or imprisonment and might even have their passports or driving licences confiscated.

In many cases, absent parents who meet their responsibilities will be better off under the new scheme. The average weekly payment is expected to fall from £38 per week to £30.50. As an example: a woman earns £300 a week as a teacher and lives with two teenage sons in a rented house, and her ex-husband, also a teacher, earns £300 a week. Under the present scheme, he pays £75.50 a week; under the new scheme this will fall to £60 a week.

But we should not throw our hats up in the air too high. 'To avoid the problems which occurred when the current system was introduced too quickly,' said Alistair Darling, the new system will not start until 'towards the end of 2001' – and even then it will, at first, only apply to new cases. As the *Daily Telegraph* said in a headline announcing the news: 'Long wait before CSA is overhauled.'[4]

In the meantime, the only sensible rule remains: however bitter the breakdown of your marriage may have been, try and sort out things direct with the other parent. Mediation and compromise must, if at all possible, be the name of the game – for the benefit of all parties, adults as well as children.

To help you bring that about, here are useful people to contact, wherever you live, in addition to the Solicitors Family Law Association already mentioned in the previous chapter:

One Parent Families at 255 Kentish Town Road, London NW5 2LX (Tel: 0800–0185026); Families Need Fathers at 134 Curtain Street, London EC2A 3AR (020 7613 5060); Eye to Eye Family Mediation at 231 Camberwell New Road, London SE5 0TH (020 7701 1114) and Divorce Mediation and Counselling Service at 38 Ebury Street, London SW1W OLU (020 7730 2422). The Child Support Agency has its own telephone enquiry line on 0345–133133.

In the words of the old Swedish proverb, 'Children are certain sorrow but uncertain joy.'

Notes

1 This, of course, is apart from very extensive court powers to put children who are at risk from lack of parental control into the care of a local authority, but that is outside the scope of this book.

2 I once asked Mrs Justice Lane, at my client's request, not to ask a 10-year-old girl the specific question with whom did she want to live, her mother or her father, and received the magisterial (and justifiable) reply: 'Mr Bresler, do please credit me with *some* intelligence.'

3 The Agency assists to make any absent parent, whether father or mother, contribute towards the maintenance of a child for whom they are responsible; but it has never lost its original emphasis on making absent fathers pay for their neglected offspring.

4. The Government's final plans for the reform of the CSA are contained in its Child Support, Pensions and Social Security Bill, published at the beginning of December 1999.

PART 2

YOU AND YOUR JOB

11

BASIC EMPLOYMENT LAW

Employment law has changed out of all recognition in recent years. It is the fastest-growing part of the law with which we will have to deal in this book. A splurge of legislation and case-made law that began in 1963 with the Contracts of Employment Act has continued unabated right up to the present time – and even beyond, with the latest example of this legislative overdrive, the 1999 Employment Relations Act spawning more rules and regulations that have not yet been brought into effect. In many respects, the law has become almost too complicated for its own good. This is not because it confers too many rights on the nation's workforce, far from it; it is because its complexity means that it is difficult for workers and middle-management executives, whom it is primarily designed to protect, to understand it or even to know fully what their rights are.

Senior management and top executives have always enjoyed a strong bargaining position and are able to negotiate advantageous service agreements with generous built-in 'golden handshake' provisions, backed up if necessary by the financial clout to sue for breach of contract or wrongful dismissal if things go grievously wrong. They are not really in need of further help.

Ironically, the same is often true of the average worker at the opposite end of the income range if he or she is a member of a trade union or is fighting sexual discrimination, in which case the Equal Opportunities Commission is only too happy to provide expert legal assistance. Senior management, the unions, the Commission – and, on the employers' side, large corporations – all have easy access to the new breed of skilled (and often expensive) specialist employment lawyers.

But, as so often in Britain today (unlike other parts of the law, modern employment law is the same throughout the entire United Kingdom), it is the man or woman in the middle, the middle-management executive and the middle-class small businessman (for he too has rights!) who are most in the dark and have to rely on their own resources for their protection.

Yet the modern law, for all its complexity, which I shall try to simplify as much as anyone can, is still a great deal better than what went before. Until the mid-1960s, when employment law reform first came powerfully on to the political agenda, the law of master and servant (as it was then called) had changed little since Victorian times. The employer was – quite literally – the 'master', with the legal right to expect, and demand, that an employee turn up for work on time, put in a full working day, not take time off without proper authorisation and do his job conscientiously and to the best of his ability: if not, he could expect to be sacked without apology or compensation. The employer had virtually unbridled 'power of hiring and firing'.

Many people might think that, in some respects, those were the Good Old Days but, of course, the other side of the coin was not so appealing: an employee was, truly, a 'servant'. He had, in almost all circumstances, to do his master's bidding and accept his working conditions with very little redress to the law. His legal rights, if any, were only those given him by his contract of employment, which he usually had to accept on a take-it-or-leave-it basis and of which he did not even have the legal right to demand a written copy; and his personal safety at work was only protected, apart from specific Acts like the 1937 Factories Act, by the judge-made general principle, grounded in late Victorian notions of social philanthropy, that, as Lord Herschell laid down in 1891, an employer must 'take reasonable care to provide proper appliances, to maintain them in a proper condition and so to carry on his operations as not to subject those employed by him to unnecessary risk'.

The process of change accelerated when Harold Wilson's first Labour Government came to power in October 1964, but there has been a bipartisan approach with varying degrees of support from successive Labour and Tory governments. Alongside the traditional courts presided over by a judge in robes and steeped in legality, a whole new nationwide network of local 'industrial tribunals' (a name changed more appropriately to 'employment tribunals' in 1998) has been created to which the employee can go to assert most of his or her new-found rights. These tribunals are staffed by a legally qualified chairman flanked by two lay members, one from employers' organisations and the other from employees' organisations. These can overrule the legal chairman, and quite often do so. However, the law comes more into its own on appeal to the Employment Appeal Tribunal (EAT) in London, where the two lay members almost never overrule the legal President who, although never robed and only called 'Sir' and not 'Your Lordship', is always a High Court judge on secondment.[1]

This was originally supposed to be an area of the law where lawyers were intended to have little or no place. 'Industrial tribunals will be like industrial juries,' forecast one early pioneer of the new system. It has not worked out like that. Legal aid is not available and, even if you win, the tribunal will hardly ever order the losing side to pay your costs, which is the general rule in the normal courts. Nevertheless, many low-income employees obtain skilled representation through their trade union or the Government-funded Equal Opportunities Commission in sex discrimination cases. It is the middle-income employee or the small business owner who most often has to try to argue her own case because she simply cannot afford a competent lawyer. For all the tribunals' deliberately low-profile atmosphere, sitting in plain, almost austere rooms with no legal robes or ceremonial, the middle-ranking employee – or small employer – arguing her own case is undoubtedly at a disadvantage. It has been estimated that only 22 per cent of applicants are represented by lawyers; when they are not, their chances of winning are diminished. With representation, the success rate is 49 per cent; without it, the success rate, if opposed by lawyers, is down to 29 per cent.

Enough of preliminaries: what are employees' legal rights today? I do not write specifically of employers' rights, whether those of large or small businesses, because one cannot discuss employees' rights without also touching upon employers' rights: the two are inextricably interwoven. Similarly, when writing about employees or the owners of small businesses, I shall write 'he' for both sexes except when logic dictates that I specify one sex rather than the other. This is nothing to do with being politically incorrect (my natural impulse) or correct: it is merely a matter of convenience. The subject is complicated enough already without using more words than are absolutely essential.

So where shall we begin?

For a start, there are three different kinds of rights with which we are concerned:

- those which an employee enjoys merely by virtue of being an employee, however short the period of time he may have been working for that particular employer;
- those to which he is entitled only after working continuously for at least three or six months for the same firm; and
- those to which he is entitled only after working continuously for at least one or two years for the same firm.[2]

In the rest of this chapter, we shall deal primarily with the first category: i.e. your rights merely by virtue of being an employee. In the next two chapters we shall examine exclusively those for which you need to have worked for the same employer for a specific length of time.

SO WHAT ARE YOUR RIGHTS SIMPLY BECAUSE YOU ARE AN EMPLOYEE?

A written statement of the main terms of your contract

You are entitled to this, even though the contract may have been by word of mouth and nothing was said about putting it in writing at the time. The 1996 Employment Rights Act (which contains most of the current statutory law, so I shall henceforth simply call it 'the 1996 Act') says that, within two months, an employer must give every new employee working for at least eight hours a week 'written particulars' of certain specified details. The most important of these are pay and sick pay, holidays, hours of work, place of work, notice periods, date when the employment began, job title, disciplinary procedures, and, when the employment is not intended to be permanent, for how long it is expected to last.

A specific word is needed on *sick pay*. Irrespective of what is said in the written particulars, every employee is entitled to *statutory sick pay* . The figures are minimal but still better than nothing. The subject is excessively complicated, although a helpful free leaflet (SD1) is available at all local Social Security offices and many public libraries.

In essence: to qualify, you must have worked for the same employer for at least three months and earn at least the lower earnings limit for National Insurance contributions of £66 a week. The amount of statutory sick pay increases slightly every year and is currently around the £58 mark but is usually not paid in respect of the first three days of absence. It must be paid by your boss for up to 28 weeks at a time, although the employer gets a refund from the state. After twenty-eight weeks, you normally become eligible for Invalidity Benefit.

Do you need a doctor's certificate before claiming? The position is much the same as with non-statutory sick pay when, as usually happens, the written particulars of your contract specify the circumstances in which your employer will continue to pay your wages while you are off sick. If an employee phones in sick and wants to be excused work for a few days because he is (allegedly) not feeling well, most employers will not ask for a doctor's certificate except when dealing with someone known to make a habit of it; but after a week they may well do so. With statutory sick pay, if the illness is for less than a week, most employers will accept a self-certificate: a form that you fill in yourself confirming that you are ill and specifying what you think is wrong with you: a bad cold, food poisoning or whatever.

Similarly, irrespective of what the written particulars may say about the notice period, the 1996 Act gives you a statutory right to *minimum notice* when dismissed without any fault on your side. You are entitled to one week's notice if employed for at least a month, two weeks' notice if employed for at least two years and one additional week's notice for each further year of service up to a maximum of 12 weeks.

What about employers, if an employee suddenly walks out on them or only gives them a couple of days' notice? Especially with a small firm, that can sometimes cause major inconvenience. But there is no statutory minimum notice period to which an employer is entitled. According to Parliament, what is sauce for the goose is not sauce for the gander. Technically, the more robust rules of judge-made Common Law *do* give employers equal rights with employees to sue if their business is damaged or disrupted by staff walking out without adequate notice, and once many years ago in Marylebone County Court in London, on behalf of a client, I won £50 damages in exactly such a case: I am not sure whether my client ever got his money and it certainly cost him far more than that to bring his lawsuit but I remember him saying that he was well pleased 'as a matter of principle'. Nowadays, for similar stout-hearted employers, the small claims court would seem an ideal, inexpensive venue for just such an action.

If, as an employee, you do not receive your written particulars within two months, you should write a polite letter asking for them (and keep a copy of your letter). If you still do not get them, you can apply to an industrial tribunal and your boss will be ordered to supply you with them. If you disagree with any specific term, you can ask a tribunal for a ruling. This right has existed since an Act of 1963 and a good example dates back to 1976 when written particulars gave a job title as 'Planner and associated duties' and a new employee thought it should have been

'Senior Planning Engineer'. The tribunal gave a Solomon-like judgment that it was 'Planning Engineer'.

But do not go over the top on this. There is no point in running the risk of antagonising your boss unnecessarily. You are only entitled to details of the specific terms referred to in the 1996 Act. There may be many other important terms that a tribunal could rule at a later date may have to be implied, but this will not always be to your advantage. This happened in a 1992 case where the Appeal Court ruled that British Telecom had rightly withheld a branch manager's wages for four days when she had taken part in *unofficial* strike action: the appeal judges held that she had acted in breach of a term to be implied in any manager's contract that the employee would faithfully serve his or her employer and not wilfully disrupt his business.

There are two popular misconceptions about employment contracts that we ought to get out of the way at this early stage:

There is a maximum working week   It has never existed in Britain – and, in a sense, still does not. Going back in history, the European Union in November 1993 formally adopted a Working Time Directive and gave member states three years to implement it. It imposed a maximum 48-hour working week, four weeks' annual minimum holiday and an eight-hour limit on night work on all countries within the Union.

David Hunt, then Employment Secretary in John Major's Tory Government, promptly called this an attempt to impose 'arbitrary legal limits on British working hours' and, for so long as the Major Government was in power, it refused to implement the Directive on one pretext or another. Then on 1 October 1998, within 18 months of Tony Blair's Labour Government's taking over, it enacted the Working Time Regulations, based on the five-year-old EU Directive. These apply to all workers except the self-employed and those working in transport sectors, sea fishing or other work at sea, and doctors in training.[3]

'The Regulations provide new rights for workers ensuring they do not have to work excessive hours,' proudly declared the Department of Trade and Industry in an explanatory leaflet. But this was a typical example of Government spin-doctoring, ignoring the salient fact that the Regulations specifically permit employers to contract out of a 48-hour week by inducing their staff to sign 'voluntary' written agreements to that effect – although the original EU Directive contains no such escape clause.

Everyone is entitled to a paid Bank Holiday   In fact, that has never been the law. Until the Working Time Regulations, no employee had any statutory right to a paid holiday, not even Bank Holidays. It was all down to the individual work contract.

But the Regulations have muddied the waters. They are typical of the slipshod way in which both Labour and Tory governments have made new English law based upon EU directives. When one gets to specifics, the bad drafting – never submitted to fine-tuning in Parliament – frays at the edges.

The Regulations' central framework is that most 'workers' should not work more than 48 hours a week, averaged over 17 weeks, and have three weeks' paid annual leave (including Bank Holidays), which was increased to four weeks as from November 1999. But these 'weeks' take no account of any Bank Holiday falling within them. The actual phrase appears nowhere in the Regulations.

In fact, Bank Holidays have existed ever since a Victorian Act of 1871 named the days on which banks and other public institutions were closed and financial obligations due on that day were made payable on the following day. Public Holidays – different from Bank Holidays – date back even further: to judge-made Common Law. They are exclusively Good Friday and Christmas Day.

But despite this long history there has for many years been no statutory right to *paid* Public Holidays and Bank Holidays.

Even so, irrespective of the strict word of the law, except for certain specialised trades, employment contracts generally conceded this entitlement and allowed staff to take their normal paid holidays plus Bank Holidays. It may well be that the 1998 Regulations will change all that. When rewriting staff contracts, some employers may be tempted to follow this new pattern of including Bank Holidays as part of the staff's annual leave, and many workers will lose out. The Regulations may prove to give with one hand while taking away with the other.

Physical safety in your job

Modern judges have gone beyond Lord Herschell's already quoted cautious words in 1891 about an employer's legal duty to take reasonable care not to subject his employees to 'unnecessary risk'. Nowadays there is widely accepted case law that anyone injured in an accident at work can sue his employer for damages if the accident occurred through the employer's failure to take reasonable care for his safety and provide him with a safe system of work including safe equipment, plant and premises, adequate supervision and proper training where necessary.

And an employee is bound to get his money, however small the employers' financial resources may be. Few people realise that the 1969

Employees' Liability (Compulsory Insurance) Act says that *every* employer in Britain must insure against liability for bodily injury or disease sustained by her employees in the course of their employment.

In addition, the 1974 Health and Safety at Work Act imposes a general duty on all employers 'to ensure, so far as is reasonably practicable, the health, safety and welfare at work of all their employees'. For years, this Act and two others (the 1961 Factories Act and the 1963 Offices, Shops and Railway Premises Act) imposed detailed health and safety standards at work. But, prodded (as so often) by enlightened European Union directives, they have been upgraded and modernised by six sets of Health and Safety at Work Regulations applying to almost all non-domestic workplaces, including factories, shops, hotels, offices, sports halls and theatres: home workers are exempt. The Regulations originally came into force in January 1993 for all new workplaces but employers were given three years, until January 1996, to bring existing workplaces into line with the onerous new requirements.

In the words of an editorial in the *Solicitors Journal*, 'People spend more of their waking day at work than they do at home. A nine-to-five job in an office means that a minimum of thirty-five hours a week is spent in one location. Not at any other time in the week, except when you are asleep, do you spend so much time in one place.' Supported by an approved Code of Practice and by guidance issued by the Health and Safety Executive, these regulations have greatly enhanced standards in the nation's workplaces. Anyone, whether employer or employee, wanting specific further information can write to the Health and Safety Executive Information Centre for a set of helpful free leaflets: the address is Broad Lane, Sheffield S3 7HQ, Tel: 01742–892345, Fax: 01742–892333.

There are three specific matters you may be particularly interested in:

Visual Display Units   Some seven million people in Britain work with VDU screens, while the number of machines in operation has more than doubled in the last 14 years. Under the Regulations – specifically the Display Screen Equipment Regulations – employers are under a legal duty to protect 'habitual users' of VDUs from the health threat posed by their work. Screens must be glare-free with no flicker and have adjustable brightness and contrast. Firms must provide suitable office furniture, including specially designed chairs and matt-surface desks, and rooms must have adequate lighting and ventilation. Free spectacles must be provided for those specifically needing them for VDUs (but not merely for normal reading) and 'regular' free eyesight tests, although no precise time scale is laid down. And the daily work routine must be broken up by breaks or changes of activity that do not involve the screen.

Repetitive strain injury (RSI)   Some people may remember the wide media publicity given to Judge John Prosser QC's remark in the High Court back in October 1993 – 'RSI has no place in the medical dictionary' – when throwing out a claim from a former Reuters sub-editor that Reuters had caused his RSI through failing to provide advice on correct working posture when using his VDU keyboard or on the necessity to take regular breaks. Prosser's remark stuck in the popular consciousness but, in fact, both before and since, there have been several cases where RSI sufferers have recovered substantial compensation from their employers.

Indeed, less than three months later, a record out-of-court settlement of £79,000 was awarded in January 1994 to a former Inland Revenue typist who developed RSI after working for years on an electric typewriter for over seven hours a day with only a 30-minute break. Mr Clive Brooke, General Secretary of the Inland Revenue Staff Federation, which had supported her claim and was said to be actively pursuing more than 150 other cases against the Inland Revenue, told a reporter: 'Judge Prosser was out of touch with the pain and reality of life of many workers suffering from RSI. There is a growing army of RSI sufferers.'

Mr Brooke was correct. In May 1998 five former Midland Bank workers at the bank's processing centre at Frimley, Surrey who had suffered 'considerable pain' in their arms, necks and shoulders were awarded damages totalling around £60,000 in an important test case. In a reserved judgment at the Mayor's and City of London Court, Judge Byrt QC ruled that the bank had breached its legal duty of care to its staff. He said that a combination of management pressure for the women to increase their work rate and lack of sufficient breaks from keyboards had caused their injuries. His ruling was hailed as a 'tremendous break-through' by the banking union UNIFI which had backed the case, and one of the women proudly claimed: 'We have been vindicated. Everyone says that people who complain about RSI are crackpots. It is nice it has been recognised.'

Over a year later, in July 1999, the Appeal Court rejected the Midland Bank's appeal and Mike Watson, a senior partner with Lawford & Co., the successful claimants' solicitors, told the magazine the *Lawyer*: 'I am sure we shall get a lot more keyboard operators from other areas mounting claims now.' Within weeks, he was proved right. In September 1999, a graphic designer who claimed that she suffered RSI from using her computer mouse won £25,000 damages from her employers, the oil company Shell UK, at Colchester County Court. Twenty-six-year-old

Michelle Gould was awarded the money when Judge Nicholas Brandt
ruled that the company was at fault in failing to correct the 'bizarre' way
she held the mouse, with hand, wrist and forearm unsupported. 'In my
opinion the way in which she was using the mouse should have been
picked up on,' he said. Who says we do not live in a nanny state?

Smoking at work   Some people cannot stand it; others cannot work – or
live – without it. What does the law say? It undoubtedly favours the non-
smokers. In January 1993 a woman worker at Stockport Borough
Council accepted an out-of-court settlement of £15,000 after claiming
that she had developed chronic bronchitis as a direct result of working in
a smoky atmosphere. Though the settlement did not set a legal precedent
because it was resolved out of court, it increased the pressure building up
on employers to implement and enforce smoking policies.

There is as yet no decisive ruling by the Employment Appeal Tribunal
but, as a matter of principle, such policies can apply to either all or part
of the premises but they must always be 'reasonable' in all the
circumstances. A ban should not be imposed overnight nor should it
discriminate against one section of the company at the expense of others:
for example, allowing directors to smoke in their offices but not their
secretaries. With that caveat, anti-smoking policies are likely to be
upheld by the law.

REFERENCES

'Will you at least give me a good reference?' is the question many people
ask when told they are being sacked. The law on the subject may therefore be of some interest to both employers and staff.

It is deceptively simple: an ex-employee has no right to demand a
reference and, if requested, an ex-employer is under no legal duty to
supply one – or to explain the refusal. Indeed, if employers do not want
to give a reference because it would mean telling the unpleasant truth
about someone, they should refuse and give no reason.

If the ex-employee still presses for something in writing to show a new
prospective employer, the request can either be ignored – impolite but
legally watertight – or an enigmatic reply given to the effect that the
employee would not want the only reference that could truthfully be
supplied.

BUT if a reference is given – not only in an employment context –
anyone supplying it must take reasonable care to ensure it is factually
correct. If not, they risk being sued for libel.

For instance, if an employer gives a man a glowing testimonial, and then it transpires that he was sacked because he was strongly suspected of embezzlement, the reference-giver could find herself paying damages to a new employer who, relying on the reference, gave the man a job – and he stole from him.

It also works the other way round. If you give a bad and untrue reference which damages, not a new employer, but the ex-employee, he can sue you. The House of Lords gave that ruling in 1994 when the untrue reference for an insurance company's sales director was 'so strikingly bad as to amount to . . . a kiss of death to his career in insurance'.

However, it is worth remembering that employers can protect themselves by stating in the reference that it is given with a disclaimer of liability. Of course, that may put people off. But warning an ex-employee that a reference will only be given on that basis may make him think again about asking for it.

ONE LAST WORD ON DIRECTORS

Many directors of small companies are uncertain as to their precise duties and responsibilities. 'It sounds nice being a director,' a friend recently told me. 'But I know that in the end I am really an employee just like anyone else.'

That is an over-simplification of the legal position.

Directors are more than company employees; indeed part-time (non-executive) directors are usually not employees. But all are under a legal duty to act solely in the best interests of the company and of its staff members, and not for their own private gain.

They must not deceive any outsider. If so, they can be made personally liable for compensation, as when the director of a company installing flooring in a new office building wrongly assured architects that the flooring met certain specifications. The architects had to pay damages for the inadequate flooring to their clients, the building owners – and Mr Justice Forbes ordered the director to indemnify them out of his own pocket.

Directors must also not allow their company to continue trading while insolvent. The 1986 Insolvency Act calls this 'wrongful trading' and, if the company goes bust and the liquidator can prove a director knew or ought to have known that 'there was no reasonable prospect of the company avoiding liquidation', that director – and any similarly negligent colleague – can be made to contribute to the company's debts and may be disqualified from serving again as a director.

Furthermore, all directors must ensure that the company's accounts, annual returns and notice of any change of directors or secretary are filed at Companies House. If not, they commit a criminal offence and can be fined up to £5,000. This is not a technicality. An average of 1,000 directors are convicted every year, and it is no excuse to say that the company's accountants were dealing with it. A Companies House publication menacingly tells directors: 'Accountants and financial advisers don't get prosecuted or penalised. You do.'

Notes

1 There is a further right of appeal, with the leave of the EAT or the Appeal Court itself, to the Appeal Court, which is, of course, solidly within the framework of the normal court structure and from there in rare cases to the House of Lords, the highest court in the land. There are, of course, women High Court judges but so far none has been appointed President of the EAT, but, when that does happen, they will be called 'Madam' and not 'Your Lordship'.

2 With these three length-of-service qualifications, you do not need to have held the same job for the requisite period; merely to have worked for the same employer during all that time, although you may have gone from one job to another.

3 Domestic workers are excluded from much of the Regulations but, if continuously employed by the same boss for more than 13 calendar weeks, they have holiday rights on a sliding scale pegged to their working hours: for instance, a cleaner who spends one morning a week cleaning a flat and ironing shirts is entitled to one and a half days' paid holiday a year. How many people know this?

12

MATERNITY RIGHTS

Few things in the law are simple but it is little short of a disgrace that the law on something so basic and important for so many working women as their rights when they have a baby should be quite so complicated or intricate as unfortunately it is. Shortly before Christmas 1998, Lord Justice Ward joined the long line of judges to criticise the exceptional complexity: 'It is surely not too much to ask of the Legislature,' he said, 'that those who have to grapple with this topic should not have to have a wet towel around their heads as the single most important aid to the understanding of their rights.'

Every human resources officer and employees' adviser in the country will surely agree.

But I suppose we should be thankful for small mercies. There were no minimum legal rights at all for pregnant working women until twenty-five years ago when, on the same day in 1975, the Sex Discrimination Act and that year's Employment Act came into effect. Until then, unless a woman's contract of employment specifically gave her the right to take paid leave to have a baby and assured her of her job back afterwards, she had absolutely no legal redress if having her baby meant that she lost her job. Motherhood all too often came with a price tag.

Nowadays women's employment contracts often spell out generous maternity rights but that is still not the norm. At least, the modern law – with a minimum of five later Acts complicating the initial two (plus a European directive incorporated into British law) – does give a certain minimum measure of protection to many (but still not all) working women. The trouble is that even one of our most distinguished judges has admitted he does not always understand it!

In 1983, Mr Justice Brown-Wilkinson, now a law lord but then presiding over the Employment Appeal Tribunal (EAT) in London, was one of the first senior judges to bemoan his lot:

> These statutory procedures are of an inordinate complexity. We find that especially regrettable bearing in mind that they are regulating the everyday rights of ordinary employers and employees. We feel no confidence that, even with the assistance of detailed arguments from skilled advocates, we have now correctly understood them: it is difficult to see how an ordinary employer or employee is expected to do so.

Where judges fear to tread, the rest of us can only follow on tiptoe. I regret that this chapter will not be fun reading but do not blame me, blame the law-makers. Here is, I hope, a useful guide, which takes into account not only the existing law but so much as possible of the future law when the 1999 Employment Relations Act comes fully into effect:

Ante-natal care   Any pregnant woman – full-timer, part-timer, no matter how short a period she has worked for the same firm or how little she earns a week – is entitled to reasonable time off, with pay, to receive ante-natal care. An employer can ask to see a medical certificate confirming the pregnancy and a woman's appointments card.

No dismissal for pregnancy   This is a special form of unfair dismissal, which we shall examine in general in the next chapter, but one cannot emphasise sufficiently that it is never legal to sack a woman simply because she is pregnant.

The 1996 Employment Rights Act says that sacking is *automatically* unfair – and therefore unlawful – if 'due to or connected with pregnancy'. But, as with all unlawful dismissal cases, the woman must, at least since June 1999, have worked continuously for the same employer for at least one year.

There was a case in October 1998 where an employment tribunal ordered a Swindon caravan centre to pay £1,500 compensation to a 20-year-old sales assistant whom they had sacked after only half an hour in her job. They claimed that they had only just discovered she was five months pregnant and said that justified her dismissal because it would prevent her lifting heavy loads.

She was only able to get so much money for a job that lasted such a short time because the EAT ruled back in 1985 that dismissal for pregnancy may not only be unlawful dismissal. It may also be sex discrimination, outlawed by the 1975 Sex Discrimination Act. And awards are not restricted by length of employment or financial loss. Furthermore, uniquely in English law, compensation can include an element for 'injury to feelings'. This somewhat vague legal concept has proved extremely popular with claimants; but not with many employers.

Sacking a pregnant woman without good cause can be expensive. As Lord Griffiths, then a senior law lord, laid down in the House of Lords back in *Brown* v. *Stockton-on-Tees BC,* reported in (1988) 2 All England Law Reports at page 129:

[Protection against dismissal for pregnancy] must be seen as part of social legislation passed for the specific protection of women and to put them on an equal footing with men. I have no doubt that it is often a considerable inconvenience for an employer to have to make the necessary arrangements to keep a woman's job open for her whilst she is absent from work in order to have a baby, but this is a price that has to be paid as a part of the social and legal recognition of the equal status of women in the workplace.

So when a care supervisor on a Youth Training Scheme had been made redundant because she was pregnant and would soon be claiming maternity leave, the lords overruled both the EAT and the Appeal Court and held that her redundancy also amounted to unfair dismissal – for which you get a higher rate of compensation than redundancy alone.

In 1993, Parliament went beyond even Lord Griffiths's trenchant statement and said in the horribly entitled Trade Union Reform and Employment Rights Act (now re-enacted by the 1996 Act) that a woman's protection against a pregnancy-related dismissal extends from the start of her pregnancy through to the end of her maternity leave and even possibly four weeks beyond, if she produces a medical certificate that she is still not fit to return to work. Even if she does not ask for it, an employer has to provide a sacked pregnant woman with a written statement of the reasons for her dismissal, however short a time she has worked for him, and, if not, he is liable to pay her two weeks' extra pay.

She is also given special protection against being unfairly made redundant while she is away on maternity leave and being victimised by being sacked on her return from it; and there is no exemption for small businesses, no matter how hard they may be hit financially.

How does sex discrimination come into the picture? In the 1985 case when the EAT ruled that, although a woman might not qualify for unfair dismissal because (for instance) she had not worked for the same employer for long enough, she could still claim sex discrimination: so long as she could show that a man employed by the same firm and, like her, temporarily unable to work through physical incapacity would not have been dismissed as she was.

In June 1993, for instance, the Equal Opportunities Commission (EOC) helped a 32-year-old project manager with GEC-Plessey, Britain's biggest electronic firm, to win an out-of-court settlement of £7,000 after she was fired when medically unable to return to work on the due date after having had her baby. The basis of the case was that a male employee taking sick leave after a sabbatical would allegedly not have been treated as harshly. An EOC lawyer commented afterwards: 'We hope this settlement sends signals to employers that they must consider carefully how they treat pregnant employees.'

Maternity leave   There are now two kinds:

(1) 14 weeks' maternity leave[1]   Every pregnant working woman, irrespective of how long she has worked for the same employer, is entitled to this. If she wants to claim it, she must write to her employer at least 21 days before the start of her proposed leave telling him that she is pregnant and giving the expected week of childbirth. There is no mystique about this: an ordinary letter in ordinary language – 'Dear Mr Smith', 'Dear Jim', 'Dear Susan' or whatever – will do, although it would be prudent to keep a copy. She must also give the date on which she would like to start her leave but technically she only needs to put this in writing, if asked to do so. Also, if her employer asks for it, she must supply a copy of her maternity certificate (form MAT B1) which her midwife or GP will give her. She does *not* need to say in her letter that she wants to come back to her existing job when her leave is over: that will be assumed although, if she knows that she definitely will want to come back, there is no harm in saying so.

If she cannot give 21 days' written notice, perhaps because she suddenly has to go into hospital ahead of time, she must write her letter as soon as she reasonably can.

The choice of when she starts her leave is entirely up to her: an employer has no say in the matter. The only restriction is that it cannot start earlier than 11 weeks before the expected week of childbirth. A woman can even work right up to the week of childbirth, if she wants to. The only exception is that if she is off work for a pregnancy-related reason during the last six weeks of her pregnancy, she may find herself forced to start her leave ahead of time even if she was only off work for one day.

When her 14 weeks are up, she is entitled to come back to work and does not need to claim that right in her original letter saying she wanted to take maternity leave. In fairness to her employer, however, who may have taken on substitute staff during her expected period of absence, if she wants to come back to work earlier, she must give him written notice at least seven days beforehand. If not, he can send her away for seven days or until her leave was due to end, whichever date is earlier.

If her baby is born very late and her leave has already run out, she can extend it by two weeks from the actual date of birth and, if there are any other complications, she should tell her employer to see if they can work out a satisfactory compromise. Bearing in mind the sex discrimination aspect, the employer would be a fool not to take a reasonable line. In case of trouble, she should consult her local citizens' advice bureau or trade union representative.

(2) Forty weeks' maternity leave This used to be the only kind of maternity leave and, although still available, is of limited application. It used to apply only to women who worked for the same employer for two years full-time, but for women whose expected week of childbirth falls on or after 30 April 2000 the period is halved to only one year. This is because the Maternity and Parental Leave, etc. Regulations are made under the 1999 Employment Relations Act.

Eligible women need to have a calendar in front of them. They can claim a total of up to 11 weeks' leave before the expected week of birth and up to 29 weeks after the birth, with this latter period capable of extension for a further four weeks on production of a doctor's certificate. As with 14-week maternity leave, it is the woman and not her employer who has the right to say when it shall start; but it cannot be earlier than 11 weeks before the expected week of childbirth. There is also a similar need for her to write to her boss at least 21 days before the proposed commencement date claiming her leave and, if asked, giving the starting date but, unlike the other written notice, she *must* specify that she will be wanting her job back afterwards. She should do this even if she is not yet sure that she really wants to return: this may be dishonest but it is essential to guarantee her legal right to come back, if afterwards she decides to do so.

Maternity pay during maternity leave Until most women actually begin to plan for their pregnancy, or even much later, they probably do not realise that state maternity pay is available for less than half of a 40-week maternity leave – but for four weeks longer than the 14-weeks version. Crazy! As Christine Gowridge, Director of the charity Maternity

Alliance, has said, 'This is bound to confuse everyone. The Government has created a muddle.' What did she expect? That is par for the course.

Anyway, during both kinds of maternity leave, all of a woman's contractual rights continue, including holiday entitlement, pension rights, company car, etc. – except for her entitlement to wages! Unless her firm has a better scheme than the Government's, as many do, she is only entitled to be paid State Maternity Pay (SMP), and only for a maximum of 18 weeks. This is ridiculous: she is not covered at all for the remaining 22 weeks of a 40-week leave whereas, if her leave is only 14 weeks, she loses the last four weeks of her entitlement. It makes precious little sense, on any basis.

But not every pregnant working woman is entitled even to this. SMP is restricted to women who have worked for the same employer for at least six months before the end of the 15th week before the baby is due, which is Civil Service jargon for at least 41 weeks before the expected week of birth, *and* who earn more than the threshold weekly salary for National Insurance contributions of £66 a week.[2]

How much is it? A woman gets 90 per cent of her average pay for the first six weeks but for the remaining 12 weeks she is only entitled to a miserly £57.70 a week; and that is an increase on the previous rates! Most of the cost comes from the nation's employers with no contribution from the Government. But 'small employers', defined as employers paying £20,000 or less annually in gross national contributions, will continue, as before, to be reimbursed by the state.

Coming back to work afterwards   Life moves on. Nothing stands still. Few employers, large or small, especially nowadays, can preserve their work patterns in embalming liquid. According to the 1996 Act, a woman is entitled, as of right, to return to her old job. Great! But what is that job? The Act merely says that it is sufficient for her to be offered employment on 'terms and conditions not less favourable' than before. If not, she can claim reinstatement or compensation for unfair dismissal.

But often an employment contract only defines an employee's job in wide terms. So unless the written job description is very specific, a woman will have to accept a similar job as long as the pay, hours, holidays and other terms are the same. If her job description, for example, is 'secretary' but not secretary to a named person or designated executive (e.g. 'sales manager'), she can insist on being taken back as a secretary on the same 'terms and conditions' as before but not necessarily as secretary to that same person or designated executive.

This can cause problems: for instance, before taking maternity leave a woman was a Grade 13 bookkeeper looking after the accounts of two companies. When she came back from leave, she was offered a post on the same grade but dealing with only one company while her former part-time assistant now dealt full-time with the other. An industrial tribunal rejected her claim that she had, in effect, been unfairly dismissed because she was still a Grade 13 bookkeeper, albeit with reduced responsibilities.

But grading – and even pay – is not everything. When an established C63 clerk in the Building Section of a local public transport authority returned to work as supernumerary C63 clerk in the Traffic Research and Development Section of the same authority, another industrial tribunal ruled that she *had*, in effect, been unfairly dismissed. It was not the same kind of job. She no longer had her own desk, she was no longer getting a full day's work and there was a drop in job security, supernumeraries being more at risk in the event of redundancies.

On the other hand, if others with the same job description receive a pay rise while a woman is away having her baby or their terms of employment improve in some other way, she will automatically be entitled to the same benefits when she returns.

There is, alas, yet one more complication. If it is not 'reasonably practicable' for a woman to return to her exact old job or one with the same 'terms and conditions', an employer can offer her a suitable *alternative* job, which she must accept. But this is not meant to be an easy option. When the manageress of an exclusive shoes outlet in a luxury department store was offered a job as sales assistant in the sports shoe department in the same store on her return to work, she received £3,996 compensation.

The only exception is with small firms employing no more than five people. If it is not 'reasonably practicable' for such a firm to give a woman her old job back or even a suitable alternative, she will have no legal remedy.

How is a woman to make sure of such rights as she has? With the 14 (or soon to be increased to 18) weeks' maternity leave, there is no problem: it is automatic. But the 40-week leave calls for even more paperwork. Once the woman has had her baby, she must finally make up her mind whether she wants to return to work or not. If yes, she must give her employer at least 21 days' written notice of her intended return date. If she has not yet done this within seven weeks of the baby being born, he can write asking whether she still intends to return to work and, if so, she must confirm back to him in writing that she wants to do so. These 'written notices' are all perfectly ordinary letters just stating the essential facts: for instance, 'I intend coming back to work in my old job as secretary to Mr Smith from maternity leave in four weeks' time, on 4 November 2000'. But all these dates that I have given are absolutely vital.

The woman who lost her job – by two days

Back in 1980, a woman working for a telecommunications company expected to have her baby on 2 April. She notified the company in proper time and took her 40-week maternity leave. Unknown to the company, her baby was actually born 18 days late, on 20 April. Twenty-nine weeks from that date expired on 8 November but 29 weeks from her expected birth date expired on 27 October. As the law then stood, an employee had to give seven days' written notice of intention to return, not 21 as now.

But she made a mistake and only gave five days' notice on 22 October to return on the 27th. That was two days too few.

The company took advantage of those vital two days and rejected her right to return at all – and the Appeal Court ruled, with considerable reluctance, that they could legally do so. She had given inadequate notice and it was irrelevant that she would have had sufficient time to give the full seven days' notice, if she had wanted to return on the last day she was entitled to, 8th November. She had chosen the earlier date and her notice was two days short: that was all there was to it.

The principle of this stern ruling still stands. It is unfortunate that, with all the subsequent changes in the law made by Parliament in the intervening years, no attempt has been made to comply with these notice requirements to render less devastating failure. They are a snare for the unwary. Regulations to be made under the latest (1999) Act may ease the situation but I would not count too much on it.

ONE FINAL THOUGHT: WHAT ABOUT PATERNITY LEAVE?

From 1982 until 1999 the EOC called without success for at least five days' statutory paternity leave for working men when their wife or partner had a baby. Private schemes are on the increase, including such market leaders as Tesco, Gateway, Marks & Spencer, Littlewoods, Nissan and Ford, not to mention British Rail, Rowntree, United Biscuits, the BBC and Cable and Wireless. But until the 1999 Employment Relations Act comes into effect, Britain remains one of the few European states that has no such state system. Of course, without any formal scheme, many businesses will allow a man a few days off when his wife or partner has a baby. It all depends on how reasonable everyone is.

However, soon 'reasonableness' may not be enough on its own. When fully implemented, the 1999 Act will give thirteen weeks' parental leave to both mothers and fathers – but it will be unpaid. The Maternal and

Parental Leave, etc. Regulations, which we have already met on page 145, contain detailed provisions which will take time to work out in practice, and which I will deal with in the next edition.

Notes

1 Increased under the 1999 Maternity and Parental Leave, etc. Regulations to 18 weeks where the expected week of childbirth falls on or after 30 April 2000. These regulations made as recently as December 1999, have also made some minor changes to the printed text on maternity leave.

2 Maternity Alliance has calculated that 20 per cent of all pregnant working women are excluded from SMP by this National Insurance threshold requirement. In effect, the lowest-paid women, who most need it, are denied the benefit of the scheme.

13

REDUNDANCY AND
UNFAIR DISMISSAL

Losing your job is like a kick in the stomach. The pain is great and the trauma does not easily go away. In recent years too many people in the nation's workforce have been experiencing this particularly unpleasant body blow. It is bad enough for anyone, whatever their individual circumstances, but at least those at shop-floor level may be feather-bedded to some extent by their trade union and the legal obligation upon employers whenever possible to consult with labour and keep it well informed of large-scale sacking.

But for the executive at middle-management level and above, losing your job at the stage when it looks as if you're really starting to go places or perhaps have at last arrived can have a decidedly cruel edge to it. For a middle manager in middle age, finding an equivalent job may prove virtually impossible or, at least, extremely difficult. His whole lifestyle, and that of his family, may be destroyed overnight.

Some are lucky enough to have contracts that give them reasonable severance pay or even the proverbial 'golden handshake' of a large tax-free (up to the first £30,000) farewell gift. But if you are not one of those fortunates, what are your basic legal rights? The answer is, in general, much the same as with most of our modern employment law. Some protection from the chill blasts of economic reality is provided, there is a basic legal framework of remedies – but in many respects the law is unnecessarily complicated (as if grudgingly handed down by a reluctant Parliament successfully lobbied by big business interests, irrespective of which political party is actually in power) with the sums allowed by way of compensation sometimes grossly inadequate.

It is truly a legal minefield. The aim of this chapter is to provide a portable mine detector, helping to guide you along a perilous path.

There are two main aspects of the problem: redundancy, which can hit large numbers of people at the same time, and unfair dismissal, which more often occurs on an individual basis.

REDUNDANCY

No sector of the business community is immune. Banks, supermarket chains, financial houses and computer firms are just four new areas that have recently joined the more traditional victims such as the construction industry, car manufacture, shipbuilding, coalmining and aerospace, where redundancy has long been an occupational hazard.

Employment contracts and house agreements may themselves provide for redundancy. But the 1996 Employment Rights Act (again, I shall refer to it subsequently in this chapter simply as 'the 1996 Act') lays down the general rule that someone who has worked continuously for the same employer, whether part-time or full-time, for at least two years can claim statutory compensation if made redundant.

But what is the legal definition of 'redundancy'?

Apart from stipulating that there must be a written redundancy notice, the 1996 Act gives no definition of this deceptively simple word. Section 139 merely trots out this boring mumbo-jumbo:

> An employee shall be taken to be dismissed by reason of redundancy if the dismissal is attributable wholly or mainly to:
>
> (a) the fact that his employer has ceased, or intends to cease, to carry on the business for which the employee was employed by him or has ceased, or intends to cease, to carry on that business in the place where the employee was so employed, or
>
> (b) the fact that the requirements of that business for employees to carry out work of a particular kind, or for employees to carry out work of a

particular kind in the place where he was so employed, have ceased or diminished or are expected to cease or diminish.

The verbiage is appalling but the principle is reasonably clear: you are entitled to redundancy pay if, through no fault of your own, your job ceases to exist or changes so fundamentally that it is no longer your job as you have known it. In practice, this arises in four different types of situation:

All or part of your employer's business closes down   If one factory in a group shuts down, the employees become redundant if not given suitable alternative employment elsewhere in the group.

The business is moved   But if a contract contains a 'job mobility clause' saying you will work wherever required, you will not be redundant at one workplace if asked to move to another.

The business is sold or taken over   Here the European Community complicates the issue immensely. On top of the 1966 (and 1997!) Acts, back in 1981 the Thatcher Government had to enact the Transfer of Undertakings (Protection of Employment) Regulations because it was based on a European Community directive to which they were committed. As Gwyneth Pitt, Senior Law Lecturer at Leeds University, has commented: 'Unfortunately no one bothered to ensure that the Regulations made sense in the context of existing redundancy law. The result is two overlapping sets of provisions whose operation may be inconsistent.' Surprise, surprise.

You will need to seek skilled help in any particular instance but, as a general rule, there is a difference between where a business is transferred as a going concern (complete with stock, goodwill, existing contracts and customer contacts) and where only the assets are sold and the business does not continue as a going concern. In the first case, there is no redundancy as the contracts of the workforce pass to the new owners along with all the other existing contracts *but* if anyone is dismissed *solely* because of the transfer, they may be able to claim compensation for unfair dismissal.

Yet if only the assets are sold, regardless of any possible unfair dismissal situation, there usually is a redundancy and the normal rules apply.

Your work is reduced   No business can stand still if it hopes to survive in these competitive times. Reorganisation, rationalisation and new working methods can all lead to a reduction in the number of staff required or in the need for the particular work done by any specific employee. This will all too often mean that people will be sacked. As we shall see in a minute, they may well have a good claim for unfair dismissal but have they been made redundant? Not necessarily. Reorganisation and all the rest only create a legal redundancy if the actual amount of work to be done by any particular employee is reduced. Merely changing the hours of work is not sufficient.

The two women police clerks

In 1973, two women police clerks in Nottinghamshire worked a five-day week, from 9.30 to 5.30 each day. Then the local police authority asked them to work two daily split-shifts, six days a week, in alternate weeks. They claimed redundancy but Lord Denning ruled sternly: 'The change in the hours of work was not due to redundancy but to a reorganisation in the interests of efficiency. The same work was done by the ladies afterwards as before. But they did it at different hours.'

There are four other matters that have to be considered:

You are laid off or put on short time   This does not often happen at middle-management level but it may still be useful to know that if an employee has been laid off (i.e. told not to come to work and not been paid) or put on short-time working (i.e. been paid for only half a week's work or less), she may, in effect, declare herself redundant in writing to her boss and therefore become entitled to redundancy pay. Sections 147 and 148 of the 1996 Act are, of course, devilishly complicated and you should really seek skilled advice before committing yourself.

Time off to look for a job   Once you have been served with a redundancy notice, Sections 52 and 53 of the 1996 Act say that your employer must give you 'reasonable' time off during paid working hours 'to look for new employment or to make arrangements for training for future employment'. How much time is 'reasonable'? It all depends on the circumstances: your needs have to be balanced against your employer's business demands. Technically, you can complain to an employment tribunal if you think he is being unreasonable but the most a tribunal can do is order him to pay you an extra two days' wages!

Voluntary redundancy   It has become very common for employers to ask for voluntary redundancies to try and cut down the number of compulsory sackings, and it generally poses no legal difficulties. Even with enhanced severance payments, voluntary redundancy still counts as a dismissal as the employee is taken to have volunteered to be dismissed – which is still not the same as volunteering to resign. But be careful about early retirement! That does not count as redundancy and you should ensure that the deal includes full recompense for giving up your job, for that is all you are going to get: in 1985, when a lecturer accepted an early retirement scheme from a university forced to make staff cuts, the Appeal Court ruled that he could not later also claim redundancy pay.

How much is redundancy pay?

Redundancy pay has two positive advantages: (1) it is usually tax-free and (2) it does not matter if you start another job the very next day, you are still entitled to your full money. *But* it is not calculated on a very generous basis. It depends on how old you are when sacked, your gross wages at that time (calculated on a weekly basis, even if you are paid monthly) and how long you have worked for the firm. Full details are readily available in the free Department of Trade and Industry booklet *Redundancy Payments* (PL 808 (REV 5)), one of a range of useful employment law pamphlets obtainable at local job centres. However, although they are excellent, I strongly advise anyone worried about exactly how much they are entitled to in their own specific circumstances, to telephone the DTI's Redundancy Helpline on 0500–848489, open Monday–Friday, 9 a.m. to 5 p.m. It offers a valuable free service on all redundancy problems.

In principle, if you are between 41 and 65, you should get 1.5 weeks' pay for each year of work, one week for each year if 22 to 41 and half a week's money if you are between 18 and 22. Service below the age of 18 does not count, although many people start work at 16, and, if you are made redundant after 64 (whether man or woman), you lose one-twelfth of the payment for every additional month up to your 65th birthday. So if you are sacked, say, when aged 64 years and 9 months, you will not lose three-quarters of your *total* redundancy pay (that would be ridiculous, even though some books state this!) but, as I have specifically checked with the Department of Employment, you will lose three-quarters of the compensation due *for that last year*.

But please note two other important restrictions, for which no one has been able to give me a satisfactory explanation: (1) you cannot claim redundancy pay for more than 20 years, even if you have worked for the same firm for much longer, and (2) any weekly wage over £220 is disregarded, even if you have earned considerably more. The maximum redundancy pay possible, even if you have worked the full 20 years, is $20 \times 1.5 \times £220 = £6,600$. And that is whatever the individual circumstances or however much you have, in fact, earned over the years.

An example of how the system works

A youth joins an engineering firm straight from school at 16. He works his way up the ladder until 22 years later at the age of 38 he is earning £500 a week as senior projects manager. He is then sacked as redundant. Although he has worked for the same firm for 22 years, he can only claim compensation for 20 years – i.e. since he was 18. According to the official sliding scale, he should then be entitled to 20 weeks' wages as redundancy pay. But this will not be calculated at the rate of 20 × £500, his actual wage, which would total £8,250, but only at the rate of 16.5 × £220, which, as we have seen, totals less than half that amount: i.e. £6,600.

It is usually the employer, not the state, who pays: most employers used to be able to reclaim half the amount from a state Redundancy Fund but this rebate system was whittled down to firms with fewer than ten workers getting back 35 per cent of the money until that too was abolished by the Thatcher Government in 1989.

When can you expect your money? Undoubtedly, many firms hand it over without question but the 1996 Employments Rights Act states that you should receive your pay on your last day of work. An employer can stagger payment, provided it all comes in 'within a reasonable time'. What is 'reasonable' depends on all the facts. But if you threaten to go to your local employment tribunal for a ruling, you may find that speeds up payment!

Payment must come with a written statement of how it is made up. If not, an employer commits an offence carrying a £200 fine. Citing Section 165 of the 1996 Act to a reluctant employer may make her supply this vital document.

If seriously worried about non-payment, you can either write within six months to the firm demanding your money or take them to an employment tribunal. You should fill in form IT1, available at all job centres, and send it to the Secretary to the Tribunals, Central Office of Employment Tribunals (England and Wales) at 19–29, Woburn Place, London WC1H 0LU (Tel: 020 7273 8666) if you live in England or Wales, or to the Secretary of Tribunals at Eagle Building, 215 Bothwell Street, Glasgow G1 2RY (Tel: 0141–204 0730) if you live in Scotland. They will then allocate your case to a local tribunal.

There is also another way. Once you have asked your employer and a reasonable time has gone by without payment (perhaps because she has gone bust), Section 166 of the 1996 Act says you can write direct to the Department of Employment at Sanctuary Buildings, Great Smith Street, London SW1P 3BT. The Department will then pay you out of public funds, taking their chance on getting back the money, or some of it, from your ex-employer – or her remaining assets.

Who cannot claim redundancy pay?

Apart from those who have worked for the same firm for at least two years since they were 18 or who work less than eight hours a week, certain types of employee are specifically exempted from the state scheme:

(a) If you normally work outside Great Britain or are self-employed, a partner in a firm, a share fisherman, a merchant seaman, a Crown or public servant, a policeman, a member of the armed forces or a domestic servant working for a close relative (except a spouse);

(b) If you are 65 or older unless there is an earlier 'normal retiring age' in your job in which case that age applies;

(c) If you are on a fixed-term contract of two years or more and you have specifically waived your right to a redundancy payment in writing. But all other people employed on a fixed-term contract are covered if they have, in fact, worked for at least two years before the contract is not renewed. And it does not matter that you thought the contract might not be renewed when you first started the job.

The lecturer who won his case

An ex-teacher was given a one-year contract as a lecturer in a teacher training college run by Nottinghamshire County Council. He realised that, because of Council policy, there would be a diminishing need for lecturers. In fact, his contract was renewed for a further year but at the end of that time he was told to go. The Appeal Court ruled that he was still entitled to redundancy pay.

(d) If – and this is *very* complicated! – you unreasonably refuse suitable alternative employment offered by your employer to follow on within four weeks of your old job ending or, having accepted a four-week trial period in the new job, you then unreasonably refuse to carry on with it, you will lose your rights to redundancy pay. But your employer or 'an associated employer' (e.g. another company in the same group) must offer you the new job: it is not enough for them to find an outsider prepared to take you on.

Furthermore, the standard of what is 'suitable' alternative employment is set by you, the employee, not your employer:

The school cleaners' case

Gloucester County Council unilaterally reduced its school cleaners' working hours. It offered them alternative employment at higher pay but for fewer hours. Two cleaners thought they could not get through their work to a satisfactory standard in that time and claimed they had been made redundant. An employment tribunal said they had acted reasonably but, on appeal, the EAT ruled that it was not for the cleaners to set a satisfactory standard but their employers. The Appeal Court then overruled the EAT and upheld the claim.

But the offer of the new job must specify the material facts: remuneration, status, job description and the like. It cannot just be airy-fairy. You are entitled to be told exactly what you are being offered.

Yet, even if you are not in an exempt category, merely because you have been made redundant does not necessarily mean you are entitled to redundancy pay. You must also prove that you were *dismissed* because of that redundancy. This may seem simple but it does not always work out like that.

DISMISSAL

Whatever you do, do not 'dismiss' yourself. Hang in there, if at all possible. As far back as 1967, in the early days of the state redundancy scheme begun only two years earlier by the first Wilson Labour Government, Lord Parker, then Lord Chief Justice, ruled that a foreman in a fabric company who, having been told he would 'shortly' be made redundant, found himself another job and handed in his notice, had effectively dismissed himself and was not entitled to redundancy pay. Lord Parker ruled that for a notice of impending redundancy to rank as 'dismissal' it must give a date of termination of the employment – or at least state facts from which that date can fairly be inferred. Simply to warn that redundancy is on the way is not dismissal.

But even if an employer specifies a date, that does not mean you can safely leave before that date and still qualify for redundancy pay. When an engineer faced with a three months' redundancy notice, resigned rather than working out his notice – seldom an easy thing to do – he was ruled to have dismissed himself and not be eligible for redundancy pay.

So the moral is clear: do not jump the gun. Unless you really can find another job with sufficient salary and perquisites not to worry about redundancy pay, wait until you are unequivocally 'dismissed' and your employment is finally at an end. The 1966 Act says that you *can* give written notice that you are opting to leave early; but the procedure is complicated and your boss can serve a written counter-notice demanding that you work out your time and your redundancy pay may be reduced.

However, this is not to say that you cannot be 'constructively' dismissed. If your position has really been made impossible so that you cannot do your work properly and you are made forcefully aware of the fact that the company is trying to 'squeeze you out', you do not have to wait until you feel your ribs are actually cracking beneath the pressure before you write (keeping a copy of the letter) to your immediate superior setting out the behaviour of which you complain and saying that it has been made impossible for you to continue with your duties. You should use some such phrase as: 'I consider, in the circumstances, that the firm has constructively dismissed me.' On no account should you write: 'I, therefore, resign.' That may only confuse matters.

You are then free to pursue a claim for breach of contract, redundancy or unfair dismissal, depending on the circumstances.

These cases are often difficult to argue on behalf of a claimant – but it can be done: as in a merger where an executive had worked for taxi operators for over 30 years, rising to general manager. Then they were taken over by a larger concern and, as often happens, his face no longer fitted. The company told him that he would keep his salary but would no longer be general manager or authorised to sign cheques – and would eventually be put in charge of a workshop at new premises.

He left, claiming that they had forced him out. Of course, they retorted that he was too sensitive and had sacked himself. But they had to pay out. If after a take-over or merger the new regime offers a senior employee an alternative post with a significant loss of status, that can amount to a repudiation of his contract of employment entitling him to claim 'constructive dismissal'.

It does not matter that the salary is unchanged. The law accepts that conscientious staff do not work for bread alone. As Lord Griffiths said: 'A change of status may be a change of such a nature as to show repudiation of the contract.'

So far we have only been talking about *pure* redundancy and the maximum £6,600 compensation payable for it. But if you have not merely been dismissed for redundancy but *unfairly* selected for that dismissal, you will qualify for the much greater compensation payable in cases of unfair dismissal: i.e. a maximum £50,000 compensatory award[1] as well as a basic £6,150 award.

In fact, the average awards made by employment tribunals for redundancy and unfair dismissal come nowhere near these maximum amounts but the average for unfair dismissal is still much more than for 'pure' redundancy. Even so, you will not get two lots of compensation: your redundancy pay will be swallowed up in the greater unfair dismissal award. Yet it is usually worthwhile, when filling up form IT1 and making your application, to put that you are claiming for 'unfair dismissal or redundancy or both' – leaving the employment tribunal that eventually hears your case to decide what is the most appropriate award in your circumstances.

There is one other important difference between 'pure' redundancy and unfair dismissal, whether for redundancy or for any other cause, and this relates to *time limits*. As we have seen, you have six months in which to make a redundancy claim, but with unfair dismissal, you only have half that time. This three-month rule is strictly applied and will be extended only in exceptional cases when a tribunal considers it was 'not reasonably practicable' for you to have applied earlier. This usually arises because you received bad or inaccurate advice or because your application was mislaid in the post. If bad advice is the cause, the legal position depends on who gave you the advice: if it came from your own lawyer or other outside person, such as a citizens' advice bureau worker or a trade union official, you will be stuck with it and unable to pursue your claim (although you may be able to sue the person responsible for negligence) but, if it came from a clerk or someone else on the tribunal's own staff, the delay will be overlooked and your claim allowed to continue.

As for claims sent by post, the High Court has ruled that, as a general legal rule, when documents are sent by first-class post, they are expected to arrive by the second working day after posting but, with second-class post, it is the fourth working day. Yet with unfair dismissal claims you can never be too careful, as this EAT decision shows:

The claim that took too long in the post

A woman shop assistant was dismissed on 5 February 1992. Her solicitor sent her claim to the Secretary of Tribunals at the Central Office on 25 March. On 27 July of that year, enquiries revealed that the application had not been received and the solicitor re-submitted it on 4 August. An employment tribunal later ruled that, because that first application had been lost in the post, it had not been 'reasonably practicable' for the woman to have submitted her claim in time: i.e. by late April, within three months of 5 February. But the employers appealed – and won their case.

The EAT ruled that the tribunal had erred in accepting that there was a presumption that a posted letter (whether first or second class) would be delivered in time or at all, without expressly considering whether reliance on that presumption was reasonable in the particular circumstances. In the present case, it would have been reasonable for the solicitor, not having heard anything from the authorities for some time, to have checked long before 27

July whether the first application had arrived. (The law report does not state whether the woman then sued her solicitor for negligence but the ruling stands as a stern warning to us all not to trust blindly to the post.)

So, what is unfair dismissal?

There is no easy definition. As a past President of the Employment Appeal Tribunal has said, 'Unfair dismissal is in no sense a common-place expression capable of being understood by the man in the street . . . In fact, it is narrowly and, to some extent, arbitrarily, defined.' An employer who has sacked a grievously incompetent or even dishonest employee may find himself paying unfair dismissal compensation because he acted too quickly or because of a technical failure in his dismissal procedure while an honest, decent employee may be deprived of remedy because, through no fault of his own, he did not make his claim within three months or because he was too quick to give up his job under adverse pressure.

Justice is by no means guaranteed. As Judge Timothy Lawrence, when President of Employment Tribunals for England and Wales, admitted to *The Times*: 'The system has become increasingly legalistic.' Perhaps that was only to be expected: for the whole concept of unfair dismissal and the legal infrastructure for dealing with it was brought in hurriedly by the new Tory Administration of Edward Heath in its 1971 Industrial Relations Act to try and steal some of the clothes of the previous Labour Government's legal pro-worker policy and was then re-enacted by the next Labour Government in its own 1978 Employment Protection (Consolidation) Act without any concerted attempt to iron out many of the wrinkles that had by then already appeared. Tony Blair's subsequent Labour Government has erased some of the wrinkles but created new ones of its own. That is often the way major pieces of social legislation are cobbled together in this wonderful country of ours.

In principle, the current legal position is that, if you have worked for the same employer for at least one year and can prove to an employment tribunal that you have been 'dismissed' – and this means the same as with redundancy (including the advisability of not resigning but obstinately remaining until you can claim 'constructive dismissal') – the employer must then satisfy the tribunal that you were not dismissed 'unfairly'. If you have been dismissed because of your membership of a trade union or refusal to join a trade union that counts as *automatically* unfair but, in most other cases, an employer must prove that she had a 'fair' reason for dismissing you, which the 1996 Act defines as a reason relating to one of these five categories:

redundancy;

your capability;

your conduct;

a statutory restriction on your doing your job (e.g. a long distance lorry driver who is banned from driving for a year); or

'some other substantial reason'.

But that is not all. An employment tribunal must also be satisfied that your employer acted 'reasonably' in deciding to sack you *for that reason*. If he gets his reason wrong, he is in trouble. Furthermore, a sacked employee should always put his ex-boss on the spot by availing himself of his right, under Section 92 of the 1996 Act, to ask – preferably in writing – for a written statement of the reason for his dismissal. For his or her part, an employer should never treat such a request lightly, although too often they do. In fact, they should at once seek skilled legal advice, if they have not already done so, because the reason that is given in the statement will tie ones hands for ever after.

This imperative need for an employer to act 'reasonably', even when he or she has a fair reason for sacking someone, has proved the bugbear of the system, so far as many employers are concerned. For example, if an employee of mine ever told me to 'Fuck off!' I would sack him on the spot, whatever the circumstances. I just would not tolerate that sort of behaviour from anyone – let alone someone whose wages I paid. But I have to tell you that I am *not* a 'modern' employer. If that person had worked for me for at least one year, a tribunal would probably order me to pay him compensation for unfair dismissal.

For several EAT decisions have laid down that, when an employee uses bad language to his superior, he should not be sacked on the spot. Instead the employer must be 'reasonable' and ask such questions as: Who was the person insulted? How senior was his status? Had such an incident occurred before? Was the employee given a chance to explain and apologise? Was he given a formal warning that repetition would lead to dismissal?

As Lord Bridge said in the House of Lords in 1988, when giving general guidance to employers: 'In the case of misconduct, the employer will normally not act reasonably unless he investigates the complaint of misconduct fully and fairly and hears whatever the employee wishes to say in his defence or in explanation.'

What then does this much overused word 'reasonable', so beloved of lawyers, mean in the context of modern employment relations? Section 98 (4) of the 1996 Act tried to spell it out but only succeeded in getting lost in its own well-intentioned verbiage. It says that reasonableness

(a) depends on whether in the circumstances (including the size and administrative resources of the employer's undertaking) the employer acted reasonably or unreasonably in treating it as a sufficient reason for dismissing the employee, and (b) shall be determined in accordance with equity and the substantial merits of the case.

Originally employers had to prove positively that they had satisfied this test but in its 1980 Employment Act the Thatcher Government tried to ease their burden by saying that the onus of proof with regard to reasonableness is neutral. This means that neither side has to prove its case one way or the other. Tribunals are left to form their own conclusions on the evidence, and this is still the law under the 1996 Act, but they still tend to be far more gentle than many an old-fashioned type of employer.

In practice, nowadays the reasonableness test usually means that an employer must not have acted precipitately. She must, as we have seen, have consulted beforehand where appropriate with her employee before sacking him or effectively warned him that he must improve his performance and that time is running out or have followed a fair disciplinary procedure. She must also, except in the case of summary dismissal for gross misconduct,[2] usually give two clear warnings in advance (the first can be merely oral) before dismissing. As Mr Justice (now Lord) Browne Wilkinson said, when EAT President, in 1983:

> In many, though not all, cases there is a band of reasonable responses to the employee's conduct within which one employer might reasonably take one view, another quite reasonably take another. The function of the industrial tribunal, as an industrial jury, is to determine whether in the particular circumstances of each case, the decision to dismiss fell within the band of reasonable responses which a reasonable employer might have adopted. If the dismissal falls within that band, the dismissal is fair: if it falls outside the band, it is unfair.

Even if an employment tribunal rules that an employer has 'reasonably' used a 'fair reason' for dismissal, that is still not an end of the matter. The employee will only get full compensation if the tribunal is satisfied that he has not been guilty of what is called in lawyers' jargon 'contributory fault'. For Section 123 (6) of the 1996 Act states: 'Where the tribunal finds that the dismissal was to any extent caused or contributed to by any action of the complainant, it shall reduce the amount of the compensatory award by such proportion as it considers just and equitable having regard to that finding.'

It is legally possible for a 'successful' applicant's award to be cut by 100 per cent because of his contributory fault; but tribunals are rarely so bold. Usually reductions of at the most a half or a third are made, as when a waiter at a north London restaurant who was 'frequently insubordinate' to the restaurant's woman owner and literally threw coins at customers who left inadequate tips won his case for unfair dismissal because the owner had not followed correct disciplinary procedures but had his award cut by a third. She still had to pay out £900 to an employee who, as she told the tribunal, 'stole money from customers and was rude and abusive to everyone'.

For the sake of completeness, I should add that compensation is not the only available remedy for unfair dismissal. A tribunal can order that you be given your old job back on the same terms ('reinstatement') or be re-employed but in a different job and on different terms ('re-engagement'). But these are alternatives to compensation: you cannot both be given a cash award *and* reinstatement or re-engagement. In fact, they are very rarely ordered: there is generally too much bad feeling or tension in the workplace to make either a practical possibility.

So how does it all work out in practice? We need to look, in turn, at the five 'fair reasons' for dismissal laid down by the 1996 Act:

Redundancy   In this context, this word has an extra edge. It is not enough for you merely to be redundant. Your employer must also prove that she was fair in her selection of employees to be sacked. Selection criteria must be vigorously adhered to. A simple policy of 'Last in, first out' is not always enough. There must be a comparative, objective analysis of all the relevant information before a decision is made.

An employer must also, as a general rule, consult with her workforce and consider whether other options are available, such as redeployment elsewhere within the organisation. Failure to do so will usually make the dismissal unfair. Many experts are of the view that lack of consultation is the single greatest source of trouble in this area.

Where 20 or more employees are concerned, there is a set timetable. An employer should consult with employees' representatives or recognised trade union representation at least 30 days before redundancies are proposed to take effect. With 100 or more employees, the period is 90 days.

In highly exceptional circumstances where no amount of consultation would have altered the final result, redundancies may still be fair even without prior full consultation. The EAT has, for instance, ruled that it was fair when a foreman painter was dismissed as redundant after 18 years' service when his employers had not even thought about consultation. The objective reality was that they had waited until the last possible moment and only sacked him when, owing to the recession, no further work came in.

Because bigger companies often cannot afford to leak information about redundancies in advance, they sometimes ignore the need for consultation and dismiss without prior warning. No doubt, very understandable. But consultation still remains the norm. Non-consultation will only be upheld by an employment tribunal if it considers that the employer could reasonably have concluded, in the light of the situation as then known, that consultation would have been 'futile' or 'would serve no useful purpose', to quote two law lords in a 1988 case.

Recently, a university research assistant whose fixed-term contracts had been renewed for nearly seven years was told that his last contract would not be renewed because he was redundant. There was no consultation and he claimed unfair dismissal. The local tribunal dismissed his complaint. But the EAT said that non-consultation and not taking reasonable steps to find him alternative employment meant the university had acted unreasonably, and sent the case back to another tribunal for a rehearing.

As Lord Bridge ruled back in 1987: 'An employer will normally not act reasonably unless he warns and consults any employee affected.' That is without doubt the usual rule, and Lord Bridge's statement deserves to be better known.

Your Capability   You may be doing your very best but you are still not up to the demands of the job in these highly pressured times: what then? If your employer sacks you 364 days after you started with him, you will only be entitled to the notice payment provided in your contract of employment but, if you have clocked up the full year, you may well be able to claim compensation for unfair dismissal. This comes fully within the 'reasonableness' yardstick: an employer will generally be expected to do all he can to help employees. They should be given a chance to improve their performance and receive proper encouragement and training from management. They should also usually be sent at least one letter (of which an employer should, of course, keep a copy) clearly warning that they will lose their job if they do not improve their performance.

How long should they be given? It all depends on the individual circumstances. In one case, three months was held to be enough for a sales director who had been employed for two years; in another case, six months was appropriate for a works director who had been six years in the job. But five weeks have been held insufficient for another works director with six years' service.

Particularly difficult, and sad, cases arise when sickness or ill health prevents someone doing their job well – or even at all. Of course, if the individual employment contract or a union house agreement specifies in detail what is to happen if illness strikes, everyone knows where they stand. Otherwise, there simply is no hard and fast rule as to when management are entitled to say: 'Enough is enough.'

The legal principle evolved by the courts ever since a pioneering decision of Sir John (later Lord) Donaldson, when sitting as President of the Industrial Relations Court in 1972, is that an employer can dismiss staff without fear of a claim for unfair dismissal when things have reached such a stage that the employment contract has been 'frustrated' by events so that, through no fault of either party, the contractual obligation has become impossible or radically different from that foreseen by the contract.

Each case will turn on its own facts. How much longer is the employee expected to be away from his normal duties? How long has he already been off duty? What do his medical reports say? Can any suitable alternative job be found? If so, has it been offered and what was his reaction? and so on. You can really use your own common sense to find the answer.

Unfortunately everyone, including EAT judges and employment tribunal chairmen, can have their own different ideas of what is common sense. For instance, in 1977 Mr Justice Phillips, then EAT President in London and a kindly, wise man whom I remember well, said in a case where there was no prior discussion with an ailing borough surveyor before he was sacked: 'The employee has to be consulted and the matter discussed with him ... One thing is certain. If the employee is not consulted, an injustice may be done.' But three years later the EAT in Edinburgh ruled that where a barman at a Shetland camp for North Sea oil riggers who had been ill with asthma for six months was told by telephone that both his own doctor and the firm's medical officer agreed that he was medically unfit to continue and this was followed up by a letter sacking him, that was *not* unfair dismissal. The President of the Scottish EAT ruled that, since it had been overwhelmingly proved that the barman had become medically unable to do his job, no consultation was necessary. 'The purpose of consultation is to establish the facts of the case, and if it is clear that purpose cannot be achieved, the need for a consultation diminishes or disappears.'

The fact is that neither party can demand anything. It is all a question of balance and of fairness to be worked out on the basis of the specific situation. Indeed, comparatively few disputes ever get as far as an employment tribunal for the very reason that the general principles of law are so well settled. Sometimes an executive will feel the need to consult his solicitor and bring them into the negotiations: indeed, I know of one such recent case within a well-known central London firm of solicitors. But usually the parties work things out satisfactorily for themselves.

Your conduct   This can range from insisting on keeping your office door closed, persistently coming back late or drunk from lunch, wearing clothes (or a hair-style) to work that the boss considers inappropriate and an unhelpful reluctance to work occasional overtime right through to downright dishonesty, bad language, violence or flagrant disobedience to orders. The basic yardstick in all these cases is whether the conduct complained of adversely and unreasonably affects life at work and the efficiency of the work unit.

Fine lines are drawn. In one case, a married chargehand and a young female worker were often seen fondling each other in their workshop and in the factory canteen. Gossip spread, they were both sacked – and a Bedford tribunal rejected their claim of unfair dismissal. 'We take the view that this is the kind of misconduct for which there can be no explanation,' said the tribunal chairman. An important factor was that 'other girls were being embarrassed by misconduct on company premises'.

But in another 'love at work' case, a couple had done nothing to provoke the gossip – indeed, they had not even been having an affair. A Birmingham works superintendent had formed a one-sided infatuation with a woman clerk but she had done nothing to encourage him and it was his own secretary who had spread untrue stories about him (one wonders why!). He lost his job and a local tribunal ruled that he had been unfairly dismissed.

Human relations are very important in a work environment. 'A boss's relationship with his personal secretary must be one of complete confidence,' Mr Justice Bristow once said in the EAT. 'They must respect each other. They must treat each other with consideration. I suspect they must like each other.' So when a middle-aged woman secretary walked out on her boss after he had called her a 'bitch on Monday mornings', Bristow ruled that she had been constructively dismissed because their working relationship had been 'shattered' by that one ill-advised, intemperate remark and upheld her £3,756 award. Similarly when, during 'a trivial argument' between a turf accountant's woman cashier and her branch manager, he called her a 'bloody fat sod and a stupid stuck-up bitch' – and he had once before sworn at her in front of customers – she was also held entitled to walk out and claim constructive dismissal.

Can you be told what to wear at work? Do male bank clerks have to wear ties? Can female office workers be sent home if they turn up for work in trousers? Can you be told to 'get your hair cut'?

The efficient running of the work unit is still the main yardstick – but now there is another dimension: that of freedom and personal choice. A 20-year-old female typist in a Midlands co-operative society office was rebuked by her boss for wearing trousers to work. To avoid trouble, she wore a skirt thereafter – until she had to go to a college training scheme in the afternoon and wore trousers to the office in the morning. Result: she was handed a letter saying she was 'redundant'. But she was awarded compensation for unfair dismissal; the local tribunal's chairman saying that her departmental head had 'antiquated ideas on dress'. Similarly, a Suffolk tribunal ruled that a local engineering firm's 60-year tradition of 'neatness, tidiness and smartness' was not broken by a 32-year-old fitter's refusal to obey his managing director's ultimatum to shave off his beard or be sacked.

And a computer engineering firm in Slough, Berkshire has been ordered to pay £4,351 to a 36-year-old engineer who had lost his £32,000 a year job because he refused to cut his 12-inch long hair. 'I would have tied my hair in a pony tail if it meant keeping my job but the option was not offered me,' he told a central London tribunal. He fought the case himself and afterwards urged others to follow suit: 'There are a lot of closet long-haired people out there just waiting to pop out,' he told a reporter. 'They should stand up and be counted.'

If you are sure of your ground, that is good advice: employment tribunals seldom order unsuccessful redundancy or unfair dismissal applicants to pay their winning ex-employer's legal costs. So, if you genuinely think you have a worthwhile case and have the courage to go it alone, you are at little financial risk – and your ex-employer could well be advised by her solicitor that it is worth her while to offer you a reasonable out-of-court settlement to buy you off. Cynical but true! *Employment Tribunal Procedure* (ITL 1) and *Unfairly Dismissed?* (PL 712 (REV 8) are two excellent free DTI pamphlets available at job centres.

The other side of the coin is that every employer, no matter how small the firm, should, in sheer prudence, have her own set procedures for dealing with these matters: even if it is only something so basic within a very small firm as the boss calling in the person to see her, perhaps offering to let him bring someone with him and then listening patiently to all that he has to say. The Advisory Conciliation and Arbitration Service (ACAS), an independent official body charged with promoting the improvement of employment relations, has issued a Code of Practice for Disciplinary Practice and Procedures in Employment (CP01). In employment relations terms, this is rather like the Highway Code for drivers: it is not illegal to fail to observe the Code but an employer who does so will find herself in trouble when facing a claim for unfair dismissal.

It is, in fact, one of the fundamental documents of modern employment law and all commentators emphasise its importance. The problem is that they usually do not bother to tell you how to obtain a copy, and it took me several phone calls before a helpful ACAS official told me that the Code is available at £2.95 for a single copy (and at lesser rates for bulk orders) at branches of the Stationery Office, whose local address you will find in most phone books. It is also available from ACAS Reader Ltd, PO Box 16, Earl Shilton, Leicester LE9 8ZZ (Tel: 014555–8522252).

The Code is too detailed to go into here but, whether employer or employee, if this problem really affects you, it is well worth investing in a copy.

A statutory restriction on doing your job   The most obvious example is where a chauffeur or long-distance lorry driver is disqualified from driving for a year or more for a serious motoring offence – or for only six months under the 'totting up' procedure for minor offences. But, even with this seemingly straightforward category, reasonableness is all. An employment tribunal would want to know the answer to such questions as: How long is the ban? Could a temporary replacement have been found? Could the banned driver have been offered another job in the meantime? and so on.

'Some other substantial reason'   This is a catch-all provision. The courts have deliberately left vague this phrase in the 1996 and earlier Acts. It means almost whatever you – or rather an employment tribunal – want it to mean but, in practice, it has worked out to favour employers far more than employees. So it has been used to make fair the dismissal of a female employee who had upset her male colleagues by frequently boasting of her sexual exploits with a younger man; an employee in an old people's home whose behaviour, though not deliberately offensive, had upset the elderly residents, and an office worker sacked for refusing to do reasonable voluntary overtime because a tribunal ruled that the needs of the business required that the overtime be worked.

This is also the heading under which sacking because of reorganisation and modernisation have been held fair. As Lord Denning said in 1977 in a case involving a local county secretary employed by the National Farmers' Union, 'It is important that nothing should be done to impair the ability of employers to reorganise their workforce and their terms and conditions of work so as to improve efficiency.' But the overall need for reasonableness remains, and this may sometimes call for prior consultation or the offer of a suitable alternative job – even at a lesser salary. So, for instance, a bed upholsterer working for a firm going through a period of economic difficulty was held not to have been unfairly dismissed when he refused an offer of a new job doing much the same work at a lesser rate – and all the other upholsterers (and their union) had accepted a similar proposal.

The actual framework of the law undoubtedly has its shortcomings and the old idea of an employment tribunal as a sort of jury dispensing informal common-sense justice has long been exposed as a myth. But I would like to end this chapter with these words from a judgment of Mr Justice Bristow back in 1982. It still gives the tone of modern employment law at its best, although I am far from saying that it always reaches this standard:

[The law] is concerned only with the reasonableness of what you do, not how you do it. But very often the way in which you do something affects or may affect the question: 'Was it reasonable for you to do it at all?' If you dismiss a senior employee or one of long standing at a moment's notice with no consultation whatsoever, you are not simply treating him with discourtesy: you are depriving yourself of the opportunity to explore with him the possibility of finding another slot in which to place him and leaving yourself open to the accusation of having acted unreasonably.

Notes

1 This was increased from the previous maximum of £11,000 by the 1999 Employment Rights Act. Employers must have heaved a sigh of relief: before Stephen Byers took over from Peter Mandelson as Trade Secretary, the Government's White Paper *Fairness at Work*, on which the Act was supposed to be based, had proposed no limit whatsoever to this type of award.

2 A 1991 example was where a shop steward deliberately used an unauthorised password to gain access to sensitive information stored in his employer's computer. The EAT ruled that unauthorised use or tampering with computers is an extremely serious industrial offence.

14

SEX DISCRIMINATION AND SEXUAL HARASSMENT

As Julie Mellor, the Chairwoman[1] of the Equal Opportunities Commission (EOC), wrote in its latest Annual Report in June 1999, 'While the position of women and men has changed dramatically since the EOC was set up in 1975, it is hugely frustrating that many of the fundamental barriers to true sex equality remain.'

In fact, the 1975 Sex Discrimination Act covers all forms of discrimination on the grounds of sex but claims over discrimination in the workplace are the most likely to succeed. Not only is there no qualifying period of employment; you can claim simply because you have *not* been employed. Uniquely in English law, a successful claimant can receive an award for 'injury to feelings'. Whereas in all other employment cases there is no compensation for 'injury to feelings' but merely a hard-nosed assessment of what the employer's unlawful behaviour has cost you in material terms, in discrimination 'injury to feelings' is a factor in every case.

This somewhat vague legal concept has proved extremely popular with claimants but not with many employers. The judges are not too keen on it either. As Mr Justice Morison has said, 'It is not automatically to be made whenever unlawful discrimination is proved or admitted.'

However, there is no limit to the total amount of compensation payable. It used to be capped, whatever the circumstances, at £11,000. But in August 1993, in a case brought (with EOC help) by a 62-year-old woman dietician in a Southampton hospital forcibly retired three years earlier than her male colleagues, the European Court of Justice at Luxembourg ruled that a financial limit on sex discrimination claims by public employees was contrary to European Community law. Ministers could have responded by merely removing the ceiling for public employees but, as a junior Employment Minister said: 'The Government believes that all types of unlawful discrimination should be liable to the same penalties.'

So the law was changed to remove all limits on claims for sex and race discrimination in both the public and private sector. Since then awards of several tens of thousands of pounds have become not infrequent. It can often be a profitable business being discriminated against at work.

'We don't want to see businesses going under because of sex discrimination cases,' an EOC lawyer told the press after an award of over £24,000 in March 1994. 'We want them to be taking it seriously in the first place and making sure that it doesn't happen. But, if they are going to discriminate, they now know that they will lose not just a good worker but they can lose £24,000 as well.'

Another point of view was expressed by a spokesman for the Institute of Directors, who said that such awards could put small firms out of business.

The essential – and laudable – principle of the 1975 Sex Discrimination Act, passed during the third Labour Government of Harold Wilson, is that no employee is to be treated at work in a different way from any other employee on account of their sex.

Except when sex is 'a genuine occupational qualification for the job' (such as when a man is wanted by a department store to play Father Christmas during the Christmas season), this applies throughout the whole range of employment activities. The Act applies to recruitment procedures, pay differentials, promotion or transfer prospects, holidays and time-off allowances: everything. It even applies to social engagements involved with one's work: I can point to no specific tribunal decision to prove my point but it is quite clear, on the basis of case law as it has evolved, that it is unlawful sex discrimination for an out-of-date employer to perpetuate the unpleasant practice of not allowing female staff to bring their husbands or boyfriends to the firm's Christmas party – so long as the same embargo is not also put on male staff's wives or girlfriends.[2]

It is clearly in most cases unlawful sex discrimination to differentiate between married and single staff in terms, for instance, of promotion and transfer prospects, unless the same restrictions apply to staff of both sexes.

Job advertisements must also not be 'discriminatory'. The 1975 Act says: 'Use of a job description with a sexual connotation (such as waiter, salesgirl, postman or stewardess) shall be taken to indicate an intention to discriminate, unless the advertisement contains an indication to the contrary.' That is why you see newspaper advertisements for male or female ground hostesses, male or female chambermaids, waiters/resses, male or female night porters, and the like. Adverts with job descriptions that are sexless or use the bland unisex word 'person' abound: there was once an advert in the London *Evening Standard* for a 'Person Friday'. Robinson Crusoe would have turned in his grave! Employers sometimes have to resort to subterfuges to get what they want: if school governors want to advertise for a male sports teacher, they might get away with saying 'rugger essential'.

Until very recent years, the whole thrust of the EOC's endeavours to encourage compliance with the Act was to protect women from sex discrimination at work. Men hardly came into it. But the nation's recurring economic slow-downs have changed all that. A 'significant number' of complaints received by the EOC are from men claiming to have been unfairly turned down for jobs in favour of women. One successful claimant, helped by the EOC, told a reporter: 'There's no reason why clerical work should be regarded as women's work. But I think executives like to be surrounded by attractive young girls.'

And it is not only clerical staff. A retired admiral and former surgeon-general to the armed forces has withdrawn his claim of sex discrimination against the Health Department and a local healthcare authority after a woman, who he claimed had no previous medical experience, was preferred to him as chairman of a local county healthcare trust. There was no formal admission of liability but he accepted an undisclosed amount in compensation, and the Health Department said it would review guidelines that called for more women to lead such trusts.

There are two specific aspects of the problem that we should look at:

EQUAL PAY

Despite significant advances, this has proved a bitter disappointment for many women. The 1970 Equal Pay Act says that women are entitled to equal pay with men working for the same employer if they do (1) 'like work' with the men, (2) broadly similar work with any differences not of 'practical importance', (3) work of 'equal value' and (4) work rated as 'equivalent' under a job evaluation scheme.

That is the theory but, as the EOC admits: 'Women on average still earn less than men. Women working full-time earn 80% of the hourly earnings of full-time men and only 72% of their average weekly earnings.'

The reason is not only the determined opposition of many employers but an appalling legal complexity made worse by protracted delays. The basic problem for claimants is that an employer has the defence that any pay differential 'is genuinely due to a material factor which is not the difference of sex'. For instance:

- when duties are different, as when men warehouse workers loaded and unloaded whereas women in the same warehouse did light work such as sorting, packing and labelling;
- when responsibilities are different, as when a man and a woman were employed as production schedulers by industrial manufacturers and the man, who was paid more, handled more expensive products and a mistake would have had far more serious financial consequences;
- when hours are different, as when men and women night workers were paid the same but this was higher than that paid women working the day shift. Equal pay claims go to employment tribunals and must be made while still in the job or within six months of leaving. Tribunals can award up to two years' pay arrears.

I know that I sound gloomy about possible success and the EOC itself says that claims are complicated and need expert advice but anyone who really believes they have a case should telephone the EOC's Manchester headquarters on 0161–833 9244 and ask for the Equal Pay Unit. They will give free advice and may even pursue the claim themselves on the applicant's behalf.

SEXUAL HARASSMENT

For many women – and some men – this is a curse of their everyday working lives. It is not even good for employers: in the words of a study by the European Commission, 'It has a direct impact on the profitability of the enterprise. . . where employees' productivity is reduced by having to work in a climate in which an individual's integrity is not respected.'

Yet surprisingly there is no legal definition of sexual harassment, even though it is a pernicious form of sex discrimination. I cannot improve on the European Commission's 1991 dictum: 'Unwanted conduct of a sexual nature or other conduct based on sex affecting the dignity of women and men at work, including unwelcome physical, verbal and non-verbal conduct.'

In France and Spain it is a criminal offence, but not in this country. Even so, an employer who tolerates such behaviour must expect to pay substantial sums by way of compensation. Anyone – male or female – who believes they have been subjected to sexual harassment should complain to the Equal Opportunities Commission's head office at Overseas House, Quay Street, Manchester M3 3HN (Tel: 0161–833 9244). It will investigate and, where appropriate, assist presentation of the claim.

Here are some typical awards of out-of-court settlements: £7,182.50 to a 22-year-old female typist from Portland, Dorset whose male employer offered her £10,000 for sexual intercourse; £2,500 to a 19-year-old shopgirl in Leeds whose 25-year-old manager pestered her to go out with him, asked her to strip off to attract customers and quizzed her about her underwear; £10,000 to a 34-year-old married manageress of a dry cleaning chain in Rochester, Kent whose male area manager told her that there was a 'special chemistry' between them and constantly pestered her for sex; and £10,000 to a female firefighter in Dorset who was subjected to childish and barbaric behaviour, such as when she was thrown on to the bonnet of a Land Rover while a fireman stood between her legs pretending to have sex with her.

You can also claim compensation if sexually harassed at a recruitment interview for a job you did not accept, as in the case of a 20-year-old student from Shoreham-by-Sea, West Sussex who won an award of £1,710. She had turned down the offer of a summer job after her prospective employer had said she could have it if she had sexual intercourse with him twice a week.

Many women are frightened of complaining to senior management because they are scared they will lose their job, as undoubtedly does happen. But 'You have to be brave to do this because it's such a sensitive and emotional thing,' said a 25-year-old Rochester salesgirl who won a 'substantial' out-of-court settlement after being sacked for refusing to spend the weekend with her male boss.

There is also this practical consideration: if you are sacked because you complain or you leave because you simply cannot stand the pressure and resentment that your complaint has caused, that may increase your compensation! For instance, the 34-year-old dry cleaning manageress from Rochester whose boss spoke of their 'special chemistry' was told, when she complained to head office, that she had been made redundant and her allegations were unsubstantiated. Yet she won her £10,000 award, then only £1,000 under the limit.

One final note: harassment does not come only from the opposite sex. In June 1990, a 17-year-old girl cook made legal history as the first woman in the UK to win an award (£1,000) because of harassment by another woman: her middle-aged married supervisor in an Isle of Wight restaurant. Three years later, in June 1993, came the first man-to-man case when a 21-year-old male security guard was awarded £4,500 compensation after being sexually harassed by his supervisor, a 50-year-old married man, in the ultra-macho setting of a steel plant in Newport, Gwent.

But even today, when so many people are ready to put a money value on everything and try to turn every misfortune in life into financial gain, there is a limit. Employers will be pleased to learn that staff still have to use their common sense. An Exeter employment tribunal has thrown out as 'trivial' a case brought by a 19-year-old packaging machinist. She complained that her 50-year-old production manager, a married Northerner, had used terms of endearment such as 'darling', 'love' and 'sweetheart' and was constantly touching her arms and shoulders. The tribunal accepted that such words were 'natural in the North of England' where people also tended to be much more tactile. 'I feel I have been branded a sex pest and I did nothing wrong,' said the production manager afterwards. 'It could happen to any man in a work situation. You are treading on eggshells. The accusations have changed my life. The tribunal was a nightmare. I will be a lot more cagey in future and save the words "sweetheart", "darling" and "love" for my wife.'

Rightly or wrongly, in today's climate, that is good practical advice.

Notes

1 Like all her predecessors, she calls herself the 'Chair' of the EOC but I cannot bring myself to write such an abomination. She is not a piece of furniture on which people sit.

2 Mind you, staff-only Christmas parties also have their problems. Every spring there is a crop of sex discrimination cases with employees complaining about unwanted sexual advances by drunken bosses.

PART THREE

YOUR HOME

15

BUYING AND SELLING

Most readers, even if they have not yet personally suffered the trauma of buying or selling their home, will know the general framework:

If you are a buyer, you offer 'subject to contract' to buy the property at a certain price, which the seller then refuses or accepts – or finally accepts at a mutually negotiated higher price. At that stage, you may be asked for a small returnable deposit – again, 'subject to contract' – of £50–£100 as a token of your genuine interest in the property. You will also, if not before, find the necessary finance by negotiating a mortgage. Eventually the seller's solicitor will send your solicitor a draft contract of sale, together with proof of her client's ownership of the property. She will also send the seller's solicitor 'preliminary enquiries' into the past history of the property and (if not done before) make 'searches' of the local authority as to any matters, such as local traffic schemes or development plans, which may affect the value or desirability of the property.

Then, when all queries have been resolved and the seller's solicitor has received your signed contract and your solicitor's cheque for the deposit, for which you have put her in funds usually amounting to 10 per cent of the purchase price, 'contracts will be exchanged' with signed copies of each side's contract being delivered to the other. The actual 'exchange' is no longer a physical operation: the two solicitors merely speak over the telephone making a note of the date and time of day. At this stage – and not before – a binding contract comes into being between buyer and seller.

The signed contracts will state a 'completion date' when the balance of the purchase price is to be paid and you at last become the owner of the property. The Law Society's latest (1995) *Conditions of Sale*, which forms the basis of most home purchase contracts, states that the completion date is 20 working days from exchange – but the parties can write in their own date.

If you are a seller, events will follow the same pattern but it is your responsibility – usually, of course, delegated to your solicitor – to prepare the draft contract of sale and to answer truthfully a Seller's Property Information Form. This is a questionnaire that your solicitor will send you asking detailed questions about the property, to which you must carefully consider your answers, as we shall see below.

How long does all this take? It is a slow process – too slow. It takes on average twelve weeks for a home to change hands in England and Wales, twice as long as in Sweden, the US and Canada. Scotland has a different system where the seller's acceptance of the would-be buyer's offer counts as a binding contract.

Now let us look at some of the major problems that may arise in practice.

SURVEY

Even though buying a house or flat is most people's biggest investment, almost two-thirds of homebuyers do not bother to spend money on commissioning their own survey – as distinct from the mortgage lender's – before they hand over their hard-earned cash. This is false economy. A good survey will pinpoint most major flaws like damp or rot or the sort of thing that happened to me recently when my surveyor reported that a ground-floor flat I was keen on buying was right on top of the block's boiler with the likelihood of intermittent noise throughout the year and excessive heat in the summer. Armed with expert information as to any defects, you can either pull out of the deal before it is too late – as I did! – or use it to persuade the seller to knock something off the sale price to cover the necessary repairs.

Please do not be tempted – as an estimated 80 per cent of potential buyers are – to save money, not bother with your own survey and simply rely on the mortgage lender's survey. That is dangerous nonsense. It is not really a survey anyway but a valuation report to ensure that the property is sufficient security for the mortgage, so that if you were to default in your repayments the lender could sell the property and get its money back. For a start, the monetary value in which the lender's surveyor is interested is not how much you actually paid for the property but the amount of the mortgage, which can be much less. Also a valuation will contain only a brief description of any obvious problems and not go into the sort of detail that you, as someone wanting to live in the place, will need to know.

Without labouring the point: get your own survey!

TITLE DEEDS

Many people may be surprised to learn that nowadays these exist for only about a quarter of properties in England and Wales. The reason is that three-quarters of property today is 'registered land': i.e. registered at the Land Registry, an institution set up in 1925 to keep a register of ownership. Eventually, all land will be registered and title deeds will finally disappear.

So how to prove ownership of 'registered land'? All the details and proof are held by the Land Registry, which is in four parts:

- the property register, which describes the property;
- the proprietorship register, which names the proprietor (i.e. owner);
- the charges register, which contains such things as mortgage details and charges protecting a wife's rights in her home in a divorce situation;
- the filed plan, which shows the location of the land and its boundaries – though not necessarily to the actual inch or centimetre.

When you become the new owner of a property, the Land Registry issues a new Land Certificate stating who is the registered proprietor – and that is your 'title deed', guaranteed by the state.

DELAY IN COMPLETION

This can be a nightmare, both for buyer and seller. As we have just seen, the Law Society's Standard *Conditions of Sale* specify 20 working days from exchange of contracts as the date of completion. But, in legal jargon, 'time is not of the essence'. This means that one party's failure to complete on time does *not* automatically give the other the right to cancel or claim compensation. They must first serve a written 'notice to complete' on the defaulter specifying a new date, usually 10 or 14 days ahead. This at last makes 'time of the essence' and, if completion does not then take place, both can assert their full legal rights.

These will depend on who is to blame.

If the seller defaults, the frustrated buyer can cancel the contract, recover his deposit (plus interest) and sue for damages for his loss. This can include the increased cost of buying an alternative property of the same type and location, the rent of a temporary home, wasted legal and other professional costs – and compensation for distress and inconvenience.

If the buyer defaults, the seller can similarly cancel the contract. She can keep the deposit – and sell the property elsewhere. Even if she sells at a higher price, the buyer still cannot claim back his deposit. In the present property hothouse, sellers can make a substantial profit on buyers not completing!

THE SELLER'S PROPERTY INFORMATION FORM

The seller's solicitor will ask her clients to fill this in as part of the legal paperwork between an offer 'subject to contract' being accepted and exchange of contracts. It specifically asks three questions, which can be difficult to answer truthfully: 'Do you know of any disputes about this or any neighbouring property? Have you received any complaints about anything you have, or have not done, as owners? Have you made any such complaints to any neighbour about what the neighbour has or has not done?'

The form states that, if any answer is, 'Yes', you must give details. And it warns: 'Incorrect information may mean the buyer can claim compensation.'

There was, in 1996, a well-publicised case at Portsmouth County Court which shows how careful one must be in answering these questions. An elderly widow had to pay £16,000 damages plus costs for not saying in her answers that she had had a running battle with her neighbours about noise. The problem was that she had actually written a formal letter of complaint to the council so, when the new owners' lives were made hell by the same noisy neighbours and they sued her for her 'incorrect information', a judge had little difficulty in holding her liable.

SOLICITORS

This is one instance where we nearly all use a solicitor. Few of us take on the task of do-it-yourself conveyancing and the comparatively new breed of licensed conveyancers are still used only by a minority.

Conveyancing is the basis of many solicitors' livelihood. But there is still a great deal of anecdotal evidence about the high cost, the delays and sometimes staggering incompetence.

Solicitors' charges

According to the Law Society's own Code, solicitors must tell their clients at the outset 'the best information possible about the likely overall costs' and their basis for charging. With conveyancing, there literally are no rules. In a survey by the Consumers' Association, 400 solicitors were asked to quote for services by telephone. Prices varied considerably: one solicitor charged £20 for drawing up a lease, while another quoted over 17 times that amount – £350. On a £75,000 house, the conveyancing costs ranged from £117 to £750.

It should be offered but, if not, do not be too embarrassed to ask for an estimate of the likely cost. Preferably, try and get a firm 'quotation' which cannot then be varied. Do not be afraid to negotiate or to shop around. Some people think that there is a fixed rate, depending on the price of the house but, in theory, that ended over 20 years ago. Yet many solicitors still use 1 per cent of the purchase price – or 0.5 per cent, if you are lucky – as a starting point (and for some a final point!) for talking about fees. Solicitors are supposed to charge what the Law Society calls 'fair and reasonable fees' depending on the work entailed.

With a really straightforward transaction, you can sometimes find solicitors charging as little as £350 plus VAT and out-of-pocket expenses. Not everyone realises that solicitors lost their conveyancing monopoly in 1985, since when licensed conveyancers can also act; and they tend to charge less.[1] But remember that, with both these professionals (as in life generally), cheap is not necessarily the same as good.

Your final bill may still exceed what you were told but you can query it with the Law Society. In cases like this which do not involve court work (where different rules prevail), any client dissatisfied with fees should complain to their solicitor and ask him to obtain 'a remuneration certificate' from the Law Society that his fees are 'fair and reasonable'. DO NOT PAY NOW AND COMPLAIN LATER. The general rule is that you cannot ask for a certificate once you have paid the bill in full –

but you must first pay half of the solicitor's fee plus VAT and 'disbursements'(i.e. expenses). As everyone who has sold a property will know, your solicitor at the end of the transaction will send you a completion statement – which shows that he has already deducted his fees in full. Which means you cannot then ask for a remuneration certificate.

How to get round this? As I recently advised someone, there is a perfectly valid way: if you anticipate the possibility of being overcharged, write to your solicitor before completion stating your anxieties and instructing him only to deduct half his fee and all his disbursements before sending your completion statement. He is then bound to follow your instructions and the complaints procedure is available to you.

Solicitors' incompetence

Many, if not most, solicitors provide an impressive service but sadly one cannot always count on it.

A tale of incompetence

A man was looking for a house in Belsize Park, north-west London and thought he had found the perfect place. But he missed out on it because on the morning when both sides' solicitors were to clinch the deal and exchange contracts over the telephone, his solicitor refused to interrupt a consultation with another client to phone the seller's solicitor.

It was highly urgent because the seller had been holding out for £225,000 and now suddenly said he would take £200,000 – but insisted on an immediate response. Despite repeated phone calls, the solicitor would not make that vital phone call, so the seller offered the house to another keen purchaser – who immediately clinched the deal for only an extra £2,000, which the first buyer would have been very happy to pay.

Sometimes a dissatisfied client will go so far as to sue her solicitor for negligence: i.e. failure to take reasonable professional care in the discharge of his duties. It used to be said that one solicitor would be reluctant to sue a colleague on behalf of a client but several London solicitors have assured me that this is no longer true. However, I have a lurking suspicion that it may still occur when both solicitors are practising in the same small country town where professional and social links could be closer than those in large towns and cities.

Undoubtedly, whether this is so or not, successful negligence cases against solicitors are on the increase.

A successful negligence case

A retired lorry driver in London bought a council flat with his younger son under the Right-to-Buy scheme. The father put up 70 per cent of the purchase price and the son funded the other 30 per cent with a mortgage. But their solicitors did not warn them of the two different legal scenarios when two people buy property together: tenancy in common where, if one dies, his estate takes his half or joint tenancy where the survivor automatically takes everything and the other's next-of-kin get nothing.

Without consultation or explanation, the solicitors made them joint tenants. So when the father died in his seventies, the son automatically became sole owner.

But there was an older son living in Dorking who believed that his father had meant him to inherit his share. A local solicitor took on his case for professional negligence but the London solicitors denied liability. The Dorking solicitor persisted – and won an out-of-court settlement of £9,000 damages plus legal costs.

GAZUMPING

This is the biggest curse of modern homebuying. You think you have a deal because the seller has accepted your offer, so you go ahead with plans to sell your own property. But the seller's estate agent keeps the property on the market and in due course the seller dumps you for a higher offer from someone else.

One London buyer of a flat in Camden Town had her offer of £120,000 accepted. She put her own flat on the market, spent a week showing it to potential buyers and took another week off work to sort out her mortgage and other paperwork. But a few days later the seller accepted an offer £5,000 higher than hers, and she was back where she had started.

The gazumper, aided by his agent, can strike so quickly that no 'sale' is safe. Another buyer was hours away from clinching a deal on a six-bedroom house in Kensington, west London, for which he had agreed to pay just over £1 million. Then someone else made an offer of more than £1.25 million in cash and exchanged contracts within 24 hours.

Gazumping is completely legal in England and Wales. Since, as we have seen, all offers are made 'subject to contract', the seller is under no legal obligation to sell the property until contracts are exchanged. In fact, agents are legally obliged to pass on higher offers to their client, the seller. This applies even if the agent puts 'Under Offer' on her details of the property which she leaves in her window – perhaps to impress passers-by with how busy and successful she is. If someone then comes in and wants to see the property, she cannot refuse to show it to him – or to pass on to the seller any higher offer that results. If the seller accepts – of course, 'subject to contract' – that new offer, the original offeror has no legal comeback.

So what then is the legal significance of stating 'Under Offer'? There is none. It merely means that someone has made an offer which the owner has either accepted or is considering.

So long as the house purchase system remains as it is in England and Wales, gazumping will remain a real possibility with sought-after properties. Even so, the agent in such a case may have committed a breach of her own professional code – if she belongs to one of the three professional bodies, National Association of Estate Agents, Royal Institute of Chartered Surveyors or Incorporated Society of Valuers and Auctioneers. Their Code of Practice says that, if members want to continue to market a property after a 'subject to contract' offer has been accepted, they must obtain specific instructions to that effect from the seller and tell the would-be buyer what they are doing.

I wonder how often this happens. But I have a tip for prospective home-hunters. If making an offer to purchase, you should always say that it is on the basis that the agent will not show anyone else the property before exchange. By agreeing to that, the agent accepts a duty to you as well as the seller and you may be able to sue if she breaks her word. I cannot point to any reported case when saying this but, to my mind, this is both good sense and good law. It is certainly worth having a go!

'E X C L U S I V I T Y'

This is a word that has crept into estate agents' jargon over the past few years. It is supposed to be a way around the problem of gazumping. What happens is that, when accepting a 'subject to contract' offer on his client's behalf, the seller's agent says that the seller has agreed to give the buyer 'exclusivity' for, say, 10 working days from the receipt of draft documentation, which should be sufficient time for the solicitors on both sides to exchange contracts. During this period the seller legally cannot accept any higher offer from anyone else.

To be honest, the exact legal status of this device has not yet been tested in the High Court but it probably is legally binding. It is a sort of updated, shorthand version of a full 'lock-out agreement' signed by both parties with the seller undertaking to 'lock-out' any other prospective buyer for a stated period, usually 10 working days. The Appeal Court accepted the validity of such agreements back in June 1993 in *Pitt* v.

PHH Asset Management Ltd, reported in (1993) 4 All England Reports at page 461.

But I must warn you that, whether with full-blown lock-out agreements or 'exclusivity', if contracts are – for whatever reason – not exchanged within the stated period, a seller can thereafter accept a higher offer with perfect legality. It is by no means a complete answer to the problem of gazumping.

STOP PRESS

The Government has announced its intention of bringing in new legislation that will carry out root-and-branch reforms to the system of home purchase in England and Wales which will speed up the process and hopefully remove the potential for gazumping.

It is proposed that a 'seller's pack' will be required before a property goes on the market. This pack will contain title documents, local council searches and a draft contract of sale. It will also include planning and building control approvals for extensions and conversions, all guarantees and warranties for items such as damp and wood treatments – and, most controversially, a full survey report on the property.

The details of this new scheme still need to be worked out and no one knows the exact date when it will become law. But it looks as if, at long last, change is in the air. It cannot come too soon.

Note

1 Anyone wanting further information about licensed conveyancers should contact the Council for Licensed Conveyancers at 16 Glebe Road, Chelmsford, Essex (Tel: 01245–349599).

16

ESTATE AGENTS

The law on estate agents is like the curate's egg in the old *Punch* cartoon: only 'good in parts'. Although the modern estate agent is as honest and straightforward as any other decent businessman or business-woman, the fact remains that there are no legal qualifications required to put up your plate and call yourself an estate agent. As Hugh Dunsmore-Hardy, chief executive of the National Association of Estate Agents told a reporter in September 1999: 'Malpractice and dishonest behaviour are bringing the profession into disrepute.'

He was only repeating what John Bridgeman, Director-General of Fair Trading, had just said in an official press release: 'It is extremely disappointing that some undesirable practices from the late 1980s are making a comeback. Agents should take note that, if I have evidence that they are failing to meet their obligations, I can ban them from practising.' That is no great threat. In the first nine months of 1999, Mr Bridgeman banned four estate agents and, in the whole of 1998, only two.

A certain breed of estate agent does not shrink from flouting the law – and all too often they get away with it.

In truth, estate agents law is inadequate and, in many ways, ill-fitted to cope with the increasingly harsh realities of the modern property world. Until 1979 there was no statute on the subject. But the Estate Agents Act of that year dealt only with a few isolated matters. Clients' money (deposits, etc.) must be paid into a separate account with interest payable if the deposit is over £500 and the interest at least £10 (figures that, of course, have little relevance to today's property values); estate agents must declare any personal involvement in a transaction; they must keep properly audited books and accounts; and they must tell their clients their fees before taking them on. It is this Act which gives the Director-General of Fair Trading his rarely exercised power to ban rogue agents for 'undesirable practices'.

Unfortunately, the Act failed to make much practical difference and, in 1991, following a highly critical report by the then Director-General of Fair Trading, Sir Gordon (now Lord) Borrie QC, the Estate Agents (Provision of Information) Regulations came into being. As a result, estate agents now have to explain in writing the meaning of three vital phrases habitually used in their contracts and and obtain their clients' written acceptance of their terms before starting to market their property.

The Office of Fair Trading, in its handbook *Using an Estate Agent* states: 'Usually estate agents work for sellers, not buyers. Sellers are the clients. They pay the fees and their interests are an agent's priority.' That is absolutely correct but it masks a more complex reality.

There are three principal areas of possible dispute:

COMMISSION

Estate agents' commission is a straight percentage of the price for which the property is sold. It is not normally paid until the sale is completed.

There are three main contracts:

Sole agency You say only one agent can sell, and pay the lowest rate: 1.5 per cent to 2.5 per cent. This is usually the best deal – at least, for a try-out period. BUT if during that time you sell through another firm, you will have to pay *two* sets of commission.

Joint sole agency You sign up with two agents who agree to share one commission, whoever makes the sale. Typical rate: 2–3 per cent.

Sole selling rights To be avoided. Only the agent can sell the property. If you sell it privately, you still have to pay his commission.

What event triggers liability to pay commission?

The question is deceptively simple. The answer is complex. In the main, judge-made Common Law prevails and over the years the courts have contrived to achieve something of a delicate balancing act. On the one hand, there has been a realisation that estate agents put in a lot of work and expense on trying to set up deals that eventually through no fault of their own may go awry. No sale takes place and the question arises: what happens to the money and time they have uselessly expended? On the other hand, the client has only engaged the estate agent's services in order to sell his property, so why should she have to pay anything, if in the end there is no sale?

The amount of an agent's commission is usually assessed on a sliding scale, according to the price paid for the property (*not* the asking price!) – and the client's ability to negotiate an acceptable fee. Disbursements – for advertising, 'For Sale' boards and the like – can only be charged separately if specifically agreed beforehand in writing.

When is an agent entitled to be paid his money? Lord Justice Harman laid down in 1961: 'Before you find the commission payable, you must be satisfied that the condition on which it is payable has been satisfied.'[1]

Estate agents – or their lawyers – have expended over many years much ingenuity in trying to phrase their contract letters in such a way that they were entitled to commission merely for introducing a possible or probable buyer – even if the sale did not eventually go through. Many judges disapproved, and there was almost a running war between estate agents and the courts, with judges throwing out one form of words whereupon estate agents retaliated with another: all designed to ensure that their clients paid up, even without a sale.

Nowadays it has all simmered down to a situation where, in the words of the latest edition of the leading textbook, Cheshire, Fifoot and Furmston's *Law of Contract* : 'Broadly speaking, the intention which, as a matter of probability, the courts should impute to the parties is that if no sale in fact results from the agent's efforts, no commission shall be payable. This is the normal expectation of the vendor.'

So phrases in estate agents' letters to their clients saying that commission will be payable on introducing 'a purchaser', 'a person willing and able to purchase', 'a person ready, willing and able to purchase' and 'a person prepared to enter into a contract to purchase' have all been held to mean only a person who actually reaches the stage of exchanging contracts on the property thereby committing her legally to buying it. In other words, 'a purchaser' must be a purchaser. There must, as a general rule, be a sale.

The 1991 Regulations specify that in estate agents' contract letters they must explain the meaning of 'ready, willing and able purchaser'. Unfortunately, the Regulations are not very helpful to the average lay client. Their official explanation of the term to be incorporated in all contracts is: 'You will be liable to pay remuneration to us, in addition to any other costs or charges agreed, if such a purchaser is introduced by us in accordance with your instructions and this must be paid even if you subsequently withdraw and unconditional contracts for sale are not exchanged.'

That wording is a snare for the unwary. If you see it in a contract submitted for your approval, refuse to accept it. No law says that you must do so, and do not be bamboozled into accepting it. You should write and say you are taking your business elsewhere unless they rephrase the clause to make clear that commission is only payable if contracts are exchanged. I say 'write' rather than telephone because a cynical but experienced QC told me many years ago: 'Telephone calls never happen.' Letters, of which you keep a copy, are much more difficult to deny.

I practise what I preach. When recently trying to sell my west London flat I wrote to the agent whose office I had visited to question the wording in his subsequent contract letter purporting to define a 'ready, willing and able purchaser' – a person not even mentioned in our initial meeting. His firm's letter had said that commission would be payable on their 'introducing a purchaser who is ready, willing and able to proceed'. I did not like that, so I wrote back: 'I am unhappy about accepting such wording in the light of the definition in your explanatory leaflet accompanying your letter which says that such a purchaser is someone "prepared and able to exchange unconditional contracts." Full stop! That frightens me. Can we agree between ourselves that the vital words should be added: "and actually does so"?' He wrote back – reluctantly, I am sure – agreeing to this new wording, and that formed the basis of the contract between us.

NATURE OF THE AGENCY

Some people still do not realise the difference between giving an estate agent 'sole agency' and 'sole selling rights', as specified above. In fact, it is vital, and the 1991 Regulations say that these two terms must be explained in writing before an agent can legally accept instructions to market a property. Usually this is in the form of a letter following a preliminary meeting in the agent's office and purporting to 'confirm' the discussion that then took place – even if many of the items in the letter were not even mentioned in that initial conversation. I hate to think how many people sign this confirmation without fully understanding its often complex wordage, written in legalese more than ordinary English.

As with all small-print clauses, the only answer is to read the document carefully and, if anything is unclear, ask exactly what the words mean – and request that explanation to be put in writing. I am sorry to seem so cynical but experience has taught me that: 'Put in writing', is a sound guiding principle.

SHARP PRACTICES

There are several questionable tactics against which buyers should be on guard:

'Imaginative' written particulars

The only other statute dealing exclusively with estate agents, the 1991 Property Misdescriptions Act, makes it a criminal offence for agents to make 'false or misleading statements' about property. They can be fined up to £2,500 – whether the statement is written or only spoken.

But too many agents still paint more rosy a picture than truth requires.

Two successful prosecutions

Engineer Tony Petworth and his girlfriend dreamed of enjoying barbecues in the evening sun in the garden of the £58,000 house they were buying on the outskirts of Southampton. Their estate agents, a national chain, claimed in their written details that the garden faced south-west, which Tony knew would give plenty of evening sun. But when he took out a compass to install a TV aerial the day after moving in, he saw that the garden was north-west facing and so too cold for evening barbecues.

One of the main reasons for buying the house was to have the evening sun on the patio. So he complained to the local trading standards office, which prosecuted both the agency chain and the local branch manager who wrote the details for making a false or misleading statement, contrary to the 1991 Act. The magistrates fined the agency £1,150 with £1,000 costs and their manager £150.

Solicitor and would-be home buyer Timothy O'Sullivan was delighted when he saw an advertisement in a Bournemouth newspaper for luxury seaside flats with balconies for only £99,000. But on speaking to the estate agent, he discovered that, for that price, he would only get a ground-floor flat with a patio. A balcony flat would cost £140,000. When he expressed surprise, the agent said that if he wanted a balcony, he could 'put a fence around the patio'.

O'Sullivan, like Tony Petworth, complained to his local trading standards office. Bournemouth magistrates fined the national chain that produced the advertisement £1,250 and their local associate £1,000, with each paying £2,180 costs.

'The 1991 Act was intended to prevent estate agents from exaggerating,' Martin Fisher, Hampshire's chief trading standards officer and spokesman for the Institute of Trading Standards has told me, 'but since it came into effect the Institute has prosecuted almost every large chain of estate agents in Britain. And, since the British are generally not a nation of complainers and most people are not even aware of the Act, those hundred or so prosecutions are likely to be only the tip of the iceberg.'

Your best protection is to ask the agent to be specific: ask for rooms' precise measurements, whether a 'garden' is paved or grassed; exactly how far away is the nearest Tube station, etc. The more specific the statement, the easier to prove it 'false or misleading'.

The professional bodies disapprove of bad trading practices. Many agents belong to the National Association of Estate Agents and, if you see their logo in a dishonest agent's window, you should threaten to report her to the Association unless she starts sending you particulars on which you can fully rely. If, in a really bad case, you think that a criminal offence has been committed, you should follow Messers Petworth and O'Sullivan's example and complain to the trading standards department at your local town hall. They will investigate and may prosecute. The law is there to be enforced.

Dishonest advertising

This is the age-old way of 'hooking' potential buyers, designed to make the place seem much better or more desirable than it really is. The result is that buyers waste their time in visiting property that is totally inappropriate.

Looking to buy in central London recently, I went to see a flat described in a leading agent's newspaper advertisement as 'overlooking Queensway' – an attractive, cosmopolitan thoroughfare near Kensington Gardens. But the flat, in a modern purpose-built block, did not overlook Queensway at all. Instead, it looked out on an inner courtyard, on the *other* side of which were the flats that overlooked Queensway.

I warned the estate agent's representative that, if he repeated the advert, I would report his firm to the local trading standards office for prosecution under the 1991 Act.

A different agent in another advert in the same reputable Sunday newspaper described a flat in another block as 'a rare opportunity to buy'. I discovered that two similar flats in the same block were also on the market. How rare is 'rare'?

Using impressive words that mean nothing

Although the 1991 Act makes it an offence for estate agents to give a false description of property, it is not illegal for them to use a whole range of enticing but fundamentally meaningless words. Beware of traditional phrases such as 'desirable residence', 'deceptively spacious', 'stunning', 'spectacular views', 'conveniently situated', 'luxury kitchen', 'exceptionally well presented', and 'early viewing is advised'. If queried in a court of law, they would be dismissed as having no real value – and, therefore, as being devoid of legal significance.

Ring-fencing

In this practice, which occurs when too many prospective purchasers are chasing too few houses, the estate agent asks a prospective buyer for payment to ensure that their bid is the only one put to the seller.

The businessman who was cheated

A 32-year-old businessman paid an agent £1,500 to ring-fence a house in north London and secure a hassle-free purchase. 'I simply couldn't afford to let the deal fall through, so I suggested to the agent that I match in cash what he was receiving from the seller,' he said. 'The deal was that the agent would get his client to accept my offer and not let anyone else view the house. Of course, the seller was never told.'

Keeping back information

Agents sometimes conceal defects that would cause you to make a lower offer, or put you off the property completely.

For instance, four different estate agents in Swanage, Dorset, all failed to mention that a flat they were selling was situated on a cliff threatened by erosion. A nearby cliff had already collapsed and severe weather was expected to bring further problems. The flat's building insurance did not cover slippage and buyers would be very unlikely to get a mortgage. Yet two of the estate agents even included contact numbers for mortgage lenders with the details of the property.

Legally speaking, estate agents are not obliged to reveal negative features about a property unless specifically asked. And they can easily evade general questions such as: 'Is there anything wrong with the property?' The result is that thousands of people end up wasting time in visiting properties that are wholly unsuitable.

As so often, the only answer is to ask very specific questions, especially before going a long way to view a property.

Inaccurate measurements

For most would-be buyers, it is important to know whether rooms are big enough to take their existing furniture or what new furniture or carpets they will need to buy.

The high ceiling which 'made a room look smaller'
When an office secretary was buying a flat in Christchurch, Dorset, she queried the estate agent's measurements for the living-room of 17 feet by 14 feet. He blithely assured her that the high ceiling made the room look smaller than it really was. But after moving in, she found that a £520 carpet she had bought specially for the room was too big. She checked the measurements for herself and found that the room was only 13 feet eight inches by 11 feet 10 inches.

Christchurch magistrates fined the agent's company £1,300 for breach of the 1991 Act and awarded the secretary £216 compensation.

Some agents try and avoid liability by saying that they are merely quoting measurements given by their clients. But no one yet knows how effective is this disclaimer. There has been no test case and the High Court may well rule that agents are under a legal duty to use reasonable care to check information supplied by their clients.

HOW TO COPE WITH ROGUE AGENTS

Under the 1979 Estate Agents Act, the Government can make regulations laying down minimum legal standards for agents. But that has not yet happened and the industry's attempts to regulate itself have met with limited success.

The majority of the 12,000 firms of estate agents in England and Wales belong to the National Association of Estate Agents, the Royal Institution of Chartered Surveyors or the Incorporated Society of Valuers and Auctioneers, all of which try to maintain a professional code of conduct. Their disciplinary measures range from an informal warning to –

occasionally – expulsion from membership. BUT an estimated 3,000 agents do not belong to any of these bodies.

In recent years, there has been an Ombudsman for Estate Agents as part of a scheme which 11 corporate chains and over 380 independent agents have joined. You can complain direct to the Ombudsman at Beckett House, 4 Bridge Street, Salisbury, Wilts SP1 2LX (Tel: 01722–33306), and he can award compensation of up to £50,000. In 1998, the last year for which official figures exist, there were 3,541 complaints as against 3,039 in the previous year, with 1999's figures expected to be still higher.

But there are two drawbacks to the Ombudsman Scheme: it is purely voluntary, and independent agencies must be linked to one of the three trade associations to be eligible. So only the best agents are likely to join anyway. Furthermore, the Ombudsman in his Annual Report never publishes the names of offending estate agents. 'The real objective of the Scheme is to secure redress for the victim,' says John Bridgeman, Director-General of the Office of Fair Trading. 'It has not been set up to name and shame the guilty.'

Whyever not? Publicity is always a powerful weapon against dishonest and incompetent behaviour.

However, the best remedy would be to implement in full the 1979 Estate Agents Act and lay down minimum professional qualifications. In his 1997 report, David Quayle, then Ombudsman,[2] said that, if estate agents did not voluntarily join his scheme, 'they must reasonably expect to have a statutory scheme imposed upon them'.

Most people will wonder why on earth this still remains to be done.

Notes
1 This was in *AL Wilkinson Lrd.* v. *Brown* (1966) 1 All England Law Reports at page 510.
2 He retired as Ombudsman in June 1999 to be succeeded by Stephen Carr-Smith.

17

LETTING AND RENTING

This is a disgracefully complex and complicated subject for something that is of considerable everyday importance. Facing me in my study at this moment are the four large volumes plus index of *Woodfall on Landlord and Tenant*, the practitioners' leading textbook, heavy with statutes, case law and precedents. They do not make easy reading. All I can hope to do in the space available to me is paint the general picture and highlight a few of the special problems.[1]

For a start, let us not get hung up with terminology. You talk about 'letting' when it is from the landlord's point of view: he or she allows a tenant to enjoy exclusive possession of their property for a period of time and for a fixed price called a rent. You talk about 'renting' when you look at it from the tenant's point of view: he or she 'rents' the exclusive use of premises from a landlord.

Similarly, there is no need to get worried about the difference between a 'tenancy agreement' and a 'lease': they both refer to the written agreement between landlord and tenant, save that if the agreement is for less than seven years, it is likely to be called a tenancy agreement and, if for more than seven years, it is likely to be called a lease. Furthermore, 'landlord' means the same as 'lessor' and 'lessee' means the same as 'tenant'.

I wish the subject were always as easy as that.

THE GENERAL PICTURE

Ever since Margaret Thatcher's Tory Government took office in 1979, there has been a sea-change in the statutory law dealing with residential lettings in the private sector. Until then, in a hangover from the old Rent Restriction Acts of World War II, the emphasis had been pro-tenant and anti-landlord. Most tenancies were 'protected tenancies' and the tenants enjoyed security of tenure so that, except in strictly defined circumstances, they could not be evicted by the landlord when their tenancies expired. Furthermore, landlords were restricted to charging what the law called 'fair rents' – although many landlords considered them unprofitably low.

The result was that the private rental market was virtually stagnant, with very few properties coming on to the letting market.

To try and reverse this situation and encourage private sector lettings, the Thatcher Government brought in the 1988 Housing Act. It created two new forms of private residential tenancy called 'assured tenancies' and 'assured shorthold tenancies' for most new lettings after 15 January 1989. These were intended to curtail tenants' security and increase landlords' rental prospects. But the legal changes did not end there. Eight years later, John Major's Tory Government passed the 1996 Housing Act which amended the 1988 Act and again rewrote the law.

So nowadays there are the following types of private residential tenancies:

Old-style protected and statutory tenancies

These both stem from the old protected tenancies pre-dating 15 January 1989. A few may still exist but when they eventually expire – as virtually all now have done – and the tenant remains living on the premises, a new statutory tenancy automatically takes its place, and the old rules as to security of tenure and 'fair rent' still apply. For practical purposes, there is no real change.

If a statutory tenant continues to live in the house or flat until his or her death, a surviving spouse or partner living with him or her at the date of death may succeed to the tenancy. Alternatively, a member of the tenant's family who was living with the tenant for two years before the death may also succeed. *But this can only happen once.* If, for example, a widow succeeds her late husband as tenant, her unmarried son cannot eventually succeed her – as a member of her family – when she dies.

Assured shorthold tenancies

'Shortholds', as they are generally called, are the most popular form of tenancy. Under the 1996 Housing Act, most private residential tenancies granted on or after 28 February 1997 are usually to be treated as assured shortholds unless the landlord gives notice that the tenancy is not to be shorthold or the agreement itself says otherwise. The tenancy must be for a fixed period of not less than six months and it gives virtually no security of tenure. The landlord cannot end the tenancy in the first six months unless the tenant is in breach of covenant. But he can get back possession at the end of the tenancy if he has given two months' written notice, in a prescribed form, before then.

Assured tenancies

Since 28 February 1997, most new residential tenancies are assured tenancies and the tenant is protected very much as with the old protected and statutory tenancies. During the lifetime of the tenancy, the landlord can only obtain possession by proving a statutory ground, such as substantial rent arrears, and by obtaining a court order. When the tenancy ends, a statutory tenancy is automatically created and the tenant can remain living on the premises until such time as the landlord can prove a specific ground of possession and obtains a court order. The rights of succession on the tenant's death are also similar to those on the death of a pre-1988 Act protected or statutory tenant.

RATIONALE

Shortholds are understandably popular with landlords because they confer almost no security of tenure. On the other hand, a tenant with security of tenure – i.e. an assured tenant – may agree to pay a higher rent just because he has that security. So if a landlord wishes to maximise his rent but is not too concerned about the tenant having security, he will probably prefer to offer an assured tenancy.

NOTE: Lettings by resident landlords, company lets, student lettings, occupational lets (e.g. porters' flats in apartment blocks) and most holiday lettings are the most important exemptions from the above rules.

RENT CONTROL

Old-style 'fair rent'

This still applies to long-standing protected and statutory tenancies. The rent that a landlord may legally charge for the property is fixed as the 'fair rent' by a local authority official named the rent officer who enters it in an official register. The phrase, a brilliant example of 1960s spin-doctoring, is said to have been coined by the late Lord Goodman, the then Prime Minister, Harold Wilson's, shrewd personal solicitor. The rent officer takes account of various specified factors, such as location and type of accommodation, but is forbidden to consider what a market rent would be or to consider if there is any shortage of properties in the area. There is a – rarely exercised – right of appeal to the local rent assessment committee, whose decision is final. No application for a new 'fair rent' will be heard within two years of the last registration.

Shortholds

There is no question of the rent being assessed at a rent lower than the market rent for the premises. A landlord is at risk of a lower rent being fixed only if he is charging 'significantly' more than the market rent. The rent officer is not involved and application has to be made direct to the local rent assessment committee. In practice, applications are few and far between.

Assured tenancies

Similar provisions apply but no application for a new rent can be made until the original tenancy has expired and a new-style statutory tenancy has taken its place.

LANDLORDS' RIGHTS TO REGAIN POSSESSION

Old-style protected and statutory tenancies

Not of great practical importance for most readers but roughly the same as set out below for assured tenancies.

Assured tenancies

Proper notice   A landlord must serve a written notice on the tenant, in the terms laid down by Section 8 of the 1988 Housing Act.

Specified grounds for possession   On grounds 1–8 in the Housing 1988 Act, a judge *must* make an eviction order. She cannot refuse to do this. But, on grounds 8–17, she must also be satisfied it is *reasonable* to do so. She has a discretion, depending on her view of the circumstances. The Act specifies 17 possible grounds for obtaining possession.

(i) *Where the judge must make an eviction order*

Ground 1: The landlord lived in the premises as his (or his spouse's) only or principal home, or now either one or both of them wants to do so; has given written notice of these facts to the tenant at the beginning of the tenancy; and has also served two months' notice of the court proceedings.

Ground 2: A mortgage lender wishes to obtain possession to foreclose on the property and exercise its power of sale with vacant possession. Again, notice of the fact that the property was mortgaged should have been given by the landlord to the tenant at the beginning of the tenancy and two months' written notice of the proceedings must also have been given.

Ground 3: In certain circumstances, the property is wanted for holiday lettings. [A landlord can let a property to a non-holiday tenant for a fixed term of not more than eight months provided that the tenant was told in writing that it would be required for a holiday let for four months (usually the summer period) after the eight-month period *and* the property had been let as a holiday home in the year before the tenancy began.]

Ground 4: The property belongs to an educational institution which normally lets it to students, and wants it back again for that purpose.

Ground 5: The property is normally used by a minister of religion and is required again for that purpose.

Ground 6: The landlord intends to demolish the whole or a substantial part of the property and the works cannot be carried out with the tenant in occupation.

Ground 7 : The tenant has died and the person living on the premises is not entitled to succeed to the tenancy.

Ground 8: There are arrears of rent which exceed 13 weeks, if rent is payable weekly or fortnightly, or three months if payable monthly, quarterly or yearly.

(ii) *Where the judge has a discretion whether or not to make an order*

Ground 9: Suitable alternative accommodation is available for the tenant if an order for possession is granted.

Ground 10: Some rent is in arrears but not for so long as set out in Ground 8.

Ground 11: Persistent delay in paying rent.

Ground 12: Breach of covenant by the tenant.

Ground 13: Deterioration of the property through the tenant's waste or neglect – which can apply not only to the premises occupied by the tenant but also to the common parts. It also applies if someone living with the tenant is responsible for the deterioration.

Ground 14: The tenant, or anyone residing with the tenant, has been a source of nuisance or annoyance to neighbouring occupiers.

Ground 14(A) : Domestic violence where the landlord is a registered social landlord (usually a housing association) or a charitable housing trust.

Ground 15: The tenant has damaged the landlord's furniture or this has been done by someone living with the tenant – and the tenant has failed to take reasonable steps to remove the offender.

Ground 16: The tenant was an employee of the landlord and the employment has ended.

Ground 17 : The tenant induced the landlord to grant the tenancy in the first place by misrepresentation, such as a false reference.

Shortholds

The tenant has virtually no security of tenure. But the landlord cannot just sit back and wait for the tenancy to expire. He must still go to court for an eviction order – *and* give the tenant at least two months' prior written notice of his intention to do so. Lawyers and estate agents call this a 'Section 21 notice' because it was created by Section 21 of the 1988 Act. If this notice has been served, the judge has no alternative but to grant an eviction order. But depending on the circumstances, she may give the tenant as long as four weeks to pack his bags. A landlord's chances of getting his rent paid for that time are not too great.

SOME SPECIAL PROBLEMS

Harassment and unlawful eviction

The 1977 Protection from Eviction Act makes it a criminal offence for a landlord, however much he may feel justified by events, to harass any residential occupier of premises – not only a tenant – with the intent of making her leave against her will or physically to evict her without a court order .

The Act defines harassment as any action likely to interfere with the peace or comfort of the residential occupier or any member of his or her family. It also covers withdrawal of services reasonably needed for residential occupation. It includes such things as changing the locks, uttering threats, accumulating rubbish on the premises and removing light bulbs in common parts.

This anti-social and retrogressive behaviour is also a civil wrong, and judges can award substantial damages to deter unscrupulous landlords. In one case, a tenant who was forced out of her bedsitter was awarded £31,000: her landlord had woken her at 2 a.m. to ask for rent, played loud music, entered the bathroom when she was using it and changed the locks when she finally fled. He then smashed her belongings.

Rent books

Do you have a legal right to a rent book for your bed-sit? The 1985 Landlord and Tenant Act says that, except where the rent includes a 'substantial' payment for board, every weekly tenant of residential premises – furnished or unfurnished – must be given a rent book stating the landlord's name and address and providing space for acknowledgement of rent payments.

The Act makes it an offence for any landlord (of whichever sex and including a company) not to supply such a rent book – or to demand or receive rent without it. Anyone denied a rent book should complain to the tenancy relations officer at their local town hall. They will investigate and the culprit may be prosecuted in a magistrates' court and fined up to £2,500.

This is probably one of the best known pieces of everyday landlord and tenant law but an official at a London Borough Council has confirmed to me that 'from time to time' landlords still fail to comply with this basic legal duty.

Landlords' duty to repair

This will usually be spelt out in a lessor's covenant in the lease or tenancy agreement. But whatever that document may say, Section 11 of the 1985 Landlord and Tenant Act imposes an obligation on the landlord in all residential tenancies of less than seven years to keep the structure and exterior of the property, including drains, gutters and external pipes, brickwork and stonework, in good repair.

But this does not apply if the tenant causes the blockage, for instance by putting inappropriate matter down the lavatory.

Working from home

Tenancy agreements and leases often contain a clause restricting use of the premises to a private residence only. But nowadays many people, whether because made redundant in their salaried job or for lifestyle reasons, prefer to work from home. How is this compatible with 'user restriction clauses', as they are called?

Discretion is the name of the game. If you were to put up a plaque with a business name outside the front door of your house or the entrance to the block of flats where you live, the landlord would be within his or her rights in asking you to take it down – and even in asking you to stop working at home altogether.

But if you work over the telephone, by fax, post, e-mail or on the Internet, you would almost certainly be all right. Similarly, you should try and avoid a regular stream of business visitors, but an occasional work visitor would be unexceptionable.

Basically, the premises must still remain a private residence with you working from home *as a home*.

One final point: if the landlord – or her agent – accepts rent from you knowing of your new set-up, she cannot thereafter complain. She will be deemed in law to have waived her right to complain of any possible breach of your 'user restriction clause'.

Getting back your deposit at the end of a tenancy

Landlords' non-return of deposits can be a major problem. The National Association of Citizens' Advice Bureaux estimates that outgoing tenants could together be losing £80 million a year. But the law is clear: subject to the wording of any particular tenancy agreement, landlords must return deposits in full, subject to an allowance for lost or damaged items: 'fair wear and tear' excepted.

What does that well-known expression mean? It or its sister expression 'reasonable wear and tear' should be in all short-term residential tenancy agreements – and no prospective tenant should sign one without it. They both mean that a tenant cannot be held responsible at the end of the tenancy for the property's condition caused by what the House of Lords has called 'reasonable use of the premises by the tenant and the ordinary operation of natural forces' (i.e. the passage of time).

Some outgoing tenants avoid the problem by simply deducting the amount of the deposit from their last payment of rent – but, except when done with the landlord's consent, this is unlawful. Technically, the landlord could sue for the return of the money but that is hardly a realistic proposition.

The quality of furniture in a furnished letting

The law imposes no overall standard – except that the 1988 Furniture & Furnishings (Fire) (Safety) Regulations, which came into effect on 1 January 1997, say that anyone renting out residential premises (including bed-sits) as a business has to supply fireproof furniture. This does not apply to one-off ventures, such as letting your home while working temporarily abroad.

But you do not have to supply *all* new furniture. The Regulations do not apply to older furniture manufactured before 1 January 1950 and, even after that date, only to furniture, furnishing and other products that contain upholstery. Upholstery is considered the primary fire risk, not furniture as such. So, for instance, a landlord of furnished accommodation would have to buy new pillows but not new pillowcases; padded beds, head-boards and mattresses but not new bedclothes (including duvets). Curtains and carpets are also not included.

What about buying secondhand upholstered furniture? If manufactured before 1 January 1950, the Regulations do not apply. If of later date, they must have been re-upholstered to comply with the Regulations – except when bought non-retail for non-business purposes. So that you could buy – if prepared to take the risk – secondhand furniture not re-upholstered at a car boot sale or in answer to a private person's newspaper advert for your own home. But not for premises you intend letting out as a business.

Finally, all furniture, whether new or secondhand, sold during the course of business must be supplied with an official label saying the items comply with the safety requirements of the 1988 Regulations.

Making tenants pay through the nose for gas

The old days of landlords legally making money out of their tenants' gas have long gone. Nowadays they cannot charge more than a 'maximum resale price' laid down by the Director-General of Gas Supply. Gas meters must be set at roughly the same price as landlords themselves pay and, if they want to recover standing charges in addition, the amount must be divided up among the various meters and billed separately.

Ofgas, the Government watchdog for the gas industry, publishes a leaflet, *Selling Gas to Tenants*. This explains tenants' rights in full and is available, with other advice, from a free Ofgas Helpline on 0800–887777.

Covenants against the tenant assigning or subletting

Restrictions in leases on assignment or subletting are of two kinds: absolute, where subletting is not allowed in any circumstances and conditional, where the landlord's consent is stated to be required. Even then, the 1927 Landlord and Tenant Act says that a landlord cannot 'unreasonably' refuse consent – and decided cases have established that refusal generally must relate to the personality of the assignee or subtenant or the effect on the use or occupation of the premises. A desire to be 'bloody-minded' and cause maximum inconvenience to the tenant is most certainly not enough.

What happens if a tenant considers his landlord's refusal 'unreasonable'? He can either go to court for a declaration to that effect and an award of damages or, if he has the courage of his convictions and can persuade others to follow suit, he can carry on with the assignment of subletting regardless – leaving it for the landlord to challenge it in court. But such tactics are only for the brave – or the foolhardy.

So far, we have primarily been dealing with fairly short leases or tenancy agreements. In the next chapter we shall move on to consider long leases of 21 years or more. They bring their own batch of legal problems.

Note

1 A reasonably priced (£10.99) specialist paperback, the *Which? Guide to Renting and Letting*, is currently on the market.

18

LONG LEASES

Long leases are leases whose original length was for 21 years or more. It does not matter how many years have passed since they first began: a 99-year lease may have only five more years to run but it still counts legally as a 'long lease'. More flats than houses are held on long leases, and people owning long leases on their flats often call themselves 'flat-owners', and that is what I shall most frequently call them in this chapter – but they are nothing of the sort. In law, they are merely glorified flat-owners. They do not own the freehold. They – or their children or grandchildren – will eventually have to hand back the flat to their landlord: i.e. the individual or company that owns the freehold of the ground on which stands the building containing the flat. All that these flat-owners – myself included! – actually own is their long lease.

And there are half a million of us in London alone.

Sadly it is undoubted fact that the law dealing with our rights is inadequate, out of date and urgently in need of reform.

I do not often quote politicians but Nick Raynsford, then Tony Blair's London Housing Minister, spoke nothing less than the truth when, in May 1998, he told an all-party group of 57 MPs set up to promote

leasehold reform that 'existing leasehold law in this country is fundamentally flawed'. He said: 'There is an all too significant minority of
landlords whose styles range from the incompetent to the criminal.
Although the value of their freehold can be as little as a fraction of 1 per
cent of the value of the flats, the present law gives them far too much
control and potential to extort money.

'Piecemeal legal changes in 1985, 1987, 1993 and 1996 have solved
some problems but created others, leaving landlords with too many
opportunities for disreputable behaviour.'

He promised 'comprehensive reform' and declared grandly: 'Our
overall objective is to provide leaseholders with the opportunity to reap
the full benefits of owner occupation and to have control over the way in
which their homes are managed.'

Needless to say, as with many politicians' promises, we are still
waiting to know when these wonderful new laws will come in and what
exactly they will say. Meanwhile we will have to continue to make do
with enforcing such rights as we have. Indeed, if you are prepared to be
persistent, they are not all that bad – but, in a really serious case, you will
almost certainly need help from a solicitor, accountant or surveyor,
which can be expensive. However, useful free advice can be obtained –
whether you are landlord or tenant – from the Leasehold Advisory
Service (LEASE) at 8 Maddox Street, London W1N 9PN. This is an
independent agency, funded by both Government grant and private
sector contributions, and is staffed by officers with legal training. Its
telephone number is 0207–493 3116; but LEASE prefers you, if possible,
not to call in the first instance but to write stating the specific issues on
which you need its help.

These are the main problem areas:

EXCESSIVE   SERVICE   CHARGES

Service charges, whereby flat-owners in a block contribute to the expense
of maintaining, repairing and insuring the building, are an essential part
of any long lease. But too many dishonest or incompetent landlords and
their managing agents use these charges as a device to make extra money.
Disputes usually occur over the standard of work done, its high cost or
the extent to which it is really necessary. Russell Conway, a specialist
London solicitor, was quoted in the *Sunday Times* in May 1999 as saying:
'I have cases at the moment where the landlord, managing agent and
builder are all related; they all make money from each other by ripping
off their tenants.' That does not surprise me. Some landlords carry out no

work for several years then put in swingeing service charges which they intimidate their flat-owners into paying. Others even make a profit out of the property's building insurance. It is common form in long leases for the landlord to have to arrange this cover, the cost of which they then get back from the flat-owners as part of the service charge; but there are reports of some landlords choosing the most expensive policy because they know they will get a kick-back from the insurance company.

So what does the law say?

It used to say almost nothing on the subject. Flat-owners were easy prey for dishonest landlords or managing agents. But in 1985 the Thatcher Government changed the law on residential long leases. In its Landlord and Tenant Act of that year, Sections 19 and 20 lay down that (1) service charges must be 'reasonable' with work done to a reasonable standard; (2) before new expenses are incurred, landlords must give their tenants or any residents' association[1] at least two different written estimates one month before spending over £1,000 for the whole building or £50 multiplied by the number of flats, whichever is the greater, and invite their comments upon them; (3) if these estimates are not given, landlords cannot claim more than £1,000 or the relevant multiples of £50; and (4) they cannot claim at all stale service charges relating to costs incurred more than 18 months earlier.

Until 1997 you had to sue in your local county court to obtain your rights under these two sections, with all the formality and built-in potential for delay often entailed in court proceedings. But in September 1997, to try and make it easier to obtain justice, the process was made more user-friendly when jurisdiction was transferred to the more informal, and less expensive, leasehold valuation tribunals (LVTs). Nowadays these handle all disputes over the reasonableness of service charges, insurance problems and cases where the management problems are so intractable that, as we shall see, flat-owners apply to take over the management themselves or nominate someone else as manager.[2]

LVTs normally consist of a lawyer, a valuer and a lay person, with the chairman always a lawyer. Hearings are 'semi-formal' and evidence is not on oath. Their official handbook says: 'Applicants do not have to be represented by a solicitor or barrister, although professional assistance is recommended.' Even so, articulate and intelligent residential owners do occasionally conduct their own cases – and win.

So much for civil law but the 1985 Act also, for the first time, brought the criminal law into this arena:

Section 21 (1) gives a tenant or the secretary of a residents' association the right to ask the landlord to supply a written summary of the costs incurred over the past 12 months on which she has based her most recent service charges. If the landlord then fails to comply with such a request within one month or within six months of the end of the last accounting period, whichever is the later, she commits a criminal offence for which she can be fined up to £2,500.

Furthermore, the next section of the Act, Section 22 (1) says that, when such a written summary has been supplied, a tenant or residents' association secretary can ask the landlord in writing to afford 'reasonable facilities' for inspecting the accounts, receipts or other documents supporting the summary and for taking copies or extracts from them. If she fails to provide such facilities for inspection, she commits another offence with a maximum £2,500 fine.

Flat-owners or residents' association secretaries can themselves prosecute for these offences in the local magistrates' court, but that seldom happens. The Act says that the local council can also prosecute. Anyone who thinks an offence has been committed with regard to their property should complain to the Tenancy Relations Department at their local town hall.

All this may read very well but, alas, the courts tend not to treat these cases with the seriousness they deserve – as, for instance, in this typical case:

An inadequate fine

In August 1997, a property company which showed 'a rigid, high-handed, obstinate and pedantic' attitude towards flat-owners in a block in St John's Wood, north-west London and 'wilfully and deliberately' refused to give them details of their service charge was fined £350 with £978 costs by local magistrates. The company appealed to the Crown Court but abandoned its attempt in the face of overwhelming evidence. Judge Leo Charles, QC said it was 'a great shame' that the appeal had been brought and increased the fine to £1,000 with £1,778 costs. Two years before the company had been convicted in a similar case over another one of its properties.

So why did the original magistrates only hand down a £350 fine and why did Judge Charles not increase the amount to much nearer the £2,500 maximum? Even that figure is peanuts to most property companies. For penalties really to sting, Parliament should increase the maximum amounts fourfold: a £10,000 fine is far more likely to teach unscrupulous landlords proper respect for their flat-owners' rights.

NOT KNOWING THE LANDLORD'S NAME AND ADDRESS

Readers may be amazed to know that many flat-owners do not know the name and address of their freeholder – and managing agents deliberately often keep them in ignorance. This can be infuriating. Apart from anything else, how are you to complain effectively about the managing agents' failures?

In fact there are at least three ways in which the law imposes a duty upon landlords of residential property to give their tenants, whether on long or short leases, their name and address.

1. Section 1 of the 1985 Landlord and Tenant Act is straightforward. It says that a residential tenant is entitled – at any time – to make a written request for the landlord's name and address to 'the last person who received rent' (which includes ground rent) or 'to any other person acting as his agent'. And if that person does not 'without reasonable excuse' supply the information in writing within 21 days, he or she commits a criminal offence and can be fined up to £2,500.
2. Section 2 of the same Act says that, if the landlord is a limited company, you can ask the company or its managing agent for the name and address of every director and the company secretary. Failure to give this information within 21 days 'without reasonable excuse' also attracts a fine of up to £2,500.
3. Furthermore, Section 48 of the 1987 Landlord and Tenant Act says that a written rent or service charge demand 'must contain the landlord's name and address' – even without your asking for it. If not, the service charge is not payable until the name and address are given!

This is all powerful stuff – but how many people know about it? I have a question and answer column on homes and property law in the London *Evening Standard* and this recent extract reveals an appalling lack of knowledge on the part of lawyers and others who should know better:

When lawyers do not know the law

I am the leaseholder of a flat in litigation with the company that owns the block over serious housing disrepair and noise nuisance, but my solicitor's attempts to discover the name and address of the company secretary and any other directors have been ignored. He tells me that I can start proceedings for myself in the local magistrates' court. I telephoned the court but they said they do not deal with such offences and advised me to telephone the local county court where they told me much the same. I then contacted a legal advice centre whose details I found in the phone book but they also could not help. Can you please tell me which court to go to?

I am amazed at this general ignorance. This aspect of landlord and tenant law is obviously not so well known as it should be. The people whom you consulted at the magistrates' court and the legal advice centre should have known – or bothered to look up! – that Section 2 uses the phrase 'summary offence'. This can *only* mean an offence prosecuted in a magistrates' court.

They should also have known that, if prepared to take the financial risk, private citizens can themselves bring such a prosecution.

Furthermore, they and, with respect, your own lawyer should also have known – or checked – that, as well as being able to do it yourself, Section 34 of the 1985 Act states quite clearly that prosecutions for any offence against the Act 'may be brought by a local housing authority'.

You should contact the Tenancy Relations Officers at your local Town Hall and see if they are prepared to bring proceedings. If not, go back to your local magistrates' court and tell them what the law is!

SACKING MANAGING AGENTS

Despite paying heavy service charges, many flat-owners remain aggrieved with the general standard of maintenance of their building and some adventurous souls believe they are capable of taking on the job themselves. The 1987 Landlord and Tenant Act gave them the right to apply to the local county court – ever since September 1977, the local leasehold valuation tribunal – for an order sacking the existing managing agents (or the landlord) and handing over the management to them or their nominee.

So long as a building contains two or more flats, the owners – or joint owners of a single flat – can apply, although obviously the more who do so, the greater the likelihood of success. But applications will succeed only where you can prove that the landlord is in breach of a management obligation in the lease or has demanded or is likely to demand unreasonable service charges or has failed to comply with a Government-approved code of practice (such as that produced by the Royal Institution of Chartered Surveyors) *and* it is 'just and convenient' for the order to be made.

Furthermore, Section 23 of the 1987 Act excludes any application where there is a resident landlord or in certain other specified cases, including a local authority, urban development corporation or housing association.

BUYING A SHARE IN THE FREEHOLD

Long leaseholders of houses have long been able to force their freeholder to sell them the property – if they can afford to buy it. For decades long leaseholders of flats campaigned successive governments to change the law to allow them a similar right to club together with others in the same building and jointly buy the freehold from the owner. Finally, John Major's Government brought in, with some reluctance,[3] the 1993 Leasehold Reform, Housing and Urban Development Act to achieve exactly that purpose, and nowadays 'leasehold enfranchisement', as it is properly called, is often resorted to.

Regrettably, the subject is extremely complicated and anyone contemplating it really should consult a solicitor or specialist surveyor. The Blair Government is committed to revising the system and making it more accessible to ordinary flat-owners; but they still have not even reached the stage of draft legislation.

However, this is an outline of the current legal framework, as it has existed since 1993:

The right to buy the freehold only arises if at least 90 per cent of the floor space of the block is residential: no more than 10 per cent can be used for shops or offices. Then the only flat-owners who qualify are those with leases of over 21 years paying a low ground rent. But that is not all. At least two-thirds must agree to join the scheme *and* half that number must have lived in their flats as their main or only home for the past year or for a total of three years out of the past ten.

But once that essential half of consenting residential leaseholders exists, other flat-owners who do not live in the block but merely have their flats as an investment can come in on these residents' backs.

We then come to the vital question: how much is the freehold likely to cost?

There are some strange ideas currently in vogue. I know one local estate agent in central London who airily tells clients: 'It will cost you half the present value of your flat.' That is nonsense. The 1993 Act lays down a very strict formula by which the price is to be calculated.

The basic concept is that the landlord should not lose out on the deal and is entitled, as a starting point, to the present market value of his freehold, calculated as if the Act was not forcing him to sell. This is assessed on the basis of his ground rents and the eventual value of the property when your leases run out and it reverts to him.

But that is not all. You will also have to pay his share (approximately 50 per cent) of what the Act calls the 'marriage value' of the property. This is even more complicated. It is supposed to reflect the net increase in value to you and your colleagues of 'marrying' your leaseholds with the freehold. This involves a valuation of your existing leases (inevitably diminishing as time goes by) and balancing that against the increased value of the freehold you will be acquiring.

So, putting it bluntly, the landlord gets not only the existing market value of his freehold but also half the increased value of your leases. It is little wonder that many flat-owners take the view that the Act is weighted in favour of the landlord.

Sometimes one sees, when estate agents are advertising flats for sale, the phrase: 'Enfranchisement available'. How is this possible if the buyer will have to live in the flat for at least one year in order to qualify?

The answer is simple. The 1993 Act's residential qualification only applies to *starting* the legal process. That has to be done by serving the freeholder with a written notice claiming the right. Once that notice has been served, the claim can then easily be passed on to a new flat-owner. He or she must notify within 14 days the flat-owner nominated by the others to buy the freehold on their behalf – and can then carry on as if nothing had happened.

The position of a resident landlord has also to be considered: he is treated with greater consideration than someone who does not live on the premises. The 1993 Act, therefore, exempts resident owners from the legal duty to sell the freehold, if the block is a converted property containing no more than four flats and the resident landlord (or an adult member of her family) has lived in one of the flats as their only or principal home for the last 12 months. But if the block is purpose-built, the exemption does not apply and the mere fact that the owner of the block lives in one of the flats is irrelevant.

NOTE: Even with converted blocks of less than five flats, flat-owners, although unable to buy a share in the freehold, still have the right to buy 90-year extensions of their individual leases.

NINETY-YEAR LEASE EXTENSIONS

These are an alternative to clubbing together to buy the freehold. The 1993 Act confers a totally separate right to demand from the freeholder a 90-year extension of one's lease at a cost to be worked out in accordance with the Act. But the residential qualification is not quite the same as with buying the freehold. Except where the landlord is a charitable housing trust, nearly all flat-owners qualify for the extension if they have lived in the flat as their main or only home for the past three years or for periods totalling three years in the last 10 years. And it does not matter if 90 per cent of the block is not residential.

As always with this Act, the procedure is extremely complicated with rigid time limits but, in principle, it works like this:

You serve a notice on your landlord formally asking for a 90-year extension (it cannot be less!) and making an offer of what you want to pay. The landlord then has two months in which to respond, either (rarely) saying you are not entitled to an extension or (more usually) accepting your entitlement but disputing your suggested price and putting forward her own figure.

If you cannot, within a stated time, agree the price, you both have to go before a leasehold valuation tribunal which will give a definitive ruling. If you then produce the money required, the freeholder cannot refuse your extension. There is no question of 'holding out' against it, as some freeholders threatened to do in the early days of this legislation. It is inevitable. That is the whole point of the Act.

Furthermore, if you are buying the long lease of a flat where the seller has already clocked up her three years' minimum residential qualification and started the legal procedure to extend the lease, you can take over the seller's application – without having to live there yourself for at least three years. This has, of course, very much increased the value of many existing long leases whose time is running out.

One final question: is there a formula by which the price of the new lease is calculated or is the freeholder free to charge any price?

As I have already said, the answer is extremely – and unnecessarily – complicated and you will undoubtedly need professional help from a specialist solicitor or surveyor. So that you will know some of the pitfalls involved, I strongly recommend that you write to the Leasehold Advisory Service (LEASE) at 8 Maddox Street, London W1N 9PN asking them to send you their two explanatory booklets *Lease Extension – Getting Started* and *Lease Extension – Valuation*. Both are free and you need only enclose a self-addressed A4 envelope bearing a 60p stamp.

Having said that, an easy rule-of-thumb method is to look in local estate agents' windows, see what a similar flat in your area with a 63-year lease and another with something like a 153-year lease would cost, halve the difference and that will be a very rough (but still reliable) indication of what an extended lease would cost under the procedures laid down by the 1993 Act – especially for leases with more than 50 or 60 years still to run.

RIGHT OF FIRST REFUSAL

Sometimes flat-owners are shocked to discover that the property company which owns the freehold has sold the block over their heads. Often the first they know is when a new firm of managing agents sends them a service charge demand naming a new owner. Is this legal?

Part 1 of the 1987 Landlord and Tenant Act says that, if a non-resident landlord (with very few exceptions, such as a housing association) wishes to dispose of property where more than half the internal floor area is let to residential flat-owners, he must serve them with a written notice of his intentions and give them 'a right of first refusal'. He must also tell them the price and other principal sales terms.

He can name his own price, which the flat-owners can either accept or try to negotiate down. Only if negotiations fail, can he then sell the property to anyone else – but the price must be not less than that at which it was first offered to the flat-owners.

If the landlord does not offer his flat-owners first refusal, he commits a criminal offence for which he can be fined up to £5,000 and, where the landlord is a company, any consenting director can also be fined.

As always, the provisions of the Act are extremely complicated. If flat-owners find their block has been sold over their heads, they should consult a solicitor as soon as possible – and they may be able to unscramble the deal and buy back the freehold from the so-called new owners.

FINAL THOUGHT

It will have become apparent that I am no great lover of the modern system of long leaseholds, but then few people, apart from large property companies, are. I leave you with this extract from the Leasehold Enfranchisement Association's open letter to Prime Minister Tony Blair in September 1999 commenting on his Government's seeming reluctance to change the system to any great extent: 'Long leasehold is a flawed and abusive form of land tenure, which is not now tolerated in any country in the world except England and Wales (Hawaii, the only other harbourer of it in recent times, now having outlawed it)'.

Notes
1 Unless leases state the contrary (which is rare), managing agents cannot insist on dealing only with a residents' association if it does not represent all the residents. They must treat all residents as having equal rights and, if that means they have to deal with the association and then with each resident who is not a member, it is their tough luck.
2 LVTs still do not have the jurisdiction to make monetary awards. They can

only rule on whether service charges are 'reasonable' and leave it to the parties to sue in the local county court for the payment of any moneys due because of that ruling.

3 It nearly cost the Tory Party the financial support of some of its most traditional friends in the ranks of the landed aristocracy and other large property owners.

19

NEIGHBOURS

The traditional view of the average Englishman or woman is as a reasonable sort of person. 'Live and let live' is supposed to be their motto. They are thought to be always ready to see the other person's point of view.

This may all be perfectly true. But it does not seem to apply when they are living next door to each other. As G.K. Chesterton wrote a long time ago, 'Your next-door neighbour is not a man; he is an environment. He is the barking of a dog; he is the noise of a pianola; he is a dispute about a party wall; he is drains that are worse than yours or roses that are better than yours.'

The Law Reports – and daily newspapers – abound with tales of the most unseemly battles between neighbours. Noise, smoke, smell, fumes, leaking drains, late-night parties, do-it-yourself disasters, vibrations from nearby factories and workshops, broken-down fences and hedges, overhanging branches of trees, disputes about dustbins and parking space, marauding pets, windows broken by cricket balls: all these, and much more, have led to court cases between warring neighbours. And when I say warring, I mean warring.

In one case, a man could not stand the noise when the music teacher next door gave piano lessons. So he banged on trays and whistled and shrieked whenever lessons were being given. Result: a High Court judge granted an injunction ordering him to stop and ruled he must pay damages as well.

In another case, a woman living in a maisonette complained that her life had been made 'absolutely intolerable' by hammering, stamping and jumping on the floor above. The people upstairs retorted that she banged on her ceiling, interfered with their part of the garden and had once stuffed a dead mouse through their letterbox. *Both* were ordered to stop causing what is technically called 'an actionable nuisance' to each other.

The second case is very recent, the first was over a hundred years ago in nineteenth century England. Human nature has not changed very much.

The Common Law, that part of our law which is made up by the decisions of our judges over the years, has always insisted that reasonableness must be the keynote of the law of neighbours. Victorian judge Vice-Chancellor Knight-Bruce may sound pompous (and prematurely anti-European Community) to modern ears. But what he said in 1851, in the case of *Walter* v. *Selfe*, is still – perhaps incredibly – the current legal yardstick:

> Ought this inconvenience to be considered in fact as more than fanciful, more than one of mere delicacy or fastidiousness, as an inconvenience materially interfering with the ordinary comfort physically of human existence, not merely according to elegant or dainty modes and habits of living, but according to plain and sober and simple notions among the English people?

In April 1994, the defence lawyer used this very quotation in his final speech to the magistrates at Wetherby, West Yorkshire to help obtain the acquittal of an aviary owner in a nearby village accused of causing a nuisance after a neighbouring couple had bitterly complained about the 'incessant' chirruping from his 40 budgerigars. The hearing lasted for seven days, was reported in all the daily newspapers and cost Leeds Council, which had taken up the neighbours' case, an estimated £100,000 in legal costs.

The application of Knight-Bruce's venerable principle varies from locality to locality. As a later Victorian judge said in 1879 (still quoted in all the law books): 'What would be a nuisance in Belgrave Square would not necessarily be so in Bermondsey.' Similarly, in 1935, an Appeal Court judge laid down: 'A reasonable person would not expect precisely as much light in Mayfair as he would get in the country and he would not expect precisely so much light in the City of London as he would get in Mayfair.'

It follows that people living in the country can expect different standards from those living in London or other large cities. For instance, Judge Deirdre McKinney overruled at Bournemouth Crown Court an earlier order by magistrates in Wimborne, Dorset ordering Mr Dereck Orman, a local smallholder, to dispose of a stag turkey called Bernard and four cockerels. His family had kept poultry on the smallholding since the turn of the century without any complaints but when a couple retired from London to a nearby bungalow they soon found the noise too much. The local magistrates agreed but, on appeal, their counsel successfully quoted to Judge McKinney this extract from a leading article in the *Daily Telegraph* :

> The appropriate noises of nature should be left alone. If Mr Orman had blasted his new neighbours with loud pop music over the garden fence, then it would be easier to feel some sympathy for their case. If people living in the country object to its immemorial sounds, they should retreat to the man-made cacophony of city life.

Judge McKinney's ruling confirmed that was the attitude of the law. Crowing cockerels, barking dogs, smells from drains, cesspits and pig farms are typical countryside 'problems' which neighbours usually have to put up with. Country-dwellers often keep several cockerels or dogs on the premises and 'country smells' are a fact of rural life.

But there is a limit. In one case, cockerels who sounded like 'a football crowd cheering a cup-tie' were ruled to be a nuisance and when three neighbours in deepest Berkshire joined forces to sue over the noise from over 90 dogs in newly opened training kennels for greyhounds, Mr Justice Hinchcliffe came down at 8 a.m. from the High Court in London to hear for himself the barking chorus. Later, back in court, he ruled with some feeling: 'When country dwellers are unable to open a window or to enjoy working, resting or pottering about in the garden, when the barking of dogs can be heard above the sound of a washing machine, when rest is interfered with and one has to leave for peace and quiet – then a substantial nuisance has been caused.' He awarded the plaintiffs an injunction and damages.

Yet there is a delicate balance to all this. The mere fact that any particular activity has been going on for years before someone comes to an area does not, *in itself*, prevent a newcomer from complaining of an 'actionable nuisance' if it is objectively unacceptable. That was first decided by the Appeal Court in 1879 and in May 1994 there was an interesting modern example at Slough County Court:

The case of the village cricket club

A couple came to live in a house overlooking a Buckinghamshire village green where cricket had been played at weekends for the past seventy years. Soon cricket balls were being hit into their garden and the couple found it most unpleasant. They asked the village cricket club to put up two huge 25-foot-high nets as protection but the club claimed it did not have the money and the nets would be an eyesore. Negotiations broke down and the couple sued for an injunction preventing the club from continuing to play any more cricket – without the two nets.

They lost their case. Judge Nigel Hague said: 'An injunction would deprive many people of the pleasure they obtain from watching cricket and the focus of social life. The mere fact that cricket balls sometimes penetrate and even fly into the grounds of nearby houses does not mean that the playing of cricket is an actionable nuisance.'

It might have been different if someone had actually been hit by a cricket ball or the house itself damaged in some way with windows broken or roof tiles dislodged. As it was, the risk of serious injury or damage was 'minimal' and the interference to the plantiffs' enjoyment of their property not undue. 'Such interference is a consequence of the character of the neighbourhood. Nearly all of us have to put up with a certain amount of annoyance from our neighbours.'

Let us now have a quick look at some of the most frequent causes of complaint, whether in town or country:

Trees Do the branches of your neighbour's trees overhang your garden? If so, you may lop them off at the boundary without even warning her beforehand – although it would clearly be more polite to do so. As long ago as 1895 in the classic case of *Lemmon* v. *Webb* Lord Macnaughten ruled: 'A man is not bound to permit a neighbour's trees to overhang the surface of his land.'

The same principle applies to tree roots spreading out below your land. If they endanger your foundations, you can cut them back to the boundary – but you must take care not to damage the tree itself. In fact, you should first complain to your neighbour and offer her facilities to do the job herself. If she refuses, you then have a much freer hand to engage contractors yourself and recover the cost from her. Furthermore, if you warn that her roots are creating a potential danger, this will make it easier to claim compensation for whatever damage they cause. Poplar trees, in particular, figure highly in the reported cases.

But please remember that if you cut offending branches yourself, you cannot use them for firewood or eat any of the fruit. Both branches and their natural attachments remain your neighbour's property. The strictly legal position is farcical: she cannot insist on coming in to reclaim her property and, if she enters without your consent, she commits trespass for which (technically) you could sue her. But you cannot pick them up or use them yourself! That would be a trespass on your part. Your only legal right is to let them lie there to rot. The law sometimes favours the bloody-minded.

(This same principle applies to balls and other such objects hit accidentally on to your land. Technically, the couple in the village green case need not have handed back the cricket balls hit into their garden, although they usually did. They could have insisted on the balls lying where they fell. When some years ago a golfer in Harwich insisted on going on to private farmland to retrieve a golfball despite the farmer's objections, the police were called and the golfer ended up being bound over by the local magistrates to keep the peace.)

Reverting to trees, their owners must take reasonable care of them and lop or trim them when safety requires it – or risk being sued if the tree falls and does damage. Not everyone can afford this. In one recent case, an elderly widow living on a modest pension could not pay an expert to lop a large old tree, even though her neighbour warned it was unsafe and might fall and hit someone in his garden. She explained her financial position and said she would be happy to allow a contractor to come in and do the job if her neighbour paid the bill. And that is what happened, even though legally it was her responsibility.

But no one can come on to your land and cut down your tree without your permission, as happened in discreet, respectable Kensington in August 1979. A woman complained to her neighbour that three plane trees at the back of his garden partly overhung her land and blocked the light to her house (we shall see about 'the right to light' in a minute). While the tree owner and his wife were away on summer holiday, she instructed a tree surgeon to go into the next-door garden and 'thin' the trees but, because one was diseased, his workmen felled the whole tree. Result: after Mr Justice Woolf had visited the garden (which often happens in this type of case), he held the woman and her tree surgeon jointly liable to pay £750, the value of the 40-foot felled tree.[1]

What many people may not realise is that you can be fined for cutting down a tree in your own garden. The 1990 Town and Country Planning Act says that when you live in a conservation area, you cannot cut down, lop, top or uproot any tree standing on your own land without the local authority's consent – except when the tree is dead, dying or dangerous. The penalty is a fine of up to £5,000, although usually nothing like this amount is handed down.

The same prohibition applies, even outside a conservation area, if a local authority has imposed a tree preservation order on a particular tree because of its 'amenity value'. So it is prudent to check with your local town hall before taking drastic action: in 1980 the High Court ruled, on an earlier piece of similar legislation, that ignorance of a tree preservation order is no defence.

Animals often cause immense problems: so much so that they deserve a chapter all to themselves, as you will see in Chapter 21.

Fences Arguing about who should keep a garden fence in good repair is another frequent cause of contention. But here at least there is usually an easy remedy: the title deeds may give the answer but, if not, go out into the garden and look at the fence. The law presumes that it will originally have been built up to the very limit of its owner's land. So, if the supporting stake is on your side, the fence belongs to you and you have to maintain it. If it is on the other side, the fence is your neighbour's liability. If there are no supports on either side and there is nothing in the title deeds, you and your neighbour share responsibility.

Barbecues and garden bonfires Contrary to what many people may think, the 1956 Clean Air Act does not apply to domestic gardens. So, in the absence of any local by-law, no one can threaten you with prosecution for an occasional smoky bonfire or over-pungent barbecue. But if you make a persistent habit of it, you could be sued for an actionable nuisance.

Sometimes people complain about their **right to light**. This is what the law calls 'ancient lights' and can be enjoyed only if there is a specific legal agreement to that effect or if you, or previous occupants of your property, have enjoyed it for at least 20 years. This excludes most new properties, and many houses on modern estates have a clause in the title deeds preventing a right to light accruing even after 20 years.

But, once the right exists, it is of considerable value. If, for instance, your neighbour builds an extension, even if it is not large enough to require planning permission, you may well be able to sue. But, as with all actionable nuisance, your inconvenience must not be trivial: your light must have been *substantially* reduced. And it is only light to a building that is protected. You cannot complain merely because there is less sun in your garden.

However, in 1978 the Appeal Court ruled that a garden greenhouse was a 'building' for the purposes of this rule. So a Rochdale house-owner, who had built a fence alongside his neighbour's greenhouse and parked his caravan behind it so that, although the neighbour could still work in his greenhouse, the light was not enough to grow his more exotic plants, had to take down the fence and remove his caravan.

Incidentally, there is a limit to what you can legally do *in your own garden*. You can bury your dead pet there[2] and, if not prohibited by local by-laws or other regulations, even a dead human being. Diana, Princess of Wales, Dodi Fayed, her last lover and Alan Clark, the diarist and politician are obvious recent examples. But I would advise first checking with your local town hall.

Sun-worshippers should note that you cannot strip off and sunbathe in the nude in your own garden, if there is a risk of a neighbour seeing you from an upstairs window and reporting you to the police for a possible breach of the peace or indecent exposure. And some neighbours would take pleasure in doing so.

Nor can you make love on your own back lawn, if anyone can see. 'I love my wife and I cannot see why we should not show some affection to each other,' a 39-year-old instrument maker in Norwich once told the police. It had been his regular practice to have sexual intercourse with his wife in their bungalow's back garden, as and when the mood took them. Unfortunately, the next-door garden was separated only by a row of flowers and one afternoon, unknown to them, their neighbour's two small children saw what was going on, told their mother – and she called the police.

Local magistrates fined the husband £50 for indecent exposure and gave his wife a conditional discharge for aiding and abetting. Some cases could only happen in Britain.

But of all the reasons for neighbourly dissension, **noise** is far and away the most frequent. As a nation, we are getting increasingly selfish and complaints about noisy neighbours have risen greatly in recent years: barking dogs, screaming children, thumping music and DIY noise are the most common causes. Not that offending music, as between neighbours, has necessarily to be loud. In a case in Leicester where a young single mother was fined for subjecting her neighbours to a continuous stream of music from BBC Radio One, the actual decibel level of the noise was not great but, as a local environmental health official explained, 'There is a peculiarly irritating characteristic of music coming through a wall, particularly if it has lyrics. The brain cannot help latching on to them. A 10 decibel level against background hum isn't irritating. A singer at the same level is.'

Parties are a particular noise menace. If an excessively noisy party ruins your evening or prevents you sleeping, you can – even on a one-off basis – complain to the police and, if resources permit, they will send an officer along to knock at the door and ask them to quieten things down. You have the right to demand this as part of the legal duty cast upon the police to keep the peace. Nor does this only happen in the deprived areas of our inner cities. In July 1993, exhausted neighbours called police to a pensioners' Darby and Joan party in respectable Aylesbury, Bucks where the doors were left open because of the heat. The party had started at 5.30 p.m. and was still going strong well after midnight. As a neighbour said: 'We've had Max Bygraves and now we are on to Frank Sinatra.' Later, the police issued a discreet statement: 'When our officers arrived they found the party was still going strong but the noise was not excessive and no action was taken.'

With most people a polite visit from the police will, in itself, be enough to quieten things down. But if noisy parties persist, it can amount to an actionable nuisance. Some years ago, at Clerkenwell County Court, a man whose rowdy parties every third Saturday night always disturbed a couple across the street was ordered to stop and pay them £50 damages (now it would be much more).

Burglar alarms are in a special legal category. As a *Times* leading article has said, 'Burglar alarms have come to epitomise the worst menaces of urban life, malfunctioning at every conceivable occasion, invariably waiting until a Friday night, when the owners are away and untraceable, before unleashing their aural violence.' False alarms have become a curse of modern living – and the law is largely inadequate to deal with them. The names of two key-holders able to reach the property within half an hour are supposed to be lodged with the police and 'it is desirable that' alarms should be fitted with an automatic cut-out device after 20 minutes but these requirements do not have the force of law. They are contained in a *Code of Practice on Noise from Audible Intruder Alarms* of which most people have never even heard.

The police, though frequently telephoned by anguished neighbours, have no effective or speedy right of forcible entry to turn off an alarm, nor have local environmental health officials and, of course, neighbours cannot sue for nuisance because the inconvenience suffered, although intense, does not usually last (at the very worst) for all that long and so does not count as 'substantial' within Vice-Chancellor Knight-Bruce's 1851 ruling.

Noise from building works is also in a special legal category but here the law is quite effective. Section 60 of the 1974 Control of Pollution Act gives local authorities extensive powers to control the hours within which building work can take place, the type of plant or machinery used and the level of permitted noise. If your life is being made wretched by building work, speak to the site manager or phone up his head office and say that, unless they curb the din, you will complain to the environmental health department at the local council under Section 60 of the Act. You should quote the actual number of the section and the name of the Act:

they will realise that you know what you are talking about.

Unfortunately, the Act does not apply to the nuisance caused by the many building workers and house decorators, not only those on building sites, who seem unable to work without their radios blasting out pop music at top volume. Some councils have by-laws about noisy radios and stereos so a complaint to the local environmental health department may bring results, although I doubt it. Our understaffed police will also usually not intervene, even if you say the noise is causing a breach of the peace. They have their own priorities.

But, in general, what are your practical remedies when your neighbour commits a legal nuisance and makes your life miserable?

Self-help Obviously you should begin by politely asking the neighbour to stop or tone down whatever she is doing. If that does not work, some people now turn to mediation: you could try telephoning Mediation UK, an independent charitable organisation representing over 500 mediation services in the UK. The number is 0177–9046661.

Yet the law is quite robust. If you do not protect your own interests, when you physically can, you may find yourself penalised in court. Some years ago, a man sued his neighbour in Lowestoft County Court for £500 for damage done to his house by a plant that had encroached from next door. It must have been a ferocious weed, because it grew up through the floorboards and was sprouting through the wallpaper and up the staircase before the neighbour was finally made to remove it with a mechanical digger.

But 'the plaintiff could have saved himself much money if he had taken steps to deal with the matter earlier,' ruled Judge Evans, and cut his claim to £50.

Yet there is a limit. In June 1993, a 30-year-old scaffolder on night work who could not get to sleep because of his neighbour's blaring pop music finally smashed up his stereo with an axe. The noise had been so loud that the pictures were jumping about on his bedroom wall as he lay awake. Result: he pleaded guilty at Hatfield magistrates' court to criminal damage but the chairman of the Bench said he had been 'provoked' and let him off with an order for £25 costs – ignoring the neighbour's request for £1,000 compensation for his ruined hi-fi system.

You can sue for an injunction and damages This may sound awesome but you can do so inexpensively in your local low-cost small claims court where the judge can award up to £5,000 damages and grant an injunction banning future excessive noise on pain of imprisonment for breach of this order. Sometimes a strongly worded solicitor's letter threatening to sue will do the trick.

You can complain to the environmental health department at your local town hall In practice, this is what most people do and it is the most cost-effective way of dealing with the problem. Sections 79 and 80 of the 1990 Environmental Protection Act, improving upon earlier legislation, set up a really good system of 'abatement notices'. It is primarily invoked by people complaining about noise (which includes vibration) but is also available to deal with complaints about smoke, fumes or gases and about dust, steam, smell or other effluvia from industrial premises.

If, after investigation, the environmental health inspectors agree that a 'statutory nuisance' – which is the same as an 'actionable nuisance' – exists, they have no option. Under the wording of the Act, they *must* serve an abatement notice on the owner or occupier of the building requiring him to stop the nuisance. If 'without reasonable excuse' he does not do so, the council will then prosecute him in the local magistrates' court and, if convicted, he can be fined up to £5,000 with a further £500 for each day on which the nuisance continues. In extreme cases, magistrates have even ordered hi-fi sets and stereo units to be confiscated: the first instance was in January 1992 when a 16-year-old Liverpool flat-dweller's hi-fi was seized after she had made neighbours' lives wretched for months with loud music blasting out late at night and early in the morning.

The 1996 Noise Act gave greater powers to local authorities to ensure their citizens had restful nights. It created a new offence of 'excessive noise at night': i.e. 35 decibels when measured in the complainant's house. Householders can be fined £100 on the spot, their equipment seized there and then and a maximum £1,000 fine can be handed down in court, if the noise persists. The main problem, as so often, is one of resources. Not many councils have been able to afford to recruit the extra personnel needed to implement these powers.

Some councils have nevertheless, with help from Government funding, set up out-of-hours complaints services to enforce the ordinary 'statutory nuisance' provisions of the Environmental Health Act, and some even operate 24 hours a day. But the cost is often prohibitive. The result is that you can find zealous officers prowling around prosperous suburbs in the early evening, trying to find reggae parties whereas at midnight, when parties are really getting under way in the inner cities, they are usually at home tucked up in bed.

You can bring a 'do-it-yourself' prosecution Section 82 of the 1990 Act gives private citizens the right to bring their own prosecution for a 'statutory nuisance' in the local magistrates' court. But most people prefer merely to complain to their local council – and that is what I recommend. It is simpler and easier.

Notes

1 But, Solomon-like, the judge threw out the tree owner's additional claim that the felling had lopped £10,000 off the value of his £300,000 house.

2 This long-standing principle of Common Law is now subject to the 1990 Environmental Protection Act which says that where an animal dies on veterinary premises of a highly infectious disease the vet must ensure that it is incinerated as 'clinical waste'. But, if your pet dies at the vet's of old age or some non-infectious illness, you can still bring it home and bury it in the garden. 'Clinical waste' does not apply where an animal dies at home or indeed anywhere other than at a vet's surgery.

20

VISITORS

So much for neighbours; now let us look briefly at the law on visitors. The 1957 Occupiers' Liability Act says that the occupier of premises, both residential and commercial, owes all his lawful visitors a 'common duty of care' to ensure that the visitor will be reasonably safe in using the premises for the purpose for which he is permitted or invited to be there.

What does that tortuous formula mean in practice? A little-known High Court case in June 1975 provides a good example.

The DIY that went wrong

A DIY enthusiast in Hemel Hempstead, Herts converted his garage into an extra sitting room and put in two attractive glass doors. He went to a reputable local firm to buy the doors but unfortunately they sold him doors with thinner glass than specified in a trade code of practice.

Result: an eight-year-old visitor was badly injured when she ran into the door and the glass shattered.

Mr Justice O' Connor awarded her damages against both the supplier and the do-it-yourselfer. 'Far be it for me to discourage people from "doing-it-themselves",' he said. 'But if you "do-it-yourself", the law requires that the degree of skill you must bring to bear on the project is the same that a reasonably competent workman would show.'

It is never an excuse that a workman is a well-meaning amateur. You undertake DIY at your legal peril. You cannot plead ignorance, either of building methods or of the law, as a defence if something goes wrong. You should have checked things out beforehand.

For instance, when contemplating major structural work it is always sensible to ask your local town hall whether you will need Building Regulations approval or planning permission. Similarly, an enthusiast can do his own rewiring. But only a local public electricity supplier can connect it to the supply – and they will need to be satisfied that the connection is safe. So first check their requirements: their number is in the phone book.

The golden rule for all DIY enthusiasts is to know your limitations, and keep within them.

In fact, any prudent householder should make sure that her household contents insurance policy covers her (at very little extra cost) for legal liability for injury to visitors.

Valid claims can all too easily be made. Every case depends on its own facts and many are settled out of court, but any failure to take reasonable care in all the circumstances can make you liable: for instance, leaving a child's toy on the stairs when you are expecting visitors, failing to warn someone that the kitchen floor has just been polished and is very slippery or not reminding an infrequent visitor to your house that there is one step down to your ground-floor lavatory.

This question of warning visitors of possible dangers can be tricky. The 1957 Act specifically says that a warning may not be enough, *in itself*, to escape liability. It is merely one factor to be taken into account. You may, for instance, warn a guest staying overnight that the shower mixer in the bathroom is faulty and only hot water comes out but, if the water is so hot that it scalds him, you will almost certainly still be liable.

Furthermore, the Act specifies that someone who visits premises 'in the exercise of his calling' must accept any special risk normally involved with that calling. In one case, a window cleaner recovered no damages when a frayed sash cord broke and a window came crashing down on his hand yet, if the same accident had happened to a non-working visitor, almost certainly there would have been liability.

But few things in the law are simple: if a window cleaner, plumber or similar trade visitor catches her foot in a worn patch of carpet and you should have realised it was a potential danger (but had not warned her), she probably could successfully sue you.

Another special category is children: as we have seen in Chapter 3, the 1957 Act says that you must expect children to be less careful than adults, even when trespassing. An adult may have his claim reduced because of his own 'contributory negligence' in not taking reasonable care for his own safety: e.g. in not looking where he was going. With child visitors, it is different: what would not be a potential danger for an adult could easily be so for a child. Obvious examples are the sharp corner of a table left uncovered or a carving knife left lying around or, as in a 1998 case, a building site where the owners had been warned that children used to squeeze through holes in the wire-mesh fence but had failed to block them off.

So much for lawful visitors but what about the unlawful variety: **adult trespassers**? The garbled wording of the 1984 Occupiers' Liability Act attempted to impose liability on occupiers to give some sort of 'reasonable' protection to uninvited guests but there still has been no authoritative court ruling as to exactly what that means.

I wrote those last words in the first edition of this book and blithely continued, 'But it is hardly a practical issue: unless you grab a Kalashnikov rifle and shoot a trespasser between the eyes at point-blank range (which most people would agree was illegal), he is hardly likely to sue over a mishap on your premises.' That was in 1995 before Britain had gone 'compensation crazy' and too many judges began too many inappropriate claims that earlier they would have rejected out of hand, such as the case in the High Court at Leeds in May 1997 when a 37-year-old burglar successfully sued a 63-year-old farmer who had broken his jaw with a kick after catching him stealing roof slates from a piggery. The burglar was prosecuted and let off with a conditional discharge. The farmer was ordered to pay damages. Mrs Justice Smith ruled that his kick amounted, in the circumstances, to 'unreasonable force'.

This was not the first case where our present generation of judges have seemed to favour criminals rather than their victims. The seal of approval on this surprisingly benign judicial mentality dates from *Revill* v. *Newberry* in the Appeal Court in November 1995.

The pensioner ordered to pay a burglar £4,000

Retired Derbyshire miner and pensioner William Newberry, 78, had taken to sleeping in his allotment shed to protect it from vandals and thieves. At about 2 a.m. one Saturday morning, he was awakened by the sound of 21-year-old Mark Revill and another man trying to break in. The shed contained several items worth stealing. So Mr Newberry grabbed his shotgun, loaded it, poked the barrel through a small hole in the door and fired into the darkness. The charge struck the intruder in the chest. He sued for damages – and won. Mr Justice Rougier threw out the defence that Revill had been involved in a criminal enterprise but ruled that he was two-thirds to blame and therefore only entitled to £4,000, instead of £12,000. Three appeal judges upheld the award on the basis that Mr Newberry had used 'unreasonable force', with Lord Justice Tudor Evans commenting: 'The trespasser/criminal is not an outlaw.'

So how far can you go, in modern law, in defending your own home? If a burglar breaks in tonight, what can you legally do to defend yourself and your property?

Back in the early seventeenth century, Chief Justice Sir Edward Coke coined the phrase: 'An Englishman's home is his castle.' And it was another long-dead judge, Baron Parke, who ruled in a classic 1841 judgment: 'If a man find another breaking into his house, he has a right to push him out and to use as much force as necessary for that purpose.'

That is, in theory, still the law but nowadays judges tend to draw a clear line between what Oxford University Professor R.F.V. Heuston has called 'retributive' and 'deterrent' methods of house protection. You can legally 'deter' intruders by such means as barbed-wire fences, spikes, broken glass on top of walls and iron bars on your windows. The 1861 Offences Against the Person Act even allows you to place in your home – but only between sunset and sunrise – a spring-gun or mantrap capable of destroying human life or causing grievous bodily harm.

Guard dogs and electronically protected fencing are allowed, provided you display large warning notices alerting intruders to the risks that they run.

But you cannot 'punish' burglars and trespassers by wilfully shooting at them or attacking them, as if you were an avenging angel. That is presumably why the Crown Prosecution Service had earlier prosecuted the frightened Mr Newberry at Derby Crown Court for allegedly wounding his would-be burglar with intent. Fortunately the jury threw out the charge. With respect, they seem to have had more common sense than the CPS or the judges in the case.

For you *do* have the legal right to defend yourself, your home and your property – provided you use no more than reasonable force, and what is 'reasonable' will depend on all the circumstances.

Judges used to show considerable sympathy for innocent citizens reluctantly forced to defend themselves. As Lord Morris of Borth-y-Gest, a senior law lord, ruled in 1971: 'A person defending himself cannot weigh to a nicety the exact nature of his necessary defensive action. If a jury thought that in a moment of unexpected anguish a person attacked had only done what he honestly and instinctively thought was necessary, that would be most potent evidence that only reasonable defensive action had been taken.'

So this is my rough guide to what, in theory, you can and cannot do:

You can:

- shoot the intruder if you both have a gun, although, if you do not have a firearms certificate, the CPS may see fit to prosecute you. This actually happened to a Hertfordshire jeweller who was fined in September 1993, although a judge, when jailing the burglars, had earlier awarded him £300 for his bravery.
- pick up a knife, a walking stick (even, in a couple of cases, a sword) or anything else easily to hand if the intruder has a gun or is armed with any other weapon, such as a knife, hammer or cosh. That is why in 1994 the Essex coroner ruled that 33-year-old jeweller Dean Davies acted lawfully when stabbing to death with a clasp knife a masked armed burglar he found in his parents' empty home. You do not have to wait for the intruder to strike the first blow. As Lord Griffiths ruled in 1988: 'Circumstances may justify a pre-emptive strike.'
- use your fists, if you are young, fit and brave enough. But again 'reasonableness' is essential. If you are older and not so strong as the intruder is, you can again probably grab whatever is to hand.

BUT you cannot:

- booby trap your home with a home-made bomb, as did an electronics engineer in Belvedere, south-west London. A burglar almost had his left thumb blown off and the CPS threatened the engineer with prosecution for an explosives offence.
- shoot a burglar after it is all over. When a 56-year-old Nottingham man fired warning shots on seeing two burglars running away with their loot from an 81-year-old neighbour's home, he had to pay one of them £512 damages because a ricocheting bullet hit him in the thigh.
- cross what Lord Justice Ormrod once called the borderline between 'necessary self-defence and angry retaliation'. As in the tragic Old Bailey case in July 1993 when 40-year-old music teacher Bob Osborne, alerted by tyre-slashing outside his south London home, chased through the streets with a hammer the 17-year-old culprit who was later acquitted of murder after stabbing him to death with a Swiss Army knife.

I leave you with these sobering words by Lord Justice Millett in *Revill* v. *Newberry* : 'For centuries the Common Law has permitted reasonable force to be used in defence of the person or property. Violence may be returned with necessary violence. But the force must not exceed the limits of what is reasonable in the circumstances. Changes in society and in social perceptions have meant that what might have been considered reasonable at one time would no longer be so regarded: but the principle remains the same. The assailant or intruder may be met with reasonable force but no more; the use of excessive violence against him is an actionable wrong.'

21

CATS, DOGS AND OTHER PETS

We love pets. More than 50 per cent of British households have one. The *Reader's Digest* has calculated that we keep some 7.7 million cats, 6.6 million dogs, one million budgerigars and 18 million goldfish. And, as any fan of Rolf Harris's successful BBC TV series *Animal Hospital* will know, we are increasingly adopting exotic creatures such as small farm animals, snakes, tropical fish and even spiders: an estimated 2,000 households now have reptiles of one form or another.

So what does the law have to say about it?

CATS

Legally speaking, there is not much to say. They lead charmed lives. For instance, if the next-door cat attacks your chickens, you will not be able to sue. Why? Because in 1926, when a suburban house-owner in the Midlands with a chicken-run in his back garden sued a neighbour whose cat had slaughtered some of his chickens, Lord Justice Atkin ruled: 'The owner of a cat is not rendered liable by the mere fact that the animal does

damage in following a natural propensity of its kind to do damage.' The
1971 Animals Act was intended to remove the legal immunity of cats to
roam wild and unrestrained; but it has not worked out like that. I know of
no single case, ancient or modern, where a cat owner has been held liable
to compensate anyone for damage or injury caused by a pet. Cats remain
the spoiled darlings of the law.

DOGS

They are in a totally different legal category. For a start, if a dog
belonging to your neighbour (or anyone else) attacks your chickens – or
your own dog or any other animal – your neighbour will have to compensate you, if she has been negligent in controlling her pet. Indeed, the
judges accept that some breeds are more dangerous and require more
control than others: for instance, at Birmingham County Court Judge
Toyn awarded damages to an old lady whose dog had twice been savaged
in her own back garden by a Rottweiler from next door, and there have
been similar cases involving Alsatians and Jack Russell terriers.

When it comes to attacks on human beings, many people still quote the
well-known old phrase: 'Every dog is allowed one bite.' In fact, that is
now totally out of date and the legal thinking behind it was abolished by
the 1971 Animals Act. For nearly 300 years, ever since Chief Justice
Holt, obviously an early dog-lover, laid down in 1699, 'The law takes
notice that a dog is not of a fierce nature but rather the contrary', the
Common Law maintained that a dog owner was only liable to compensate someone bitten by his or her dog if it had bitten someone else at
least once before (hence, 'one bite') and the owner therefore knew of its
specific vicious propensity.

But the 1971 Act altered that charming simplicity. Section 2 says that
the keeper of any domestic animal[1] is *automatically* liable to pay
compensation when his or her pet causes damage 'of a kind which (a) the
animal, unless restrained, was likely to cause or which was likely to be
severe; (b) that likelihood was due to characteristics not normally found
in animals of that species or only in specific circumstances and (c) those
characteristics were known to its keeper or his or her servant or member
of the household under 16.'

This remarkable verbiage (and my version is cut down from the
original!) was criticised by the judges and for nearly 20 years had little
effect in practice. But then two Appeal Court decisions, one in November
1989 and the other in May 1990, belatedly revealed that a fundamental
change in the law had taken place. As a result, it is now clearly

established that the 1971 Act has made it much easier to sue a dog's keeper for an attack on a human being: the victim no longer must prove that the animal has already had one bite. *Any* potentially seriously dangerous 'characteristic' is enough.[2]

So, in the first Appeal Court case, when a normally placid bull mastiff leapt at and bit a 10-year-old boy who called it while it was being loaded on to the back of a Land Rover, the Appeal Court ruled that the dog's owners were automatically liable, even though the animal was on a lead. They knew their animal regarded the back of the Land Rover as part of its own territory – and that it was likely to react fiercely when defending its territory. So the boy's parents did not have to prove that the bull mastiff had attacked anyone else before.

In the second Appeal Court decision, a man was walking his dog along a street in Woking when another dog, also being taken for a walk, lunged at it and knocked him down in the process, breaking his leg. Both dogs were on leads but the Appeal Court overruled a High Court judge's dismissal of the injured man's claim and awarded him £7,203 damages plus interest. Lord Justice Neill said that the owner of the attacking dog, a large mongrel named Sam, knew his pet was likely to go for other animals. He also knew of the risk of another dog owner being hurt in any rescue attempt, and that was enough to incur liability under the 1971 Act.

Not enough people know about these two decisions – and they should. Taking your dog for a walk can have legal complications nowadays. I always kept a firm grip on my own late dog's lead when I saw another dog approaching.

Do not get confused with guard dogs. The 1975 Guard Dogs Act makes it an offence to have a guard dog on commercial or industrial premises without warning notices, a full-time handler or unless the dog is satisfactorily tethered. But this does *not* apply to your home or any other residential premises.

Now to some specifics.

The 1991 Dangerous Dogs Act   Many people are confused about the effect of this piece of legislation, rushed through Parliament in the summer of 1991 because of several highly publicised attacks on people by vicious dogs. In fact, it not only banned the breeding or sale of 'any dog of the type known as pit bull terrier' (which loose phraseology has cost a fortune in interpretation in the courts) and said that such a dog must be registered, insured and kept on a lead or muzzled in a public place. It also made important changes to the existing law on dangerous dogs – of all breeds.

It amended the old 1871 Dogs Act to enable magistrates to declare a dog of any breed dangerous and order its owner to keep it under proper control. Otherwise the dog would be destroyed – *without proof that anyone has been injured*. Mercifully, but only after several innocent dogs had died an unnecessary death, that harsh provision was abolished by the 1997 Dangerous Dogs Amendment Act, which says that in every case it is a matter for the magistrates' decision. They now should order a dog to be destroyed only if otherwise it 'would constitute a danger to public safety'.

The 1991 Act also – but less controversially – created a new offence imposing severe penalties on an owner or the person for the time being in charge of a dog who allows it to be 'dangerously out of control' or injure someone, whether in a public or a private place. They face a substantial fine and/or up to two years' imprisonment. If your dog snaps at visitors on private property, you can now end up in the dock of a criminal court and not merely have to pay damages in a civil court.

Dog collars, dog leads and dog excreta   The 1992 Control of Dogs Order, updating a 1930 order, says that every dog out in public, whether or not with its owner, must wear a collar with its owner's name and address – but not necessarily the dog's own name.

Many modern local by-laws make it an offence for a dog to be out without a lead, even though wearing a collar, on specific town streets named in the by-laws and identified by a small metal notice attached to lamp-posts. This offence is committed even when the animal is out with its owner.

Many by-laws also make it a criminal offence to allow a dog to foul the footpath of any street or public place, again with a small metal notice on lamp-posts identifying the specific streets or public place. The High Court has ruled that 'footpath' does not include a grass verge and public parks have their own dog rules in the large notices of park regulations displayed near all major entrances.

Irrespective of any local by-laws, the little-known 1996 Dogs (Fouling of Land) Act makes it an offence for anyone in charge of a dog in a street where the traffic speed limit is 40 m.p.h. or less to fail to remove 'forthwith' any faeces the animal drops. In such circumstances, using a 'pooper-scooper', or at least (as I carried for my own dog) an empty supermarket shopping bag, is a legal necessity. The fine is not cheap: a maximum of £1,000. The same rule applies to 'any land open to the air and to which the public are entitled or permitted to have access with or without payment', so long as the local authority has designated it as coming within the Act. This applies to London's Royal Parks and to many municipal parks, both in and outside the capital.

What about those selfish people who habitually allow their dogs to wander into the front gardens of private houses and deposit their excreta there? Because that is not a public place, the 1996 Act and local by-laws do not apply but, if an aggrieved householder could prove any one person was regularly allowing his pet to defecate in her front garden, she could, in theory, sue him for damages and an injunction for an actionable nuisance – but I know of no actual case.

Stray dogs   Bits of the 1906 Dogs Act and bits of the 1990 Environmental Protection Act must be read together to discover the legal system for dealing with stray dogs, although it is difficult to see why Parliament did not simply repeal the old Act and put the whole thing together in one new Act – but then that is how legal 'reform' so often works in this country.

Anyway, this is the basic framework of how the system works: a stray dog can be seized by either the police or a dog warden employed by the local council who must give the owner a chance to reclaim the animal. If the owner cannot be found or does not want the dog back, it will be sold or destroyed. If a private citizen finds a stray dog, she cannot just keep it for herself straight away. She must either return it to its owner (if, for instance, the name and address are on the dog's collar, as they should be) or take it to the nearest police station or give it to the local dog warden and tell him where it was found.

If she says she would like to keep the dog permanently, the police or warden will allow her to take it home for at least a month and, if during that time its owner does not claim it, she will be allowed to keep it permanently and become its new legal owner.

If a dog worries livestock, the farmer can kill it if the animal is still on his land, but if it is under no one's control at the time, he must notify the police within 48 hours.

Leaving a dog on its own, whether temporarily or permanently, without reasonable cause, if likely to cause unnecessary suffering to the animal, was made an offence by the 1960 Abandonment of Animals Act. In theory, this Act applies to all animals but in practice it is usually only invoked with regard to dogs, either when left on their own all day tethered in the garden while their owners are at work or, more often, when left in the hot sun outside supermarkets while the owner shops or alone in parked cars with the windows closed. Every summer people complain to the Royal Society for the Prevention of Cruelty to Animals who, when the circumstances justify it, are happy to prosecute. The maximum penalties, but never imposed, are six months' imprisonment and/or a £5,000 fine.

Taking a dog into a public house, wine bar, restaurant or shop There is no law which says specifically that dogs can – or cannot – be brought on to trade premises. In each case, the management can make its own rules and there is no legal requirement to provide a small ring outside the entrance to which a customer's dog can be tethered.

But where food or drink is prepared, handled, manufactured, stored or served, the 1995 Food Safety (General Food Hygiene) Regulations specify that the proprietor must ensure the process is carried out 'in a hygienic way'. This is defined as ensuring that 'all measures necessary to ensure the safety and wholesomeness of food' are taken. Most pubs, wine bars, restaurants and food shops interpret this to mean that dogs should legally not be allowed on their premises, although to the best of my knowledge no court has ever ruled on the legal correctness of this common interpretation.

However, as far back as September 1976, the Department of Health and Social Services (DHSS) circularised local authorities recommending that an exception should be made in the case of guide dogs for the blind because: 'They do not urinate or defecate while wearing harness and they ignore interesting smells. Thus they present less of a risk to food hygiene than dogs generally.'

That is why many notices on the doors of food shops specifically say that guide dogs *are* allowed.

However, if a dog – of whatever kind – is allowed entry, its owner must take reasonable care to ensure that it does not cause harm to other people. In a High Court case in the 1960s, a dog owner had to pay damages when another pub user broke his leg and tripped over his large Alsatian that was not kept on a tight lead. Basically, dog owners should use their common sense.

OTHER PETS

Until 1975, there was no restriction in English law on the kind of animal you could keep as a pet. You would be liable if they injured anyone, even if you were personally not at fault; but actually having a wild dangerous animal in your home was not, in itself, illegal.

'Beware of the lion'

That was the sign on a suburban garden gate in Worcestershire in 1975 but a young man calling in search of work thought it was a joke. So getting no reply from a knock at the front door, and seeing a light on at the rear of the house, he clambered over the 17-foot-high back garden fence. 'Suddenly something leapt out of the dark on to my back and completely floored me,' he later told the police. 'I suddenly realised, 'Good God, it *is* a lion!' One-year-old Laddo had been bought by the houseowner a year earlier as a protection after two burglaries.

But the law had not been broken. A police spokesman explained: 'We have interviewed the houseowner and we are not happy with the situation. But the caller was legally a trespasser and the lion was not loose, so there is no question of any prosecution.'

Today the answer would be different. In the following year, Parliament passed the 1976 Dangerous Wild Animals Act which states that anyone keeping a wild animal, whether as a pet or for protection, must first obtain a licence from their local council. And a licence will only be granted if veterinarians are satisfied that the animal is kept in suitable escape-proof accommodation and – most important – properly fed. I swear to you that that last requirement is actually specified in the Act. Parliamentary draftsmen think of everything.

Notes
1 The Act imposes liability on an animal's 'keeper'. This is not only the owner. It can also be someone who has temporary charge of the animal or who heads a household where an under-16-year-old owns or is in charge of it. How many people realise they are legally responsible, if their child under 16 owns a dog – or any other domestic pet?
2 Yet, as in the old Common Law days of 'one bite', it still remains inadvisable to put a warning notice: 'Beware of the Dog' on your front gate. You are in effect admitting in advance that you know your animal has a dangerous propensity! You are only making it more difficult for yourself if it then bites a visitor.

PART FOUR

YOUR CAR

22

MOTORING LAW

This is totally different from any other part of ordinary, everyday law dealt with in this book. With all other aspects of 'ordinary' law, most people have, at best, only a somewhat hazy idea of what the law has to say and what precisely are their rights. But with motoring law, those who need to know – the country's 28.1 million drivers (the official Transport Department figure) – already have a pretty good idea of what the law is and what their rights are. The Highway Code's latest (1999) edition not only outsells the Bible: it also contains, in addition to the Code itself, a simple yet comprehensive guide to the basic law.

Besides, you cannot be a motorist nowadays without automatically knowing a lot about motoring law. It would be like a cook not having his or her own private storehouse of recipes or not knowing the basic rules of cookery.

So the shape of this chapter is different from all the others. There is no point in telling readers what many of them will already know: i.e. the main framework of the system and its fundamental principles. Instead, I have selected 10 specific topics of everyday importance to motorists where the law is always changing and developing – and where sometimes even the experts do not know all the answers.

LEARNING TO DRIVE

Most people, of course, know that the basic minimum legal requirements are that a learner cannot drive on a motorway and that he must be at least 17, with a provisional licence and L-plates (D-plates in Wales from the Welsh *dysgwr* for 'learner') displayed on the car, back and front.[1] Furthermore, the accompanying driver must be at least 21 and have held a British licence to drive that type of car for at least three years.

But there is much more to it than that.

The accompanying driver is not just there for the ride. Professional driving instructors must be registered by law if they receive payment for their work. But even non-professionals cannot simply sit back and let the learner get on with it. They have a job to do: they must supervise the driving of the novice at the wheel.

If not, they can *both* find themselves in trouble with the law. Back in the early months of World War II, in 1940, when there was still a fair amount of traffic on the roads, a learner driver, overtaking on a bend, ran into a heavily laden lorry coming the other way. It was not entirely his fault. His fully qualified friend sitting beside him should have warned him not to overtake but to wait until they had first gone round the bend. He did not: so local magistrates convicted the learner of careless driving and his accompanying driver of aiding and abetting him.

On appeal to the High Court in London, the formidable Mr Justice Hilbery upheld both convictions and laid down this classic statement of the law: 'It is the supervisor's duty, when necessary, to do whatever can reasonably be expected to prevent the driver from acting unskilfully or carelessly or in a manner likely to cause danger to others.' This basic ruling still applies across the whole gamut of possible motoring offences. Technically the supervising driver may even be guilty of aiding and abetting – and therefore, also liable to be fined – when a learner commits a simple parking offence.

There was a case, in October 1980, when Judge Henry Kershaw ruled at Burley Crown Court that a driving examiner had rightly been convicted by local magistrates of aiding and abetting a driving-test candidate to drive without due care and attention while actually taking his test. The young learner had misunderstood the examiner's instructions and turned the wrong way into a one-way street but the examiner had said nothing – until they crashed into an oncoming car.

Judge Kershaw said: 'While examiners are not in the same category as supervisors or instructors neither are they merely passengers. If a candidate is so incompetent that to continue the test would be a serious danger to the public, the examiner must terminate it.'

Similar considerations apply to the question of civil liability. Other road users must be protected. The standard of driving on the road has to be objective. A learner's inexperience is no excuse if his negligent driving causes an accident and, if the accident could have been averted by the accompanying driver using reasonable supervision (grabbing the wheel, applying the brake, even just shouting out), she will have to share the bill for damages.

Can the supervising driver herself sue, if injured, or will she be met by the defence that she knew the risk she was letting herself in for? After all, *Volenti non fit injuria* ('To the consenting there is no injury') is a basic rule of the Common Law. The Appeal Court supplied the answer in 1971 in *Nettleship* v. *Weston:*

The case of the supervising driver

A woman in Sheffield wanted to learn to drive. Her husband did not want the job but he was quite happy to let her use his car. So a family friend agreed to give her lessons. She was a careful pupil and was doing well but on the third lesson she failed to straighten out after taking a left turn. She panicked. Her hands 'seemed to freeze on the wheel'. The friend grabbed hold of the handbrake and tried to control the wheel with his other hand but could not stop the car slamming into a lamppost. He broke his leg and sued for damages.

The Appeal Court upheld his claim. Lord Denning ruled that the woman learner was guilty of negligence: 'It is no answer to say, "I was a learner driver under instructions. I was doing my best and could not help it." The law requires the same standard of care as from any other driver. He may be doing his best but his incompetent best is not good enough.'

As for the *Volenti* defence, the family friend had specifically asked beforehand whether she was insured against injury to passengers (which she was), and that was sufficient to show he had not legally accepted the risk of being driven by her. Lord Justice Megaw went even further: 'The mere fact that the passenger knows of the driver's inexperience is not enough' – without any need to ask about insurance.

Even so, for their own protection, anyone today going out with a learner (whether as supervising driver or ordinary passenger) should first check that he or she will be covered by insurance. This is so that they can later *beyond doubt* refute the defence: 'You agreed to the risk of an accident.'

One final point: a learner driver cannot always count on being fully insured. If the car owner's policy allows 'any authorised driver' to drive the vehicle, he will be covered, although a claim may be subject to a substantial excess. But, if the policy only allows a 'named driver', a claim may be rejected completely unless the policy holder has informed her insurers and given them the opportunity to charge an increased premium for having a learner at the wheel.

Many people are not sufficiently aware of what they are taking on when helping a relative or friend to learn to drive.

SEAT BELTS

Ever since 1965, the law has required all new motor vehicles to be fitted with front seat belts. But surprisingly it is only since 1983 that it has been an offence, with certain exceptions (when reversing; for a pregnant woman with a medical certificate; for taxi-drivers, minicab drivers, etc.), not to wear them.[2] Indeed, the Automobile Association has calculated that a life a day is saved through 'belting up'.

Over the age of 14, it is the responsibility of the passenger, not the driver, to ensure that he is belted up. In fact, the value of wearing a front seat belt has been obvious for so long that back in July 1975, before wearing was even made compulsory, the Appeal Court ruled in the classic case of *Froom* v. *Butcher* that an unbelted driver or front passenger injured in an accident caused by another driver's negligence might have his/her damages cut because of his or her own 'contributory negligence'. As you will already know from earlier chapters, the law says we all must take reasonable care for our own safety.

So Lord Denning laid down: 'The judges should say plainly that it is sensible practice for all drivers and passengers in front seats to wear seat belts.' If not, and their injuries would have been the same despite the seat belt, their damages will not be affected. But, if wearing a seat belt would have saved them from *all* injury, their damages will be cut by 25 per cent – and by 15 per cent if the injuries would have been 'a good deal less severe'.

Since then the law has moved on. Rear seat belts now have to be fitted to most new cars and all 'small minibuses' (those with an unladen weight of 2,540 kilograms or less). Coaches and ambulances are still legally exempt and, although some are fitted with rear seat belts, there remains no legal compulsion. Furthermore, in September 1989 it was made an offence to drive a car in which a child under 14 is being carried in the rear without wearing a suitable seat belt or 'appropriate child restraint'.

But it was only in July 1991 that the marvellously entitled Motor Vehicles (Wearing of Seat Belts in Rear Seats by Adults) Regulations first made it an offence for adults not to wear seat belts in the back of a car as well as in front. A maximum fine of £500 is specified in the upgraded 1993 version of these regulations. Yet how many rear-seat passengers in fact bother to belt up? How many even know that they can be fined if they do not? The Automobile Association knows of cases where front-seat passengers have been badly injured by head butts from the rear when an unbelted back-seat passenger has been thrown viciously forward by the impact of a collision.

Yet it has not yet been authoritatively decided in the courts whether the reduced rate of damages laid down in *Froom* v. *Butcher* should apply if an unbelted rear passenger, as distinct from front passenger, is injured. There simply has been no case reported since the new law was introduced. But if the line of judicial reasoning in the 1991 Appeal Court case of *Eastman* v. *South West Thames Regional Health Authority*, decided before the change in the law, is followed, the answer will probably be 'Yes':

The case of the injured ambulance passenger

Mrs Eastman was allowed to accompany her aged mother-in-law to hospital in the back of an ambulance. A sign stated: 'For your own safety, use seat belts provided'; but she did not do so. The driver braked hard to avoid a cyclist and she was thrown from her seat and injured.

The Appeal Court threw out her damages claim. It ruled that the health authority was entitled to leave to an individual passenger of mature years the decision whether or not to use the seat belt and it was not unreasonable for the ambulance crewmen not to tell her to use the belt or to point out the warning notice.

This ruling would also seem to apply to those London taxi drivers (and no doubt taxi-drivers in other cities) who, when the 1991 Regulations came into force, warned passengers to wear seat belts but no longer bother to do so. It was at one time thought that an unbelted rear passenger could sue them if he was injured in an accident. That would now seem to be not the case.

TRAFFIC LIGHTS

Three common situations are of interest.

The traffic lights do not work

If you disobey an official set of traffic lights, whether these are working properly or not, the 1994 Traffic Signs Regulations and General Directions make it an offence for which you can be fined up to £1,000, have your licence endorsed and get three penalty points.

But there is a nuance: if the lights are jammed at red, you must either turn round and find another outlet or else stop – and remain stopped until a policeman or traffic warden comes along and countermands the red light by beckoning you forward.

However, a judge commented many years ago in a case at Hertfordshire Quarter Sessions (the equivalent of a modern Crown Court) that, if a motorist edges forward carefully in such circumstances without causing any damage or injury, the appropriate sentence should usually be only an absolute discharge. So, in practice, you are unlikely to be charged with any offence.

If the lights fail completely and no colour whatsoever is shown, you are legally better off. You can treat the junction as uncontrolled and commit no offence whatsoever, even technically, in carefully edging forward.

Traffic lights at road works

What is their legal status? Some motorists believe that they are only advisory and that, even when they are showing red, you do not have to stop if you can safely see your way ahead. That is simply not so. The 1994 Regulations give portable temporary lights at road works and temporary road-traffic-control schemes equal legal validity with permanent traffic lights. If they show red, you must stop – even if you can see that the way ahead is clear.

Aggressive windscreen-cleaners at traffic lights

How does the law treat this new curse for motorists? In nothing like so tough a way as it treats the long-suffering motorist himself. Consider this court case in Brighton in July 1993:

The driver who hit back

A BMW owner sitting in the driving seat of his car stopped at traffic lights. A burly youth approached him and started wiping his windscreen without saying anything. The driver ignored him, but the youth put his head inside the car and swore at him.

As the driver later explained, 'If someone puts their head in my car window and shouts threats at me I am going to defend myself, and that is what I did. I got out and grabbed hold of him. It was a push rather than a slap. Within fifteen minutes I went to a police box and reported what had happened.'

What happened next? No prizes for guessing that it was the motorist, not the foul-mouthed washer boy, who ended up at Brighton magistrates' court charged with threatening behaviour, contrary to Section 4 of the 1986 Public Order Act, for which he could be fined up to £1,000.

In fact, the magistrates threw out the case without the motorist even being called to give evidence and awarded him £300 costs. But a local police inspector told a *Daily Telegraph* reporter: 'We get complaints about washer boys but *criminal law does not cover that area.*'

That was then, and still is, absolute nonsense. Aggressive washer boys commit, at the very least, the exact same offence with which the Brighton motorist was charged: namely, threatening behaviour, contrary to Section 4 of the 1986 Act. And if they continue to use foul language when told by a police officer to stop it comes within Section 5 of the Act, which creates the more serious offence of 'threatening, abusive or insulting words or behaviour with intent to cause a person to believe that immediate unlawful violence will be used'. This offence carries the increased penalty of a maximum six months' gaol sentence or £2,500 fine, or both. Yet I know of no prosecution brought anywhere in the country against aggressive washer boys under either Section 4 or Section 5 of the 1986 Act.[3]

SPEEDING

Nearly all motorists are guilty of this offence. Department of Transport figures indicate that about 70 per cent of motorists exceed the 30 m.p.h. limit, despite the increasing presence of speed cameras and improved warning signs. Most of us, no doubt, like to think that we only exceed the permitted limit, whatever it may be, 'within reason'. But there is *never* a legal excuse, except when driving a vehicle for fire brigade, ambulance or police purposes.

For the rest of us, when caught, we can only throw ourselves on the mercy of the police officer who has stopped us. A lot depends on the individual officer and on your own attitude. Politeness usually pays dividends.

However, it is useful to know that there are 'flexible' guidelines within which the Association of Chief Police Officers (ACPO) advises police forces to operate. As a senior police officer attached to the Association has told me, the 'starting point' for police action is reached when the relevant limit is exceeded by '10 per cent plus 2'. For instance, within a 30 m.p.h. built-up area, you will generally only be stopped if you are travelling at more than 35 m.p.h.: i.e. 30 plus 3 (10 per cent of 30) plus 2.

Thereafter, a kind of sliding scale applies. If you exceed the relevant limit by up to 10 m.p.h., you will probably get only a warning for future behaviour. If 10 to 25 m.p.h. over the limit, you can usually expect to be offered a £40 fixed penalty – *which, as a general rule, you should accept.* It will cost much less than going to court: £40 and three penalty points as against a fine of up to £1,000 (or £2,500, if speeding on a motorway), your licence endorsed and three to six penalty points.

Only if you have exceeded the relevant limit by more than 25 m.p.h., will you usually not be offered a fixed penalty but taken to court.

What are the limits? Unless official signs show otherwise, they are 30 m.p.h. on 'restricted roads': i.e. roads in built-up areas in England and Wales with street lamps not more than 200 yards apart (Class C and unclassified roads in Scotland with lamps not more than 185 metres apart), 60 m.p.h. on single carriageways and 70 m.p.h. on dual carriage-ways and motorways.

Incidentally, if you are towing a caravan or trailer, those last two limits are lowered by 10 m.p.h. – which not everyone remembers!

But one should always remember that the speed limit alone is not the sole criterion. As Rule 104 of the latest (1999) edition of the Highway Code spells out: 'The speed limit is the absolute maximum and does not mean it is safe to drive at that speed irrespective of conditions.' Rule 124 repeats the message: 'Do not treat speed limits as a target. It is often not appropriate or safe to drive at the maximum speed limit. Take the road and traffic conditions into account . . . Be prepared to adjust your speed as a precaution.'

If you do not, you are liable to be stopped and 'booked' for careless driving, at the very least.

Most people know that nowadays you can temporarily lose your licence for speeding – but when exactly is this likely to happen?

There is no 'law' on the subject. The 1988 Road Traffic Offenders Act merely says that disqualification is 'discretionary'. So, in September 1993, the Magistrates' Association, for the first time, issued its own guidelines.

They were updated – and toughened – in April 1997 so that magistrates are now advised to consider imposing, subject to any mitigation advanced by the defendant and in addition to any fine, six penalty points or 14 to 56 days' disqualification depending on how far the motorist has exceeded the permitted limit. Again, it amounts to a sliding scale:

21–30 m.p.h. excess over a limit of 20–30;

26–35 m.p.h. over a limit of 40–50;

31–40 m.p.h. over a limit of 60–70.

The effect, of course, is that someone travelling at over 51 m.p.h. in a built-up area with a speed limit of 30 m.p.h. is as likely to lose her licence for a short while as someone travelling at over 101 m.p.h. on a motorway. Speed can kill, and the lesson needs to be drummed home.

Finally, we all know that a driver who persists in habitually breaking the law – not only by speeding – may lose her licence for at least six months. This will happen if a court, when convicting her of a motoring offence (not necessarily speeding), 'tots-up' her penalty points over the past three years – and finds that the latest offence brings the total to 12 points or more. However, it is perhaps not quite so well known that, ever since the law was changed in June 1997, new drivers who tot up only six points or more during a two-year probationary period after passing the driving test, will revert to learner status until they pass a repeat test.

ACCIDENTS

When do you have to stop in the event of an accident and what precisely are you supposed to do? This is possibly the most misunderstood aspect of everyday motoring law and is, in fact, surprisingly complicated.

Section 170 of the 1988 Road Traffic Act spells out what you must do. Your first duty is to stop. Obviously you must use discretion: if possible, you should not stop in the middle of a busy road but try to pull in to the kerb.

If another motorist is involved, he too must stop but the police need only be called if someone has been injured. If not, your only obligation is, 'if required by any person having reasonable grounds to do so' (e.g. the other driver or the owner of damaged property), to give your name and address, those of the owner of the vehicle if it is not your own, and its index number. Of course, this applies vice versa to any other motorist involved.

Many drivers think they are entitled to demand driving licence and current insurance certificate; but Section 170 says nothing at all about a driving licence and stipulates that a motorist only has to show his insurance certificate in case of injury.

But not every accident brings with it the duty to stop and give particulars. That only applies when someone besides yourself is injured, *another* vehicle or property is damaged, or any animal (except a cat!) not being carried in your own car is injured.

If you do not give particulars at the time, perhaps because no one was there to ask for them (for instance, the absent owner of a damaged parked car), it is no defence to say that no one was around. You must report the accident at a police station or to a police officer 'as soon as reasonably practicable and in any case within twenty-four hours'. The High Court has ruled that those words mean exactly what they say. You must not put off reporting the accident for up to 24 hours: you must do it as soon as 'reasonably practicable'. Only if it is not possible to report the accident promptly do you have up to 24 hours in which to do so.

Furthermore, the High Court has ruled that you cannot simply telephone a police station to report. You must do it in person. Failure to stop and give particulars to anyone reasonably requiring them is one offence and failing to report to the police is another, separate offence. You could, if really unlucky (or stupid), find yourself convicted of both. Neither is a laughing matter: for each carries a maximum six months' gaol sentence or £5,000 fine (although I know of no case where the offender has been punished so severely) and five to ten penalty points.

The only exception to all this is if you can convince a Bench of cynical magistrates that you genuinely did not know there had been an accident. This is unlikely when there has been an accident on the open road but, where you are trying to manoeuvre in or out of tightly parked cars, it is not entirely impossible. Some years ago, the Queen's cousin Lord Harewood was acquitted at Bow Street magistrates' court in central London when he successfully claimed that he had not realised he had backed into a parked car because he was listening to a Mozart wind serenade on his car radio. He explained that he might have confused the sound of a burglar alarm, set off on the parked car, with a sustained note on the clarinet.

But there is a limit. In 1989, a driver tried to avoid being convicted of failing to report by saying he did not realise there had been a mishap until 15 minutes later. It did him no good. The High Court ruled that a driver does not have to realise an accident has occurred *at the time* : later will do.

(Note: Because a cat is not an 'animal', as defined by Section 170, do not make the common mistake of thinking that you can drive on with impunity. If there is a reasonable chance of helping it, you must stop; otherwise, if you are spotted, you could be reported for causing it unnecessary suffering, contrary to the 1911 Protection of Animals Act, which *does* define a cat as an 'animal'.)

DRINK-DRIVING

You could write a whole book about drink-driving offences, and some people have; but the general requirements of the law are so very well known that I shall content myself with only one aspect of the problem that is perhaps of special interest.

When can the police breath-test you, once you have got back home? The question is simple but the answer is complex. As Lord Scarman has said, 'Parliament must be understood, even in its desire to stamp out drunken driving, to pay respect to the fundamental right of privacy in one's own home, which has for centuries been recognised by the Common Law.' It was, after all, a judge (Chief Justice Coke) who first said, in the early seventeenth century, 'An Englishman's home is his castle.'

Two basic legal propositions are easy and straightforward:

1. If you were involved in an accident which injured someone else, a uniformed police officer can enter your home by force, if necessary, and request a breath test, with the normal consequences of arrest, fine and disqualification if you refuse.
2. At a less serious level, if a uniformed police officer merely has reasonable cause to believe that, while driving, you had alcohol in your body (not even necessarily that you were drunk!) or committed a moving traffic offence (which can be as trivial as one small sidelight not working), he can knock on your door and request a breath test on your doorstep or, if you let him into your house, request the test inside – with the usual consequences for refusal.

The difficulties start if you do not let the police officer in or, once inside, ask him to leave. As any experienced police officer knows (but may not be prepared to admit), that puts him in a very sensitive legal position.

If he persists with his request, and you refuse, he can undoubtedly arrest you on the spot (even in your own home), take you to a police station and, if you then prove positive, charge you with drink-driving. The actual arrest will have been unlawful because he was a trespasser – but, as the House of Lords ruled in October 1985, that does not matter. 'A lawful arrest is not an essential prerequisite of a breath test,' said Lord Fraser of Tullybelton.

However, he added that, 'if a motorist has been lured to the police station by some trick or deception, or the police officers have behaved oppressively', a court has a discretion to throw out the charge.

Lord Fraser's words, echoed by his fellow law lords, have become the basis of the often successful defence of 'oppressive behaviour', which is

practically unknown outside the ranks of barristers and solicitors special-
ising in this sort of work. Two years later, in *Matto* v. *Wolverhampton
Crown Court*, the High Court quashed the conviction of a motorist who
had told police that they could not test him on his own driveway, to which
a police officer had charmingly replied: 'We know what we are doing. If
I wrongfully arrest you, you can sue me. OK?' Lord Justice Woolf ruled
that this was 'behaving in an oppressive manner'.

In April 1993, the prosecution itself withdrew a case at Gray's (Essex)
magistrates' court when the driver of a police car was accused of having
'tricked his way' into a motorist's house by telling her seventeen-year-
old daughter at the front door that he was going in anyway when he knew
he had no power to do so. A motorist's home is still – occasionally – her
castle, even when she is accused of drink-driving.

MOTORWAYS   (AND   HARD   SHOULDERS)

There is not much that the general motoring public does not know about
motorways and the special legal rules that apply to them: no learner
drivers, no cyclists, no riders of motorcycles under 50cc, etc. But doubts
persist, even with magistrates, about the exact legal status of a motorway's hard shoulder.

Everyone knows that it is supposed to be used only in emergencies and
that in no circumstances (unless directed so to do by official traffic signs
or a police officer) can you drive along it or use it as a short cut or
overtake on it. But when precisely are you allowed to *stop* on it?

Paragraph 7 of the 1982 Motorways Traffic (England and Wales)
Regulations says that you can stop on a hard shoulder 'by reason of any
accident, illness or other emergency' but – of course! – does not say what
constitutes an emergency.

In March 1992 Chris Timms, a High Wycombe antique dealer, was
returning from a business visit to France. He was driving his Ford Transit
van back home from Dover along the M25, having just passed its
junction with the A3, when, at around midnight his eyes 'suddenly
started bouncing', as he later told me. He realised he was a potential
danger to other drivers and himself. He thought it was too far to go to the
next junction, so he pulled on to the hard shoulder, stopped, turned off the
engine – leaving the lights on – and closed his eyes.

Next thing he knew, a policeman was asking why he had stopped. The
sequel, despite a vigorous defence by Timms acting as his own lawyer,
was a £60 fine at Woking magistrates' court for stopping his vehicle
contrary to the 1982 Regulations. In other words, his sudden tiredness

was not an emergency.

But Timms was not prepared to accept that. He fought the case himself on appeal to Guildford Crown Court, where, in October 1992, Judge Peter Slot overruled his conviction. Awarding him £30 costs, Judge Slot said: 'I see no reason to reject Timms's evidence that he felt tired after he passed the junction. It follows that what he did was within the law.'

Timms's case has a wider implication for motorists. An anonymous 'legal expert' was quoted in several national newspapers at the time as saying: 'Motorists must understand that the law has not changed. The judge simply made an exception to the rule.'

That is not so. Judge Slot did not make an exception to the rule: he applied and enforced it. For, as far back as February 1972, Lord Widgery, then Lord Chief Justice, in the case of *Higgins* v. *Bernard,* brought on an earlier but identical version of the 1982 Regulations, authoritatively defined what is an emergency for tired motorway drivers. Taking as his basis the dictionary definition of emergency as 'a sudden and/or unexpected occurrence', Lord Widgery said: 'Too much stress must not be attached to the word "sudden".' The tiredness does not have to attack the motorist at the very second before he pulls on to the hard shoulder. 'If he gets on to the carriageway at a time when, so far as he could see, it was safe and lawful for him to proceed to the next turn-off point, it is sufficient to show that something intervened which rendered it unsafe to proceed to that next turn-off point.'

So the reason why Judge Slot quashed Mr Timms's conviction was that he only felt tired after he passed the M25's junction with the A3 and he was 'stuck', as it were, on the motorway until the next junction, which was some distance ahead.

PARKING

Most of us know that yellow lines are of two kinds: those painted along the road and those on the kerb. But not everyone knows that they have a different legal function.

When painted along the road, double yellow lines mean that 'waiting' – i.e. parking – is not allowed *at any time*. In all conscience, that is straightforward enough. But the situation gets complicated with single yellow lines. These mean that you can park at any time except within restricted hours and on certain days, usually Monday to Saturday but sometimes also on Sunday.

How do you know precisely what hours and days? Every controlled parking zone has its own details stated on 'time plates' displayed on poles at the entry to the zone. But if these are different in any specific street within that zone, there must be a different time plate *in that very street*.

If no days are shown on the time plates, the restrictions are in force every day including Sunday and Bank Holidays.

The latest (1999) edition of the Highway Code says: 'Yellow or red lines can only give a guide to the restrictions and controls in force and signs, nearby or at a zone entry, must be consulted.' That is, of course, true but it is easier to find the nearest parking meter or pay & display ticket machine, where the relevant information is clearly stated.

Except on red lines along London's red routes, which we shall look at in a moment, you can always *briefly* pick up or drop off passengers even within restricted hours and days. Furthermore, white bay markings on the road with upright signs alongside indicate where parking is specifically allowed within specified times.

Loading and unloading is more complicated. It is governed by yellow kerb lines. That is their role. If absent, it means there are no restrictions. If present, two lines mean no loading or unloading at any time whereas one line means not between the hours shown on the nearest time plate.

What about parking out of hours in a residents' bay? Again, many people are unsure of the answer. In fact, non-residents can usually park there out of hours and on Sundays and Bank Holidays – but, just in case, look around for any contrary time plate. I was once caught out through not checking.

With parking meters and pay & display areas, you must buy on arrival all the time you want (usually up to two hours), with no time allowed for finding change and you cannot later 'feed the meter' or buy a second display voucher. You also cannot park on a meter showing OUT OF ORDER or covered by an official NO PARKING bag.

On some major roads in London, yellow lines have been replaced by red lines. These are the notorious 'red routes'. Red lines mean that you cannot stop to park, load or unload or even to board or alight from a vehicle – except from a licensed taxi or a car displaying an official Orange Badge for the disabled. As with yellow lines, single line restrictions are shown on nearby signs but double lines mean no stopping is allowed for any purpose at any time.

Yet even on red routes the authorities accept that a motor vehicle must sometimes be allowed to stop, however briefly. Red boxes on the road, with signs specifying the exact times allowed, indicate where you can park to load or unload. White boxes mean you can do it throughout the day.

Besides all this, it is an offence to 'leave a motor vehicle in a dangerous position' (maximum £1,000 fine, three penalty points and discretionary – but rare – disqualification) and to 'cause or permit an unnecessary obstruction' (maximum £1,000 fine alone).

In London, most illegal parking is now 'decriminalised' with 'penalty charges' replacing fines. Save for parking dangerously, on zigzag lines or on red routes, or causing an obstruction, law enforcement is not handled by the police or traffic wardens but by parking attendants employed by the local council. A similar system may eventually spread over much of the country but so far only Oxford, Winchester, High Wycombe and Maidstone have followed suit.

TOWING AWAY AND CLAMPING

This is the twin-headed monster that lies in wait for so many motorists who park illegally on our overcrowded roads.

The 1984 Road Traffic Regulation Act allows towing away when motor vehicles are 'illegally, obstructively or dangerously parked'. This is done by private firms operating at a profit. They can only act with the prior authority of a police officer, traffic warden or parking attendant but many drivers – including myself – suspect it has more to do with revenue-gathering than law enforcement.

Clamping (which, at the moment, only applies in London) again requires prior authority. Many motorists believe it can only happen to vehicles parked dangerously or causing an obstruction. Sadly, no. It applies to all cases of illegal parking on roads. The law is ruthless.[4]

THE FIXED-PENALTY SYSTEM

On-the-spot fines by means of 'fixed-penalty notices' are extensively used for motoring offences outside London and for many other offences throughout the whole country.

The system has proved both a blessing and a curse for drivers. It is a blessing because, if you have committed an offence, it provides a genuine soft option. The fixed penalty will always be less than the fine imposed after unsuccessfully fighting the case in court – when you will also have to pay your own and the prosecution's legal costs. It is a curse because it is so remorseless. In truth, most fixed-penalty notices are justified and many motorists believe it is not worthwhile querying one, even if there is much to be said on their behalf. They pay up and save themselves aggravation.

But, it is possible sometimes to beat the system – by using the system.

Let me explain.

It is pointless challenging a fixed-penalty notice on the basis that you did not commit the offence. The fixed-penalty clerk at a local magistrates' court (whose address is on the notice) will merely write back saying you must let the case go to court.

What you *should* do is write admitting that you were technically guilty but explaining why you think the ticket was unfair or unjust. Someone in authority will then reply that your representations are being considered but in the meantime you should pay the penalty, which will be refunded if ultimately they agree that 'the circumstances do not warrant further proceedings'.

You should always comply with such a request for notices are, indeed, cancelled and payments refunded in genuine cases of hardship or serious mitigation. Pregnant mothers who cannot walk too far and have searched in vain for a legitimate parking place or elderly drivers with a similar problem are among those who receive sympathetic treatment.

But there is another reason why we should all, if possible, query a fixed-penalty notice: there is always a chance that the query will disclose a technical fault which would otherwise have gone undetected.

I give an example of my own which happened in London when unlawful parking was still a criminal offence dealt with by the police under the fixed-penalty system:

The fixed-penalty cheque that was returned

At 10.10 on a Monday morning I came down to the Chelsea mews where I then lived in a small block of flats to move my car into the garage underneath the block only to find a £30 'ticket' slapped on the windscreen for parking on a single yellow line. I had been unable to put the car in the garage the previous evening because the entrance was blocked by a parked car and I could not use my local resident's permit to park in the nearby residents' parking bays since, as often happens, they were occupied by cars with no permit while their owners visited a nearby cinema.

So I wrote to the fixed-penalty clerk asking him to take no further action. I received a formal reply from the Metropolitan Police requesting me to pay the fixed penalty while the matter was considered – which I did – and eventually a further letter arrived saying that my vehicle had been illegally parked and that the notice 'was correct in the circumstances' – but I would still get my cheque back because the issuing officer had made 'an administrative error'.

And that was it! No explanation as to the nature of the error or whether it would have been spotted if I had not questioned the notice.

So I wrote back asking those two very questions and received a reply saying that the office copy of the notice had been found to be incomplete because the exact details of the parking restriction were missing: together with this fascinating piece of information was another: 'Upon receiving mitigation from a member of the public a fixed-penalty notice is checked. If it is then noted that the notice was incorrectly completed by the issuing office, it is cancelled.'

So now we know: if you do not query your ticket, they do not check and, if they do not check, you can find yourself paying when there is no legal need to do so. Which goes to show that, if you use the system, you can sometimes beat the system – even if only by a fluke.

Notes

1 There is no legal mystique about buying manufactured L-plates or D-plates in a motor accessory shop. You can make your own provided they comply with the 1996 Motor Vehicles [Driving Licence] Regulations: i.e. a red letter 'L' or 'D' 102 mm high by 89 mm wide by 38 mm thick on a white card that is 178 mm square. (The previous Regulations dating from 1981 measured everything in inches and did not require a separate 'D' plate for those in Wales.)

2 No baby under 12 months is allowed to travel in a front seat, even if securely held by an adult, unless every other seat is occupied. Children between one and 14 are only allowed to with a proper restraining device (adult belts are not enough).

3 In the summer of 1999, Westminster City Council prosecuted several washer boys for 'street trading' contrary to local by-laws. It is to be hoped that other local authorities will follow suit.

4 *Private* clamping where motorists parked unlawfully on private property have to pay an often exorbitant fee to have their cars unclamped is illegal in Scotland where, in 1992, the Court of Session ruled that it was 'extortion and theft'. In England and Wales, the Appeal Court's 1995 ruling in *Arthur* v. *Anker* applies where Lord Bingham, the present Lord Chief Justice, upheld a £40 unclamping charge on a Rover car parked unlawfully on private land in Truro on the basis that the charge was 'reasonable' and a prominently placed notice warned that cars were at risk of being clamped and specifying the release fee. Both John Major's and Tony Blair's governments have promised to bring in new legislation on the subject but – for once – Whitehall is so far silent.

PART FIVE

YOUR LEISURE

23

HOTELS AND
HOLIDAYS

Holidays should be fun. For most of us, they are also something special and should be a well-deserved rest, with no complications. But whoever said life was going to be fair? You may book well in advance, you may look forward to it with eager anticipation – but a holiday can all too easily work out badly.

At least, it helps to know that the law is basically on your side. The tone was set by the Appeal Court in October 1972, in *Jarvis* v. *Swan Tours Ltd* (reported in [1973] 1 All England Law Reports, at page 71), when a young Essex solicitor booked a two-week winter sports holiday in Switzerland. The brochure promised a marvellous time, with a whole gamut of attractions, but it turned out a disaster. When he complained, the tour operator said he was only entitled to some of his money back because he had enjoyed *some* of the holiday and he was not criticising, for instance, the travel arrangements, there and back.

But the Appeal Court ruled that he should receive substantial damages for his 'frustration, annoyance and inconvenience'. Furthermore, Lord Justice Edmund Davies declared in words that should be written over the door of every tour operator's head office:

When a man has paid for, and properly expects, an invigorating and amusing holiday and, through no fault of his, returns home dejected because his expectations have been largely unfulfilled, it would be quite wrong to say that his disappointment must find no reflection in the damages to be awarded.

There are two main aspects of the problem to be looked at:

Ever since unscrupulous innkeepers in the eighteenth century knocked their clients over the head and stole their belongings, hoteliers have been under what Lord Justice Jenkins once called 'a special liability by virtue of the custom of the realm'. Even without a booking, they cannot refuse sleeping accommodation to a respectable traveller, if rooms are available and the traveller can pay their charges. They are also automatically liable for loss or damage to the belongings of a guest *staying at least one night in the hotel* – whether or not their staff is at fault.

The 1956 Hotel Proprietors Act exempts your car – and anything left in it – from this old automatic liability and allows a hotel to limit its responsibility for other goods lost or damaged without the hotel's fault to £50 for any one article or £100 for any one guest. This is ludicrously low and, in 1994, the Consumers' Association called for the limit to be increased to £1,000 but – of course! – nothing has happened. The only saving grace is that your household contents insurance policy may fully cover you for the loss of personal items taken with you.

Furthermore, to claim the limitation, the management must prominently display a clearly legible notice headed '1956 Hotel Proprietors Act' near the reception desk or entrance. Without it, they will be responsible for anything stolen while you are staying with them, even if you cannot prove any particular staff member was to blame.[1]

But they may be able to reduce your compensation because of your own 'contributory negligence': for instance, in leaving jewellery in a dressing-table drawer instead of putting it in the hotel's safe.

Some hotels put up a notice in the room itself saying they will not accept liability for goods lost or stolen unless left for safe keeping with the management, similar to the kind of notice one finds in many foreign hotel rooms. But in England this has no legal effect. As the Appeal Court ruled in 1948, the hotel guest has by then booked in, signed the register – and completed his contract. The hotel cannot then try and impose new terms into that contract. If it wants to limit its liability for valuables only to those left in its safe, it should clearly say so in a notice near the reception desk, so that you can see it when checking in.

Another important notice that you should look for in the reception area is a list of room charges. The little-known 1977 Tourism (Sleeping Accommodation Price Display) Order says that any hotel or establishment in the business of providing sleeping accommodation (those two words 'or establishment' broaden the scope to include boarding houses, private guest houses and even bed and breakfast places) must give details of prices plus VAT for all accommodation, including any service charge, if it has at least four bedrooms or eight beds.

Many places 'forget' this notice and can be fined up to £2,500. But prosecutions are rare. Even so, the order does not require prices to be displayed in each room, as on the continent.

You are, of course, legally entitled to expect that you will get what you pay for. And this applies both in criminal and in civil law.

In criminal law, hotels and boarding houses, etc. come within the 1968 Trade Descriptions Act which makes it an offence (with a fine of up to £5,000) to apply a false trade description to the supply of goods and services. So a West Country landlady who wrote to a would-be customer that her boarding house was 200 yards from the sea, was fined in the local magistrates' court when a trading standards officer found the real distance was 801 yards; another West Country hotel has escaped prosecution for claiming that it was only a stone's throw from the beach by employing a Hampshire fast bowler to throw a pebble on to the beach from its front entrance; and a hotel company in Bayswater, London has been fined for claiming in its brochure that it was 'newly opened' and 'modern' when in truth it had opened six years before and the building was about 80 years old, although a lift had been installed and the building had been extensively modernised. Other examples abound.

As for the civil law, in 1951, in an early test case, the Appeal Court ruled that a holidaymaker, who had booked a 'superior room with a sea view' in a Jersey hotel and was then given a room that was neither superior nor had a sea view, was entitled to damages for his 'appreciable inconvenience and discomfort'. And there have, for instance, been decisions that a room from which you can only see the sea by going out on to the balcony is *not* a room 'with a sea view'; that the term 'a lounge' in a hotel brochure does not apply to a room in which meals are served and that accommodation in an annexe will suffice only if it is near to the main building and its amenities (including the provision of meals) are reasonably acceptable.

In all these cases, the disappointed holidaymakers won damages in a civil court but that is not the only remedy available. If, when you arrive at a hotel or similar establishment, you are not offered the type of room you booked (and you should always keep a copy of the filled-in booking form, your booking letter or your written confirmation of a telephone booking), you can insist on their giving you what you asked for. If they do not, you should reclaim your deposit and walk out: provided, of course, you are reasonably sure you can get what you want elsewhere! If your new hotel costs you more than the original one because you cannot find anything suitable in the same price category, you can reclaim the difference: pursuing your demand, if necessary, into a small claims court.

(Surprisingly I can give no practical advice as to how large you can expect a 'double room' to be. Neither Parliament nor the judges have laid down any precise measurements. When the Appeal Court was faced with the problem back in 1962, it ducked the issue. It was in a case where a South Coast three-star hotel had given a couple a 15 foot × 8 foot 6 inches 'double room' hardly big enough to hold a double bed, a chest of drawers and a built-in cupboard; but the appeal judges ruled that this complied with the description in that particular hotel and at that particular price and refused to lay down any general guidelines.)

What about cancellation? What is the law on cancelling a booking?   The best-laid holiday plans can easily go wrong even at the last minute. But that does not entitle you to write, as many people do, to the hotel cancelling your booking because of illness or 'unforeseen circumstances' – and then expecting they will not claim compensation.

A hotel booking is as much a legally binding contract as any other commercial agreement. Just as the hotel cannot go back on its contract, neither can you. Unless you stipulate when making your booking that you reserve the right to cancel for illness or some such cause, which is highly unlikely, neither party to the contract can terminate it off their own bat.

On the other hand, a hotel is not entitled to present you with its bill at once. The management should write a 'holding letter' saying that you have forfeited any deposit but they will try and re-let the room and, if they fail, they will hold you responsible. If they then re-let the room for the same price, they have no case, since they have lost nothing (although they are usually able to keep the deposit).

Even if they have not re-let, they still cannot claim the whole cost of your cancelled booking. They must knock off a third for the food you have not eaten. They cannot, as it were, make a profit out of your breach of contract. In logic and in law, a forfeited deposit is not so much a profit to them as the price to you of cancelling when the contract gives you no such right.

PACKAGE TOURS ABROAD

The estimated fifteen million Britons jetting off on holiday abroad every year enjoy greater legal protection than ever before. Until comparatively recently the law had not kept pace with this massive, fast-expanding industry that some 30 years ago did not even exist. Various Acts of Parliament and test cases in the courts had built up a partial armoury of legal rights. But that was all part of general consumer protection law.

However, there now is – almost unknown to the general public – a detailed set of legal provisions that specifically applies to package tours: the clumsily titled Package Travel, Package Holidays and Package Tours Regulations that came into effect on 31 December 1992. That was literally the very last day by which John Major's Government could comply with an EU Directive dating back to June 1990 ordering all Common Market countries to enact their own package tour laws. Some lawyers and consumer-rights experts claim these Regulations do not go far enough. But at least they are a beginning. This is how they (and other laws) work:

Before you leave Britain

Cancelling   No matter what may have happened to cause it – a family death or losing your job – cancelling a package tour holiday will cost you money. Look under 'cancellation' in the booking form or explanatory details at the back of your brochure, and you will see that you will lose up to 90 per cent of your deposit, depending on how late you have left it. The sooner you cancel, the less it will cost.

Even if you took out travel insurance when booking (which you always should), that will only give you very limited cover. For instance, you must not only have lost your job but must have been made redundant. Or if you are ill, it must not be an illness which you should have anticipated.

Even so, if you have a genuine excuse and are prepared to put off your holiday, not cancel it outright, the tour operator will often do his best to help, and charge only a token 'transfer fee' (usually £15) per person. 'Always ask, they may say yes' is the best legal advice I can give – in any situation.

Surcharges   These used to be a curse but the 1992 Regulations allow no price increases whatsoever within 30 days of departure – and before that they must be tied to increased transport costs.

Overbooking   Usually only a problem on scheduled flights where airlines would habitually 'bump off' passengers with virtual legal immunity because they had sold too many seats. It can now cost them money. For if the flight originates in an EU country or was booked through an EU travel agent, the EU's 1991 Denied Boarding Regulation says you can demand on-the-spot compensation. If you have a confirmed reservation and have presented yourself for check-in 'within the required time limit', you are entitled to 150 Ecu (about £120) for a flight of up to 3,500 kilometres and 300 Ecu (about £240) for longer journeys. These amounts are halved if the next flight is available within two to four hours.[2]

Travel Insurance Do not leave home without it. New Government regulations in November 1998 made it illegal for travel agents and tour operators to insist on customers taking their own in-house (and usually expensive) travel insurance as a condition of getting a discount on package holidays. Discounts must be available to all customers, including those who buy their insurance elsewhere.

But an estimated 40 per cent of package tour holidaymakers are still talked into taking out in-house insurance because of hard-sell techniques. These contravene the spirit, if not the wording, of the Regulations and the Office of Fair Trading is currently monitoring the position.

The only answer is to be resolute, ignore the sales talk and, if you want to be insured, shop around. The problem is that you may have to find another tour operator! This is because the 1992 Package Tour Regulations do not say that holidaymakers must be insured, although many tour operators like to give that impression. In fact, just as you can choose whether or not, and with whom, to be insured, tour operators can choose whether or not to accept you on that basis. Unfortunately the November 1998 regulations do not affect that fundamental position.

Airport delays Every summer we read of outward-going passengers stranded for hours and even sometimes days.

What are your rights? Even today they are surprisingly few, despite the 1992 Package Tour Regulations. The Air Transport Users Council states in *Flight Plan*, its official passengers' guide: 'If travelling on a scheduled service with a flexible ticket, you may find the check-in staff have already arranged for you to fly with another airline. If not, ask if you can transfer. But on most other types of scheduled ticket (generally the cheaper ones), or if you are on a charter flight, you are in the hands of the airline whilst the problem is sorted out.'

Those sombre words accurately state the law.

Travellers used to believe that after two hours an airline had to give you free refreshments or a meal and, if you were kept waiting between midnight and 4 a.m., they had to put you up in a hotel. In fact, that was never the law – and still is not today. There are no rules which say that airlines or tour operators must provide food and drink or, in extreme cases, overnight accommodation while you wait. Many do. But it is entirely at their own discretion.

For package tour holidays, the brochure forms the legal basis of the contract and usually gives adequate safeguards against changes from day flights to night flights but they usually give little or no compensation for mere delay.

Nowadays most air travellers have insurance and even the cheapest, costing £20 to £30 per adult for a two-week trip to Europe, gives comparative peace of mind – and includes some compensation for airport delays. But do not cheer too loudly. Usually you will get nothing if delayed for less than 12 hours (or six hours with more expensive insurance). With run-of-the-mill insurance, the clock starts ticking at £20 for that first 12 hours with a measly £10 for each subsequent 12 hours – up to £60 per adult for two and a half days' delay.

As so often in life, you get what you pay for.

At the foreign airport

Missing luggage   Tour operators like to pass the buck. Their brochures normally exclude liability for lost or damaged luggage and say you must claim on the airline or on your own insurance.

In practice, most people are insured anyway so they can claim up to £1,500 with a £250 maximum for any one item.

If you claim on the airline, the Warsaw Convention of 1929 used to limit liability to only £13.60 for each kilo of luggage, so that someone losing the maximum weight allowance of 280 kilos was entitled to a maximum of just £280 – no matter how expensive their case or its contents. Fortunately, a few months ago, the figure was increased to £800.

But, of course, you cannot claim once on the airline and then on insurance! In fact, most luggage turns up within 24 hours and insurance generally pays out £100 for delays of only half that time: i.e. 12 hours. If insured separately, you will get your money upon your return. But with the tour operator's own insurance, their local representative will usually hand over £100 in local currency to buy essential items – swimwear, change of underwear, etc. – after those first annoying 12 hours.

At the foreign hotel

It is nothing like the brochure description   This is the most common complaint of all – with the strongest protection from the law. We have all read horror stories about 'luxury' hotels next to a sewer or 'sea view' rooms half a mile from the sea. But ever since the 1968 Trade Descriptions Act disgruntled holidaymakers on their return can complain to trading standards officers at their local town hall and tour operators have been fined heavily in the local magistrates' court for false trade descriptions. The 1992 Regulations have extended this offence to descriptions that are merely 'misleading' without being downright 'false'.

And, of course, the disappointed holidaymaker with a legitimate grievance can also sue for damages in a civil court. I wish that more people in the package tour industry knew the powerful words of Mr Registrar Delroy in the Manchester District Registry in April 1985: 'A tour operator sells a dream. If he sells a dream, he must make it come true. This is fragile; therefore it imposes on him a great obligation to take care.' (If you are interested, the name of this most useful case is *Harris* v. *Torchgrove* and it is reported in (1985) Current Law Year Book at paragraph 944).

But you must first complain in writing to the tour operator within 28 days of your return, otherwise you will be in breach of the booking conditions in your brochure.

These conditions also generally claim that the tour operator has the right to change the resort, flights and accommodation or to limit the compensation, if it makes such a change. Even so, these clauses are only valid if a judge says they are 'fair and reasonable' under the 1977 Unfair Contract Terms Act, as strengthened by the 1999 Unfair Terms in Consumer Contracts Regulations. I give those two long-winded names because it can be useful to throw them in, when writing to complain. If tour operators think you are serious, you may well find that their bite can prove much less than their bark.

To start with, they will often meet your claim with an apology and a host of excuses. But if your complaint is reasonable (backed up, as we will shortly see, with photographs, details of complaints to their local courier – *very important!* – and receipts for extra expenses), they may offer compensation or, at the least, private arbitration.

But with claims under £5,000 (and each one in a party has his or her own separate claim), your local user-friendly small claims court will have jurisdiction and, if you are a reasonably articulate person, you should threaten to argue your case there. Although only another kind of arbitration (with a district judge instead of a private arbitrator in the chair), this procedure has the great tactical advantage that, since it is a court, the press cannot be excluded. Faced with a fight in a small claims court, many tour operators cave in and offer an out-of-court settlement to avoid unwelcome publicity – but you must have a case they think you are likely to win!

The courier is useless We have all met them. The couriers who seem to be too keen on having a good time themselves to take our complaints seriously. But that is their job – backed up by the law. The 1992 Regulations say it is their duty to 'make prompt efforts to find appropriate solutions'.

But even if they are useless, you *must* complain to them, and my advice is to make a written note of the date and time, and anything that happened as a result.

Thomson Holidays say in their brochures: 'If you have a complaint, please tell your Thomson representative immediately. It is always easier to sort things out on the spot, when your representative can see and understand the exact nature of the problem.' That applies to all tour operators.

It goes further than that. If you do not complain, you are at risk of having your compensation claim cut later. When a London couple sued after their Tenerife holiday had been spoiled by bad meals and an unpleasant room, their 'substantial damages' were reduced to £400 because they had not complained to the courier.

However useless the courier may be, it will cost you money if you do not at least go through the motions of complaining.

You get food poisoning As tour operators try and hang on to their profits and at the same time keep prices low, something has to give; and very often it is quality. This can easily show itself in bad hotel food.

Jane Goulding, a Nottingham solicitor, was recently quoted in the press as saying: 'Badly cooked food, poor refrigeration and dirty crockery can all combine to cause health problems that can ruin a holiday and continue to cause serious problems after returning home.' Of course, she is quite right; and in 1998 she won £5,222 compensation from a leading tour operator for a family of five, including a Down's syndrome child, who went down with serious food poisoning on a holiday in Turkey.

When it is not just a case of individual food poisoning but many people in the same hotel fall ill, they are nowadays much more organised than before. They talk to each other, exchange telephone numbers, use cameras or camcorders to produce evidence, make careful notes and, when they get home, use the one firm of solicitors to pursue their claims. These 'class actions', as lawyers call them, have much more muscle than people complaining on their own – and are more likely to end in a generous out-of-court settlement.

You have an accident at the hotel or on an organised trip   Before the
1992 Regulations, tour operators could always say if an accident
happened abroad that it was their foreign associate's fault – the hotel or
a coach operator, for instance – and they were not liable. 'Sue the foreign
company,' they would say but, of course, no one did.

The Regulations changed all that. Now the general rule is that the tour
operator is responsible for the proper performance of its contract by its
foreign associates as well as by itself. And it can be sued in this country
for a holiday accident abroad, even though not to blame for what went
wrong.

And it is no excuse that the foreign company complied with local
safety standards if they were lower than British standards.

The young man who fell off the balcony

When on holiday with friends in Crete in July 1993 a young man from
Lancashire, aged 20, went out on to the balcony of his third-floor hotel room
at 3.30 in the morning and fell to the pavement beneath. He broke his neck
and was permanently paralysed from the neck down.

The balcony's walls were only 797 millimetres high. That was sufficient
by Cretan standards but in Britain they would have had to be 1,100
millimetres high.

So five years later, in July 1998, his Manchester-based lawyers won an
estimated £1 million out-of-court settlement for him from the tour operator –
even allowing for his being 30 per cent to blame for his own carelessness.

How best to complain?   Having laid the basis of your claim by
complaining to the courier, you should as soon as possible on return write
to the customer services department at the tour operator's head office.
The address is in the brochure – which you should have kept with you as
a guide to what you were entitled to expect.

It is always a good idea to enclose with your letter any photographs to
help prove your case: the revolting food served on your plate, the non-
view of the sea from your room, the all-night disco right under your
window, the too small swimming pool, etc. But always keep copies in
case your letter never arrives or the tour operator mysteriously 'loses' the
photographs.

Do not include the tape of any recordings you have made of excessive
noise late at night or videotapes of eyesores or dangerous hotel facilities.
These are always useful evidence but you only need write that you have
them and can produce them, if necessary. Do not risk them in the post.

The stronger you make your letter, the more likely it is to be taken
seriously and that decent compensation will be offered. But do not expect

that will happen quickly. Companies do not like paying out money. You may have to keep up the pressure with frequent reminders.

Your tour operator goes bust and you are stranded far from home

It is the ultimate horror to discover that your tour operator, travel agent or airline has gone bust and you have lost your holiday or you have already gone – and cannot get back home.

The 1992 Regulations say that all package tour companies flying people abroad must lodge a bond with an insurance company or bank sufficient to bail out their customers in the event of financial collapse. Not everyone obeys this law. But there are three trade organisations whose members you can be sure do so: the Association of British Travel Agents (ABTA), Air Travel Organiser's Licence (ATOL) and Association of Independent Tour Operators (AITO).

Their logos on premises or stationery are essential for your protection. They mean that, if the individual company goes bust, you will get your money back if you have not yet gone on holiday, or will be brought back safely if you have. So always look around for those vital ABTA, ATOL and AITO logos – and check they are not out of date. If too embarrassed to ask the individual company, phone ABTA on 020–7637 2444, ATOL on 020–7832 5620 and AITO on 020–8744 9280.

It is well worth it for peace of mind.

Notes
1 Some older hotels think it more 'atmospheric' to display a notice under the 1863 Innkeepers Liability Act, an earlier version of the 1956 Act. They are foolhardy: it has absolutely no legal effect.
2 I'm sorry to quote Ecus which no one uses now but the EU Regulation has not been updated.

24

RESTAURANTS, WINE BARS AND DISCOS

Many years ago, I was interviewing over lunch in an expensive restaurant Hugh (later Lord) Scanlon for an article I was writing for a Sunday magazine on the nature of power. I was a young man at the time and he was then one of the most powerful trade union leaders in the country.

When I tasted the wine that I had ordered, I was not sure but I thought that it might have been off. It seemed corked. What should I do? I did not want to make a fool of myself in front of Scanlon but at the same time I did not see why we should drink wine that was perhaps questionable.

So I called over the wine waiter and he was most unpleasant at the mere suggestion that something might be wrong.

Reluctantly, he tasted the wine – and immediately apologised profusely and brought another bottle. 'That's what I call power!' said Scanlon.

It helped, of course, that I knew I was legally in the right. Food and drink served in a restaurant or wine bar (or public house, for that matter) must be reasonably fit for human consumption and of the quality you are entitled to expect in an establishment of that category. You should never forget that, even in this modern era of the over-hyped 'celebrity chef' or the 'absolutely fabulous' wine bar, you are the client and, as such, you have considerable rights.

We are primarily going to look at the law on restaurants but many aspects also apply to wine bars:

RESTAURANTS AND WINE BARS

Getting in

If you have made a booking, even if only over the telephone, a restaurant is in breach of contract if it does not honour it – and you can (politely) threaten to sue them for damages for a spoiled evening in their own local small claims court. They will then usually find you a table. (An unscrupulous friend of mine does this quite often – and gets his table – even when he has not made a booking!)

But if it is vice-versa and you have let *them* down, they can sue you for the lost business. This actually happened back in 1988 when a London advertising agency booked a table for 1 p.m. for five people at Mijanou, a small but very successful restaurant in Pimlico, central London – and cancelled at 1.35 p.m. on that very day. The meeting had gone on too long, the client did not want to eat. It was an all-too-familiar scenario for the owner. 'As always, I was a bit upset,' he told a reporter. 'We only seat 30 so that's a sixth of our seating, and I had turned people away.' The agency refused compensation. So he sued and the judge ruled that, *since it was lunchtime and the table could not be rebooked*, they should pay the owner's loss of profit on the meal plus his legal costs.

But please note that italicised sentence. It means that, if the restaurant is not out of pocket – perhaps because it is very busy or very large and has easily seated waiting customers at your empty table – it has lost no profit and has nothing to sue about.

Even so, all restaurant owners understandably do not like last-minute cancellations or 'no shows' and some of the better-known establishments can afford to draw up their own private blacklist of people from whom they will not accept bookings. They are perfectly entitled to do so. The management of a restaurant, wine bar or public house can always refuse admission at their complete discretion – except on grounds of race or sex.

Hence, they can lawfully refuse admission because they say you are 'improperly dressed': no jacket and tie or torn jeans (however fashionable) for a man or any kind of trousers for a woman – or whatever. On one occasion, a bishop, wearing traditional white-necked collar and purple robe, was turned away from a smart central London restaurant and wrote a three-page letter of complaint – to no avail.

But there is a nuance: if the restaurant has accepted your booking without warning of their dress code, they cannot legally refuse a table (though not perhaps in the best position!). They should have told you of their special rules. In practice, you will avoid a lot of embarrassment by asking over the phone, when making your booking, if they have a dress code and then either choosing to accept it – or eating elsewhere.

The menu

Whether in English, phoney French or, even worse, dog-Spanish, this is a vital legal document. The 1979 Price Marking (Food and Drink on Premises) Order says that a restaurant can be fined up to £5,000 for not displaying a full menu (or at least 30 selected items, if the menu is mega-large), including prices and VAT, outside or immediately inside the door so that potential customers know in advance what they are committing themselves to.

This specimen menu does not have to include a full wine list: whether for restaurant or wine bar. The Order only relates to table wine anyway and stipulates that, if less than six kinds of table wine are supplied, the description and price of each kind (white, red or rosé) shall be given but, if more than six, the price and description of only six (again, broken up into white, red and rosé) must be given. It is fascinating to walk out into your local High Street or 'restaurant row', as I have just done, and see how few establishments comply with these strict legal requirements. Some restaurants give no wine at all, table or otherwise, some wine bars give their entire wine list while others limit themselves to table wine and 'champagne and other sparkling wines'. Yet I know of no prosecutions for breach of the wine provisions of the 1979 Order.

It is an offence against the 1968 Trade Descriptions Act for any food establishment (including restaurants, wine bars and public houses) to give a false trade description of any of their food. Everything must be what it claims to be. *Pâté maison* or *pâté du chef* must be home-made or at least made on the premises, and not come from a factory or be bought in from outside. Fresh fruit salad must consist of fresh fruit and not be tinned fruit freshly mixed. Welsh lamb must be an animal raised or at least born in Wales.

You also have to be careful about scampi. A lot of what passes as scampi on many restaurants' menus and tables is nothing of the kind. Genuine scampi should consist only of the tails of Dublin Bay prawns fried in batter but much of what is called 'scampi' today – especially at the lower end of the market – consists of bits of fish minced and bound together with starch or cereal. Prosecutions for breach of the 1968 Act are not unknown. But roast Aylesbury duck or Norfolk turkey do not have to come from Aylesbury or Norfolk: they are merely the names of a breed.

The same principle applies to wine. If they bring you a vintage different from that stated on the wine list, they are not only cheating you but committing an offence against the 1968 Act. With a quality wine, it is always worth checking the cork as well as the label: I once made a restaurant change a wine on which the château named on the label was different from that on the cork!

A menu does not legally have to spell out whether 'liver' is that of a calf, pig or lamb. If you ask the waiter or waitress, their only obligation is to give you a truthful answer. And, if you have a taste for 'bangers and mash' (which you can sometimes find on the menu in even the most fashionable restaurants), you cannot count on the sausages tasting as meaty as those at home. The meat content regulations that apply to sausages sold by retail to the general public do not apply to the catering trade.

On the other hand, if you pay twice or three times as much in a trendy restaurant as you would pay for sausages and mash in a transport café, and the sausages taste as you would expect to find in a transport café, you may be able to persuade a trading standards officer at your local town hall to prosecute for a false trade description under the 1968 Act or an environmental health officer in the same building to prosecute for the offence of selling food 'not of the quality demanded' under the 1990 Food Safety Act. Anyone fancy a test case?

You cannot rely on getting bread (or roll) and butter free. A restaurant is entitled to make a cover charge for this, provided it appears in the menu by the door. 'Cover' relates to whatever goes on the table apart from the food or drink that you actually order: i.e. clean linen, silverware, glassware, condiments, sauces and such trendy items as olives, sliced raw carrots or gherkins which appear whether you ask for them or not – or whether you like them or not.

A little-known legal quirk is that restaurants which have a liquor licence are legally obliged to serve tap water free. This is because the 1964 Licensing Act says that an implied condition of the licence is that suitable beverages, other than alcohol, including drinking water, shall be equally available with the meal – and habitual breach of this condition is a ground for local magistrates refusing to renew the licence.

Technically, merely because a cover charge is stated on the menu does not necessarily mean that you must pay for it. If any part of the 'cover' has been unsatisfactory (or you have not eaten the gherkins), you need only leave what you think the acceptable items are worth. But, of course, most people do not bother. They simply 'vote with their feet' and do not return to the restaurant because usually that is not the only thing that has gone wrong.

Quality

If the food is not cooked to one's satisfaction – for instance a steak is well done instead of 'rare' – you can insist on their taking it back and supplying what you ordered. If you asked for the steak 'well done' and it arrived rare, it is not acceptable for them merely to put the piece of meat back on the grill and cook it a bit more. A 'rare' steak is a steak that has been cooked 'rare' from raw, not merely reheated. If you complain and the management prove difficult, remind them that the 1990 Food Safety Act makes it an offence with a maximum fine of £20,000 and/or six months in gaol, to supply food 'not of the nature, substance or quality demanded'.

Of course, if the food gives you food poisoning, not only has an offence against the 1990 Act been committed but, *if you have been to the doctor* (an essential for proving your case), you can sue for damages in a civil court. And this applies to any kind of restaurant, irrespective of where it is or how much (or how little) it costs: it was, for instance, a point of honour at one famous central London seafood restaurant that only the best lobsters were served. The head chef told Judge Blagden at Westminster County Court that they were delivered live each day and any Dead On Arrival were returned at once. Yet one day an out-of-town visitor was served an 'elderly' lobster that made her violently ill. There was no way that she could disprove the head chef's confident evidence – but 'Accidents happen in the best regulated families,' said Judge Blagden, and awarded her damages.

Liability is so well established today that insurers often pay out without a case getting so far as the courts:

The case of the school curry

The chefs at an expensive public school in Norfolk were used to preparing food with a special wheat-free diet for a 17-year-old day-boy because he had an allergy to all forms of wheat protein. But in March 1992 he was served a beef curry – and the curry contained flour: kitchen workers had forgotten they had used flour to thicken the sauce.

Result: the curry gave him stomach pains and severe headaches that persisted for eight months. He blamed this illness for his poor A-level results. He sued the school and, in July 1993, the school's insurers paid him £3,000 in an out-of-court settlement.

The £100,000 pay-out

In July 1991, two cricket teams in Suffolk were hit by food poisoning after tucking into sandwiches during the tea interval at a friendly match between a law firm and an accountants firm. Nine solicitors, ten accountants and a number of spectators went down with severe diarrhoea, headaches, vomiting and stomach cramps.

It transpired that mayonnaise used in the sandwiches supplied by a Colchester sandwich bar was infected with salmonella. The sandwich bar owner had been morally blameless (the salmonella had come from raw eggs used in the mayonnaise and supplied from a batch of chickens later destroyed) and local magistrates gave her a conditional discharge and ordered her to pay £500 costs for offences against the 1990 Food Safety Act.

But a personal injury specialist with the law firm took up a civil case on behalf of his cricketing colleagues and the worst-affected other victims and in May 1994 the sandwich bar's insurers finally agreed a £100,000 compensation package for the 76 major sufferers.

Even if the food or drink is not bad enough to make you ill but you merely think it is not up to a reasonable standard for the money, you can send it back and insist on something else or you can make a deduction from the bill. But if you make a deduction, you should give your name and address and proof of identity (driving licence, for instance), so that the restaurant cannot call the police and claim you have committed the criminal offence of walking out without paying the bill.

If they want the rest of their money, they will have to sue you – if they want to risk the adverse publicity. Amazingly, this happened in one superb case some years ago:

The case of the too-expensive tea

A university economics lecturer, charged eight shillings (40p) at a teashop in Hampstead, London for two slices of apple pie and a pot of tea, insisted on leaving only five shillings (25p).

He gave his name and address and produced his driving licence, so that they could not call the police. But they actually bothered to sue him for the remaining three shillings (15p) in Marylebone County Court – where Judge Leslie ruled that the meal was worth only 7s.6d. (just over 37.5p). The lecturer's solicitor then handed over 2s.6d. (12.5p), and a crucial legal principle was reaffirmed.

The great wine scandal

As far back as September 1974, a great legal victory for wine-lovers was – supposedly – won. A government order specified that wine sold *en carafe* for consumption on the premises must be sold by capacity measurement: a quarter-litre, half a litre, three-quarters of a litre or one litre. At last, 'carafe' meant something in law.

But the catering industry's steady lobbying had not been in vain: under the Order, an establishment did not have to volunteer its carafe sizes. It merely had to give a truthful answer, if asked – and who asked?

It took another 14 years before a 1988 order said that an establishment must specify its carafe sizes in a conspicuously displayed notice or in its wine list or menu so that customers might see in advance how much they were ordering. The 1988 Order also said that wine sold in bottles for consumption on the premises must be in the same sizes allowed for carafes – and similarly displayed in a notice or wine list or menu.

As for wine sold by the glass, the 1988 Order was updated in 1995 so that nowadays wine sold by the glass must be sold in a 125 or 175 ml. (millilitre) glass (or in a multiple of those quantities) with a similar conspicuous notice or statement in a wine list or menu. But there remains no legal control on price. One establishment can legally charge, say, £2.50 for a 125 ml. glass and another £1.75 for a 175 ml. glass. You must shop around for the best value.

Yet despite the Order's strict requirements – backed up with a maximum £2,000 fine for any breach – one does not often see an establishment's glass, carafe or bottle sizes stated as legally they should. Sadly, the Order is not rigorously enforced.

Tipping

Perhaps the most ticklish question of all. In fact, it is purely voluntary. Even if warned of a fixed service charge on the menu, you can still (as with a 'cover charge') refuse to pay it if, at the end of the meal, you do not think the service was worth it.

Not enough people know their rights. In May 1990 a restaurant in west London advertised a 'set lunch for only £4.95' on a billboard outside the premises but it said nothing about a 10 per cent service charge. Trading standards officers warned the management that this constituted the offence of giving customers a 'misleading price indication', contrary to the 1987 Consumer Protection Act. When on a second visit this hidden extra was still not mentioned on the billboard, the restaurant was summoned in the local magistrates' court.

It pleaded guilty, and was fined £500.

A Code of Practice drawn up under the 1987 Act suggests various ways of including 'extras' on the menu. As with the Highway Code and breaches of motoring law, this Code is of importance when deciding if a restaurant has broken the law on misleading prices under the Act but it is neither compulsory nor does everyone heed it. 'Discretionary service charges' and 'optional service charges' are often found on menus, although the Code does not like them. In fact, you can legally ignore them, if you think the standard of service does not warrant them.

No one wants aggravation when out for pleasure but also no one wants to be taken for a ride. I once queried a mysterious 'Grat – £2.50' at the bottom of my bill in a fast-food Italian restaurant in the tourist heart of London. 'That is a gratuity, if you want to pay it,' explained the waiter. Perfectly fair, and I was happy to hand over the extra £2.50.

But I wonder how many people paid their bill without question – and then added 10 per cent for the tip.

DISCOS (WITH A QUICK LOOK AT RAVES)

There is not much to be said about discos in a book of this nature except for two things:

Disco law is based on hypocrisy For the 1964 Licensing Act only allows discos where you can drink to operate legally on Special Hours Certificates issued by local magistrates. These certificates allow them to serve drinks beyond the normal hours permitted by their liquor licence: i.e. on weekdays until 3 a.m. in London and 2 a.m. elsewhere.

But it is a special condition always imposed that the premises must have a music, singing and dancing licence *and* provide 'substantial refreshment' as well as drink. In fact, food – substantial or otherwise – is one of the last things that people go to such a disco for. Yet the High Court ruled in 1968 that 'the fact that some customers will not take advantage of either the refreshment or the music and dancing facility does not justify refusal of the Special Hours Certificate'. For many youngsters it is merely a legal way to be out drinking into the early hours of the morning.

There is widespread doubt about the minimum age of entry In fact, there is no legal minimum age. It all depends on whether the disco or club is licensed to sell alcohol.

The 1964 Act makes it an offence for a liquor licence holder or member of staff to sell intoxicating liquor to any person under 18 except beer, porter (a type of thin beer), cider or perry sold to 16- and 17-year-olds with a meal in a normal restaurant or in a restaurant in a pub not forming part of a bar. Clubs and discos make a great deal of money from alcohol sales and most would rather take strong measures (e.g. bouncers at the door) to exclude under-18-year-olds than run the risk of losing their liquor licence.

Also many clubs or discos do not want too young a crowd and, irrespective of the law, limit their membership to those over 21.

A quick look at raves

No parent, regardless of wealth or social class, can be complacent about where their teenage children go at night, and some are genuinely worried about what might happen if their young son or daughter were found at a rave. Are they liable to be arrested?

The answer is 'No'. Only the actual organisers or someone who allows a rave to take place on his premises commit an offence against the 1982 Local Government (Miscellaneous Provisions) Act, as amended by a 1990 Act, which carries an awesome maximum fine of £20,000 or six months in gaol or both. No one else commits a crime and, even if your youngster is found with a small amount of 'soft' drugs on her for her own use, the police will probably only give her a caution for that specific offence.

25

SPORT – PLAYERS AND WATCHERS

PLAYERS

Sport is a dangerous pastime. The *Daily Telegraph* has calculated that in an average year some 370,000 people need hospital treatment for football injuries, 78,000 for injuries on the rugby field, and there are 20,000 injured hockey players and 15,000 injured basketball players. And these are all non-professionals, playing the game for fun!

Indeed, the traditional attitude of English (and Scottish) law has always been that anyone engaged in sport is presumed to know what they are letting themselves in for. You are expected to realise that in certain kinds of sport there is always a risk of injury. Very little Parliament-made law exists on the subject but the consistent attitude of the judges, many of whom took part in sport at school and university, has been that by agreeing to take part in a sporting activity you are voluntarily accepting the risk of injury from 'a normal incident of the game'. As the Ancient Roman lawyers said in Latin, and modern British lawyers still do, *Volenti non fit injuria*: 'To the willing there can be no injury.'

In a vague sort of way, there has somehow always been the feeling among the judges that only 'sissies' sue over a sporting injury. It must be all those cold showers at school when they were young; but there is a general notion pervading the judgments in the comparatively few cases where players have sued over sporting mishaps that it somehow 'isn't done' to sue over such a matter. 'Judo is a robust and manly sport,' said Lord Justice Sellers sternly in the Appeal Court when quashing a £5,500 damages award to a judo novice hurt in his very first practice lesson.

Yet it was this same Liverpool-born lord justice who gave us our classic statement of the modern law on sporting injuries. It was back in 1962 in a case where the Appeal Court threw out a claim for damages over an incident involving one of the horses at an international horse competition. Lord Justice Sellers laid down: 'There is no liability unless there is negligence. Provided that the competition or game is being performed within the rules and requirements of the sport and by a person of adequate skill and competence, another player does not expect his safety to be regarded.'

Exactly! In one of my last games of geriatric squash before a bad car smash ended my sporting days for ever, three times within 40 minutes I hit my opponent with the ball. That was something of a record, even for me. But the galling thing for my opponent was that each time, according to the rules of the game, it counted as my point because my ball was heading for the right section of the front wall and *he* got in the way. Yet even if he had wanted to, he could not have sued me – however badly I might have 'crocked' him – for I was not playing *negligently*. After more than 30 years, I was still playing with 'adequate skill and competence', although I did not win the game.

What then is negligence in sport? Later in his 1962 judgment, Lord Justice Sellers gave us this answer:

> If the conduct is deliberately intended to injure someone, or is reckless and in disregard of all safety of others, so that it is a departure from the standards which might reasonably be expected in anyone pursuing the competition or game, then the performer might well be held liable for any injury his act caused.

Until recent years, before the increasing (and frightening) aggression of several professional sports such as football, rugby and tennis began to seep into the amateur sector, almost the only sporting cases that came before the courts involved golf. Why this should be I really do not know. Perhaps the reason is that so many judges have always played this game, which is one that you can continue to enjoy well into late middle age. Or it may be because golfers tend to come from the more prosperous sections of society and are therefore more likely to accept the financial risks of suing, certainly in the years between the 1920s and 1970s from which most of the reported cases date.

Whatever the reason, these are just three typical British golfing cases:

- In Belfast, a golfer put all his power into a drive but did not shout 'Fore!' until he saw the ball heading straight for the wrong green. By then, it was too late. The ball knocked out the eye of a fellow player trying to sink a putt. The judge ruled that it was a 'a clear case of negligence', and awarded damages.
- 'This is the way to do it,' said a golfer to her partner demonstrating a shot – and had to pay damages to the caddy she struck with her club.
- A golfer in the North Country, playing in a foursome competition, sliced a shot and it landed smack on the head of a player in a group in front. He had not shouted 'Fore!' and Mr Justice Brabin ordered him to pay £3,333 damages. Brabin was unusually vehement: 'He made the mistake of thinking the party ahead had played their second shots and were moving off. He misjudged the distance. I think it was an idiotic thing to do. He misread the whole scene. He drove the ball at a time when it was dangerous to do so.'

'Duffed' shots, sliced shots, pulled shots: they have all had their sequel in court. In the early 1930s, Mr Justice Swift, himself – naturally! – a golfer of some accomplishment, said: 'A ball may be hit without negligence and strike a spectator or a player. But if negligence could never be brought home to anybody, an injured person could never recover damages. No player or spectator takes the risk of a negligent stroke.'

Even so, most of the cases before the mid-1970s had something of an old-world grace to them. They were all very gentlemanly affairs. I know of my own knowledge of a cricketing incident on a village green some 30 years ago when a batsman made a wild sweep at the ball, knocking it into the crowd and hitting a spectator. He was happy to hand over £25 in cash to keep the matter from going any further: it was a really stupid stroke and he realised the risk of a judge ruling, however reluctantly, that he had been negligent.

Of course, cricket balls then and now are often hit into the crowd and even beyond -but they are normally splendid shots, not reckless play. Consider, for instance, this case in the early 1950s:

The cricket ball that soared over the wall

A woman was waiting at a bus stop outside a cricket ground in Manchester when a ball came soaring over the wall and hit her on the head. As a judge commented in a later case, the batsman had 'received the right kind of ball and dealt with it in the right kind of way'. But the unfortunate woman was badly hurt. She did not sue the batsman but she sued the club for the inadequate layout of its ground.

She lost her case. A club official testified, 'The hit was altogether exceptional' and evidence was produced to show that only about six times in the previous 28 years had a ball been hit out of the ground. So Mr Justice Oliver ruled: 'The possibility of injury occurring was too remote', and (after the Appeal Court had overruled him) the House of Lords said he was perfectly correct.

But faulty layout *can* make a sporting club responsible, as in this 1930s case of a Northern golf club:

The wayward golf ball

A man was hit by a golf ball when walking along a road adjoining a course and sued the club for its negligent siting of some of its greens. Neighbours came forward to testify that balls were continually being hit out into the road, which the club had done nothing about.

So Mr Justice Croom Johnson ruled: 'The club officials should have realised their course was dangerous and re-planned some of their greens away from the road.' He awarded damages against the club. But the player was not sued – he had merely been enjoying a pleasant round of golf and using all reasonable care.

In the more materialist times in which we now live, a senior London insurance claims manager tells me that some golfers, knowing that clubs are nowadays almost always insured, claim against even their own club for injuries sustained as the result of alleged negligence in laying out the course: 'The 18th hole is too near the fairway on the 17th. That sort of thing.' He did not know of any case actually getting to court but he knew of several out-of court settlements: with consequent changes of layout.

Earlier in this chapter I commented upon the increasing (and frightening) amount of violence and sense of aggression that has seeped into some parts of amateur sport from the professional sector. This is particularly true of football and rugby. The very first case in which a non-professional footballer received damages for being injured by a deliberate foul was as far back as 1941, when a Blackburn policeman received £150 for a foul during a wartime charity match. It took another 29 years before the second award was made: in April 1970, when an uninsured 17-year-old plumber was ordered by Mr Justice Rees to pay £5,400 (in instalments over the next 40 years!) to a 27-year-old civil engineering foreman whom he had deliberately kicked during a game at

Eastbourne. But the 1980s and 1990s have sadly seen several such cases – and they have not been defeated by the defence of *Volenti non fit injuria* because the judges have ruled that, even given today's lower standards, a foul is still not to be treated as a 'normal incident of the game', the risk of which you accept by taking part in the game.

Sir John (later Lord) Donaldson, then Master of the Rolls, made a positive ruling to this effect in April 1985, in *Condon* v. *Basi,* when upholding a £4,900 damages award by a county court judge to a player whose leg had been broken by an over-the-ball tackle in a local league game in Leamington. Lord Donaldson said: 'The defendant was clearly guilty of serious and dangerous foul play which showed a reckless disregard of the plaintiff's safety and which fell far below the standards which might reasonably be expected in anyone pursuing the game.' In other words, an amateur sportsman does not accept the risk of being fouled or recklessly kicked: not even today.

What about *professional* sport? For a time it was uncertain whether Lord Donaldson's decision also applied to professional sportsmen who lost their livelihood through injury caused by aggressive play by an opponent that was not so bad as a foul, and one or two insurance payouts were made on the basis that it did. But then, in June 1994, Mr Justice Drake ruled in the High Court that *Condon v. Basi* did apply to professional sportsmen and that they enjoyed no higher legal standard of protection. This was in a case where ex-Chelsea player Paul Elliott sued Liverpool player Dean Saunders after his career had been ended by a tackle in a Liverpool–Chelsea match in September 1992. Mr Justice Drake ruled that Saunders had gone for the ball, not the man, when he made contact with Elliott's knee and that his action was not reckless or dangerous. The conclusive factor was that the referee at the time did not see it as a foul; so why should a High Court judge nearly two years later?

But, as ever, the law moves on. In December 1996, ex-Stockport County midfielder Brian Stockford became the first player to win damages for a foul that had ended his career. During a Second Division game in 1993, Swansea City captain John Cornforth had brought him down in a tackle that broke his leg in two places. Giving judgment against both Cornforth and Swansea City AFC Ltd, his employers, Mr Justice Ian Kennedy said that the making of a tackle judged to be an intentional foul and causing injury to another player, amounted to 'a serious mistake or misjudgment', even if it could not be described as reckless. It was still inconsistent with every player's legal duty to take 'reasonable care' for others in the game. 'It is a contact sport,' said the judge, 'and speed brings its own hazards and can have dreadful consequences.'

In fact, sporting fouls amount to criminal assaults as well as giving the right to sue, and several football and rugby players, both amateur and professional, have been gaoled in recent years. That is why anyone injured through a particularly bad foul should report it to the police so that he can, like any other victim of violent crime, then claim compensation from the Criminal Injuries Compensation Authority without having to sue in a civil court.

As the Authority's predecessor, the Criminal Injuries Compensation Board, wrote in its 1987 Annual Report: 'We consider that it is in the interests of everyone that people who commit criminal offences on the playing fields should be prosecuted. Anyone who considers that an injury upon him was caused by a criminal offence should draw the attention of the police to it. If he does not do so, he is unlikely to receive compensation from the Board.'

It is, of course, possible to insure against sporting injuries or loss or theft of sports equipment and any serious sports player should do so; but individual policies vary and you should hunt around for the best cover. And you should not be embarrassed by reading the small print intently before you make up your mind:

The story of the golf clubs and the small print

In January 1994 the *Daily Telegraph* carried the story of a golfer in Surrey who was refused a payout after his golf clubs were stolen from a parked car outside a course because the company claimed the clubs had not been removed from public view. In fact, they were on the back seat covered by two kitbags and loose wet weather jackets.

Yet a company spokesman claimed: 'We have an exclusion which says golf clubs must be in a locked boot and these were in the back seat of the car which was in public view.'

Are golf clubs 'hidden from view', if they are lying covered on the back seat of a car which is *not* hidden from view? It is a nice question. The Surrey golfer was threatening to complain to the Insurance Ombudsman Bureau. I do not know the outcome; but anyone who considers herself the unjust victim of insurance small print (not merely in a sporting context) should write to the Bureau at City Gate One, 135 Park Street, London SE1 9EA (Tel: 020 7928 4488).

WATCHERS

If you are watching sport, you cannot complain if you are injured through a normal hazard of the game – a six being swept into the crowd at a cricket match – but you can complain if either (a) the player has been negligent, as in a High Court case in 1981 when a 19-year-old tennis player's bat flew out of his hand at a tournament in Hornsey town hall, west London and damaged a spectator's eye, or (b) the occupiers of the ground have been negligent.

The classic case of occupier's liability was in 1932 when there was an accident at Brooklands, a famous speed car racing track of the years between the two world wars. A car had run off the track and sliced into a group of spectators, killing two and injuring many others. A test case brought in the High Court against the Brooklands Auto-Racing Club was successful – but on appeal the decision was reversed. Lord Justice Greer ruled: 'The person paying for his licence to see a cricket match or a motor car race takes upon himself the risk of unlikely and improbable accidents. There is no absolute warranty that the premises are safe but only that reasonable skill and care have been used to make them safe.'

This basic test has now been written into the 1957 Occupiers' Liability Act which, as we saw in Chapter 20, imposes a 'common duty of care' on all occupiers of land to ensure the reasonable safety of lawful visitors. The principle of *Volenti non fit injuria* does not apply to this liability. As Lord Denning explained in 1972 in a case where a spectator had been killed in a 'jalopy' car race near Gloucester and he was commenting on the earlier Brooklands ruling:

> No doubt the visitor takes on himself the risks inherent in motor racing, but he does not take on himself the risk of injury due to the defaults of the organisers. People go to race meetings to enjoy the sport. They like to see the competitors taking risks but they do not like to take risks on themselves. Even though it is a dangerous sport, they expect, and rightly expect, the organisers to erect proper barriers, to provide proper enclosures and to do all that is reasonable to ensure their safety.
>
> If the organisers do everything that is reasonable, they are not liable if a racing car leaps the barriers and crashes into the crowd. But if the organisers fail to take reasonable precautions, they cannot excuse themselves by invoking the doctrine of *Volenti non fit injuria*.

Nor can they exempt themselves from liability by claiming to do so on their tickets or on prominently displayed public notices. The 1977 Unfair Contract Terms Act specifically renders invalid any contract term or notice purporting to exclude or restrict liability for death or personal injury caused by breach of the earlier Act's 'common duty of care'.

But note that this only applies to cases where premises are occupied *for the business purposes of the occupier*.

In Lord Denning's 1972 case, a jalopy racing club had erected at their meeting large notices headed: 'WARNING TO THE PUBLIC. MOTOR RACING IS DANGEROUS' and stating that all persons were present at their own risk and that no liability would be accepted for personal injury (whether fatal or otherwise) 'howsoever caused'. A safety rope got entangled in a car's rear wheel and there was a ghastly accident, killing a spectator. His widow's claim failed because of the notices.

That was before the 1977 Act and the race was in aid of charity. Would a similar case be thrown out today? Probably yes: I cannot see how raising money for charity comes within the phrase: 'Using premises for business purposes'.

Even when it comes to sport, the law must inevitably concern itself with the proper meaning of words.

PART SIX

YOUR PURCHASES

26

SHOPPING

In Victorian times, there was precious little to be said and the little that there was was, of course, said in Latin: *Caveat emptor*, 'Let the Buyer Beware!' Many people still use the expression; but they are totally out of date except in the much more casual sense that you should always be careful when spending your hard-earned money to ensure that you are getting what you really want. The maxim no longer means that you have to watch out for yourself because the law gives you precious few rights or even none at all.

Far from it.

Consumer protection has been virtually a growth industry over the past 30 years or so, with Parliament constantly enacting new and ever-stronger legislation to counterbalance the built-in preference of the old judge-made Common Law for the sturdy entrepreneurial instincts of industry and commerce. As Lord Chancellor Lord Cairns said in a classic mid-Victorian judgment in 1867: 'Some allowance must always be made for the sanguine expectations of the promoters of a commercial adventure. Some high colouring and even exaggeration may be expected.'

That has now all changed. Modern consumer law takes a much more vigilant stance to protect the interests of the public. A buyer must still, to some extent, 'beware' but mainly in the sense that he should be alerted to what his rights are – and how best to achieve them.

Your basic rights are contained in the 1979 Sale of Goods Act, as amended and improved in one particular respect by the 1994 Sale and Supply of Goods Act. This then is the current position:

1. *Goods sold must be the seller's to sell*
That may seem obvious but it needs to be spelled out. In my young days at the Bar, I used to do a fair amount of work defending men charged with 'receiving stolen goods'. Nearly always the defence was that the items had been bought for cash, at a good price, without a receipt, from a man in a public house. Few of my clients were convicted – for it was then, and still is today, with the modern offence of 'handling stolen goods', for the prosecution to prove positively that you actually knew or believed the goods were stolen. Suspicion was – and still is – not enough.

Yet it is the civil and not the criminal law that, in practical amoral terms, should make one wary of buying possibly stolen goods. For the simple reason that, in the vast majority of cases, you do not become the legal owner. The law says, again in Latin, *Nemo dat quod non habet* : 'No one gives what they have not got.' If the person selling you the goods is not the owner or has not the owner's authority to sell, he cannot legally transfer the ownership.

So you will be at risk for at least the next six years – the relevant Limitation Act period – of the true owner claiming them back from you; and you will not have a legal leg to stand on. It does not even matter that both you and the person you bought them from were totally innocent. The villainy of the original thief affects you all.

But there is one major exception to this rule – which relates solely to cars, motorbikes and other motor vehicles. Normally anyone buying goods on hire purchase has no legal right to sell them until they are fully paid off: they still belong to the finance company. But the 1974 Consumer Credit Act says that any private person (*not* a dealer) who buys a car, motorbike or other motor vehicle for £15,000 or less without knowing of the existence of a hire purchase agreement or that it has not been paid off, gets a good legal title, even though, as always with hire purchase, it was not the hire purchaser's to sell but still remained (until the very last payment) the property of the finance company. In such a case, the company's sole remedy is against their own customer: if they can find her and she is worth pursuing through the courts.

That is not all. A dealer, even though innocent, will not get good title but, if she sells on to an innocent private person, that private person will become the new legal owner. It is only the dealer who is penalised. That is why, in practice, dealers usually check with a company set up by the finance companies and called HPI (Hire Purchase Information) which has a register of all current motor vehicle hire purchase agreements.

2. *The description of goods must be accurate*

Again, this is obvious: a shirt sold as 100 per cent cotton should not be a mixture of cotton and polyester and a '1991' model of a car must first have been registered in that year and not in 1990. It does not matter if you have selected the goods yourself, as in a supermarket: if the wrapper on pre-packed bacon says that it is Danish, it must come from Denmark. There is still no statutory definition of 'Blue Stilton': if ever there were a prosecution (and I know of none so far), a magistrates' bench would have to consult a dictionary and make up their own minds what the phrase means. It used to be the same with 'organic': there was only the *Oxford Dictionary* definition, 'produced without artificial fertilisers or pesticides'. But since January 1993, 'organic' is legally defined as 'food produced in accordance with the European Community Regulation 2092/91', and several traders have already been warned by trading standards officers for using a false trade description by calling food 'organic' although not produced according to this Regulation.

Indeed, the requirement by the 1979 Sale of Goods Act that 'goods must correspond with their description' is not merely a matter of civil law. The 1968 Trade Descriptions Act also comes into it: car dealers have been prosecuted for selling cars with 'rolled-back' mileometers or false year of manufacture, tour operators have been convicted of inaccurate descriptions in package tour brochures, there has even been a prosecution for 'crab sticks' which contained only 3 per cent crab and another in East Anglia when Tydeman's Late Orange Apples were sold as Cox's Orange Pippins, although both brands looked very much alike and the trading standards officer making the purchase was himself not sure which was which.

FOOD SHOPPING

The 1996 Food Labelling Regulations specify the legal description under which most foodstuffs can be sold, with a maximum fine of £5,000 for any breach. These Regulations give statutory force to the 'use by' and 'best before' labels we see on food displayed in supermarkets and other food shops.

What exactly do they mean? 'Use by' (until 1992, the formula was

'Sell by') means: 'the date up to and including which the food, if properly stored, is recommended for use'. It applies to food 'which, from the microbiological point of view, is highly perishable and likely after a short period to constitute an immediate danger to human health'.

But typically the Regulations do not define 'highly perishable' or 'short period'. It is left to the individual packer's discretion, although the label must state 'any storage conditions which need to be observed'.

'Best before' applies to all other food, including frozen food, and the date is one 'up to and including which the food can reasonably be expected to retain its specific properties, if properly stored'. This label also must state 'any storage conditions which need to be observed'.

It is an offence to sell foodstuffs after the 'use by' or 'best before' date but, until earlier (1984) Regulations, it was *not* an offence merely to have foodstuffs still on display after that date. That loophole has now been closed and a shopper can legally insist on such food being taken off the shelf.

Incidentally, the two other labels one sometimes sees ('eat within' and 'display until') do not come within the Regulations and have no legal status. They merely provide useful information.

3 The goods must be of 'satisfactory quality'

This requirement dates from the 1994 Sale and Supply of Goods Act, a Private Member's Bill which came into effect on 3 January 1995. This had a limited but important effect on the law. It amended Section 14 of the 1979 Act in one crucial respect. In its original form, the Section had said that goods must be of 'merchantable quality', a term dating from Victorian times and with uncertain legal meaning. 'Satisfactory' is much more straightforward and easy to understand. Everything is taken into account: appearance, how much you paid in comparison with similar goods, what the shop claimed about quality or durability, etc., etc.

You are under no legal obligation to examine goods before buying them but, if you do, you cannot complain of a defect which you should have seen. Nor are stores responsible for defects pointed out to you. But, even when labelled 'shop-soiled' or 'seconds', goods must still be *satisfactory* – all things considered.

Section 14 also says that goods must be reasonably fit for the purpose for which they were bought, having regard to their description and the price. And no amount of small print in the contract, whether in the order form, invoice, delivery note or elsewhere, can take away these basic rights.

Section 14 is, in fact, although not sufficient people realise it, a full statutory guarantee.[1] Too few consumers appreciate the protection that it gives them and are ensnared by the lavish promises of manufacturers' guarantees. They overlook the substantial rights which Section 14 gives them *against the shop itself*. Have you ever noticed that little phrase: 'This guarantee does not affect your statutory rights' amid all the glib PR verbiage on manufacturers' guarantees? That statement is not there out of the goodness of anyone's heart. It is because the 1976 Consumer Transactions (Restrictions on Statements) Order makes it a criminal offence to make any statement about consumers' rights relating to quality and fitness without informing them at the same time that their statutory rights are not affected.

Nothing is for nothing in this world. You cannot expect caviare for the price of fish paste. But, however lowly priced a washing machine, electric toaster or whatever may be, it must still work reasonably well for the money. The same applies to secondhand goods and goods bought from a charity shop. They must all be satisfactory and work reasonably well.

If not, *and you act reasonably quickly*, you can take it back to the shop and demand a replacement or full refund. You do not have to let them repair it. You are entitled to goods that do not need repairing! Nor can they fob you off with a credit note or say, 'It's the manufacturer's fault.' They can keep it for their own people to check the fault but you should make clear that you have rejected the goods as faulty and are only leaving them on that basis. Demand a receipt and write on both copies (theirs and yours): 'Left for checking but rejected by the customer.' If they report that it needs repairing, you can say: 'No thank you.'

Incidentally, although you should return faulty goods as soon as you can, you have the right first to inspect them and examine them properly – if you did not do so before buying them.

The Consumers' Association, in the December 1996 issue of its popular magazine *Which?*, has written that this applies 'even several months after buying them'. It gives the example: 'If you buy skis at the end of the season, and don't use them until the next winter, you should still be able to claim your money back if you discover that they're faulty.'

With respect, I do not necessarily agree. As you will see shortly, in the High Court case of *Bernstein* v. *Pamson Motors Ltd*, the answer will depend on whether a judge considers the delay 'reasonable' in all the circumstances. I can see some judges saying that it would be reasonable not to examine the newly bought skis until the beginning of the next season, and I can see other judges saying it would be reasonable to examine them soon after you got them home. It would be different if the fault was such that it only showed itself the first time that you actually used them to ski. Then, all judges would say you could take them back with every legal justification. I am sorry if this seems pernickety – but the law is like that.

CAR BOOT SALES

Every weekend, an estimated million or so people happily go off to car boot sales looking for bargains amid a load of trash. Australians, after all, call them 'trash-and-treasure' sales. *These are not caught by Section 14*.

The Section only applies to sales in the course of business. It does *not* apply to car boot sales – or whenever buying from a private individual. The 1979 Act's only requirements for private transactions are that the seller must own the goods and they must correspond to their description. If, for instance, it later emerges that an item has been stolen, you cannot keep it – even if you 'bought' it in perfect innocence. Some years ago, a man who had paid £40 in good faith for an oil painting at a car boot sale had to return it to the Marquess of Bute when he took it for valuation to Sotheby's and it was recognised as worth up to £12,000, being the work of an eighteenth-century master stolen earlier from the Marquess.

That goods must correspond with their description does not really help much. The seller does not have to give a written description, so any dispute can easily deteriorate into word against word. Since the average boot sale item costs less than £20, it can hardly be worth going to court.

Similarly, you can insist on a seller taking back goods if his sales-pitch was fraudulent. But can it ever be worth suing over an almost certainly denied claim that a £15 stereo was 'in full working order'?

My advice is, forget the law. Just enjoy car boot sales for what they are: a fun way of buying secondhand goods that usually are well worth the little money they cost.

To return to business transactions: You cannot complain because of defects or limitations of which the seller warns you (for example, 'Do not apply to wheat or barley crops beyond the recommended crop growth stage' on a herbicide canister in a 1987 case) or which you ought to have discovered for yourself, if you had examined the goods. In fact, unless you are prepared to examine goods really carefully before buying them, you should not check them at all. A half-hearted examination may take away your right to complain later about something that you missed but should have spotted.

BUYING PRESENTS

This too can create special problems. If they prove defective, technically only you can take them back because the contract was only with you. But if you give the recipient a letter authorising her to return them on your behalf, that will probably suffice. Similarly, if at all possible, either you or the person you bought the present for should take the receipt with them but, if it has been lost, do not be put off by a salesperson telling you that no complaints are accepted without a receipt. Legally they cannot do that. That very statement is, in itself, in breach of the 1976 Consumer Transactions Order and you can justifiably retort: 'Are you calling me a liar? If so, we'll see whom the district judge at your local small claims court believes.'

But what if the person for whom you bought the present does not like it and wants to change it, even though there is nothing 'wrong' with it? A thoughtful relation or close friend may say: 'If you don't like it, here's the receipt. Go back to the shop and change it.' But that has no legal effect on the shop. If minded to be difficult, they can refuse.

In law, shops only have to exchange goods or give a refund when, within a reasonably short time, the item proves unsatisfactory and the defect is something that, if you had examined it, you should have spotted before buying it.

BUT that is the strict word of the law. Some well-known stores have a policy of exchanging undamaged goods returned for whatever reason. Marks & Spencer, for instance, if goods are brought back (whether by the original purchaser or not) with a receipt, will offer a cash refund or a straight swap for something else within the same price range. If there is no receipt, they give credit vouchers.

At Christmastime, many shops that normally have no such exchange-friendly policy display notices that they will exchange goods if brought back, unused and undamaged, within a certain number of days after Christmas. By displaying such notices, they make it a term of their contract with their customers that they will, within that stated period, exchange purchases – even if these are not unsatisfactory.

In fact, you can get the same legal effect by doing as I often do when buying a fairly expensive gift, at any time of the year. I say to the sales assistant: 'This is a present for someone. Can they change it, if they don't like it?' If the assistant says: 'Yes, as long as they bring along the receipt' (or words to that effect), that conversation forms part of the sale contract and the establishment is bound by it.

In case of doubt, you should ask the assistant's name or even request them to write: 'Can be exchanged' on the receipt.

A MAJOR DRAWBACK TO THE LAW

Once you have, in the legal sense, 'accepted' goods, you lose your right to a full refund or to insist on their being taken back. You can claim *some* of your money back and compensation for any loss or damage (when, for instance, clothes are ruined if a defective washing machine overheats or someone is hurt when a chair collapses) but a total refund is out of the question. Section 35 of the 1979 Act says that a buyer accepts goods 'when after the lapse of a reasonable time he retains the goods without intimating to the seller that he has rejected them'. That vital word 'reasonable' is strictly interpreted. You really must act fast, for look at what happened to the unfortunate motorist in:

The case of the disappointing Nissan

In December 1984, a man in North London took delivery from his local dealer of a new Nissan car costing £8,000. Three weeks and 140 miles later, it broke down on the M3 motorway. The engine seized up due to the camshaft being starved of oil because a blob of sealant had got into the lubrication system. When the motorist finally got home, tired and angry, he immediately rang the dealer to say he was rejecting the car and followed it up the next day with a letter saying: 'I do not regard the car as being of merchantable quality as defined by Section 14 of the 1979 Sale of Goods.'

He seems to have known his law but the dealer did not accept the rejection and had the car repaired without cost so that it was as good as new. But the motorist still would not have it back and sued in the High Court.

Mr Justice Rougier agreed that the car was not of 'merchantable quality' but ruled that the man had lost his right to reject it because he had had it for three weeks and driven it for 140 miles. He was only entitled to a paltry £232.90 damages for out-of-pocket expenses and aggravation.

This case (*Bernstein* v. *Pamson Motors Ltd.*) is important because of the very restricted interpretation that Mr Justice Rougier gave to the definition of 'acceptance' in Section 35:

In my judgement, this section seems to me to be directed solely to what is a reasonable practical interval *in commercial terms* between a buyer receiving the goods and his ability to send them back, taking into consideration from his point of view the nature of the goods and their function, and from the point of view of the seller *the commercial desirability* of being able to close his ledger reasonably soon after the transaction is complete. [my italics]

But what about the argument that, as soon as Mr Bernstein knew about the defect (i.e. when the car seized up) he at once rejected the vehicle? That did not matter, ruled this judge. 'The nature of the particular defect discovered *ex post facto* and the speed with which it might have been discovered, are irrelevant to the concept of reasonable time in Section 35 as drafted.'

It is a shame that Mr Bernstein did not appeal, for this remains – somewhat dubiously – the law of England until another High Court judge or (preferably) the Appeal Court pronounces upon it. The importance of this judgment is that in answer to the question: 'Can you reject faulty goods after you have allowed the seller to repair them?', Mr Justice Rougier seems to say: 'No.' Many legal commentators say that the new requirement that goods must be 'satisfactory' – instead of merely 'merchantable' – now gives judges greater leeway and that, if Mr Bernstein sued today on the same facts, he would win his case.

I hope they are right. But I suspect that even today, with another equally legalistic judge, a purchaser in like circumstances would still lose his case. Which would not be justice.

4. *The price, once fixed, cannot be changed – except by mutual consent* This entails the discussion of two main items:

What is the price anyway?

Perhaps the most frequent legal question that I have been asked over the years is: can you insist on a shop selling you something at the price in the window?

Before the 1968 Trade Descriptions Act, the answer would have been 'No.' A retailer did not legally offer to sell you goods by displaying them in her window with a price tag. She was merely, in law, inviting you to come into her shop and offer to buy them – an offer which she could then legally decline.

Shoppers have often been met with a downright refusal to take goods out of the window or with a claim that the price tag was 'a mistake' and the real price is very much more – never, it will be noted, very much less. For decades this was perfectly legal and many shopkeepers – and some lawyers – still think it is. But this is to overlook Section 6 of the 1968 Act, which says: 'A person exposing goods for supply shall be deemed to offer to supply them.' This means that, if they refuse to sell you the goods at the price 'exposed', i.e. in their window, you can legitimately threaten to report them to the local trading standards department – which may well make them change their mind.

It is also an offence against the 1968 Act if the shop does not have identical goods for sale at that same price inside or refuses to sell you those very goods in the window, if they have no more left in the shop itself. The only way they can avoid this is to display a conspicuous notice in the window saying something like: 'Goods in window are for display purposes only' or: 'Goods available in store so long as stocks last'. This brings us to:

The law of sales

In recent years this has become much more important than before. Sales used only to happen after Christmas and in June. Nowadays they seem to go on nearly all the time: autumn sales, pre-Christmas sales, whatever. Sales have become big business.

So if you bother to read the small print at the bottom of a sales advert in the press, you will often find: 'All offers subject to availability, some lines only at selected stores.' A similar announcement is often made in television commercials about so-called 'special bargains'. They are there for a reason: to give national retailers vital legal protection to prevent you from going along to any particular store and demanding, as a matter of right, to buy goods at the advertised low price. They need that legal safeguard in case stocks run out.

Two further special points arise:

(1) A shop does not have to say why goods have been reduced, except where the reason for the price reduction is that they are sub-standard. But even when items are labelled 'shop-soiled', 'slightly imperfect' or 'seconds', they must still be of a reasonable standard, all things considered.

What about those notices one sometimes sees: 'No sale goods exchanged or money refunded'? You can ignore them! They are psychological warfare by unscrupulous shop management: without any legal effect.

It goes further than that. The 1976 Consumer Transactions (Restrictions on Statements) Order, which we have already met, makes it an offence to display notices restricting your legal right to return defective goods at sales time or any time. An umbrella-maker in Shropshire has been fined for displaying a sign: 'All umbrellas must be checked before leaving till. No returns can be accepted after use.' And a dress-shop owner in Leeds has met a similar fate for putting up a sign: 'We willingly exchange goods but regret that money cannot be refunded.'

(2) How can you be sure that the price reduction is genuine? Quite simply. Section 20 of the 1987 Consumer Protection Act says that any

retailer who gives, by any means whatever, to any consumer an indication which is misleading as to the price at which any goods, services, accommodation or facilities are available, commits a serious offence for which she can be fined up to £5,000 in a magistrates' court or without limit in a Crown Court.

And the Act backs this up with a detailed Code of Practice which retailers breach at their peril. It is, for once, written in simple, non-lawyerly language – for example:

> Always make the meaning of price indications clear. Do not leave consumers to guess whether or not a price comparison is being made. If so, the comparison should always state the higher price as well as the price you intend to charge. Do not make statements like 'Sale price £5' or 'Reduced to £39' without quoting the higher price to which they refer.

Perhaps most important of all, the Code spells out that the higher price of which the sales price is supposed to be a reduction must have been available to customers for at least 28 consecutive days in the past six months. *And* :

1. that price must have been available in the same shop where the reduced price is now offered (and not at another branch in another part of the country, as used sometimes to be the case); and
2. if the higher price was, in fact, only available for a shorter time or in another store, you must be told so by a conspicuous notice saying something like: 'These goods were on sale here at the higher price from 1 October to 31 October' or: 'These goods were on sale at the higher price in 10 of our 95 stores only'.

Goods must be delivered within the time agreed

Under the 1979 Act, a retailer must deliver goods within a 'reasonable time'. This does not mean that you can reject goods if – as so often happens – the original delivery date is not honoured. You can only do that if you made clear when ordering the goods that you specifically needed them by a certain date. You do not have to use the specific phrase but you should tell them: 'Time is of the essence.'

If not, and you continue to press for speedy delivery, you cannot later turn around and refuse to take the goods. By keeping the contract 'alive' after the original delivery date, you have waived your right to claim that time of delivery was an essential part of the contract. So what you should do is give a *new* delivery date, a reasonable time ahead – and confirm it in writing. That will make 'time of the essence' and, if that new date is not kept, you can safely reject the goods.

*

Finally, going back to what I wrote a few pages ago, what exactly is the law about those tempting manufacturers' guarantees – or warranties, as they are also called? It is estimated that there are over 10 million currently in force and that one-third of consumers take one when they make a purchase, in addition to their statutory rights under Section 14 of the 1979 Sale of Goods Act. It all seems so cut and dried, and they can hardly be blamed for doing so.

But I do wish that more people would read the small print in these things. Some are great, others (as the Director-General of Fair Trading has warned) are not worth the paper they are written on.

In fact, there are three different kinds: the free manufacturer's guarantee that usually lasts for at least a year and in the event of a breakdown *can* cover the cost of parts and labour (depending on the small print!); 'extended guarantees' offered by the shop itself; and service contracts offered by the manufacturer that are supposed to pick up where your statutory rights or the manufacturer's free guarantee leaves off. Provided they are not too expensive, these can be well worthwhile – but they are not really 'guarantees' in any legal sense. They are more truthfully breakdown insurance, which is laudable in itself but you really do have to read the small print to see if what you are getting is worth the money that is charged. For example, does it cover you for transport or the cost of delivery to whoever is doing the servicing – and does it cover call-out charges?

SUPERMARKET ACCIDENTS

Products can easily get accidentally knocked off supermarket shelves and spill on the floor. If a shopper then slips and injures herself, what is the management's legal liability?

Lord Goddard, when Lord Chief Justice, ruled as long ago as 1949 when an accident happened in a suburban London department store long before supermarkets became the norm: 'A shopkeeper's duty is to use reasonable care to see that the shop floor is kept reasonably safe and, if any unusual danger is present, the onus of proof is on the management to explain how the accident happened.'

In November 1975 this dictum was applied in a case involving the Liverpool branch of Tesco's supermarket chain. A woman shopper had slipped on spilled yoghurt but the management led no evidence as to how long the yoghurt had been there, merely contending that the floor 'was brushed five or six times a day'. The local county court judge awarded damages, and the Appeal Court agreed. As Lord Justice Lawton said, 'Intent on looking to see what is on offer, shoppers cannot be expected to look where they are putting their feet . . . There must be some reasonably effective system for getting rid of the dangers which may from time to time exist.'

It did not help Tesco's case that the injured woman noticed, when shopping three weeks later, that orange squash had been spilt and, for fifteen minutes, nobody cleared it up.

Shoppers must protect their own interests. When a 38-year-old shopper slipped on a frozen chip in Iceland's Worthing store, the management argued it was still so solid that it could only have been on the floor for a couple of minutes. But the shopper and her husband tested similar frozen chips at home and found they could take up to 17 minutes to thaw. They also went around the store with a video hidden in a bag secretly filming the floors to show that other debris had not been cleared up.

In October 1997, a judge at Brighton County Court awarded her £9,600 compensation for her injuries, and again his decision was upheld on appeal.

The moral is clear: if an accident happens, do not rush to accept denials of liability but discreetly check it out for yourself.

But then that applies to so much in the law.

Note
1 This vitally important provision is not to be found in the 1979 Sales of Goods Act itself but in Section 6 of the 1977 Unfair Contract Terms Act.

27

BUYING ON CREDIT
AND ANTIQUES

There is no immediately discernible link between these two items, except perhaps that credit cards are often used to pay for antiques. However, they are together worth a chapter on their own because they form two particular aspects of the law of shopping.

With all immediate payment purchases (whether by cash, cheque or credit card), you cannot complain merely because you have changed your mind or decided that you did not like your purchase once you got it home. But, if you are buying goods for £15,000 or less by hire purchase or other credit agreement, the 1974 Consumer Credit Act says that, if you sign the agreement 'off trade premises', you can cancel within five days: for whatever reason. This is known as the 'statutory cooling-off period' and home-visit agents selling expensive products on credit often suggest that you 'do the paperwork' at their shop or office rather than sign the papers at your home. Beware! They are trying to take away your legal right to second thoughts.

If you were to sign the hire purchase agreement on the firm's trade premises, you would lose the valuable right, given by the 1974 Consumer Credit Act, to a 'cooling-off' period during which you can cancel the agreement without penalty. For 24 years, this period was a minimum of five days starting on the day after receiving your copy but in 1998 it was extended to 14 days.

Similarly, until 1998 the 'cooling-off' period only applied when the value of the goods did not exceed £15,000. Now that too has increased to £25,000.

So no wonder salesmen try and arrange that hire purchase and other kinds of credit agreements are signed on their trade premises! The customer is then under obligation from the moment of signature. In particular, door-to-door salesmen selling double glazing on credit like this ploy.

EXTRA PROTECTION GIVEN BY CREDIT CARDS

If you use your credit card – not a charge card (such as Amex) or debit card (such as Switch) – to buy goods or services costing over £100 and up to £30,000, Section 75 of the 1974 Consumer Credit Act says that the company issuing the credit card is jointly and severally liable with the retailer for any breach of contract by the retailer. This means that, if you have a just claim but do not get satisfaction from the retailer, you can turn to the credit card company, who will have to accept liability – although you may have to be persistent before they bow to the inevitable.

A credit card company that had to pay up

In August 1997, Jane Smith [this is not her real name] bought a personal computer from specialist suppliers and paid £1,132.70 with her Visa card. From the beginning, the CD-Rom did not work and the sound card had not been installed. These were fixed but soon the CD player went wrong, and other faults appeared.

In November an engineer called and replaced the CD-Rom and keyboard. He also fitted some missing parts and said Jane needed a motherboard which would have to be ordered. It was eventually fitted on 14 January but made no difference and the engineer on that occasion said she needed a whole new system. But the suppliers asked for one more chance to make the computer work and Jane reluctantly agreed. They replaced the CD-Rom with another make but that only made things worse.

So on 23 January 1998, Jane wrote to the suppliers rejecting the computer and asking for a full refund plus expenses. She received no reply and, in despair, turned to the Consumers' Association's Which? Legal Service.[1] They advised her to get an independent report on the system to prove the suppliers were, indeed, in breach of contract. A report to that effect came in – but by then the suppliers had gone into liquidation.

The Which? Legal Service then wrote to the credit card issuer who at first denied liability but, when reminded of the provisions of Section 75, sent Jane a cheque for the computer – but not for her expenses of £96.98. The Service wrote another letter and eventually the issuer collected the computer and sent Jane a cheque for £96.98.

It is the total price of the goods or services that is important. If you pay less than £100 on your card (for example, as a deposit), so long as the total price is more than £100, you will still come within Section 75. Incidentally, in July 1995, credit card issuers agreed to extend this first-class protection to faulty goods and services bought with a credit card while abroad.

BEATING A CREDIT 'BLACKLIST'

Contrary to what most people believe, there is no such thing as a credit 'blacklist' – but, in practical terms, it amounts to much the same thing. Credit reference agencies, of which there are two main ones in the United Kingdom,[2] collect and file both good and bad information on your credit history and, if you have a good track record, this can stand you in good stead just as much as a bad credit history will work against you.

Sadly, we have long passed the stage when you could count on banks, finance houses and retail organisations to respect the confidentiality of your financial transactions. Some still do but many do not – and readily pass on information about their financial dealings with you to the agencies.

There is nothing very much that you can do to stop that but, under the 1974 Consumer Credit Act, you can at least ensure that the information that the agencies keep on file about you is accurate.

This is how it works:

If you are refused credit for up to £25,000, you should write (keeping a copy of all these letters) to the shop or finance house or whatever it is within 28 days, asking why they refused you credit and asking for the name of any credit reference agency they consulted. If they do not wish to do so, they do not have to say why they refused credit but they must within seven working days give you the name and address of any agency they used.

Section 158 of the Act then gives you the right to write to that agency asking to see a copy of your file. You should state that you are writing under Section 158 and enclose a £2 fee,[3] your full name and your current and previous addresses over the past six years. The agency has seven working days from receipt of your letter to send you a copy of your file or else tell you, if that is true, that it holds nothing on you.

If you see that any details are wrong or misleading, you can then write back asking the agency to correct or remove the error, which they must confirm they have done within 28 days of receipt of your letter. If not, you have a further 28 days in which to send your own note of correction in not more than 200 words.

If the agency then refuses to accept your correction or you hear nothing for a further 28 days, complain to the Office of Fair Trading at Field House, 15–25 Breams Buildings, London EC4A 1PR (Tel: 020 7242 2858), sending full details and copies of all correspondence. They will then intervene for you.

Once their file is amended, the agency must send the corrected details to anyone who has asked for information about you during the last six months, and continue to use them in future.

The process is complicated but effective.

ANTIQUES

British antique dealers are among the most respected in the world. Perhaps that is why there is no entirely satisfactory answer to the question: 'In law, what is an antique?' There is no Act of Parliament and the courts have simply not had the opportunity to pass judgment on the matter: there have been too few cases.

'As to what "an antique" means,' Judge Andrew Phelan told a Crown Court jury in a 1977 case over whether or not an 1860 Colt revolver was an 'antique firearm' so as to require a firearms certificate, 'if one looks at the *Oxford Dictionary*, one gets perhaps a little help because there are phrases there which claim that it means something like old-fashioned, something of long standing, something ancient of bygone days – but it is essentially going to be a matter for you'.

The jury convicted the Colt owner of *not* having an 'antique firearm' so that he needed a firearms certificate, and the Appeal Court not only refused to say that Judge Phelan's somewhat woolly dictum was wrong, they specifically failed to improve on it. In effect, they passed the buck and left it to later judges to decide.

Many people believe that an antique must be at least 100 years old. But there is no legal ruling to that effect. It is merely a practical working yardstick used by HM Customs in assessing whether to let an item into the country duty-free or at a lower rate of duty than the normal.

The 100-year rule is also adopted by the British Antique Dealers' Association, whose 450 members represent the better end of the market. Anybody in Britain can call himself an 'antique dealer' without the slightest qualification, training or experience, although a few trading standards departments nowadays operate schemes where all local dealers must at least be registered with the department and keep records of all sales exceeding £100. Yet if you see a BADA membership certificate or emblem hanging up in a shop anywhere in the country, you will know that the shopkeeper has been established in the antiques trade for at least three years, has expert knowledge and has bound himself to abide by the Association's strict rules as to integrity and fair dealing.

According to the Association's by-laws, an 'antique' is 'an object which (a) was manufactured more than 100 years prior to the date on which it is offered for sale and (b) is in substantially the same condition as when originally made and has not at any time been added to or altered to any material extent . . . except for the purpose of necessary repair'.

This definition would not necessarily be accepted in the courts, and Lord Justice Eveleigh has expressly said in another 'antique firearm' appeal case: 'It has been said that an antique must be over 100 years old. I do not think it is possible to lay down any such rule. It must vary depending on the article.'

Doing the best I can in a grey area of the law, here are my own guidelines as to the protection you enjoy in English law, when you buy an 'antique':

First, irrespective of any specific age, it must genuinely be what the dealer (or stall-holder or ordinary shopkeeper) claims it to be. 'A Chippendale chair' must be a chair actually worked on by the eighteenth-century craftsman Thomas Chippendale. If, at a lesser level, it is said to to be 'a chair from Chippendale's workshop', that is also what it must be. That is why so many dealers play safe and prefer 'in the manner of Chippendale'!

Second, there must still be enough of the original article left to qualify for the description used. Restoration work is, of course, permitted – but there is a limit. Even were the courts to accept fully the BADA's view on 'necessary repair' (which they have not done to date), the object cannot be 'repaired' out of its legitimate description. It may be 'necessary' to do a great deal of repair work to ensure that a genuine Chippendale chair can still be used *as a chair* – but that still does not automatically mean that its description as a chair *made by Thomas Chippendale* survives.

Third, price is a factor. The amount of restoration you can reasonably expect when you lay out £5,000 is surely less than when you pay £500 –

provided the two items are comparable.

Fourth, delay in ascertaining the truth about a false description can deprive you of your remedy. Where both dealer and customer have been equally duped by a fake work of art, the judges tend to shrug their shoulders (in the few cases that have actually come to court) and say that, before she took delivery, the purchaser should have taken more care to ensure that she was getting exactly what she had paid for. This is one instance where *Caveat emptor* still applies with much of its old vigour.

'If a man elects to buy a work of art or any other chattel on the faith of some representation, innocently made, and delivery of the article is accepted, then it seems to me that there is much to be said for the view that, on acceptance, there is an end of that particular transaction and that, if it were otherwise, business dealings in these matters would become hazardous, difficult and uncertain,' said Sir Raymond Evershed, when Master of the Rolls, in the Appeal Court in 1950. This was in:

The case of the fake Constable

A London collector bought an oil painting of Salisbury Cathedral as a genuine work by John Constable only to discover five years later that it was a fake. The truth came out when he decided to sell it and took it to the well-known firm of Christie's to put up for auction, and they told him it was a valueless copy. He took it back to the gallery where he had bought it and demanded they take it back and return his money. They refused both requests, maintaining that it was a genuine Constable.

Eventually a county court judge, after hearing evidence from experts on both sides, decided that it was not genuine – but that the gallery owner had genuinely believed it was and that five years after the event was too late to reopen the transaction. He was upheld on both counts by the Appeal Court.

Of course, where the dealer has been dishonest and knowingly misled her customer, it is not only easier to reopen the transaction in a civil court but a criminal offence may also have been committed. As far back as 1973, when a secondhand car dealer had deliberately misled a customer as to the value of his car ('It's only good for scrap,' he said and paid him £2 although later advertising it for sale at £135), Lord Widgery, then Lord Chief Justice, ruled that the Trade Descriptions Act applied. Defence counsel had argued that the Act only governed people *selling* goods, not to those merely buying them. In words that apply equally to antique dealers looking for bargains as to secondhand car dealers with the same objective, Lord Widgery said: 'It seems to me that it is perfectly reasonable when the buyer is the expert and the seller may be the amateur, where the buyer makes an examination of the goods in his capacity as an expert and then proceeds to pronounce on their qualities or otherwise, that he should be as much liable to be restrained in his language as a seller and is to be restricted in any temptation to make false and misleading statements about them.'

One quick word before leaving the subject of antique dealers: when buying a painting – or, indeed, anything else – you should always insist on being given a receipted and dated invoice bearing the firm's name and address and (most important) a brief description of your purchase. Technically a description does not have to be in writing – but it certainly helps! This is vital to protect your interests both at civil and criminal law: so much so that at the famous Portobello Road market in London the local trading standards department has on permanent display a printed notice giving its address and telephone number and stating: 'Always ask for a receipt giving (1) Description of Goods, (2) Age of Goods, (3) Name of Seller, Address or Stall Number, (4) Date of Sale.' Also: 'If an item is a reproduction, that word *must* appear in the description.' That is good advice: but I wonder how often people bother?

So much for antique dealers – but I want to add a word on **auctioneers**. The reason is that, in a leading case in 1989, the Appeal Court ruled that an auctioneer can be sued for negligence in valuing an art work brought to him for auction. Unfortunately, the ruling also said that the courts should not be quick to find that negligence has been proved!

As Lord Justice Slade said, 'The judgment may in the very nature of things be fallible and turn out to be wrong. Provided that the valuer has done his job honestly and with due diligence, the court should be cautious before convicting him of professional negligence.' So, despite Lord Justice Slade's 'sympathy', an elderly couple in Surrey lost their award of £76,222 damages against local auctioneers who failed to identify two oil paintings of foxhounds as attributable to the famous eighteenth-century painter George Stubbs and sold them for £840 – only for the lucky buyer to sell them five months later at Sotheby's in London for nearly £90,000.

Auctioneers were also in the legal limelight the following year, when in June 1990 the High Court ruled in *Derbyshire County Council* v. *Vincent* that the Trade Descriptions Act applied to them just as much as to antique dealers and other retailers. Until then it had been generally believed that the normal disclaimer in auctioneers' catalogues that all goods are bought as viewed and that they are not responsible for errors or misdescriptions meant that no description could be the basis of a criminal prosecution. Now we know this not to be so.

Indeed, an auctioneer in the Midlands has been fined £100 and ordered to pay £50 costs after an art dealer paid £3,250 at auction for a landscape allegedly by Thomas Girton, the well-known Georgian artist, whereas it was really by William Pearson, a follower of Girton – and worth only £400.

There is no limit to 'artistic licence'.

Notes

1 This service gives unlimited phone access to experienced consumer lawyers. A year's fee for non-subscribers to *Which?* magazine costs £51, providing help and legal advice. You can call free on 0800–252 100 for an information pack, although you may have to wait to get through.

2 They are Experian Limited, Consumer Help Service, PO Box 8000, Nottingham NG1 5GX and Equifax Europe (UK) Ltd, Dept IE, PO Box 3001, Glasgow G81 2DT.

3 The 1984 Data Protection Act gives you the same right but, perhaps because it is a later Act, the fee is increased to £10. That is why you should make clear you are applying under Section 158 of the 1974 Act.

PART SEVEN

YOUR SPECIAL PROBLEMS

28

LODGERS,
SQUATTERS,
TRAVELLERS AND
RAVERS

This chapter and the next are different from the others that have gone before. They do not follow any major theme but deal separately with some individual topics which, although mostly unrelated to each other, I have found over many years in legal journalism to be of special interest.

LODGERS

Letting out a room in your own home has become much simpler since the 1988 Housing Act came into effect in January 1989. Before then, it was easy enough to take lodgers in but getting them out could be a problem. If their time was up or you gave them reasonable notice and they refused to go, you had to go to your local county court and get an eviction order – which could be time-consuming and expensive.

But now, if they refuse to go, you can simply change the lock on your front door and only let them back in on the strict understanding that it is temporary and solely for the purpose of packing their belongings and leaving for good. Until the 1988 Act, you could not have done this. A lodger, even though not a tenant, was deemed 'a residential occupier' under the 1977 Protection from Eviction Act, and you would have been guilty of unlawful eviction and could have been gaoled for up to six months or fined up to £2,000.

Even today, you would be well advised to have a friend present when you expect your ex-lodger to come back to a front door where the lock has been changed, if only for your own protection in case they use violence, or as a witness, in case they afterwards allege that *you* used violence (which would be an offence against the 1977 Criminal Law Act).

There used to be a vital legal distinction between a lodger and a tenant. A lodger is someone who does not have the right to exclusive possession of any part of your home, not even her own room, to which she usually does not have a key. Technically, you could walk into her room at any time although usually, of course, you would be expected to knock. As Lord Templeman said in a 1985 case, 'A lodger is entitled to live on the premises but cannot call the place his own.'

On the other hand, a tenant, even though, like a lodger, she may share the kitchen or bathroom, does have the right to exclusive possession of her own room. In addition to a front door key, she will usually have her own key to that room and is legally entitled to a rent book. With all letting arrangements made with a resident landlord since 15 January 1989, her position in law is nowadays little different from that of a lodger – except that it tends to be more formal and there is usually a written 'tenancy agreement' spelling out all the terms and obligations on both sides.

Yet even with a 'mere' lodger, it is better to have written rules. The minimum basic set-up is a furnished bedroom with access to kitchen, bathroom and living-room. But there are many variations, with price usually a determining factor. Some people offer only bed and breakfast, others an evening meal and perhaps Sunday lunch as well; some clean the lodger's room, others merely supply weekly clean linen. There are no legal restrictions as to what a landlord can charge and he is perfectly entitled to take up references before letting a stranger into his home and to insist on a refundable deposit against breakages that amount to more than 'reasonable wear and tear'.

Most lodgers have their own front door key and can come and go as they please – but some landlords insist on no noise between 11 p.m. and 7 a.m. and ban smokers, pets or overnight visitors. Some may allow local phone calls free but most insist on international calls being paid for there and then. The reason is simple: too many landlords receive nasty shocks when their phone bill comes in after a lodger has left and they find several international calls charged to their account. They are legally liable to pay although, if the position is explained, the telephone company will usually allow extended time for settlement of the account in case the money can be recovered from the departed caller.

I have said there are no legal restrictions as between you and your lodger; but this is not so as between you and other people. If you rent the property or have a mortgage, your lease or mortgage will probably say you must first obtain the consent of your landlord or building society before you take in a lodger. In fact, this will nearly always be granted, but with such a personal arrangement few bother to ask and, to be honest, the worst that can happen to you, if found out, is that you will have to tell your lodger to go. Usually no lasting damage will have been done.

Insurance can, however, prove a problem. Rules differ from one company to another but they all stress that you should let them know if you are taking in lodgers. The reason is simple: as a spokeswoman for Legal & General, one of the major companies, has told the *Daily Telegraph*, 'Landlord and lodger rarely know each other in advance, and people are often more careless about security if they do not own the house themselves.' The result is that most companies will exclude cover for theft or accidental damage on a home contents policy, once you tell them you have lodgers – or refuse to pay out in the event of a claim, if they later discover the truth. In practice, many people take a chance and simply say nothing – which may be ethically wrong but makes a certain kind of pragmatic good sense.

You are also supposed to tell the Inland Revenue that you have lodgers because – obviously – any profit derived from the lodgers should be disclosed as part of your income. To encourage honesty and discourage unlawful tax evasion, the Inland Revenue has been operating since 1992 a scheme called 'rent-a-room relief'. This allows you, after deducting all proper expenses, to earn *gross* up to £4,250 a year from lodgers without paying any tax on it. You must, of course, keep written records to justify your expenses but the relief is automatic. If gross rents received in any year are less than £4,250, you simply tick the relevant box in the land and property pages of your self-assessment tax return, and that is it.

But it may be more advantageous for anyone having lodgers on a permanent or semi-permanent basis to opt for what is called the 'alternative basis'. Tax is then charged on the excess of annual gross rents over the magic figure of £4,250.

The scheme is fully explained in an Inland Revenue leaflet called *Letting and Your Home*, obtainable at most local tax centres.

One final point: what about council tax? Who has to pay: you or the lodger? It is difficult to find any clear answer in the available literature from my own local authority but this is what a helpful official at the Royal Borough of Kensington and Chelsea had to say:

> Many people are confused. They still mix up the situation with what it used to be under the old poll tax where there was a counting of heads and, as a general rule, each adult living in a property – including any lodger – had to pay his own poll tax. It does not work like that any more. Only one person in any property is responsible for paying the council tax and that is usually the 'head of the household'. The amount is solely based on the value of the property, not upon how many people may be living there.
>
> Taking in lodgers does not affect a householder's council tax at all – except in the one case where until a lodger was taken in the householder was living on his or her own and claiming the normal 25 per cent discount for sole occupancy. Once they have a lodger, they should tell us because they are no longer entitled to the discount. Do they make the lodger make up the shortfall? We never get involved in that: it is entirely a matter for the householder and lodger to sort out between themselves. So far as we are concerned, no lodger has to pay council tax.

SQUATTERS

It is a national disgrace that, despite all the old-fashioned notices that still threaten: 'Trespassers Will Be Prosecuted', trespass is *not* a criminal offence. In December 1984, well over a year after Michael Fagan had caused a public outcry by breaking no law when getting into the Queen's bedroom in Buckingham Palace because he had not broken or damaged any part of the structure (he had merely shinned up a drainpipe and pushed wider open an already partly opened first-floor window), Leon Brittan, then Home Secretary, announced that the Government was going to make trespassing on residential property a criminal offence. This was just one more unfulfilled political promise.

Despite his successor-by-two, Michael Howard's, assurance to cheers at the Conservative Party Conference in October 1993 that the Government was at last going to get tough with squatters and others who take advantage of our archaic laws on home protection, the 1994 Criminal Justice and Public Order Act, passed the following year, still does not make it an offence for an unauthorised intruder to enter your house or property *so long as he does not use force* – which has always been the case.

It still remains the law that strangers can walk uninvited into your house through an unlocked door or clamber in through an open window, read your letters and open your drawers and commit no offence – so long as their intention is not to steal, damage or rape. You can use 'reasonable force' to evict them; but that is all. If any of us should wake in the night to find a homeless person sitting on the edge of the bed, not having got in through force, despite the sense of terror, violation and anger we would all feel we could seek no recompense in our legal system. The police would not even be under a legal obligation to come and help us evict them. No crime has been committed.

An even more bizarre (but little known) fact is that a foreign ambassador and her family enjoy greater legal protection than the rest of us. In 1977, after a series of embassy break-ins, the Callaghan Labour Government passed through Parliament the Criminal Law Act which makes it a criminal offence for a trespasser to be found in the home of a foreign ambassador – but still today not in yours or mine. The wife of the ambassador of the smallest Third World country is safer in her bedroom than the Queen.

Squatting in someone else's property remains, despite all Mr Howard's rhetoric, a civil wrong and not a criminal offence. Ninety per cent of squatting is said to occur in public sector housing and 9 per cent involves commercial property, usually vacant shop premises. Squatting in private homes amounts to about only 1 per cent of the total but, as Mr Geoffrey Cutting, chairman of the Small Landlords Assiociation, has said, 'There are dozens of cases of people whose vacant home is up for sale, and cases where someone who has gone to hospital or who has died have been squatted.' Yet they cannot call the police for help unless they can prove that violence or damage has been used to gain entry – which is virtually impossible.

In practice, until the 1994 Act came into effect, the only remedy for anyone who, say, comes home from holiday to find her home taken over by squatters was to sue them in her local county court for an eviction order which the court's bailiff would enforce.

But the 1994 Act has reformed the law in two important respects, short of making trespass a criminal offence:

(1) Aided by new court rules, it has simplified the procedure of suing for an eviction order. Previously it could take several weeks to get an order at a cost of several hundreds of pounds, which you would have stood almost no chance of getting back. Now, under the present system, you can go immediately to the local county court and, at comparatively little expense, obtain an interim order within a day. There is no longer any need for the squatters to be present or represented in court.

The squatters can then be given written notice to leave and, if they do not go within 24 hours, the criminal law at last comes into it and they commit the offence of 'adverse occupation of residential premises' for which they can be gaoled for up to six months or fined up to £5,000 or both.

Once the squatters have left, they can apply for a full court hearing. Few are likely to bother but this is a necessary safeguard to protect the very few alleged intruders who are, in fact, tenants in arrears with their rent whom unscrupulous – or perhaps desperate – landlords have categorised as squatters to get rid of more easily.

(2) It amended the 1977 Criminal Law Act so that 'displaced residential occupiers' or private security forces (or anyone else) acting on their behalf are allowed to use violence to get back into their premises and turf out the squatters. Liberty, the leading civil rights organisation, has said: 'This removes the security of the front door' – but whose front door is it: the squatters' or the rightful owners of the property's?

TRAVELLERS

The summer of 1992 was a nightmare for many people living in the country. So-called New Age travellers seemed able to flout the law with impunity. They camped illegally on farmland, desecrated huge areas with their rubbish and excreta, cut down trees, knocked down fencing, allowed their dogs to savage sheep, pilfered from villagers' cars and urinated in their front gardens.

A few were arrested for drugs and vehicles offences but that was about all. The police were sometimes able to prevent trouble in one area by putting up road blocks; but it usually only served to divert the travellers elsewhere.

The existing legislation, contained in the 1986 Public Order Act, was too cumbersome and took too long to enforce to be properly effective. So, at the October 1993 Conservative Party Conference, Mr Michael Howard, again to cheers, promised sweeping changes in the law. The result was his Criminal Justice and Public Order Act which, in practice, has proved a mixed blessing. These are its main provisions:

(1) It created the new offence of 'aggravated trespass' by 'disruptive trespassers'. The problem is that it did not do so cleanly or by using simple direct language. It took the somewhat convoluted course of first postulating that someone is carrying on some 'lawful activity' in the open air and then gave a uniformed police officer the power to arrest without warrant any 'disruptive trespasser' who did anything intended to intimidate, obstruct or disrupt that activity. In that case, magistrates can gaol the trespasser for up to three months or fine her up to £2,500 or both.

But few successful prosecutions have been brought. The agonised wording of the relevant section of the Act is full of potential loopholes.

(2) It gave the police new power to ask local authorities or, in London, the Home Secretary, to ban open-air 'trespassory assemblies' of 20 or more people which may result in 'serious disruption to the life of community' or which may damage a public monument, such as Stonehenge. There is no right of appeal and anyone in breach can be gaoled for up to three months or fined up to £2,500 or both – if their guilt can be proved.

(3) It made it a criminal offence not to leave land if ordered to do so by a police officer when damage has been caused or more than six vehicles are on the land (the 1986 Public Order Act only gave this power when there were more than 12 vehicles on the land). Again, in practice, this power has been little used.

RAVERS

Another curse of the countryside, although it is more politically correct to call raves 'outdoor music festivals'. The 1994 Act gives the police power to end such events, when unauthorised, and makes it a criminal offence to disobey a direction to leave one, with a maximum penalty of three months or a fine of up to £2,500. 'Music' is defined as sounds 'wholly or predominantly characterised by the emission of a succession of repetitive beats', which is the first legal definition of loud pop music ever attempted.

The police may enter land where an outdoor music festival is being held and seize vehicles and sound equipment which a magistrates' court can later order to be confiscated, and they can stop people within an area of five miles whom they 'reasonably believe' to be proceeding to such an event and direct them to turn back.

These provisions of the Act have had a useful, but limited, effect with the police and the courts doing their traditional balancing act of weighing the rights of the community as a whole against those of a minority who claim the right to 'do their own thing'.

29

POLICE POWERS, DRUGS AND SHOPLIFTING

The police have always had an ambivalent position in society. On the one hand, they are society's principal protection against the forces of crime and lawlessness. On the other hand, they have enormous power, the use of which can sometimes be suspect.

Quis custodiet custodes? (Who guards the guards?) is a question that has been asked since Roman times. The working classes in Britain have always had a much closer grasp of police reality but nowadays, when miscarriage of justice and abuse of police power seem to occur with sickening frequency, a new antipathy has set in between the police and the middle classes, which is a section of society where hitherto they enjoyed most respect and support.

At the Association of Chief Police Officers' annual conference at Eastbourne in June 1992, Kenneth Clarke, then for a brief while Home Secretary, slated the police and urged them to concentrate on winning back the support of 'the solid citizens of middle England', whose confidence had been shaken, so he rightly said, by rising crime and miscarriages of justice. Four months later, in a response that only a few years earlier would have been thought impossible, Sir Peter Imbert, then

Metropolitan Police Commissioner, took the opportunity when addressing an international police conference in London to accuse the middle classes of self-interest and hypocrisy in their approach to policing. He openly accused them of breaking the law when it suited them.

'They are not above ignoring motorway speed limits,' he said, 'walking the narrow line between tax evasion and tax avoidance or neglecting to pay a fine when the opportunity arises. Yet they demand guarantees of safety for property and person without always recognising the competing demands placed on the police.'

No sensible person could ever deny the debt that we all owe to the dedication, sense of duty and at times physical bravery of the vast majority of police officers in this country. But that does not alter the fact that nowadays even the most law-abiding citizen, of whatever social class, can all too easily come into contact with an individual police officer who is brash, rude and acting far in excess of his or her legitimate powers.

Ten years ago, in a book of this nature, I would never have thought of including a section headed: 'Police Powers'. Sadly, as we enter the new millennium, I am sure it will be of value.

So what is there to say?

Most of us know that the 1984 Police and Criminal Evidence Act, generally known as PACE, and the five codes of practice made under it, lay down complex rules as to how the police are to conduct their interviews, detain and arrest suspects, carry out identity parades and search property and persons. I could almost fill a whole chapter with these requirements: police cells must be adequately heated, clean and ventilated. Access to toilet and washing facilities must be provided. There must be at least two light meals and one main meal each day. The suspect must be allowed at least eight hours' rest each day. Interview rooms must be properly heated. Suspects are not to be made to stand. There must be a break from interviewing at normal meal times and, as a general rule, there should be short refreshment breaks every two hours, etc., etc.

But what concerns the average law-abiding person is fourfold:

When can a police officer stop you in the street or other public place and ask your name and address or demand to know what you are doing?

The leading case is *Rice* v. *Connolly*, decided by the High Court in May 1966. Its name is known only to experts in criminal law but the principal

judgment by Lord Parker, then Lord Chief Justice, is a classic statement
of our rights. What happened was that, on a night in Grimsby in an area
where several premises had just been reported broken into, the police
were out looking for possible suspects and they noticed a man loitering
in the shadows. They asked him to tell them where he was going, where
he had come from and his name and address, and he replied: 'Give me a
good reason why I should.'

They then saw that he had a cut on his finger, so one of the policemen
asked him again for his name and address. He had to ask it twice and then
the man said: 'Rice, Convamore Road' – which afterwards proved to be
true. The policeman then said he wanted the man's full name and address,
the man refused to give it and refused to accompany him to a police box
to confirm his identity, saying: 'Look, son, I am not moving from this
spot. If you want me, you'll have to arrest me.'

So they did. And he ended up being convicted by the local magistrates
of obstructing the police in the execution of their duty[1] – even though he
was never charged with any of the breaking offences in the area that
night. His appeal to the local quarter sessions (now Grimsby Crown
Court) was dismissed – but, on further appeal to the High Court, three
judges agreed that he had been wrongly convicted.

In particular, Lord Parker restated this essential principle of our
ancient Common Law – which has not been affected by the subsequent
case or statute:

> It seems to me quite clear that though every citizen has a moral duty or, if you
> like a social duty to assist the police, there is no legal duty to that effect, and
> indeed the whole basis of the Common Law is the right of the individual to
> refuse to answer questions put to him by persons in authority, and to refuse to
> accompany those in authority to any particular place; short, of course, of
> arrest.

The principle of *Rice* v. *Connolly* was given a ringing reaffirmation in the
recent case of *Redmond-Bate* v. *Director of Public Prosecutions* in July
1999.

Lord Justice Sedley's defence of free speech

In October 1997, Mrs Alison Redmond-Bate was preaching with other
women on the steps of Wakefield Cathedral, Yorkshire. In response to a
complaint, a police constable warned them not to stop passers-by in the street.
They were not stopping anyone at that time, so he left.

But he later returned to find that a crowd of over a hundred people had
gathered some of whom 'were showing hostility towards the speakers'.

Fearing a breach of the peace, he asked the women to stop preaching and, when they refused, he arrested them for a breach of the peace. The local magistrates convicted them and, to its shame, the Wakefield Crown Court upheld the conviction.

But on appeal to the High Court, Lord Justice Sedley and Mr Justice Collins ruled that the constable was not acting in the execution of his duty when he required the women to stop preaching and Mrs Redmond-Bate was therefore not guilty of obstructing him in the execution of his duty when she refused to comply with that requirement. Lord Justice Sedley made the point that it was the wrong people whom the constable feared might cause a breach of the peace. It was not the preachers, who had a perfect right to say what they did, but those elements in the crowd who responded angrily to what they were saying.

He continued: 'Free speech includes not only the inoffensive but the irritating, the contentious, the eccentric, the heretical, the unwelcome and the provocative provided it does not tend to provoke violence. Freedom only to speak inoffensively is not worth having ... From the condemnation of Socrates to the persecution of modern writers and journalists, our world has seen too many examples of state control of unofficial ideas.'

Of course, as we shall see in a minute, if the police choose to arrest you – and they get it wrong – you can sue the individual police officer and his or her bosses, the local police authority, for wrongful arrest or false imprisonment.

The police are our servants not our masters, and they sometimes need reminding of this. When I was out shopping some time ago with my son, who had just moved into his first flat, we were coming back to my car, which was briefly parked illegally on a double yellow line in Chiswick High Road,west London when a young policeman appeared and, with an imperious flick of his hand, said: 'You – move on!' My reply was: 'The first thing you do, officer, is call me "Sir" and then you politely tell me to move my car because I am parked illegally' – which, in surly fashion, he then did.

My son, who was then a dispatch rider, harassed like most of his fellow bikers by the police on an almost daily basis, was most impressed. 'I'd have called him a filthy pig and told him what he could do with himself,' he said. Arrogance breeds intolerance.

In particular, the police often seem to think that they have a general right to arrest someone simply because they refuse to give their name and address. This is just not so. Section 25 of the 1984 Act only allows them to arrest someone on this ground in the very limited circumstances that they have told him that they reasonably believe he has committed a minor offence (which they must designate) for which they would normally report him to be summoned to court, e.g. most motoring offences, and so they need his name and address for a summons to be served on him. *And that is all*.

The 1987 case of *Nicholas* v. *Parsonage* is a perfect example of what I mean:

The cyclist who would not give his name

A young man was stopped by two policemen for riding his cycle dangerously. Neither constable knew his name and address. They asked for his name as he was riding his cycle in a dangerous manner. He refused, was warned that he could be arrested under the 1984 Act and was asked again for his name and address. He again refused and one constable told him he was being arrested for failing to give his name and address. He tried to ride away, the constable tried to stop him and the cyclist assaulted him.

Local magistrates convicted the cyclist of riding his bicycle without due care and attention and of assaulting the constable in the execution of his duty. He appealed to the High Court against the assault charge, and this required a judicial examination of Section 25 since, if the police had not been acting lawfully, the cyclist could not be guilty of assaulting the constable *in the execution of his duty*.

The conviction was upheld. The High Court ruled that Section 25 is complied with 'if, a short but reasonable time before the arrest, it is indicated the nature of an offence in respect of which a name and address are required'.

The decision is important. It emphasises that police have no power to ask for your name and address without good reason – which they must specify to you at the time. We do not live in a police state.

When can a police officer ask you to come to the police station 'and help with our enquiries' – and how long do you have to remain there?

The police can ask you whenever they think it is necessary. Whether you have to go is a different matter. As we have already seen, a past Lord Chief Justice (Lord Parker) has said: 'Though every citizen has a moral duty or, if you like a social duty to assist the police, there is no legal duty to that effect.' A suspect would be within her rights in refusing to go to the police station and challenging the police to arrest her there and then – which would probably be very foolhardy on the police's part because, at that stage, they almost certainly would not have sufficient evidence to do so. That, of course, is what they hope to obtain by questioning the suspect at the police station.

Furthermore, you do not have to remain at a police station 'helping with enquiries' for a split second longer than you want to. Clauses 3.15 and 10 of the Code of Practice for Police Questioning under the 1984 Act are quite specific:

> Any person attending a police station voluntarily for the purpose of assisting with an investigation may leave at will unless placed under arrest. If it is decided that he should not be allowed to do so, then he must be informed at once that he is under arrest and brought before the custody officer who is responsible for ensuring that he is notified of his rights and cautioned. If he is not placed under arrest but, at some stage in the questioning it becomes clear that there are grounds for suspecting him of having committed an offence, he must similarly be cautioned.
>
> [The clumsy modern version of the caution is: 'You do not have to say anything. But it may harm your defence if you do not mention when questioned something which you later rely on in court. Anything you do say may be given in evidence.']
>
> The officer who gives the caution must at the same time inform him that he is not under arrest, that he is not obliged to remain at the police station but that if he remains at the police station he may obtain free legal advice if he wishes.

What about seeing a solicitor? From the very first moment that a person voluntarily helping the police with their enquiries enters a police station, he has the right to telephone his solicitor, ask her to come to the station and sit in on the interview – and to say nothing until she arrives. Once you have asked the police for legal help, they must not question you and you need not answer any questions until you have spoken to a solicitor. In fact, the police should give you an information sheet telling you about your rights – and if they do not volunteer it, you should ask for it. An official leaflet says, 'Make sure that you read and understand it.' That is, of course, good advice but it takes little account of the tensions of the situation.

Under the heading 'Right to legal advice', Clause 6.1 of the Code of Practice for Police Questioning stipulates: 'All people in police detention must be informed that they may at any time consult and communicate privately, whether in person, in writing or by telephone with a solicitor, and that independent legal advice is available free of charge from the duty solicitor.' Annex B of the Code says this right may be delayed if you are in police detention in connection with 'a serious arrestable offence', have not yet been charged and an officer, at least of the rank of superintendent, thinks that access to a solicitor would interfere with the evidence, alert other suspects or hinder the recovery of stolen property.

The longest you can be made to wait before speaking to a solicitor is 36 hours after arriving at the police station (48 hours with suspected terrorism).

What happens if you do not know a solicitor or cannot afford one? As you will have read a few moments ago, everyone is entitled to free legal advice at the police station, *whatever their capital or income*. An independent duty solicitor, not employed by the police, is available 24 hours a day and you have the right to ask the police to contact her on your behalf.

If you end up being taken to court, legal aid is available on a much more generous basis than in civil cases. The court itself, whether Crown Court or magistrates' court, will grant you legal aid if it decides that you need financial help in meeting the legal costs of your defence and, in the words of Section 22 of the 1988 Legal Aid Act, it is 'in the interests of justice' to do so. In practice, this phrase means that, if anyone is likely (if convicted) to go to gaol or to lose their job, legal aid will be granted. So, at least at magistrates' court level, accused motorists or suspected shoplifters generally do not qualify, although in the Crown Court – where by definition the offence tends to be more serious – legal aid is much more readily granted; and it has been said that over 97 per cent of all Crown Court defendants are legally aided.

This is not a pleasant time for anyone and it is easy to panic; but it may be a comfort to remember that there are no upper income or capital limits for *criminal* legal aid – although you will probably be ordered to make a contribution (which may be substantial), if your disposable capital is over £3,000 or your weekly disposable income exceeds £52.

When can a police officer actually arrest you – and what are your rights upon arrest?

A police officer can always arrest when he has a warrant from a magistrate, which will only be issued when there is sufficient evidence *on oath* to justify it; but the overwhelming number of arrests take place without a warrant. This is most often when the police reasonably suspect someone of having committed a serious arrestable offence (i.e. where the maximum sentence is at least five years' imprisonment) and when they see someone committing a breach of the peace or acting so that a breach of the peace is likely to occur, being drunk and disorderly in a public place or driving while disqualified or committing other major motoring offences.

Once arrested and held in custody at a police station, the 1984 Codes give you the right to have 'one person known to you' informed and, if they cannot be contacted, you can name up to two alternatives. (This right does not exist if you are merely voluntarily at the station helping the police with their enquiries, although there is nothing to prevent you making a phone call before you go off with them.) If you have not yet exercised your right to see a solicitor by the time you have been arrested, you should certainly do so now.

For, once arrested, you move on to the next stage: that of actually being charged with an offence. Arrest is merely a stage in the process. Most people do not appreciate that you then go on to be charged with a specific offence – when again you must be cautioned.

You cannot just remain at the police station indefinitely after you have been arrested. The arresting officer must take you 'as soon as practicable' (Section 37 of the 1984 Act) to the station's custody officer who is, at least, a sergeant and she will have to decide whether or not there is sufficient evidence to charge you with the offence in connection with which you have just been arrested. If she thinks there is not yet sufficient evidence, she can (a) question you further herself or (b) if she reasonably believes it necessary to secure or preserve evidence, she can order you to be kept longer in custody or (c) she can release you on bail to come back to the station at some future date for further questioning: hence, the term sometimes seen in the press, 'police bail'.

If, on the other hand, as most often occurs, the custody officer thinks the evidence justifies your being charged, she will charge you at once and then either grant 'police bail' herself or tell you of your right to ask the local magistrates' court for bail when you are brought before them at their next sitting, as must happen.

No one in this country can be charged by the police without being taken before the next sitting of the local magistrates' court for his case to be made public and for the magistrates to decide whether he is to be given bail or sent to a remand prison to await trial ('remanded in custody'). Nowadays magistrates usually only withhold bail when there is a real risk that you may abscond before trial or may interfere with witnesses. It is even granted in murder cases, which never happened when I was first called to the Bar and the seriousness of the charge was always a factor.

What happens if the police reasonably believe they have sufficient evidence to arrest you (i.e. reasonable grounds for *suspecting* that you have committed an offence) but not sufficient evidence to charge you with it (i.e. sufficient proof to obtain a conviction)? How long do they have to improve their case against you?

Section 41 of the 1984 Act says that, with ordinary offences, they can keep you at a police station for only up to 24 hours without charging you but, when 'serious' offences are being investigated and an officer of at least the rank of superintendent reasonably believes that extra time is necessary, he can authorise detention for a further 12 hours. But after that the police must apply to the local magistrates' court for a warrant authorising a final extension of up to another 36 hours, and they will get it if the court accepts that the investigation is being conducted diligently and more time is, indeed, needed.

Yet, on any basis, the total period of detention between arrest and being charged cannot be more than 96 hours (eight days) from first arrival at the police station.[2]

What are your rights, if wrongly arrested?

In theory, they are considerable: in practice, you must be articulate, determined and persevering. You can sue in the courts for wrongful arrest or false imprisonment or for malicious prosecution if the police, without what the Common Law calls 'reasonable and probable cause', actually carry things so far as to charge and prosecute you and a jury eventually acquits you – although not every acquittal (or even most) means that the charge was wrong in the first place.

You can also – or instead – complain in writing to the Metropolitan Police Commissioner or, outside London, to your local Chief Constable. Serious complaints are supervised by the Police Complaints Authority and are investigated by independent police officers. You can either write direct to the Authority's head office at 10 Great George Street, London SW1P 3AE (Tel: 020 7273 6450) or walk into any police station, not necessarily your own, where you will be seen by the senior officer on duty, probably an inspector or sergeant. Unfortunately, despite many promises of improved performance, the Authority's overall success rate remains depressingly low.

You stand a much better chance by suing in court than by following the official complaints procedure. The case of Mrs Cheryl Holland, to whom the Metropolitan Police agreed to pay £25,000 damages in Lambeth County Court in October 1993, is a good example of this:

The case of the missing tax disc

In March 1989, 40-year-old Mrs Holland, a British Telecom manager, called at her mother's florist shop in south-east London to collect a cheque book before going on to buy flowers for the shop. While she was inside, two policemen spotted there was no tax disc on the Renault car she had recently bought. Although she claimed that she gave them her name and address and said she had applied for the licence, they told her she was being arrested for 'having no tax' – which is not an arrestable offence. While she was in her mother's shop trying unsuccessfully to telephone the car dealer to verify her story, a police van arrived and she was bundled into it and taken to Kennington police station where she was detained for four hours before being charged and released on bail.

Her solicitor told Lambeth County Court that, following her arrest, the two officers made written statements in which they falsely alleged that she had pushed an officer in the chest, sworn and used abusive language and refused to leave the shop, forcing one of them to speak to her through the letterbox in the shop door.

She pleaded guilty at Horseferry Road Magistrates' Court to failing to display a tax disc for which she was fined £15 but her 'not guilty' pleas to failing to give her name and address and using threatening, abusive and insulting words and behaviour were rejected. She was convicted and given a six months' conditional discharge.

She had the guts to appeal to Inner London Crown Court where her barrister called a local postman to prove that her mother's shop had no letterbox! Her convictions were quashed and Judge Rucker commented: 'It is clear that the officers were lying. It makes my blood run cold to think that police officers are willing to perjure themselves over a matter as trivial as this.'

But a Scotland Yard spokeswoman later announced that the Director of Public Prosecutions and the Police Complaints Authority had investigated whether the officers should be charged with perjury and had concluded that the evidence did not justify criminal proceedings. 'Both officers were severely admonished by their chief superintendents,' she said.

It was left for Mrs Holland to sue for damages for assault, false imprisonment and malicious prosecution and four years after the original incident her case was settled on the basis of the Metropolitan Police Commissioner paying her £25,000 damages and her costs estimated at about £7,000 – with no admission of liability and no apology.

It remains to this day standard police practice throughout the country not to admit liability, even when the police are almost certainly guilty and agree to pay very substantial sums of money in an out-of-court settlement.

DRUGS

There is not a school in the country which has not been scarred in some way by the rampant drugs culture. There can hardly be a responsible parent who in dark moments has not wondered what would happen if a loved child got caught up in this curse of modern living.

The National Drugs Helpline on 0800–77 66 00 gives free and confidential advice about drugs, including how to talk to your children about them and the availability of local counselling. The lines are open 24 hours a day, every day.

But it may perhaps also help to know the general framework of the law, as it applies to those having unlawfully in their possession illegal drugs.[3] This includes those actually caught in the act of taking such drugs: that is the most obvious example of 'possession'.

I am not concerned in a book of this nature with suppliers or distributors. They truly are criminals – apart from 'user dealers' who, as the name implies, both use and deal in drugs in order to feed their own habit. The police and the courts generally regard these people almost as much victims as their customers.

The 1971 Misuse of Drugs Act divides illegal – the technical term is 'controlled' – drugs into three groups, depending on their degree of danger:

Class A   includes cocaine, crack cocaine, heroin and ecstasy. The maximum penalties for unlawful possession are six months' gaol and/or £5,000 fine in a magistrates' court or seven years' gaol and/or unlimited fine in a Crown Court;

Class B   includes cannabis (also known as marijuana), cannabis resin and benzedrine. The maximum penalties are three months' gaol and/or £2,500 fine in a magistrates' court or five years' gaol and/or unlimited fine in a Crown Court;

Class C   includes distalgesics and some amphetamine-type substances. The maximum penalties are three months' gaol and/or £1,000 fine in a magistrates' court or two years' gaol and/or unlimited fine in a Crown Court.

Case law has made clear that in order to 'possess' something, you must be aware of its existence. You are not criminally liable if someone slips a controlled drug into your pocket until you become aware of it. However, once you know it is there, it is no defence to say you did not know what it was – unless you can prove (and the onus is on you to do so) that you neither knew of nor suspected nor had reason to suspect that it was not legitimate. This protection is given by Section 28 of the 1971 Act.

What about parents' responsibility? Section 8 says that if anyone, 'being the occupier or concerned in the management of premises, knowingly permits or suffers' drug-taking on those premises, they commit an offence for which they can be fined or gaoled, according to the seriousness of the drug in question.

So if parents allow their teenage son or daughter to have a party at home in their absence but have no reason to believe that drugs will be taken, they commit no offence. But the son or daughter will be guilty as being 'concerned in the management of the premises', if they know controlled drugs are being used and do nothing to stop it.

Enforcement of the law

Where the police have reasonable suspicion that someone is unlawfully in possession of a controlled drug, they can stop and seach that person or his or her vehicle without a warrant. But when it comes to searching a house where they suspect that drugs are being taken at a party, they will either need to get a search warrant from a magistrate (which will take time and is not readily granted) or they must have 'some degree of knowledge' entitling them to arrest a particular individual. They cannot force their way on to private premises on general suspicion alone.

The general practice is that first offenders found in possession of a small amount of a controlled drug obviously only for their own use will be cautioned by the police and not prosecuted, if prepared to admit their guilt.

Otherwise legal enforcement is patchy and, at times, indefensible. Wealthy 'smart' white people in London's Belgravia and stockbroker Surrey who habitually snort cocaine at parties seldom, if ever, have to fear a policeman's knock on the door. Poor people of whatever skin complexion in London's Brixton and Manchester's Moss Side smoking crack cocaine are always at risk.

As usual, the middle classes are in the middle. As with the magazine editor who telephoned me in despair because her 19-year-old son had been found in possession of two Ecstasy tablets at a club. It was only after I had put her in touch with an experienced criminal solicitor that the police reluctantly agreed to caution him and not pass on the case to the Crown Prosecution Service for him to be prosecuted.

SHOPLIFTING

This is the one offence with which most innocent people can wrongly be charged. It is always serious. Do not be influenced by a 'friendly' police officer advising you to 'get it over with in the magistrates' court' or by your own feelings of embarrassment and distress persuading you to deal with it as quickly as possible. If you truly are innocent – and only you can know that – you really should use your right to insist that your case be tried by a judge and jury in your local Crown Court.

It does not matter how little may be involved in purely financial terms. Your honour is beyond price to defend. And I am convinced, after defending people I believed innocent both in magistrates' courts and at Crown Courts, that the best hope of success lies in the understanding and compassion of 12 other ordinary people who could so easily find themselves in the dock instead of the jury box.

Shoplifting is theft. It costs Britain's shopkeepers several hundred million pounds a year. The retail industry cannot be blamed for responding with sophisticated closed circuit television cameras, security guards, store detectives, hi-tech labels and other electronic gadgets.

But innocent shoppers still have their rights.

For a start, for a conviction of shoplifting it is not enough merely to prove that someone left the premises without paying. As the late Mr Eric Guest, a highly experienced London stipendiary magistrate, once said when throwing out a case against an elderly woman: 'Of course, it is proved beyond peradventure that she walked out with some biscuits for which she had not paid. But, in addition, it has to be proved beyond doubt that she did so fraudulently – that is to say, with criminal intention. It is absolutely essential to examine these cases with a microscope.'

It is so very easy for a harassed shopper to put the wrong wares in the wrong bag. Or not to notice that their small child has stuffed a small chocolate bar into their open shopping bag. As far back as April 1975, in *R* v. *Ingram*, the Appeal Court warned that the defence of 'absent-mindedness' must be taken seriously:

The case of the absentminded lawyer

A store detective in a supermarket saw a young lawyer, who was a Cambridge University research student, take two packets of ham from a refrigerated cabinet, put them in his jacket pocket and leave without producing them at the checkout. But he paid for other items which he had put into a wire basket.

When stopped, he said that he remembered handling the ham but not putting it in his pocket. He must have done so in a moment of absentmindedness.

A clearly unsympathetic judge told the jury that, when testing this defence, they should decide his alleged state of mind by looking at what he actually did. They convicted – but the Appeal Court quashed the conviction and said the judge had been too cavalier. 'The temptation to regard this defence sceptically must be resisted. A trial judge should sum up to the jury fairly in the clearest terms, balancing the case of the prosecution against that of the defence.'

Contrary to popular myth, a store detective does not have to wait until you have left the premises before she can stop you. She can stop you at any time after you have passed the spot where you should have paid for the goods, even though you may still be in the store. But wherever she stops you, you should always ask her why. You are entitled to know what you are supposed to have done – and she has to be discreet in what she then says and does. If not, you can sue for slander, as did a wealthy racehorse owner and breeder who in April 1984 in the High Court was paid £1,500 agreed damages by an Oxford Street store after she had been 'humiliated' by being publicly questioned and her handbag searched in front of other shoppers and onlookers in passing buses in this premier London shopping street.

You do *not* have to 'come with me to the manager's office', as store detectives often say, simply because they ask you to. You can refuse and at once put them on the spot. For they must then decide whether to let you go – or physically arrest you. They are not police officers. They are only private citizens and, as such, can only make a 'citizen's arrest'. This means that you can sue them and their employers for substantial damages for wrongful arrest and false imprisonment, *if it turns out that you did not steal anything.* Successful claims are not uncommon. (Police officers have greater powers: they can arrest on reasonable suspicion, even though later it is shown no offence was committed.)

Furthermore, if you do return with them to see the manager, please remember it is still not too late to avoid a prosecution. You can give him your version of events and it will be his decision whether or not to call the police. A good store manager does not necessarily accept every word his own detective says: he knows they can be mistaken.

A word of caution: anyone can be unnerved in such circumstances. You may say something you really do not mean. Such as: 'I'm sorry. I didn't mean to do it', meaning only that you did not mean to leave without paying. But it will not sound good in court.

If wrongly charged with shoplifting, it can sometimes help to telephone a special hotline staffed by the Crisis Counselling for Alleged Shoplifters (CASS) on 020 8958 8859 or 020 7722 3685. This organisation, set up by the National Consumer Protection Council, has a network of local counsellors whose advice and assistance can be invaluable: especially for someone without a sympathetic or experienced solicitor to turn to.

One final matter: most shoplifting prosecutions nowadays are brought by the Crown Prosecution Service and not privately by the shop itself, as used to be the case. But in recent years there has been a new development: in more than a third of all cases, the shop does not prosecute suspects nor hand them over to the police. Instead it bans them from its premises and circulates their name among other retailers. Estimates of people blacklisted in this way by national retail chains vary between 38,000 and 50,000 a year. This is most disturbing. It means that large numbers of shoppers are being victimised without their guilt being proven in a court of law.

But the practice, however regrettable, is legally permissible. The public has no automatic right of entry to a store. Customers are there by invitation. And that invitation can legally be withdrawn at any time, however unfairly.

Notes

1 Now an offence against Section 89(2) of the 1996 Police Act.

2 The time limits are different for those arrested under the Prevention of Terrorism Act. Once arrested, a person can be held for up to 48 hours and then for a further five days with the consent of the Home Secretary. There is no absolute right to see a solicitor until after 48 hours from arrest and the right to have someone informed of your arrest can be delayed even beyond this period.

3 'Unlawfully' means without legal justification or excuse, such as a parent finding a child in possession of an illegal drug who then either destroys the drug or hands it over to the police.

30

LEGAL TENDER, JURY SERVICE, PATIENTS' RIGHTS, LIBEL AND SLANDER

LEGAL TENDER

What does this well-known but elusive term mean? It is not the same as 'cash' or 'money'. It refers to that unique form of cash which *must* be accepted in payment of a debt – as distinct from any other form of payment, such as a cheque or credit card, which the other party may refuse. He cannot say 'No' to legal tender, if you are within the rules.[1]

Those rules are deceptively simple:

- £1 coins are legal tender up to any amount. You can insist, if so minded, on paying a £10,000 debt only in £1 coins – and cannot even be compelled to provide a suitcase for it!
- 50p and 20p coins are legal tender up to £10;
- 10p and 5p coins are legal tender up to £5;
- 2p and 1p coins are legal tender only up to a measly 20p.

There is a quirk about banknotes. The Bank of England notes – £5, £10, £20 and £50 – are legal tender only in England, Wales and the Channel Islands. But three Scottish banks also issue notes – the Royal Bank of

Scotland, the Bank of Scotland and the Clydesdale Bank (with the Royal Bank of Scotland still issuing a £1 note, although the English £1 banknote ceased to be legal tender as far back as March 1988). These, and notes issued by four banks in Northern Ireland, are not even legal tender locally but an English bank will, in practice, cash one for you, if you have been mistakenly handed one – and vice versa. There is no Scottish coinage.

Jersey and Guernsey in the Channel Islands, and the Government of the Isle of Man issue their own banknotes *and coinage* – but only the Isle of Man notes are legal tender locally. In the Channel Islands, both Bank of England and local banknotes are legal tender.

If you pay by legal tender, there is no legal right to demand change. This stems from the old Common Law rule that when I owe you, say, £5.55, I am under a duty to hand over exactly that sum. It is for me to find notes or coins of the correct denomination.

Similarly, although I can, for instance, pay for a £3.50 tub of quality ice cream with exactly £3.50 worth of 50p, 10p or 5p coins, the principle does not work the other way. Those stories that we have all heard about being able to insist on a bus conductor having to accept a £10 note for a 25p ticket are hogwash. She would be perfectly within her rights (although remarkably cavalier) in refusing to give you change and, unless you give her 25p in coins, in asking you to get off the bus.

The reason is that coins or banknotes are legal tender *up* to a certain amount. They are never legal tender *down* to a certain amount, if you see what I mean. I told you the rules were 'deceptively simple'.

LIABILITY FOR JURY SERVICE

Until 1974, juries were chosen on an outdated property qualification but nowadays everyone aged 18 to 70 apart from certain privileged professions, such as lawyers, doctors and MPs, are liable to be called to sit in judgment on their fellow citizens. Every year an estimated 300,000 people receive a letter summoning them for jury service for an average of two weeks. Their names have been selected at random from the electoral register by a clerk at their local Crown Court.

Jury service used to be regarded as an important duty, undertaken willingly in the cause of justice. But nowadays many potential jurors view it as a burden: costly, inefficient and time-wasting, or simply unimportant. A judge at Newcastle upon Tyne Crown Court has even had to dismiss a juror for thumbing through her cheque stubs and filling in a job application form while the evidence was being given.

Jurors earn a modest recompense which many observers consider totally insufficient for the major upheaval at home and at work that may be entailed: a daily allowance of up to £49.68 (to a maximum of £91.37 after ten days) for loss of earnings plus expenses that are tightly budgeted. Yet even today few people would not want to get out of their jury service entirely – although many would probably like to put it off for a while, especially if that little buff envelope drops on to their front doormat at a particularly inconvenient time. What hope of success do they have?

More than you might think: especially if you write back at once requesting postponement – and explaining exactly why. Court officials are fully aware of the yardstick laid down by Lord Justice Lawton in a 1977 Appeal Court case:

> Those summoned to serve as jurors are entitled to such consideration as it is within the power of the courts to give them. If the administration of justice can be carried on without inconveniencing jurors unduly, it should be. An aggrieved and inconvenienced juror is not likely to be a good one.

Even so, mere inconvenience will usually not be sufficient: the courts still rightly regard jury service as a public duty. But holiday arrangements that cannot easily be altered, professional or university exams, the inconvenience it will cause to someone who is self-employed, pregnancy, a forthcoming long-awaited visit from close relatives living abroad or a major and important industrial fair for a business executive are all the kinds of excuse that will receive sympathetic treatment – and it always helps to make the point that you will be only too willing to do your jury service at some later stage when this immediate difficulty has been overcome.

You would be very unlucky not to be excused for some such reason – at least, first time round.

PATIENTS' RIGHTS

There are four main matters to be considered:

The legal standard of care you are entitled to expect

It is obvious that no doctor can legally guarantee a cure or that you will not continue to feel pain despite all his treatment; but the law says that he is under an obligation to treat you with reasonable skill and care. If he fails to do so, you can sue him personally, if he is a private doctor, or, if he is an NHS doctor, you can sue his employers (the local health authority or an NHS trust) for damages for his negligence.

The yardstick of medical care was laid down a long time ago by Mr Justice McNair in February 1957:

> The test is the standard of the ordinary skilled man exercising and professing to have that special skill. A man need not possess the highest expert skill at the risk of being found negligent. It is sufficient if he exercises the ordinary skill of an ordinary competent man exercising that particular art.
>
> A doctor is not guilty of negligence if he has acted in accordance with a practice accepted as proper by a responsible body of medical men.

Not every bad diagnosis amounts to negligence. As a Scottish judge has said:

> In the realm of diagnosis and treatment, there is ample scope for a genuine difference of opinion and one man is clearly not negligent merely because his conclusion differs from that of other professional men.

But there is a limit. A doctor who failed to diagnose a broken kneecap in a man who had fallen 12 feet on to a concrete floor has been ruled negligent and a 35-year-old successful sales executive from Colchester, Essex whose life was blighted by a wrong diagnosis of cancer after her name was mixed up with test results from a genuine cancer victim has been awarded over £200,000 damages. The hallmark, as so often with the law, is reasonableness: a patient who, for instance, visits his GP because he is experiencing irritation in his eye cannot expect her to have the skill of a specialist eye consultant but he would have a legitimate grievance if the GP failed to refer him to such a consultant – if his condition would have made a reasonable GP suspect that something might be seriously wrong and the patient needed specialist attention.

The law does not expect supermen or superwomen. It *does* expect reasonable professional competence. And the standard of competence is the same for private medicine as for the NHS. Nowadays there may be a two-tier NHS, as its critics claim, but there is definitely no two-tier legal standard of medical care in the sense of the actual level of competence that you are legally entitled to expect from doctors, surgeons, nurses, anaesthetists and other medical professionals. There is no difference, in that vital respect, between what you pay for and what you do not.

Doctors, lawyers and politicians sometimes need reminding of the classic statement of the law by Lord Denning in *Cassidy* v. *Ministry of*

Health in the Appeal Court in February 1951 in the early days of the NHS:

> If a man goes to a doctor because he is ill, no one doubts that the doctor must exercise reasonable care and skill in his treatment of him, and that is so whether the doctor is paid for his services or not. If, however, the doctor is unable to treat the man himself and sends him to hospital, are not the hospital authorities then under a duty of care in their treatment of him? I think they are.
>
> Clearly, if he is a paying patient, paying them directly for their treat-ment of him, they must take reasonable care of him, and why should it make any difference if he does not pay them directly but only indirectly through the rates which he pays to the local authority or through insurance contributions which he makes to the State in order to get the treatment? I see no difference at all.

To be sure, there are some legal variations. The NHS patient has no contract with her doctor or surgeon and may be operated on by any surgeon employed by the local health authority or NHS trust: she has no legal choice in the matter. A private patient has a contract with her chosen doctor and only he, or a specifically agreed substitute, may carry out any treatment or surgery.

But, as Professor Margaret Brazier says in her book *Medicine, Patients and the Law*, 'NHS and private doctors are both obliged to do their best', and I would add that their 'best' must be of the same legal standard of reasonable professional competence and skill.

Yet only a fool or a Government minister would deny that there are the most appalling differences between the level of medical treatment that is available privately or on the state. Long waiting lists, overworked, over-tired and sometimes grievously inexperienced doctors and nurses, inadequate or out-of-date equipment, wards closed because the funds are simply not there to keep them open: none of these blemishes on a civilised service will you find in the private sector. But still the judges do what they can to enforce the law with an even hand. It has, for instance, been held no defence to a claim for medical negligence that a hospital doctor was overworked or inexperienced. As Professor Margaret Brazier has written, 'Judges sympathise with hard-pressed doctors. But a doctor who carries on beyond the point when fatigue and over-work impair his judgement remains liable to an injured patient.' In fact, in December 1990 the Appeal Court ruled that young doctors whose own health is threatened by the impossible work demands made on them can sue their own health authority for damages.

If there is a mishap in an NHS hospital, you may not be able to pinpoint the particular member of the 'team' who was at fault. That does not matter. As Lord Denning said in 1951 in the same judgment from which I have already quoted,

> The hospital authorities accepted the plaintiff as a patient for treatment and it was their duty to treat him with reasonable care. They selected, employed and paid all the surgeons and nurses who looked after him. He had no say in their selection at all. If those surgeons and nurses did not treat him with proper care and skill, then the hospital authorities must answer for it, for it means that they themselves did not perform their duty to him.

The same argument probably applies to private hospitals, except that there you will have a separate legal contract with your surgeon and your anaesthetist and, if they were negligent, you could sue them personally: irrespective of any possible liability on the part of the hospital for, say, negligence by a member of their nursing staff. Incidentally, if you are being treated privately by your own surgeon in an NHS hospital and, as usually happens, the hospital allocates staff to look after you, the result is the same: if you suffer injury through the surgeon's negligence, you sue the surgeon personally but, if it is the hospital staff who have been at fault, you sue the local health authority or NHS trust. They remain liable for their employees' failings – even though you are a private patient!

What can you do if you suffer injury through medical negligence?

Obviously, you can sue – if you have a good enough case and you can afford it or can find a solicitor prepared to take on your case on a contingency fee basis (see Chapter 31). But you should be encouraged by the fact that the Medical Defence Union and the Medical Protection Society, the two major defence organisations for doctors, tend to encourage their members to settle out of court if it looks as if they are likely to lose, although they often leave it until very late in the day in the life of a lawsuit before any substantial offer is actually made. Your own resistance is more likely to be worn down by then and you are more likely to settle for less.

You must issue your High Court writ or county court summons within three years, and this is one thing that you cannot undertake on your own. Anyone who thinks that he has suffered injury through medical negligence should consult a solicitor, preferably someone specialised in that field (your local citizens' advice bureau may be able to help with some names) and she will ask the doctor or hospital for your medical records. She will then send them to an independent specialist for assessment. This independent specialist will also examine you and it will be upon the basis of his opinion that the lawyers (your solicitor and probably a specialist barrister she has called in) will be able to advise you whether or not to proceed.

But not everyone wants to sue. Some people just want to be able to complain: to get their grievance off their chest and perhaps to ensure that an incompetent or uncaring doctor or nurse is suitably reprimanded. They need determination and perseverance.

In May 1994, an official review committee under Professor Alan Wilson set up by the Department of Health itself reported: 'Complainants can face an uphill struggle when using NHS complaints procedures: firstly, in making their views known; and secondly, in receiving the sort of response they would wish for.' As Mary Ann Sieghart has commented in a moving article in *The Times*, in which she told of her protracted and ultimately unsuccessful attempts to find redress within the system for the rudeness and incompetence of the GP treating her two young daughters, 'A doctor's terms of service are so narrowly defined as to make it almost impossible for a patient to win a case.'

But the most damning indictment of the turgid over-bureaucratic official complaints system – written complaints to the local Family Health Services Authority with regard to GPs and a complex system of 'hospital complaints procedure' and 'clinical complaints procedure' for hospitals – was provided by Mr William Reid, when National Health Service Ombudsman, in one of his annual reports:

> I cannot emphasise too strongly the importance of a strong and clear commit-ment from the top, particularly from chief executives and non-executive members of NHS authorities, boards and trusts.
>
> Unless that is recognised and put into practice, much-needed improve-ments in dealing with complaints will not happen.

Despite the fact that in 1996 the Ombudsman's remit was extended to include complaints against GPs as well as his existing jurisdiction with regard to hospital doctors, NHS managers and nurses, that overall criticism of the system still is true today.

Do you have the legal right to change your NHS doctor? When can she strike you off her list?

You can change your doctor at any time, and without giving reasons. But, in sheer prudence, you should first make sure that another NHS doctor is prepared to take you on. Once you have found a new doctor, your medical card outlines the official procedure: either you can change at once by asking your new and present GP both to sign your card or, if you do not want to involve your present doctor, you can send it to the local Family Health Service Authority which administers GPs' services in your area and whose address you will find on your card, together with a letter saying that you want to change. In that case, you will not be able to see your new GP for 14 days.

Likewise, GPs do not have to give a reason for removing patients from the lists and there are frequent stories in the press of patients being removed from their GPs' lists against their wishes. Almost predictably, the most affected are the old, the chronically sick and the mentally ill, whose need for care is the greatest.

The hazards of private healthcare and small print

Private healthcare is big business. Fears over the future of the National Health Service have led to a big rise in recent years in spending on private medical insurance – especially among the middle-aged and elderly.

As with any other growing business, where profit rules and 'market forces' prevail, all too often financial considerations can affect the quality of the service provided. There has been a disturbing trend in recent years for medical insurance companies not only to rely increasingly on the small print of policies to find an excuse to reject claims outright but also to use delaying tactics in settling even the claims that they accept, hoping their worn-down customers will eventually accept less than the full amount. One medical insurance broker has been quoted as saying: 'Insurers are looking for ways to reduce costs. They have cut back on cover and are much harder on claims than they used to be.'

I was not at all surprised to read that. Far too many people do not read the small print exclusion clauses in their policies until they actually want to make a claim – and then they discover that they cannot claim at all or only for a very limited amount. These clauses have always excluded things such as chronic or incurable conditions, conditions already exist-ing at the start of cover, normal pregnancy and childbirth, normal dentistry, AIDS, cosmetic surgery, infertility treatments and conditions caused by dangerous sports.

But nowadays there is a new nuance: for instance, some exclusion clauses used to say bluntly 'alcoholism' as a condition with regard to which the company would not accept a claim, so at least everybody knew where they stood – that is, if they bothered to read the policy. But now you will often find the bland phrase 'addictive condition' instead. It means the same but is not so obvious. The only answer to small print is to read it.

Then, when you have read it, you must stand by your interpretation of what it means. For instance, the *Sunday Times* has told the story of a 38-year-old pregnant secretary who lost her baby after developing septicaemia and whose claim for medical expenses was rejected by BUPA, Britain's biggest medical insurer, because they said she had had a 'normal pregnancy' and the claim was therefore excluded. Yet she persisted and after a six-month battle BUPA paid up. 'I believe I only got paid because I wasn't prepared to give in,' she said. 'I contracted septicaemia, lost my baby and nearly died. If that's a normal pregnancy, what would BUPA consider an abnormal one?'

If you are battling with a company over an interpretation of their rules, your best ally is your GP. A survey by *Which?* magazine has shown that, of 660 patients with health insurance claims, one in seven had to pay part of the cost. It told of a patient from Norfolk who developed complications during prostate surgery and urgently needed 12 pints of blood. BUPA agreed to pay the cost of the operation with no difficulty but refused the extra cost of dealing with the complications, which amounted to £2,000. The patient's GP then intervened on his behalf – and they paid up.

Sometimes the support of your GP – or even a consultant – is not sufficient. Then, if the amount involved is large enough, only the courts or arbitration can resolve the dispute. I do not know of one major dispute that has got so far as a full court hearing. But I am sure that some have been started, although no one can say how many, and then settled before coming to trial: no leading insurance company would welcome the bad publicity of a defeat in open court.

Arbitration, though, is a different story: it is not in public and is very much cheaper than litigation. Perhaps that is why the two leading British medical insurance companies, BUPA and PPP, state in their rules that any dispute is subject to the jurisdiction of the courts 'or, at the election of both parties, to arbitration under the rules of the Personal Insurance Arbitration Service of the Chartered Institute of Arbitrators'. A helpful official at the Chartered Institute has told me that it has been approached by other medical insurance companies with a view to starting similar schemes for their own customers.

Here is the story of one such arbitration. Sadly, it is not binding (unlike a judge's ruling, an arbitrator's award creates no legal precedent for other cases); but it points the way that other decisions may go. It concerns the vital question: whose clinical judgement of a patient's condition is to prevail, that of the insurance company or the patient's own medical advisers?

The case of the rejected £11,806 hospital bill

In December 1990, 83-year-old Mrs Joan Lyall who had for years paid the then top annual London BUPA rate of over £1,000, spent six weeks in the private Lindo Wing at St Mary's Hospital, Paddington, west London after a stroke. She had first been admitted to the NHS part of the hospital because no bed was available in the Lindo Wing but she had asked to be moved.

Her daughters telephoned their local BUPA office and were told that their mother would be covered for up to three months, provided they supplied a letter from her consultant confirming that she was having 'active medical treatment'. The consultant sent the letter within days.

But when BUPA eventually received the bill for accommodation, consultant's fee and physiotherapy totalling £11,806, they rejected it, saying that, despite the consultant's letter, Mrs Lyall had received only nursing care and not 'active medical treatment'.

After months of wrangling, the claim went, with the consent of both parties, to the Personal Insurance Arbitration Service, which ruled that BUPA should pay the bill. The arbitrator said that the company was not bound by Mrs Lyall's daughters' telephone conversation with its local office as that merely amounted to a reiteration of its conditions regarding claims but that it still had to honour the claim because it could not substitute its own clinical judgement for that of the patient's consultant.

Patients' rights are the same as any others: you must be prepared to fight for them.

LIBEL AND SLANDER

Libel and slander have largely ceased to be important legal issues strongly debated and explored in court. They have become highly entertaining courtroom theatre where the payouts for unfounded and scurrilous accusations used to be astronomical – like Elton John's £1 million because the *Sun* falsely said he used rent boys or fellow pop singer Jason Donovan's £200,000 because the *Face* magazine implied he might be homosexual – or a bizarre case when a dispute between two Syrian businessmen over a letter sent to a Saudi prince earned financier Wafic Said a staggering £400,000.

Almost alone in civil lawsuits today, libel and slander cases are not decided by a judge alone but by a judge and jury: with juries having the sole right to assess the damages. And sometimes their awards have been so high as to be meaningless:

- In December 1989, Lord Addington won £1.5 million damages when wrongly accused of war crimes but then found that writer Count Nikolai Tolstoy could not pay.
- In July 1994, an award-winning yacht designer in the West Country, his wife and their company were awarded £1.485 million against IPC Magazines for a scathing review of their revolutionary new trimaran in the magazine *Yachting World*, although the judge immediately put a stay of execution on the damages pending a possible appeal.

The general public does not realise it, but those days of excess are now over. In December 1995, another libel case involving Elton John came before the Appeal Court. This time he had obtained a total of £350,000 damages against the *Sunday Mirror* for an untrue story that he was on a strict diet that required him to spit out rather than swallow his food after chewing it. Mirror Group Newspapers, the *Sunday Mirror*'s owners, appealed and Sir Thomas Bingham, the Master of the Rolls, giving the court's judgment on behalf of himself and his two fellow appeal judges (a rare event limited to major rulings) cut the award to £75,000 and said that, although the article was 'false, offensive and distressing', it did not attack the singer's integrity or his artistic reputation.

But that was not all. Sir Thomas also laid down important guidelines for the future. For years, commentators – myself included! – had written how appalling it was that those complaining of being libelled could receive much higher awards than people who had lost an eye, leg or other limb in an accident at work or on the road. At last, Sir Thomas now ruled that judges should feel free to give juries examples of accident awards so that they could keep a proper sense of proportion when saying how much the victims of libel or slander should recover. He also said that, in future, a judge should give the jury some idea of the sort of damages he would have awarded in that particular case – although stressing that the ultimate decision was for them.

The result has been that awards are now much less than they used to be even though, by the very nature of their often sensationalist evidence, libel and slander cases still remain high theatre.

But if the stakes are no longer so high as they were, the fees of the professional players remain on a mountain plateau. A leading specialist QC can still earn up to £50,000 on delivery of his or her brief before the case even starts in court, plus between £5,000 and £10,000 'refreshers' for every day the hearing lasts.

Specialist solicitors, needed to brief the expensive QCs and their juniors, also earn vast sums. Indeed, many solicitors are not prepared to take on libel or slander cases unless the client pays a very substantial sum up front. No down payment – or collateral – and you run the risk of not being represented: at least, not by a flyer.

After all, libel lawyers know that they can very easily get burned. A loser, faced with a combined bill of £500,000 for both sides at the end of a ten-day hearing (not uncommon in a really top-drawer case), may well prefer to go bankrupt – and some have! – rather than pay the full terrifying bill. Sometimes, in the end, 'accommodations' are undoubtedly made.

The idea of being able to sue for libel (or slander, which is the spoken version and much less frequent) is superb, and well established. It was back in 1840 that Baron Parke coined the classic definition of defamation (the legal term for both libel and slander): 'A false statement of fact that holds the plaintiff up to ridicule, hatred and contempt among right-thinking members of society generally.'

Unless, which seems highly unlikely, the Government introduces a law of privacy, taking the offender to court remains the only way of protecting one's reputation from hurtful and untrue attack. (The Press Complaints Commission, with no legal authority or power, cannot adequately protect the royal family's privacy let alone anyone else's.)

If a newspaper or magazine genuinely makes a simple factual mistake and commits what the law calls 'unintentional defamation', it is not so bad. You can promptly write or fax the editor a letter, quoting the 1996 Defamation Act and demanding a full apology and correction, to be given the same prominence as the original offending item. In a really bad case, you can also claim compensation – to be assessed by a judge alone, without a jury. A solicitor's letter may have more impact; but I know of apologies that have been printed on the strength of a letter from the aggrieved person alone.

Otherwise, however, it is a rich man's club. Few ordinary people can afford to sue or, indeed, do so. Although the authoritative Faulks Committee recommended as far back as 1975 that legal aid should be allowed, successive governments have steadfastly refused to do anything about it. The idea somehow persists that libel and slander cases are in some besmirched way 'gold-digging' actions, brought because of the hugely tempting awards available if you win. And undoubtedly some cases are. But so what? That is no reason for refusing legal aid to those genuinely in need.

However, as we know, extending legal aid to cover libel and slander would not be enough to bring justice within the reach of most of us. What would help more is for lawyers to put their own house in order. There simply is no justification for the vast courtroom costs in these cases. With all respect to the specialist lawyers concerned, I cannot believe that their fees for this type of work should be, on average, more than double the normal fees for ordinary High Court litigation, which are in all conscience high enough anyway. Fighting or defending a libel or slander case is no more difficult, time-consuming or arduous than any other High Court case where the issue in dispute basically boils down to who is telling the truth. For most of us, the law's protection is like some splendid stately home lived in by others but only to be walked through and admired by us on special 'Open to the Public' days. By all means, you can write a letter threatening to sue, or pay a solicitor £50–£100 to do so for you. But most high-powered defendants know that, although two leading London specialist solicitors have offered to take on cases on a 'no win, no fee' basis, few others are likely to follow their lead – and you will need to have a cast-iron case. For the most part, tabloid newspapers and sensationalist magazines will continue to know that you will almost certainly not have the resources to persist to the door of a court. You may – perhaps – get some kind of financial offer as 'nuisance money' and, if that happens, good luck! You should think long before rejecting it.

But more than that is unlikely. Sad but true, I assure you.

Note

1 Yet if a shop or restaurant displays a notice on its front door or window indicating that it accepts a particular credit card or bank Switch card, then it must do so: provided, of course, that the card is valid and in funds. But this has nothing to do with legal tender. It is merely part of the ordinary law of contract.

PART EIGHT

YOUR LITIGATION

31

CONDITIONAL FEES

The average middle-class Briton can forget about getting legal aid to take his or her case to court – except for wives in a divorce situation pursuing a claim for property division or maintenance. For the rest of us, we are all too 'rich' to qualify. As a general rule, anyone with a net disposable income of more than £7,940 (or £8,751 in personal injury, i.e. accident, cases) after various deductions or disposable capital of more than £6,700 (£8,560 in personal injury cases) is ineligible, however worthwhile his case or however strong the justice of his claim.

Nor is that all. Under a provision of the 1999 Access to Justice Act expected to come into effect in April 2000, even those so poor as to qualify for legal aid will find it withdrawn from all civil cases claiming money or damages – which is what most 'ordinary' cases are all about.

Clement Attlee's Labour Government of 1949, to its immense credit, created the modern legal aid system. Tony Blair's Labour Government of today is intent on destroying it. 'State legal aid is the Charter of the Common Man to the British courts of justice,' said Labour's then Attorney-General Sir Hartley Shawcross, QC in 1949. 'The poor can expect no special privileges when it comes to bringing cases to the courts,' said today's Labour Lord Chancellor Lord Irvine of Lairg in 1997 when first announcing his proposed legal aid 'reforms' that two years later found their place in his Access to Justice Act.

Not everyone will see that as progress.

WHAT IS TO TAKE ITS PLACE?

The highly questionable system of conditional fees – otherwise known as 'no win, no fee' – brought in by his predecessor, the Tory Lord Chancellor Lord Mackay of Clashfern, in July 1995.

For the first time, lawyers in England and Wales were then allowed to take on cases on the basis that their fees were conditional on their winning. They were only to get paid if their client won, and they would not get paid if she lost.

Under the traditional system where you paid your solicitor win or lose, you took a tremendous gamble if you lost. Not only did you have to pay your own legal costs but also the other side's, and the two together could easily amount to thousands of pounds. Conditional fees immediately knocked out this first hazard because you no longer had to pay your own solicitor if you lost, but the second hazard remained. But, in August 1995, a new kind of legal insurance called 'after the event insurance' came on the market giving, for the first time, unsuccessful litigants cover against the other side's legal costs and even against their own solicitor's out-of-pocket expenses which otherwise they would have had to pay. At last, there was double protection.

Since July 1995 many thousands of people have signed 'no win, no fee' agreements, and a Law Society spokesman has commented: 'Conditional fees seem to be working better than the Law Society dared to hope. Many of these new claims would never have got off the ground before. Many people were frightened of taking legal action.'

Until now, the scheme was limited to accidents, insolvency and human rights cases. But now, under the 1999 Act, it will be extended to all kinds of civil case. As an old-fashioned London solicitor said to me recently, 'We are all going to be ambulance chasers!'

A contrasting view was expressed by a Northamptonshire solicitor who has built up a big conditional fee practice over the past five years: 'The client loves the fact that we are putting our money where our mouth is and I support them on that. That is very much something that they enjoy!'

Even if your financial circumstances change halfway through a case, you can still switch to a conditional fee basis. A lorry driver in the

East Midlands banged his head badly when cages containing goods in his trailer broke loose, through faulty strapping, as he was unloading them. He suffered headaches and blurred vision for several months. He had a reasonable case for damages and got legal aid to pursue a claim against his employers for their staff's negligence in strapping the cages insecurely – but then his legal aid was withdrawn because his earnings increased. So his solicitor continued on a conditional fee basis, and he won over £2,000 damages with the other side paying his legal costs.

You no longer have to be very rich – or very poor – to seek justice. It is no longer *you* who take the risk when suing, but your lawyer. But there is a drawback to all this sunshine and light. I cannot express it better than in this long quotation from Richard Miller, chairman of the Legal Aid Practitioners Group, in an article in *Solicitors Journal* in August 1999, shortly after the Access to Justice Bill received the Royal Assent:

> Those who have straightforward claims will have solicitors clamouring to represent them, while those whose claims are less certain will have difficulty finding someone who can afford to take a chance on them. Many people who have suffered minor accidents at work or relatively trivial whiplash injuries in road accidents will be encouraged to sue when previously they would not have bothered.
>
> Meanwhile those cases with difficult points of law or evidence, or even simply where the client is inarticulate or unable to present their case well to the solicitor or to undertake initial enquiries themselves, will not proceed. How many solicitors can afford to work on a case for six years and then not get paid a penny for it? I do not call this access justice.

TRACK RECORD SINCE 1995

The first English 'no win, no fee' case to reach court and not settle by the wayside, as most do, was a medical negligence case at Nottingham County Court in July 1996. A middle-aged married woman from Derby won £7,500 damages from the local health authority after the Derbyshire Royal Infirmary's hand clinic had carried out the wrong operation on the nerves of her wrist some four years earlier.

Her solicitor Paul Balen recalls: 'We all believed that the case was indefensible but the hospital still ran the case. She was a private client and we started it before the conditional fees system came in; but, as soon as it did, we offered her a "no win, no fee" agreement. Otherwise, she would have had to drop the case.

'In the end, the defence didn't even bother offering any evidence at the trial and that's a pretty fair indication, certainly to us, that they had obviously spotted that the client hadn't got legal aid and were hoping and hoping and hoping that she would go away; and so they spun it out. But she was secure in the knowledge that she had her solicitor and barrister working for her for no fee.'

Insurance companies were quick to feel the impact of the new system. I know from my years at the Bar that some companies are reluctant to pay out and are skilful in using every possible delaying tactic in the hope that the aggrieved party will eventually lose heart or be frightened off the ultimate step of suing because of the financial risks involved if they lose. But now, with solicitors putting forward claims which insurance companies know they can happily take right into court, companies are settling more cases than ever before. As, for instance:

- A middle-aged golfer in the Midlands was struck in the face by a ball hit by another player driving from a neighbouring tee. He suffered severe facial injuries and lost a tooth which had to be bridged. The player admitted that he had not seen the injured golfer before teeing off and his negligence seemed obvious but his insurers still denied liability. A solicitor took the case on a conditional fee basis and, without going to court, the insurance company settled the claim by paying his legal costs, all the medical expenses and £1,000 compensation.
- A 48-year-old public house manager in St Albans was on his way down to do some work in the cellar when he tripped over a vacuum lead. A cleaning lady had pulled its lead taut across the cellar door. He fell down the stairs right into double-glazing glass panels stored in the cellar. His solicitor claimed that his employers were liable because of the cleaning lady's negligence and because the panels should not have been left in such an unsafe position. At first, insurers denied liability but eventually they settled for £6,000 and his legal costs.

SUCCESS FEES

Cynics may think that this is all too good to be true: lawyers are generally not renowned for their altruism. So what's in it for them? Simply that, if they win, they are entitled, as in Scotland since 1992, to charge *twice*: their basic fee for the case, worked out on an hourly charging rate, plus a 'success fee' – which can be up to double the basic fee!

This attracted much adverse comment when Lord Mackay's original scheme was debated in Parliament. Critics were worried about our becoming a second United States where, according to some British lawyers, ethical and professional standards are low in comparison with Britain; primarily because American lawyers take cases on what they call a contingency basis. This means that they get nothing if they lose but, in the 'contingency' of their winning, they take a hefty percentage of their clients' winnings: as high as 30 per cent to 40 per cent. To some British lawyers, myself included, it all seemed far too commercial.

The late Lord Taylor, then Lord Chief Justice, even thundered in a speech in the House of Lords, 'This alien creature should not be allowed to run amok' and warned, 'There is a danger of real conflicts of interest and possible lowering of standards.'

To lawyers such as myself, the scheme, for all its potential value to the general public, seemed to undermine one of the most fundamental pillars supporting the integrity of the legal profession in England: that no lawyer should have a direct pecuniary interest in the outcome of a case in which they are engaged.

Barristers more than solicitors took this view. As legal journalist Fiona Bawdon has written, 'Large sections of the Bar remain at best sceptical and at worst hostile to conditional fees.' Daniel Brennan, QC, chairman of the Personal Injury Bar Association, was speaking for many of his colleagues when he wrote to the *Guardian* newspaper in August 1995: 'The Bar has been unhappy about the introduction of conditional fees. We have grave doubts whether allowing lawyers to take a larger share of the client's damages is the best way to provide access to justice for the public.'

But Lord Mackay of Clashfern would not budge. He refused to put any legal 'cap' on the possible 100 per cent success fee. Yet the Law Society has drawn up a model conditional fee agreement which 'recommends' that solicitors' success fee should be not more than 25 per cent of the client's total winnings: i.e. the actual damages recovered or the amount accepted in settlement of the claim. This is also the recommendation made for Scottish solicitors by the Law Society of Scotland.

Perhaps significantly, the Bar Council says that English barristers' success fee should not exceed 10 per cent of the damages whereas the rule for Scottish advocates – as barristers are called in Scotland – is even stricter. No cap is specified but, in the words of an advocate's clerk in Edinburgh: 'Fees charged can be in no direct relationship to the amount recovered. If, for example, an advocate's normal fee for a particular type of case was £750, in the event of winning his fee might iron out at £1,000 – irrespective of the damages recovered.'

A solicitor friend admits it is 'a confusing area' but says: 'The cap as a percentage of damages only comes in as a final protective measure for the client. Your starting point is to exclude both the level of damages and the percentage because it is *not* a contingency fee, as in the United States. You are not taking a percentage of the damages. It is only a percentage increase of the solicitor's normal fee which cannot amount to more than a certain proportion of the client's winnings; and that is totally different!

'Say we charge £100 an hour, do 10 hours' work and have a 50 per cent success fee, our success fee would be £500 – if we did not take into account the amount of damages. But it does not work like that. If, for example, the client only won £1,000 damages or settled out of court for that figure, we would then apply the cap and limit our success fee, *in that case*, to £250. In other words, our total fee would not exceed 25 per cent of his winnings. That is written into the Law Society's model agreement.'

The Act will change the law by allowing judges to order that successful litigants should recover the success fee from the losing party. It will be interesting to see how this works out in practice.

INSURANCE

In all conditional fee cases, the client is protected by 'after the event insurance' policies if he loses, and he does not have to seek them out for himself. The solicitor usually arranges it and, when the 1999 Act comes into effect, a judge will have the power to order that the cost is reimbursed by the losing side.

There are four types of this specialist insurance:

Accident Line Protect (Tel: 0500–19 29 39). This is run by the Law Society and is the cheapest, costing a £148 premium for road traffic accidents and £315 for other injuries. Two thousand specialist solicitors in England and Wales are available on this policy and, if necessary, they often put up the £85 themselves, relying on getting it back from the other side if they win.[2]

But this does not cover medical negligence claims. The chances of success or failure are more difficult to assess in such cases because of the complexities of medical science. Even so, one can get cover from two other sources: **Litigation Protection Ltd** with premiums starting at £1,000 for the first £10,000 damages and, only in England and Wales, **Action for Victims of Medical Accidents**, a smaller organisation whose premiums start at £850 for the first £10,000. (Litigation Protection Ltd also offers non-medical insurance starting at £175 for the first £10,000.)

FUTURE PROSPECTS

Despite the misgivings of traditionalist lawyers like myself, an important question of principle is involved here: namely, the public's right of access to our courts.

In May 1997 Sir Richard Scott, the Vice-Chancellor and one of the most senior judges in the land, told a conference in London: 'Legal rights to which individuals are entitled must, if they are to have and retain respect for the rule of law, be perceived by them and by others as being enforceable in the courts of law.' He claimed that conditional fees had proved so successful that they should be more widely available, and he called on the Lord Chancellor to extend their scope beyond accidents, insolvency and human rights cases to cover nearly all civil disputes.

Lord Irvine has taken that advice. One can only hope that he was right to do so.

Notes

1 In Scotland, so-called speculative fees, where the lawyer does not charge if he loses but only if he wins, have been permitted for hundreds of years. However, in August 1992, nearly three years ahead of England and Wales, Scottish solicitors were allowed, if they won, to raise their basic fee by up to 100 per cent.
2 In Scotland, **Compensure**, a similar scheme run by the Law Society for Scotland, has a minimum premium of £115.

32

SMALL CLAIMS COURTS AND ALTERNATIVE DISPUTE RESOLUTION

With the ordinary courts barred to most of us – except on a 'no win, no fee' basis, and then only if we can find a lawyer who thinks we have a good case – the only avenues to justice that remain open are small claims courts and what it has become fashionable to call 'alternative dispute resolution'.

SMALL CLAIMS COURTS

Everyone calls them this – but really they do not exist. They are not 'courts', as such, at all. They are merely a service provided by an ordinary county court (in Scotland, a sheriff court) and they are now officially called, in current legal spin-doctoring language, 'the small claims track'. They are meant to be quick, cheap, easy to use and generally free of lawyers, except for the judge.

Their launch in 1973, in response to a report *Justice Out of Reach* by the now defunct Consumer Council, was hailed as a breakthrough for consumers, despite their original ridiculously low limit of £75. Within a year this was increased to £100 and over the next near-three decades successive governments have come to regard them as a sort of 'bargain basement justice'. They do not cost much to run. The jurisdiction now stands at £5,000 (with £1,000 the limit for personal injuries cases) and the range of case has widened to embrace many non-consumerist issues, such as disputes between landlords and tenants, neighbours, holiday-makers and their package tour companies, employer–staff disputes, and so on.

Reading the legal journals nowadays, it seems to me as if almost every week the Lord Chancellor's Department is announcing the appointment of new district judges from the ranks of local solicitors to preside over these courts and deal with the growing number of cases.

The higher-paid circuit judge – called 'Your Honour' – presides only over hearings in the 'proper' county court itself. District judges – called only 'Sir' – are junior in rank as well as pay and act more as arbitrators than as full judges deciding points of law. They do not sit in a courtroom with a public gallery but in a private room, with the public present only if they and the parties agree. They can, and do, not only sit in court but on site, for example at your home or business premises because your claim relates to work done there. They are not robed. They do not insist on the normal rules of evidence. The atmosphere is informal and relaxed. Some district judges are more helpful than others and question the parties at length themselves; others simply listen and let both sides get on with it, each explaining their case and calling witnesses virtually without interruption.

Once each side has presented their case, the district judge will usually give judgment at once. There is no anxious waiting while he makes up his mind. This may not be well thought-out justice but it is always quick justice.

Contrary to popular belief, both sides are allowed to use lawyers but not many do, and for two reasons. *One*, the whole atmosphere is 'anti-lawyer' with the emphasis on both sides being allowed to present their case in their own way, not filtered through lawyers. And, *two*, even if you win, you will not get your lawyer's fees paid by the other side – as usually happens with a normal court.

So how does the system work?

Going to court, even a small claims court, should always be a last resort. And the way to ensure that is to write what lawyers call 'a letter before action'. This is one last letter to the person with whom you are in dispute in which you state that, unless you receive your money or they accept liability or whatever within seven days, you will institute proceedings in your local small claims court without further notice. And you must mean what you say. It is like dealing with a child: if you threaten – or if you promise – you must carry out your threat or your promise. Otherwise, in both situations, you lose all credibility.

If your letter fails to elicit the desired reply, you will have no choice but to go along to your nearest county court and get an official form for a small claims summons. You can either complete it there and then or preferably take it away and fill it in at your leisure, perhaps with help from your partner, a friend or a local law centre or citizens' advice bureau. Basically, you will have to state what you are claiming, against whom and why.

You should then take the completed form for your summons back to the court office where the staff will go through it and make sure it is in order. At this stage, for the first time, you will have to pay a court fee. This is the 'issue fee' which the court will charge for 'issuing' your summons: i.e. sending it to the proposed defendant. This is calculated on a sliding scale of £20 to £100, depending on the amount of your claim.

The court office will then send the summons to the defendant who has 14 days within which to send back a written defence. If he or she fails to do so, you can apply immediately for judgment 'in default', and the office staff will tell you how to do this.

If, however, the defendant sends in a defence, the court office will 'allocate' your case for a hearing. This will cost a further court fee of £80[1] and start the process whereby, within three to six months, your case will come before the district judge for a full hearing. During this time there will be a preliminary hearing in which the district judge will clear the decks by making sure that copies of all necessary documents are produced in good time so that no one is taken by surprise and by deciding other important issues, such as which expert witnesses need to be called: for instance, a mechanic in a dispute over expensive car repairs.

At least seven days before the hearing, both sides must send details to their opponent and the court of all witnesses, expert and otherwise.

Your best way to prepare for the hearing itself is to think it through as much as possible in advance. Leave little to chance. Make notes, not so much of your actual speech – that can be dangerous, committing you mentally to a fixed form of words – but of the essential points that you want to make. Get clear in your own head the most important facts in your case: do not clutter your mind – or be at risk of cluttering the district judge's – with unnecessary detail. Make sure you have all the relevant documents with you – and in their proper order – and please do not forget to take with you a notepad. You will need it to jot down important thoughts as they occur to you during the hearing.

If you feel that all this is going to be too much for you, you can ask a friend – in legal jargon, a 'lay representative' – to come along to help. But you must notify the court in advance.

If you win, the district judge can order your unsuccessful opponent to pay your expert witness's fees (up to £200) and out-of-pocket expense of up to £50 for the lost earnings and reasonable travelling expenses of yourself and any non-expert witnesses. You will also get back the court fees you have paid.

If you lose, you can appeal – but, except in the rarest possible case, I would not advise it. It goes against the grain of this kind of instant justice. In addition, you will have to take on the uphill task of satisfying the resident circuit judge that a district judge in his own county court has made a major mistake of law or permitted a serious irregularity in the proceedings. Furthermore, if you lose the appeal, the ordinary court rules apply and you could find yourself having to pay your own costs and also your opponent's, including his or her (expensive) fees for legal representation. It really is not worth it.

So much for small claims courts. We now have to consider briefly other ways of resolving legal disputes without going to a normal court. In recent years it has become a veritable growth industry.

ALTERNATIVE DISPUTE RESOLUTION

This is often shortened to ADR and means any method of resolving a dispute which does not entail going to court. It can take the following forms:

Mediation

A neutral mediator helps the parties in dispute to negotiate their own settlement. He or she is not a judge. He does not impose his own views upon them. He merely provides a sympathetic forum in which they feel free to talk to each other and find their own solution to their problem. *But* this is only available where both parties agree.

How to find a mediator? There are three main sources: Mediation UK is a national umbrella organisation representing over 500 local mediation services around the UK. If you telephone its office at Bristol on 0117–9046611, helpful staff will give you details of the nearest service to you. It is a registered charity and deals mainly with disputes in the community, especially between neighbours. Most of its mediators make no charge. The Centre for Dispute Resolution (CEDR) is a commercial organisation based in London (Tel: 020 7600 0500) and offers a day's mediation for £450 plus VAT per party where the amount in dispute is under £20,000. The Alternative Dispute Resolution Group (0117–9467180), also based in Bristol, offers local mediation at a cost of £125 plus VAT per party for one hour where the amount in dispute is £25,000 or less. You should call both these numbers and discuss which type of service is best suited to you – and your pocket.

Arbitration

Except when using the small claims court procedure, this also requires both parties' consent. An independent arbitrator will consider the evidence, either looking only at the paperwork or also hearing witnesses, and decide what he thinks the answer should be. With some schemes, his decision is legally binding so that you will not be able to go to court afterwards. A registration fee is charged but, even if you lose, you may not have to pay the other side's costs. To find out more on the subject, you should consult the Chartered Institute of Arbitrators at 24 Angel Gate, City Road, London EC1V 2RS (Tel: 020 7837 4483).

Citizens' Advice Bureaux

Locally-run charities with offices all over the country, these are staffed mainly by trained volunteers, are free and advise on most kinds of problem. They will help you write letters and negotiate with the other party and some may even represent you in court, if the dispute gets that far. To find your nearest branch, look under Citizens' Advice Bureaux in your local phone book.

Law Centres

Mainly funded by local authority grants, they offer similar help to citizens' advice bureaux but usually limit themselves to social welfare law, such as housing, employment, disability rights and debt. They are also listed in local phone books.

Note

1 This 'allocation fee' of £80 – which has to be paid whether the claim is large or small – is a recent innovation and has been criticised as impeding rather than increasing access to justice. The Civil Justice Council within the Lord Chancellor's Department is said to dislike it and a spokesman for Lord Irvine has commented that he is 'considering the position with care'.

PART NINE

YOUR DEATH

33

WILLS, INTESTACY AND DEATH ITSELF

Some time ago the Law Society commissioned research into why so many people – at least a third of the adult population of this country – have not made their wills. The answer? Some have never thought about it, some simply have not yet got around to it, many think they are too young (although road accidents and terminal illness are not a monopoly of the middle-aged or elderly), some believe their husband or wife will automatically inherit everything anyway (which is not true) and one in 10 do not want to think about dying.

Even multimillionaires can feel this way. When Robert Holmes à Court, the Australian media magnate, died suddenly at the age of 53, leaving a £330 million estate, it was discovered that he had carried a draft will in his briefcase for 18 months but never signed it.

This is all very understandable – but totally indefensible. If you care about your loved ones and what is to happen to them after you are dead or even, at a more mundane level, what is to happen to your money when you have gone, you simply must make a will. It is your only way of trying to exert some control over your assets and to ensure that your estate is properly divided up between the people – or charitable organisations – you care about.

If you die intestate (i.e. without having made a will), your estate will be distributed in accordance with fixed rules laid down by at least four Acts of Parliament. These take no account of your wishes and, indeed, may have exactly the opposite effect.

THE LAW OF INTESTACY

There are two main problems: *one*, the rules totally ignore unmarried partners who have no rights of inheritance whatsoever and can only go to court and seek to persuade a judge that they are entitled to 'reasonable provision' from the estate; and, *two*, even when a married person dies without a will, their widow or widower does not, as many people believe, always automatically inherit all their property. This only happens if they survive their deceased spouse by at least 28 days *and*:

the total estate is not more than £200,000; or
there are absolutely no other surviving close relatives: no children, grandchildren, parents, brothers, sisters, nieces or nephews – which is somewhat rare.

In all other cases, the position is complex, arbitrary and can be unjust. All age and social groups may be affected: a surviving spouse may be forced to leave the family home in which he or she has lived for years, a solitary parent left with young children may lose control of sufficient money to bring them up, even though the deceased in his lifetime may have been comfortably off, an elderly and ailing widow or widower is left with insufficient income to provide adequately for their nursing and other needs or an unmarried partner is left with no share whatsoever in the estate of someone they may have lived with for years, although, as again we shall see later, they may be able to go to court and claim 'reasonable provision' from the estate.

This is how the rules work:

(1) If there are children (legitimate, illegitimate or adopted) who are at least 18 or have married earlier, surviving spouses take all personal belongings – furniture, cars, jewellery, clothing, household goods but nothing used for business – plus £125,000 free of tax (with interest payable until payment) and a life interest in half the rest of the estate. This means it is put in trust and your surviving spouse merely enjoys the income during their lifetime after which it is shared out between your children or, if any have by then died, their children.

What happens to the other half in which the surviving spouse does not have a life interest? They have no rights. It is divided between the children or, if any are already dead, their children take their parent's share.

These provisions may put the family home at risk for, as the Law Commission has pointed out, there is no law saying that a surviving spouse must be entitled to, at least, the family home – which the Law Commission has without success recommended. Where the house has been in joint names, there will usually be no hardship as the surviving spouse automatically takes the other's interest in the property, but hardship may occur where they were only tenants in common or the house was in the deceased's sole name. Then the deceased's interest in the family home forms part of their estate and, depending on its value in proportion to the total amount of the estate, the home may have to be sold so as to provide the surviving spouse with his or her statutory legacy of £125,000 or the children with their half-share of the total assets.

(2) If there are no children but there are parents, brothers and sisters or their children, surviving spouses take all personal belongings, £200,000 free of tax (with interest) plus full ownership of half the rest of the estate. The other half is shared out among the others.

If there is no surviving spouse, the entire estate will go to:

- the children, if any, but, if none,
- any parents who are still alive and, if none,
- brothers and sisters in equal shares (with the children of any deceased sibling taking their parent's share) and, if none,
- half-brothers or half-sisters or their children will inherit and, if none,
- grandparents and, if none,
- full uncles and aunts or their descendants and, if none,
- half-uncles and half-aunts or their descendants.

These categories are all self-contained so that, if someone survives in any one category, no one in the next category gets anything. A famous recent example was in July 1999 when, three months after television presenter Jill Dando had been shot dead on her doorstep, it was announced that her entire estate valued at nearly £1 million net had gone to her elderly father, Jack, a widower. She had died, aged 37, intestate, unmarried and without children. In accordance with the rules, neither her fiancé, gynaecologist Alan Farthing, nor her only brother Nigel inherited a penny.

Finally, if no one is left at all, the entire estate passes to the Crown and the Treasury Solicitor can make a compassionate payment to anyone he considers morally entitled to a share. Until recently, this would have included – but only on a discretionary basis – an unmarried partner who could not prove financial dependency so as to ground a claim for 'reasonable provision' from the estate. But the 1995 Law Reform (Succession) Act now provides that anyone living with the deceased 'as man and wife' for the last two years can claim this – as a right.

In the first case under this new Act in December 1998, Mr Justice Neuberger awarded £24,000 or £2,500 a year for life to be paid out of a £200,000 estate to a 67-year-old woman who had lived with a retired teacher for 10 years, cooking and looking after him but not sharing his bed. He ruled that, in all the circumstances, they were living together 'as husband and wife'.

Who looks after an intestate's estate?

The job goes to the 'administrator'. This is the closest surviving relative in order of priority: widow or widower, children over 18 in order of seniority, parents, brothers and sisters, etc. It is not automatic. They have to apply for what is called 'a grant of letters of administration' to their local probate registry – whose address and telephone number are in the local phone book or can be obtained from a citizens' advice bureau. If the nearest relative does not want to apply, they renounce their right – without forfeiting their inheritance – by completing a 'form of renunciation' from the probate registry. Many people ask a solicitor to act for them but, if you want to do the job yourself, the probate registry will give you a most helpful leaflet (Form PA 2) which will tell you exactly what to do.

Incidentally, this leaflet will also explain that if someone dies with an estate worth less than £5,000 you may be able to wind up their estate without formal appointment as 'the administrator'.

THE LAW OF WILLS

It is not enough simply to make a will: you must do it properly, and I am afraid that this means you must ask a solicitor to draft one for you. The cost varies from about £100 or £125 plus VAT for the *very* simplest will up to several hundreds of pounds. But it is always money well spent. You are buying peace of mind for yourself and for your loved ones. Even if the solicitor is negligent and makes a mistake – which, with a complicated will, can happen even with an experienced lawyer – a beneficiary wrongfully deprived of their inheritance can sue her for compensation. This has been the law ever since a pioneering decision by Sir Robert Megarry, then Vice-Chancellor of the High Court's Chancery Division, in *Ross* v. *Caunters* in June 1979.

Other less satisfactory options are available: some banks and insurance companies offer a will-writing service but they usually insist on being appointed as executor who does the same job as the 'administrator' when there is no will: i.e. he winds up the estate. This will almost inevitably increase the cost but, not content with that, they also sometimes try and sell you life assurance! Several large charities publish advice on will-making hoping that you will leave some of your money to them, although they cannot insist on this.

Also in recent years a new breed of professional will-writer has set up in business trying to undercut solicitors; but I would be wary of using them. Unlike solicitors, these people require no legal qualifications and their standard varies considerably. In October 1991 an Institute of Professional Will Writers was set up to try and enforce minimum standards – but the organisation is voluntary and many firms are not members.

The one thing you should definitely *not* do is try and write your own will, although many people still persist in doing this. Inexpensive do-it-yourself will packs and will forms are readily available in the shops – but please do not use them. You could be setting up the most awful problems for your nearest and dearest at a time when they least can cope: in the aftermath of your death. As a judge once said about a do-it-yourself will that ended up in the High Court: 'The testator filled in the will form and signed it, and no doubt thought he had done a good day's work – as for the legal profession he had!'

There are two main hazards:

(1) You will not get the will properly witnessed – which can easily happen despite the fact that the printed form generally spells out how it should be done. Namely, you must have at least two adult witnesses who do not have to be present when the will is actually written out or typed (in fact, they do not even need to read it, you can cover it up when they appear) – but they must both be present when you sign the document and then they must immediately sign it themselves.

If you are too frail or infirm to sign with your name, you may simply put an 'X'. This is known as 'making your mark' and, when the will is drafted by a solicitor who supervises the proceedings, it causes no problems.

But no one who is given a legacy in the will *or their spouse* should be asked to sign as witness, for that will invalidate the legacy. (It was their negligence in failing to advise their will-making client of this basic legal requirement which made the solicitors in *Ross* v. *Caunters* pay damages to the client's sister-in-law when she lost her legacy after they allowed her husband to witness the will.)

Technically a will does not have to give the witnesses' names and addresses or state their qualifications, although nowadays it often does; but do not worry if you discover that an elderly relative's will made many years ago does not give these details. The will is still valid. Similarly, it does not matter if by the time a testator dies, the witnesses are also dead: the validity of the will is not affected.

There is one category of people who do not need to have formal witnesses for their will or even for it to be in writing: soldiers and airmen on actual military service and sailors and mariners when at sea. So long as their words are intended to be a will, they are given the status of a will:

The case of the young army officer

On 6 July 1917, during World War I, a 20-year-old army lieutenant told his fiancée: 'If I stop a bullet everything of mine will be yours.' He was then on embarkation leave immediately before being posted to France. Three months later he was killed in action.

Two years later, in the High Court, Mr Justice Horridge ruled: 'It is not necessary, in order to establish the validity of a soldier's will, to prove that he knew he was making a will but merely that he intended deliberately to give expression to his wishes as to what should be done with his property in the event of his death.' He accepted the fiancée's evidence as to what the young officer had said, ruled that while on embarkation leave he was already 'on actual military service' – and upheld the validity of his 'soldier's will'.

This case (*In Re Stable*) still applies today. Lord Denning has said that you can be on 'actual military service' even in peacetime. So, for instance, soldiers serving in Bosnia or in Kosovo or in Northern Ireland or even, in the recent past, army bomb disposal experts trying to make an IRA bomb safe on the British mainland, all come within Mr Justice Horridge's ruling back in 1919.

(2) The second main hazard in DIY will-making is that it is so easy to get the wording wrong. Many phrases have a specific legal meaning which you use at your peril: you may think that you know what normal-sounding phrases such as 'money', 'all my personal jewellery', 'all my stocks and shares' and 'all my cash at the bank' mean but these, and many other seemingly straightforward expressions, have all led to protracted and costly lawsuits.

It is not only legal terms. The meaning of everyday expressions may also vary depending on the context, and an astute solicitor will be on the alert to pre-empt potential problems. For instance, a legacy to 'the children of Joyce and Hilda' could result in the gift going to Joyce's children and to Hilda's children but it could also go to Joyce's children and Hilda alone. It would depend on what the judge thought the testator intended.

At least, that is the theory. The reality is probably nearer to the famous aphorism of Mr Justice Eve in the early years of the twentieth century: 'I shudder to think that in the hereafter I shall have to meet those testators whose wishes on earth have been frustrated by my judgments.' Sometimes they even give up the battle to try and make sense of the will-maker's wishes, as in the case of the elderly lady in Australia, where the law is similar, who left her estate to 'my two brothers, Percy Ernest Evans and Mark Evans'. The trouble was that Percy Evans was her cousin and her only two brothers were Mark Evans and Luke Evans. So whom on earth did she mean?

The Supreme Court of Victoria ruled the gift void for uncertainty.

Anybody who is over 18 and of sound mind can make a will. But what does 'of sound mind' mean? The law is remarkably understanding of the frailties of age: an elderly person may have fantasies and delusions about some aspects of reality ('Don't we all?' you may ask) but, so long as these do not affect the subject matter of his will, they will not be sufficient to enable other people disappointed by the will to challenge its validity. As far back as 1870 in *Banks* v. *Goodfellow* Lord Cockburn, then Lord Chief Justice, ruled:

> A form of unsoundness of mind which neither disturbs the exercise of the faculties necessary for such an act, nor is capable of influencing the result, ought to take away the power of making a will.
>
> In the case before us two delusions disturbed the mind of the testator, the one that he was pursued by Spirits, the other that a man long since dead came personally to molest him. Neither of these delusions had, or could have had, any influence upon him in disposing of his property.

So the will was upheld.

Of course, if a will is made in someone's favour through 'undue influence', it can be challenged and ruled invalid. In 1883, Lord Justice Lindley gave this classic definition of 'undue influence':

> Some unfair and improper conduct, some coercion from outside, some over-reaching, some form of cheating and generally, though not always, some personal advantage obtained by a donee placed in some close and confidential relation to the donor.

That is why the judges have often said that, whenever an old and infirm person makes a will – or, even more so, a new will – their solicitor should ask their doctor to be present and preferably sign the will as a witness: to avoid any subsequent dispute as to their mental condition or any undue influence. Of course, difficulties may arise if the doctor himself benefits under the new will, as the courts tend to view with suspicion new wills made by elderly people disinheriting close family members in favour of their doctor, solicitor, nurse, housekeeper or any other newly acquired confidant. But, as a solicitor friend of unimpeachable integrity has told me, 'If I see that the doctor himself benefits under the terms of the will, I always ask for a second opinion.'

WILLS AND FAMILIES

A death in the family can bring out the best – and the worst – in human nature. Sometimes 'grieving' relatives do not even wait for the body to be cold before arguing over their inheritance or stealing a march on their rivals by lifting coveted goods from the home of the deceased. From the beginning of civilised time this has been the human condition, and from the start of will-making as we know it, in Ancient Rome, law-makers have been concerned to prevent families squabbling over what they consider their 'rightful' inheritance.

That is why Roman law, which is the basis of most modern Western European civil law (and, in this respect, Scottish law as well), laid down a *jus uxori*, a widow's right to a fixed proportion of her dead husband's estate. The same applied to children. A man could not disinherit his family: whatever his will said, they were entitled to something. It was their inalienable right. Eventually this also became true when it was a woman who died.

But until 1938, English law knew no such restrictions on a person's freedom to leave his assets to whomever he liked. Hence William Shakespeare's famous will showing his wife Anne Hathaway exactly what he thought of her by leaving her only 'my second-best bed'. That was completely legal in 1616 and, depending on the circumstances of their marriage, could still be so today.

For even today if you want to disinherit your partner, whether married or not (or your children) that still remains your prerogative. No one can tell you what you should or should not do with your own property. If no one complains, the will is valid.

But Parliament by several Acts starting in 1938 and culminating in the 1995 Law Reform (Succession) Act now gives substantial protection to these groups of people: a surviving spouse; a divorced spouse (if not remarried); a child of whatever age (whether illegitimate, adopted or 'treated as a child of the family', which includes stepchildren); a dependant maintained by the deceased immediately before his or her death (which includes both a mistress, who may well not have actually lived with the deceased and an unmarried partner who probably did) and anyone living with the deceased 'as man and wife' for the last two years.

If anyone in these categories considers they have been unreasonably treated by a will – *or by the fixed intestacy rules, if there is no will* – they can go to court (whether county court or High Court) and ask a judge to make 'reasonable provision' for them out of the estate. Contrary to popular belief, grandchildren do not qualify, nor nieces and nephews. And surviving spouses generally fare better than other dependants, for 'reasonable provision' in their case means a fair share of the family assets while for others it only means reasonable provision for maintenance – which is a lower yardstick.

How does a judge decide what is 'reasonable'? It is a typically English compromise. It is left to his individual discretion. He must 'have regard to' the testator's reasons in acting as she did, whether explained in the will itself or in an accompanying letter, but he is not bound by them. In one notable case, a husband left his wife nothing because, as he explained in his will, he believed she had committed adultery. She complained to the court. A judge heard the evidence, ruled that the dead husband had been wrong and his wife had not been unfaithful – and awarded her half the estate.

In another case, a 54-year-old spinster who devoted 15 years of her life to her ailing mother won an extra £7,000 and £800 a year after Mr Justice Megarry was told that the spinster was left with only £7,500-worth of assets while most of the £112,000 estate went to her mother's favourite daughter. A young second wife who left her husband of more than twice her age at the onset of his final illness was awarded £2,000 after he chose to leave his entire estate to his two children by his first marriage and a close friend who had nursed him in the last remaining months of his life. A 52-year-old woman who married a retired stockbroker aged 75 and left him after only a few months when she found (so she alleged) that he was mean not only with his money but with his sexual favours, received an undisclosed sum from his estate after settling her claim against his daughter.

The first successful case brought by a mistress for a share of her deceased lover's estate was in May 1979. Four years earlier, the 1975 Inheritance (Provision for Family and Dependants) Act had made such a claim possible. The case is pure copybook because it shows that the claimant does not have to be the dear departed's sole dalliance and confirms that he or she does not need to have actually lived with him.

The case of the Birmingham womaniser

According to his younger brother, a Birmingham insurance broker who died in 1977 leaving an estate of £899,000, had 'lived for women'. He 'usually had four girlfriends on the go at once, a couple of regulars and two casuals'. He also had a wife who was one year older and a Common Law wife who was 24 years younger.

When the 1975 Act was passed, the broker told one of his regular girlfriends, a 34-year-old auxiliary nurse with whom he had had an affair for the past ten years, that he was not going to leave her anything in his will – but he handed her a copy of the new Act. 'I think he was too embarrassed to put me in the will,' she later explained, 'but I sincerely believe he expected me to go to court to fight it.'

And when he died, that is what she did. She qualified as a dependant – it does not have to be a *sole* dependency – by proving that he had given her a holiday flat in Malta, a white MG sports car and a flat worth, at the time of the lawsuit, some £17,500. Furthermore, she was not an ex-mistress with a dependency only in the past – which would not count – because this 'generous and considerate' man had continued to pay her a £65-a-month allowance right up to the date of his death.

She was awarded £19,000 from the estate.

All claimants must act promptly. Claims must be made within six months of the grant of probate, which is when the will is officially accepted as valid; and anyone thinking they may have a claim should, in sheer prudence, consult a solicitor as soon as possible after the death. He can then lodge a notice at court ensuring he is notified when probate is granted and the six-month clock starts ticking.

What does it cost? If the estate is not too small, judges usually order a claimant's legal expenses to be paid of the estate, even if the claimant loses.

Some may doubt whether this is entirely fair, for the estate also usually pays if the claimant wins. So, in a sense, the only one who really loses is the person who made the will: she has to pay posthumously for others to dispute her own final wishes as to what is to happen to her own property. I hope that never happens to my will.

Wills are a very important subject. In my various legal advice columns in the press over the years more people have written to me about wills than on any other single topic so, before we move on, here is a quick résumé of some of the points I have most often been asked about:

• Wills have an obvious value in reducing the impact of **inheritance tax**, which many people still call death duties but experts refer to as IHT. It is currently charged at 40 per cent on estates over £223,000 and, although this is a considerable sum, property and investments bought some time ago may have risen in value. This is a highly specialised branch of the law and you really do need a skilled and experienced solicitor's advice on how best to use your will to reduce your IHT burden. For instance, many people think that they merely have to put their home into a son or daughter's name and then survive for at least seven years to avoid IHT being paid on the value of their home. It is nothing like so simple. A gift to a child of your main residence does not save IHT, even if you live for seven years or more – if there is any understanding that you will be allowed to go on living there rent-free. You cannot have what is called a 'reservation of an interest in the property'. But there are still some ingenious manoeuvrings that a specialist solicitor or expert tax-planner may be able to suggest to you.[1]

• If you have young children, it is always useful to name their **guardian** in your will in case you die before any of them reach 18. That, in itself, counts as their formal legal appointment. My wife and I made a will when we were both young for this very reason alone: at that time we had no money or other assets worth worrying about.

• A **codicil** is a useful way of keeping a will up to date without incurring the full expense of a whole new will. For instance, you may wish to increase the amount you have given your grandchildren in your will. You can easily achieve this minor alteration by a short formal document of two or three sentences stating the new amount and confirming that, in every other respect, your will remains the same.

But please do not do it yourself. The exact wording is vital and a codicil must be formally signed in front of two witnesses, just like the original will. A solicitor may charge about £75 plus VAT – but it is money well spent.

• You should **review your will at regular intervals**. Do not go so far as the distinguished old lady who is reputed in her *Who's Who* entry to have stated her hobby as: 'Changing my will'. But circumstances change and you should keep abreast of them. The sad fate of Benny Hill's will is a warning to us all:

The case of the famous TV comedian

In January 1992, in a newspaper interview, Benny Hill told a reporter that, as his close family had all died, he intended to make two named loyal fans his principal beneficiaries. 'Sadly all my family have gone now,' he said, 'so I must make a new will and I can safely say they will be No.1 and No. 2 in it.'

But when he died of a heart attack three months later, aged 67, no new will could be found. There was only an old will dating back to 1961 in which his

£7 million estate was left to his parents, his brother Leonard and his sister Diana Olive – but they had all died before him.

So what happened? His estate was shared equally between his dead brother's two sons and two daughters and his dead sister's two sons and a daughter.

• **Keep your will in a safe place** and tell your nearest relative or closest friend where it is. Many people keep their will in their solicitor's safe or at the bank but there is also an official will-deposit service for England and Wales at the Principal Registry of the High Court's Family Division. For many years this was at Somerset House near London's Law Courts but its new address is First Avenue House, 42–49 High Holborn, London WC1V 6NP (Tel: 020 7936 6000. You can write to the Record Keeper there and he will send you a large envelope and instructions how to complete it. You then return it with your will and a small fee and he will send you a deposit certificate which has to be produced before the will can be withdrawn.

• People sometimes say they are going to leave someone something in their will, and then they never hear anything more about it. **How can you find out if you are named in a will?** The original will or a certified copy is always available for inspection at First Avenue House – and you do not have to give any explanation. It costs nothing to look at the will but there is a small charge per page for photocopies. If you cannot journey to London, send a £5 cheque to the York Probate Sub-registry at Duncombe Place, York YO1 2EA giving such details as you can, and you will receive a copy post-free in about four weeks. (In Scotland you should write to the General Register House, Edinburgh.)

• How can you **donate your organs** for transplant or your whole body for medical research? You can either state your wishes in your will itself or, with organ donation, sign a donor card and keep it among your effects, or, with a gift of your whole body, contact, in London, the London Anatomy Office at Charing Cross Hospital, Fulham Palace Road, W6 8RF (Tel: 020 8846 1216) or elsewhere get in touch with the anatomy office of your nearest medical school whose address you can easily get from your local hospital.

But after you are dead, you do not own your own body or any part of it. In practice, whatever the will or any other document may say, doctors will usually not remove organs or dissect a body if the immediate family objects. By that time, your body no longer belongs to you but to your next of kin;[2] yet this is a grey area within the law and it is by no means clear whether the doctors must first ask the next of kin for their consent before they wield the scalpel or whether, once you have given your own agreement in your lifetime, they can simply proceed assuming that there will be no objection.

- **After divorce**, it is always better to make a new will. Marriage invalidates a will (a useful point to remember) but surprisingly divorce does not have this effect: it merely invalidates any gift to the former spouse or their appointment as executor. This can easily throw the whole will off balance. So you may as well have a complete rethink and make a new will.

- Many people name a close relative or friend as their **executor** in the will itself, sometimes without the sensible precaution of first asking if they want the job. But even if you have agreed to be someone's executor while they were still alive, there is legally nothing to stop you changing your mind afterwards. The local probate registry will supply you with a simple form to fill in. Some testators name their bank or solicitor as executor (at one time the Government hinted that it might also allow building societies and insurance companies to offer this service but so far nothing has come of this).

Solicitors and, even more so, banks can be expensive executors but solicitors, as in all their non-court work, are supposed to charge only a 'fair and reasonable' fee. So an executor has the same right as any other client, on receipt of a solicitor's bill which he considers excessive, to write to her within 28 days (preferably by recorded delivery) saying he is dissatisfied with the bill, refusing to pay it – and asking her to obtain a 'remuneration certificate' from the Law Society confirming that it is, in fact, 'fair and reasonable'. The Law Society cannot increase the bill but it can – and sometimes does – reduce it. If you are in any doubt about this, you should telephone the Law Society at its office at 113 Chancery Lane, London WC2A 1PL on 020 7242 1222.

It does not always have to be a solicitor *or* close relative or friend as executor, as if the two were mutually exclusive. There is nothing to prevent you, as executor, using the specific services of a solicitor as and when you think necessary. Her fees will, of course, be borne by the estate but, in this way, it is much easier to monitor the charges, as they occur. That is what I did when I was my late father-in-law's executor. The great secret of dealing with solicitors is: Never be frightened to ask, 'How much?'

- Getting a will **'admitted to probate'**. This is the first essential step needed to enforce the will as a valid legal document. It is the job of the executor or his solicitor but, if you are doing it yourself, the same useful leaflet (Form PA 2) which you can obtain from your local probate registry when applying to be administrator in the case of an intestacy will tell you what to do in these circumstances as well.

• **Living Wills**. Technically these are not wills at all. They have no relevance as to what is to happen to your property after death. They merely relate to the way in which you wish to die. The law on 'advance treatment directives', as they are properly called, is still evolving. Only in June 1992 did Lord Donaldson, when Master of the Rolls, first declare: 'Every adult has the legal right and capacity to decide whether or not he will accept medical treatment, even if a refusal may risk permanent injury to health or even lead to premature death.'

Living wills are much more popular in the United States (among other famous people, Richard Nixon and Jacqueline Kennedy Onassis were allowed to die with dignity because of their living wills) but in this country the Terrence Higgins Trust provides living will forms and the British Medical Association supports their use. These forms are not restricted to those with HIV infections or AIDS and are free to individual applicants, although professional firms are asked for a donation. The Trust's address is 52–54 Gray's Inn Road, London WC1X 8JU (Tel: 020 7831 0330).

Now we come to the most awesome topic of all.

DEATH

At once, we must face up to the question: when can someone legally say that they want to die and that the doctors and nurses should stop all their efforts to keep them alive? Suicide ceased to be a criminal offence in 1961 with the Suicide Act of that year. As we have just seen, Lord Donaldson has proclaimed the legal right of all of us to refuse further medical treatment, even if it means that inevitably we will die.

But what about others: doctor, nurses and, even more heart-rending, loved ones who are asked to assist in the process and positively kill someone who is in pain and despair and knows that they are dying? This is not the place to discuss the medical ethics of 'mercy killing' or euthanasia. The law is quite clear: there is a fundamental difference between killing and letting someone die. The former is murder,[3] the latter is not a crime: indeed, I was in this situation myself over 40 years ago when, as a young man in my early twenties, I was called to the London nursing home where my 82-year-old grandmother was living. She had been in failing health for some time and now she had suddenly been taken desperately ill. 'I can let her go tonight or I can keep her for a week,' her gravel-voiced Austrian-born doctor told me. 'What shall I do?' I did not hesitate. I knew my parents were out of town but I did not think of them. I thought only of the old lady lying in front of me, obviously *in extremis*.

'Let her go tonight,' I said and within half an hour she died, as I sat beside her bed.

I have thought about that scene many times and wondered if I did the right thing. I never told my mother, her daughter, what had happened and, to be honest, I did not even consider what the law would have said. Yet I am now reasonably sure (not that it matters a great deal, I must admit) that neither that pleasant doctor nor myself committed a crime.

But what about the situation where a terminally ill patient is in great pain and a doctor knows that certain drugs will alleviate the pain but may hasten death: what is her legal responsibility then? Again, the answer is clear: if the *primary* purpose of administering the drugs is to lessen the pain, then she commits no crime even if the drugs cause death. As a spokesman for the Crown Prosecution Service told the House of Lords Committee on Medical Ethics in June 1993: 'The administering of pain-killing, though life-shortening, drugs to terminally ill patients is rendered lawful if the doctor is acting in the best interests of the patient, despite the fact that the patient will die as a consequence.'

Fine lines are drawn and delicate decisions taken every day in hospitals up and down the country. In a study by Cambridge researchers reported in the *British Medical Journal*, almost half the 300 doctors questioned said they had been asked by patients to take active steps to end their lives – and a third had agreed to do so. This is a potentially dangerous area for doctors, as shown by the case in September 1992 of Dr Nigel Cox, a courageous consultant rheumatologist at the Royal Hampshire County Hospital in Winchester:

The case of the compassionate doctor

Dr Cox had cared for 70-year-old Mrs Lillian Boyes for 13 years. Finally she was lying dying slowly and painfully in his hospital of a wasting disease. She had borne intense pain with remarkable courage until five days before her death when she asked him to 'finish her off' with an injection. Reluctantly he gave her twice the lethal dose of potassium chloride and mercifully she died. Her suffering was over.

But the Crown Prosecution Service prosecuted him for attempted murder – and a jury at Winchester Crown Court convicted him. Why? Because his 'primary purpose' was not to relieve his patient's pain but to end her life as the only way of relieving her suffering. Mr Justice Ognall rejected defence counsel's impassioned plea for an absolute discharge and gave the doctor a 12-month prison sentence, suspended for a year.

'What you did was not only criminal. It was a total betrayal of your unequivocal duty as a physician,' Mr Justice Ognall told him. Not everyone will agree.

In February 1994, the House of Lords Select Committee on Medical
Ethics agreed unanimously that there should be no change in the law to
permit euthanasia, and doctors still have no statutory guidelines.

In fact, in May 1999, in the first case of its kind, Dr David Moor, a
family doctor who had recently retired from practice in Newcastle upon
Tyne, was prosecuted in the local Crown Court for murder. He had given
large doses of the painkilling drug diamorphine to an 85-year-old patient
grievously ill with bowel cancer. The jury took only just over an hour to
acquit him, accepting that rather than setting out to kill his patient, he had
been trying to ease the patient's suffering.

Prior to his trial, Dr Moor had admitted that he had helped up to 300
of his terminally ill patients to die and, in a statement welcoming his
acquittal, the Voluntary Euthanasia Society praised the verdict as lifting
'a dark cloud from doctors' consciences'. It claimed that up to 100,000
patients a year are quietly helped to die and its General Secretary
commented: 'Patients can be given sufficient pain relief even if this
might hasten their deaths, as long as the doctors claim they did not intend
to shorten life. This defence of double effect is a valid one.'

And so the matter remains: a typical British compromise compounded
of common sense and, with all respect, a kind form of benign hypocrisy.

Now what about death itself?

When legally do we 'die'? Perhaps surprisingly, there is no legal
definition, neither in any Act of Parliament nor in any pronouncement by
a judge. The law, faced with the technological sophistication of modern
medical science, throws up its hands and leaves it to the doctors to
decide. Nowadays doctors say that we 'die' when our brain stem suffers
total and irretrievable damage and can no longer control our bodily
functions, even though this may be achieved artificially; and the judges
go along with that view.

As in February 1993 in the classic case of *Airedale NHS Trust* v.
Bland, when the House of Lords ruled that the doctors committed no
criminal offence in withdrawing artificial feeding from the tragic young
football fan, 21-year-old Tony Bland. He lay helpless in his hospital bed
in a persistent vegetative state unable to think, speak, see, swallow or feel
anything (including pain or hunger) after his brain and lungs had been
damaged in the crush that killed 95 others in the Hillsborough stadium
disaster nearly four years earlier. Lord Browne-Wilkinson said:

'Until recently there was no doubt what was life and what was death.
A man was dead if he stopped breathing and his heart stopped beating.
There was no artificial means of sustaining those indications of life for

more than a little while. Death in the traditional sense was beyond human control. Apart from cases of unlawful homicide, death occurred automatically in the course of nature when the natural functions of the body failed to sustain the lungs and the heart.

'Recent developments in medical science have fundamentally affected these previous certainties. In medicine, the cessation of breathing or heartbeat is no longer death. By the use of a ventilator, lungs which in the unaided course of nature would have stopped breathing can be made to breathe, thereby sustaining the heartbeat. Those, like Anthony Bland, who would previously have died through inability to swallow food can be kept alive by artificial feeding. This has led the medical profession to redefine death in terms of brain stem death, i.e. the death of that part of the brain without which the body cannot function at all without assistance. In some cases it is now apparently possible, with the use of the ventilator, to sustain a beating heart even though the brain stem, and therefore in medical terms the patient, is dead: "the ventillated corpse".

'I do not refer to these factors because Anthony Bland is already dead, either medically *or legally*. His brain stem is alive and so is he. Provided that he is artificially fed and the waste products evacuated from his body by skilled medical care, his body sustains its own life' [my italics].

But five law lords unanimously agreed that he should no longer be fed and 27 days later he finally 'died' medically and legally when, with his body deprived of all food, his brain stem ceased to function. You could say that the law allowed him to be starved to death; but he felt nothing and knew nothing. He died with dignity and without suffering.

Yet the law lords were uneasy, and understandably so. They ruled that in all future cases of withdrawing life-prolonging treatment (such as artificial feeding) from patients in a persistent vegetative state the approval of the courts must first be obtained. They were clearly worried by the serious legal, moral and ethical issues raised by the case and, as Lord Mustill said, 'The whole matter cries out for exploration in depth in Parliament.' Predictably, this has not yet happened.

But what about the many, many cases when doctors 'turn off the switch' on a life support machine: do they have to go and get the consent of a judge every time? Not at all. People in a persistent vegetative state, as Tony Bland was, are still medically and legally *alive*: part of their brain stem is still working. But when doctors 'turn off the switch', the whole brain stem is dead. It no longer functions. The apparent 'life' of the patient is entirely artificial: turn off the switch and *at once* that semblance of life will cease.

As far back as March 1981, in the cases of *R.* v. *Malcherek* and *R.* v. *Steel*, the Appeal Court accepted that turning off the switch did not 'kill' a patient: they were already dead. In both cases, a person had been criminally attacked and apparently died from their injuries but, for a while, they had been put on a life support machine until the doctors satisfied themselves incontrovertibly that irretrievable brain damage had occurred and there was no hope whatsoever of continued life or recovery. Both attackers were convicted of murder and sentenced to life imprisonment but they appealed on the basis that they had not 'killed' their victims: the doctors had done so when switching off the life support machines.

Lord Lane, then Lord Chief Justice presiding over the Appeal Court, would have none of it. Both murder convictions were upheld. He said:

> Where a medical practitioner adopting methods which are generally accepted comes bona fide and conscientiously to the conclusion that the patient is for practical purposes dead, and that such vital functions as exist (for example, circulation) are being maintained solely by mechanical means, and therefore discontinues treatment, that does not prevent the person who inflicted the initial injury from being responsible for the victim's death.

So much for death itself. I began this book with the law dealing with our bodies before we are born. Now let us end with a brief look at the law dealing with the disposal of our bodies after we are dead. On the whole, it is remarkably straightforward:

If death happens at home

If a doctor is not already there, call one at once. If he can, he will immediately confirm the cause of death and give you a free medical certificate stating the cause of death in a sealed envelope addressed to the Registrar of Births and Deaths and a formal notice saying he has given you the certificate and explaining the procedure for registering the death. You must take the sealed envelope to the nearest registrar of births, marriages and deaths within five days (or up to 42 days for a stillbirth) and register the death. The registrar will then give you a formal death certificate and a green 'disposal certificate' that allows you to arrange the funeral.

If the doctor did not see the deceased during her last illness *or* within the past 14 days *or* he thinks the cause of death is uncertain *or* it was sudden, violent or caused by an accident or industrial disease, he will report the death to the coroner and inevitably the funeral and burial arrangements will be held up.

If death occurs in hospital

If you were not present at the time of death, the ward sister will telephone you as soon as possible but, if the deceased was brought in as the result of an accident, the police may inform you and ask you to identify the body.

If the cause of death is clear, a hospital doctor will give you the same free medical certificate and formal notice as when someone dies at home. But if there is some doubt as to the exact cause of death, she may request your permission to conduct at least a partial post-mortem. You may refuse but, as she will warn you, this means that she must inform the coroner, who will arrange for his own post-mortem to be held – and there will be even more delay before you can bury your loved one.

If the cause of death is uncertain (and the next of kin will not agree to a hospital post-mortem) or the death was sudden, violent or caused by an accident or industrial disease or if it occurred during an operation or while the deceased was under an anaesthetic, the hospital must inform the coroner and again there will be delay.

What happens if the coroner is informed?

Despite what many people believe, there does not always have to be an inquest but there will almost certainly be a post-mortem conducted by an independent forensic pathologist reporting directly to the coroner. Unlike a hospital post-mortem, the next of kin cannot object to this, although they can ask for their own doctor to be present. As with a hospital post-mortem, the whole body does not have to be dissected. There may be a partial examination of the dead body, limited to certain vital organs such as the heart or liver: some grieving relatives find this easier to bear.

If the coroner's post-mortem, whether full or partial, satisfies him as to the cause of death, the coroner – not your own or the hospital's doctor – will supply a cause of death certificate and a green disposal certificate for you to register the death and arrange the funeral.

However, if, despite his post-mortem, the coroner is still not satisfied as to the cause of death or if the death was violent, accidental or resulted from an industrial disease, he may decide to hold an inquest. If this happens, he will normally hold a preliminary hearing within a week or so for purposes of identification only and will then usually release the body and issue the relevant certificates for burial. The full inquest will usually follow several weeks later and relatives have the right to be present and to be represented by a lawyer, although the actual role that their lawyer will be allowed to play in the proceedings is entirely a matter for the individual coroner – and some are very autocratic.

Coroners, who must be either lawyers or doctors (a few are both), are virtually a law unto themselves. They begin by questioning each witness themselves and then it is entirely their own choice whether they allow any questions from anyone else – or even any speech by a lawyer representing interested parties. Sometimes they sit with a jury but, as the late Dr Gavin Thurston, himself a distinguished London coroner, once wrote: 'It is indisputable that juries make no contribution to most inquests. Jurors have been heard to voice the opinion that their time has been wasted.'

Inquests are only as valuable as the quality of the individual coroner, and most people who have any experience of their courts would agree that the standard varies enormously up and down the country.

The very end: burial or cremation

You may state clearly in your will – or in detailed written instructions in a separate document – your exact wishes as to how you want to be buried or whether and where you wish to be cremated. *These have absolutely no legal effect.* Once you are dead, your body no longer belongs to you and your next of kin can arrange whatever lawful kind of disposal they care for. There are many sad stories of families at last getting their own back on some selfish or domineering old person after death and disposing of the body in ways completely contrary to the deceased's express wishes.

You can be buried in a churchyard you have never heard of, cremated although you were totally opposed to the idea or buried with great pomp in a magnificent marble tomb, although you specifically said in your will that you wanted to be cremated with as little fuss as possible.

The only legal requirement for cremation is *not* that the dead person specifically wanted to be cremated, although in many cases this is undoubtedly so, but that there is no improper reason for wanting the body irretrievably destroyed in the furnace of a crematorium: in other words, you have not been murdered or caused deliberate physical suffering.

The next of kin must, in effect, prove this by giving a crematorium no fewer than three signed forms under the 1902 and 1952 Crematorium Acts:

- Form A, which is the formal application for cremation, countersigned by a householder who knows the next of kin personally;
- Forms B and C, which are on the same piece of paper. Form B is completed by the doctor who attended the deceased during his last illness, although not necessarily the one who signed the cause of death

certificate, and it details the deceased's treatment and states whether the doctor benefits financially from the death. Form C is a confirmatory certificate completed by a doctor who is totally independent, although often recommended by the Form B doctor. She will have seen the body and made a careful external examination (this form is not required where a post-mortem has taken place).

• But that is not all. There must also be a fourth form (Form D) which is, in fact, the formal authority to cremate signed by the crematorium's own medical referee after she has read Forms B and C. If she is unsatisfied for any reason, she may refuse authority to cremate or may herself order a post-mortem or refer the matter to the coroner. The relatives have no right to prevent this. If they do not want a post-mortem, they will have to forgo cremation and have the body buried instead.

No one's body can just be left to rot. If your next of kin choose to bury you rather than cremate you, they can assert your legal right to be buried, if there is room, in the graveyard of the parish in which you had your last home or died – whether or not you were even a Christian! But this legal right does not extend to a memorial or headstone: that has to be paid for privately. There is no law which says your last resting place must be marked in some way. Sadly, many people lie in unmarked and untended graves.

Church of England law says that, if a headstone exists, it must fall within legal guidelines for the preservation of the dignity of graveyards. These guidelines are supervised by church consistory courts presided over by bishops' judges called diocesan chancellors, and cases are sometimes brought when local vicars refuse to allow headstone inscriptions using such homely but 'undignified' words as 'Dad', 'Mum' or 'Grandma'. There was one such case in Lancaster in July 1994, and the same general principles even apply to the many cemeteries run by local authorities. As recently as June 1998 at a local authority cemetery near Mablethorpe, Lincolnshire, a grieving mother was ordered to remove a cross from the grave of her seven-year-old daughter who had died from Batten's disease because, according to local diocesan regulations, 'Crosses are discouraged, as excessive use of the supreme Christian symbol is undesirable.'

Even at the very end, we cannot escape the law.

Notes

1 Even after death, tax may be cut by a deed of variation in effect rewriting parts of the will but this needs the consent of everyone who loses out as a result of the

variation and must be made within two years.

2 Technically the expression 'next of kin' only applies to your nearest *blood* relative. If you are married, your husband or wife is legally your nearest relative but not your 'next of kin'. In practice, hospitals and doctors treat as 'next of kin' whomever the patient nominates for that role, irrespective of the nature of their relationship: lover (gay or straight), brother or sister, whomever. You put down on the form that you fill in and sign when admitted to hospital whomsoever you want.

3 Although it may be reduced to manslaughter on account of 'diminished mental responsibility' in the case of a husband, wife, lover or child because of the appalling mental anguish they will have endured. This defence is not open to a doctor or nurse: they are supposed to be coolly professional.

INDEX